The Resistance

The Resistance

The Resistance

The Dawn of the Anti-Trump Opposition Movement

EDITED BY DAVID S. MEYER

and

SIDNEY TARROW

AFTERWORD BY JACOB S. HACKER

OXFORD
UNIVERSITY PRESS

OXFORD
UNIVERSITY PRESS

Oxford University Press is a department of the University of Oxford. It furthers
the University's objective of excellence in research, scholarship, and education
by publishing worldwide. Oxford is a registered trade mark of Oxford University
Press in the UK and certain other countries.

Published in the United States of America by Oxford University Press
198 Madison Avenue, New York, NY 10016, United States of America.

© Oxford University Press 2018

CIP data is on file at the Library of Congress
ISBN 978–0–19–088618–9 (pbk.)
ISBN 978–0–19–088617–2 (hbk.)

1 3 5 7 9 8 6 4 2

Paperback printed by Webcom Inc., Canada
Hardback printed by Bridgeport National Bindery, Inc., United States of America

To our children, their generations, and the futures they build.

CONTENTS

PREFACE

This book owes its origin to a conversation between the editors at Notre Dame University in the spring of 2017 as they contemplated the presidential elections of 2016. Both together and separately, we had devoted most of our professional careers as social scientists to analyzing the role and the potentialities of social movements in Europe and America. We prided ourselves on the fact that we had avoided the cardinal sin of reifying movements and thus ignoring their place within the broader canvas of contentious politics. To both of us it had seemed that we would continue to do the kind of work we had been doing for decades, as our country transitioned from one moderately-progressive administration— that of Barack Obama—to the even more moderate one of Hillary Clinton. Nothing prepared us for the political earthquake of the election of Donald J. Trump to the presidency of the United States in November 2016.

Colleagues in American politics, equally stunned, soon turned to the well-honed tools of political science to try to understand the Trump phenomenon. They used survey tools and ecological analysis to divine what had led to the election of a TV celebrity and shady businessman to the highest post in the land. Political theorists, schooled in the finer points of democratic theory, joined the debate, arguing that American constitutional institutions were not working as had been intended. Comparativists, especially those who had cut their teeth on the de-democratization of once promising new democracies, joined the chorus with powerful analogies to the dangers to American democracy of a president with no respect for the rule of law and no experience in the finer points of political practice. What, we asked, could two social movement specialists add to this debate?

Since the publication of our book, *The Social Movement Society* in far-off 1998, we had been arguing that modern democracies were becoming "movement societies" in which organizations of civil society were bringing movement-like ways of thinking and acting into the heart of the political system. But neither in that book nor in our subsequent research had we contemplated the effect of the election of a figure like Trump—with a movement-like following and an indifference to the norms of democratic politics—to the highest position in a democratic state. Nor were we prepared for the political opportunity he offered to denizens of the darkest corners of American life.

It was the vast wave of protest that followed Trump's election, beginning with the Women's March the day after his inauguration, that convinced us to undertake this effort. Here was something we knew about—or thought we did: the beginning of what one of us has called "a cycle of contention" (Tarrow 2011) and which the other had traced in his work on the dynamics of "movement/countermovement interaction" in an earlier cycle of contention (Meyer and Staggenborg 1996). At first reluctantly, and then with growing passion for the task and increasing fear for our country, we decided to turn our perspective on the social movement society to the Trump phenomenon and the resistance to it. This book is the result of that passion and of that fear.

We would not have gotten very far in this endeavor without the help and advice of numerous people and of several institutions. Our thanks go first to our collaborators in this volume, who allowed themselves to be diverted from their enduring projects to lend a hand to this enterprise. Thanks are also due to our home institutions: to the University of California at Irvine's social movement/social justice seminar; to the Cornell Law School for hosting a symposium on the Trump phenomenon; and to a talented group of scholars who came together under Suzanne Mettler's leadership in Ithaca and at New America in Washington, DC to ponder the future of "Our Republic—if we can keep it." We also thank Donatella della Porta, who—in addition to serving as "den mother" for generations of social movement scholars—encouraged our work through a visiting lecture that eventually became Chapter 9 of this book.

We are grateful to David McBride, who overcame the habitual caution of University Press acquisition editors to encourage a project, the subject of which was changing even as we pursued it, and to two anonymous readers who employed a fine combination of praise and criticism that encouraged us to pursue it. We thank our families for their forbearance as we struggled to temper our political passions with academic reserve—often at the cost of domestic comity.

Finally, we want to express our gratitude to the thousands of ordinary Americans who have been resisting autocracy and defending democracy, sometimes in the streets, often in the courts, and increasingly in the electoral arena.

David S. Meyer
Professor of Sociology
UC Irvine

Sidney Tarrow
Emeritus Professor of Government
and Adjunct Professor at the Law School
Cornell University

April 2018

CONTRIBUTORS

Marie Berry is Assistant Professor of International Comparative Politics in the Joseph Korbel School of International Studies at the University of Denver. She currently serves as Research Director of the Inclusive Global Leadership Initiative at the Sié Chéou-Kang Center for International Security and Diplomacy.

Megan E. Brooker is a PhD Candidate in the Department of Sociology at the University of California, Irvine, and a Fellow of the Center for the Study of Democracy there. Her dissertation examines how presidential elections offer institutionalized political opportunities that give activists access to political parties and candidates and help their ideas to become incorporated into the political agenda.

Erica Chenoweth is Professor and Associate Dean for Research at the Joseph Korbel School of International Studies at the University of Denver. Together with Maria Stephen she won the 2013 Grawemeyer Award for Ideas Improving World Order for their book, *Why Civil Resistance Works.*

Michael S. Chu is an associate at Kramer Levin Naftalis & Frankel, LLP, in New York City, and a graduate of the Cornell Law School. As an undergraduate, he worked in a research lab where he studied how to implement social–emotional learning techniques in local schools. During the summer of 2016 he served as an intern to Justice Barry T. Albin on the New Jersey Supreme Court.

Michael C. Dorf is the Robert S. Stephens Professor of Law at Cornell Law School, where he teaches constitutional law. In addition to the blog he administers (dorfonlaw.org), he is the coauthor, with Laurence H. Tribe, of *On Reading the Constitution* and, most recently, with Sherry Colb, of *Beating Hearts: Abortion and Animal Rights.*

Dana R. Fisher is Professor of Sociology and the Director of the Program for Society and the Environment at the University of Maryland. She is the author of *National Governance and the Global Climate Change Regime* (2004) and of *Activism, Inc* and *Urban Environmental Stewardship and Civic Engagement* (2015). She is currently completing *American Resistance*, for Columbia University Press.

Jacob S. Hacker is the Stanley B. Resor Professor of Political Science and the Director of the Institution for Social and Policy Studies at Yale. His most recent book, coauthored with Paul Pierson, is *American Amnesia: How the War on Government Led Us to Forget What Made America Prosper.*

Hahrie Han is the Anton Vonk Professor of Political Science at the University of California, Santa Barbara, and was the inaugural cochair of the Civic Engagement Working Group at the Scholars Strategy Network. Her most recent book is *How Organizations Develop Activists: Civic Associations and Leadership in the 21st Century.*

David Karpf is Associate Professor in the School of Media and Public Affairs at the George Washington University. He is the author of the award-wining book, *The MoveOn Effect: The Unexpected Transformation of American Political Advocacy* and of *Analytic Activism: Digital Listening and the New Political Strategy.*

Doug McAdam is the Ray Lyman Wilbur Professor of Sociology at Stanford University and a former Director of the Center for Advanced Study in the Behavioral Sciences. He is the author of the prize-winning *Political Process and the Development of Black Insurgency, 1930–1970*, and, most recently with Karina Kloos, of *Deeply Divided: Racial Politics and Social Movements in Postwar America.*

David S. Meyer is Professor of Political Science and Sociology at the University of California at Irvine and the author of *The Politics of Protest: Social Movements in America*. In 2017 he was awarded the John McCarthy Prize for Lifetime Contributions to Social Movement Scholarship. He blogs at politicsoutdoors. com.

Michelle Oyakawa has her PhD in Sociology from Ohio State University and is currently a postdoctoral scholar at the University of California, Santa Barbara, where she is working on a study titled "Leadership, Strategy and Organization." From 2009 to 2010, she worked as an organizer for ISAIAH, an ecumenical, multiracial congregation-based community organization in the Twin Cities region of Minnesota.

Kenneth M. Roberts is Richard Schwartz Professor of comparative and Latin American Politics at Cornell, where he specializes in the political economy of Latin America and the study of political parties, social movements, and populism. His latest book is *The Resurgence of the Latin American Left* (2011). He is currently engaged in a study of Latin American and Southern European populism.

Sidney Tarrow is Maxwell Upson Professor Emeritus of Government at Cornell and Adjunct Professor at the Cornell Law School. A fellow of the American Academy of Arts and Sciences, he was awarded the John McCarthy Prize for Lifetime Contributions to Social Movement Scholarship. His most recent book is *War, States, and Contention* (2015).

Sophia J. Wallace is an Associate Professor of Political Science at the University of Washington, where she specializes in Latino politics, representation, social movements, and immigration policy. She is cofounder and co-organizer of SPIRE, Symposium on the Politics of Immigration, Race, and Ethnicity. She is currently at work on a book, *United We Stand: Latino Representation in Congress*.

Nancy Whittier holds the Sophia Smith Chair of Sociology at Smith College, where she teaches courses on gender, sexuality, social change, introductory sociology, and statistics. Among her books are *Feminist Generations, Feminist Frontiers 5*, and *The Politics of Child Sexual Abuse*, which was awarded the 2010 Charles Tilly award for the best book in collective behavior and social movements by the American Sociological Association.

Chris Zepeda-Millán is Assistant Professor of Ethnic Studies and the Faculty Chair of the Center for Research on Social Change at the University of California at Berkeley, where he teaches social movements, immigration, race politics, and interdisciplinary research methods. His first book, *Latino Mass Mobilization*, was recently published by Cambridge University Press.

The Resistance

Introduction

DAVID S. MEYER AND SIDNEY TARROW

On January 21, 2017, people of all backgrounds—women and men and gender nonconforming people, young and old, of diverse faiths, differently abled, immigrants and indigenous—came together, 5 million strong, on all seven continents of the world. We were answering a call to show up and be counted as those who believe in a world that is equitable, tolerant, just and safe for all, one in which the human rights and dignity of each person is protected and our planet is safe from destruction. Grounded in the nonviolent ideology of the Civil Rights movement, the Women's March was the largest coordinated protest in U.S. history and one of the largest in world history.[1]

What is most remarkable about this statement, which came from the group who organized this march, is that its claims were only slightly exaggerated. Consider first the claim that the march was "the largest coordinated protest in U.S. history." Figure I.1, based on a crowd-sourced archive of reports on participation in protest events following the election of Donald Trump, tells the dramatic story.

Figure I.1 shows that this claim may have been true: In the six-month period that saw thousands of protest events organized over a wide range of issues by a broad spectrum of groups and organizations that we collectively call "the Resistance," the Women's March towered over the rest, both for the number of citizens participating and for the diffusion of the events it inspired, as Marie Berry and Erica Chenoweth's chapter shows.

Although the Women's March was just that—a march—this one event helped to trigger a contentious repertoire of forms of action, using that term as it was developed by the late Charles Tilly to mean "arrays of performances that are currently known and available within some set of political actors" (Tilly and Tarrow 2015:14). Many of these forms were as familiar as the march and the demonstration, but others were innovative and disruptive, like the "die-ins" in the halls of Congress by opponents of the Republican health care plans that went down to defeat in July 2017.[2] Although the organizers were women, self-conscious in

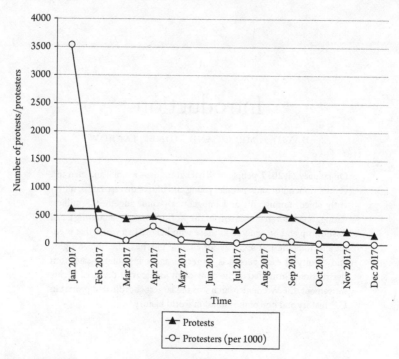

Figure I.1 Timeline of Numbers of Protests and Estimated Protesters, January–
December 2017.

Source: Chan Suh and Sidney Tarrow, "The Repression of Protest in the Age of Trump: State
Legislators, Protest Threat and Political Realignments," ms. in preparation, Fig. 1.

ensuring an ethnically and racially diverse profile, they defined women's issues
broadly. Their "Unity Principles" comprised eight major goals aimed either at a
broader audience or elucidating general principles.

Although the march was planned by a small group of American women
responding to a current threat, it had deep historical and broad transnational
resonance. The organizers claim to have inspired 673 "sister marches" across
the globe, and the campaign was recognizable as a version of the "Left-populist"
movements that exploded in Europe after the financial crisis of 2008–2009.[3] In
addition, there were strong domestic precedents: the performance of a "March
on Washington" also evoked the 1940s and the 1960s civil rights marches.[4]

Like all movement focal points,[5] the Women's March came in the early part of
a dynamic cycle of contention. It provided a focus for the continuation of organized political activity on the left, including Black Lives Matter demonstrations
against police violence, direct action targeted at Trump's earlier campaign
rallies, and more conventional political activism on behalf of Bernie Sanders's
presidential bid—among many other efforts. It both politicized normally qui-
escent citizens and reactivated veterans of previous cycles of protest. Many

women moved on from women's organizing to other groups at the heart of the Resistance—such as Indivisible. The massive turnout for the second Women's March a year after the initial one showed that the spillover to other organizations did not lead to a "spill*out*" from women's organizing to other sectors of the Resistance (Hadden and Tarrow 2007). On January 20 and 21, 2017, as Chenoweth and Jeremy Pressman estimate, "In the United States alone, between 1,856,683 and 2,637,214 people in at least 407 locations marched, held rallies, and protested . . . Although there was a decline from the numbers in 2017, given expectations of burnout, this was a very significant show of strength."[6] Women continue to be at the heart of the Resistance.

But the massive turnout of anti-Trump mobilizing also helped to trigger a countermovement, drawing mainly on men—particularly white men—who had found in Barack Obama and Hillary Clinton threats to their status and in Donald Trump a hope for its revival. In the language of Meyer and Staggenborg (1996), writing about an earlier period: The Women's March was a key flashpoint in a broader sequence of movement–countermovement interaction.

We begin this book with this brief account of the Women's March to help frame the debate we hope to advance about the Resistance.[7] We begin with three challenges that the Resistance poses for both scholars and citizens: its challenge to our understanding of social movements, its challenge to the politics and policies of the Left, and its challenge to the future of democratic norms and institutions. We then survey three of its most important predecessors—the Latino movement for immigrant rights, the Occupy movement, and Black Lives Matter—before turning to the Sanders–Clinton contest for the Democratic nomination in the 2016 election and its role in shaping both the force and the divisions in the Resistance. We turn from there to its forms of organization and mobilization, some of them familiar from the past of American contentious politics, whereas others are new and unfamiliar. We then examine the dynamics of the movement, its interaction with the Trumpian countermovement, and its possible outcomes for American democracy.

Three Challenges

The advent of the Trump administration has brought so many challenges to America and the world that providing a list would preclude anything resembling analysis. Importantly, the election of Donald Trump represents an attack not only on the Democratic Party, or the Left more generally, but also presents a clear threat to well-established bipartisan policies, the independence of institutions in the American Constitutional order, and America's place in the world. In this context, it is not surprising that a diverse and volatile opposition quickly emerged.

This Resistance, however, calls up an entirely new set of challenges to scholars of social movements, to political activists, and to citizens. Activists want to understand how to be effective not only in countering the Trump administration, but also how to promote a more effective alternative agenda. This broad concern generates questions about what to focus on (goals), how to organize and express political action (tactics), and which potential allies inside and outside government to trust (organization). Students of social movements, covering much the same ground, want to understand the complicated relationships between protest and institutional politics.

A Challenge to Social Movement Theory

Since the 1960s social scientists have developed a coherent field built around the concept of social movements. At first, these efforts were embedded in a variety of disciplinary homes, from social history to the sociology of collective action, producing the diversity of approaches and findings that enriches the field to this day. But, like many new areas of study, the social movement field soon developed its own culture, characteristic methods, and internal disagreements. This has enabled social movement scholars to leave behind many popular images of movements—for example, that they are extreme expressions of "dysfunction" in society—but it has also led to an inward-looking perspective that elided some of the links between movements and other forms of participation. A particular elision has been the scant attention given until recently to the connections between social movements and elections.[8]

The Trump election and the Resistance that followed provide scholars with an important opportunity to bridge the elision between the study of movements and the study of elections. Briefly:

- Trump's election campaign, with its racist dog-whistles and its flag-waving nationalism, enlivened the extreme right-wing fringes of the American social movement scene, as Tarrow argues in his chapter.
- Trump himself, with his combination of extreme claims, savage denunciation of his opponents, and demagogic appeals, emerged as a movement leader—not very different from populist leaders in Latin America and Southern Europe, as the chapter by Kenneth Roberts argues.
- Among many sectors of American society—women, environmentalists, immigrant rights advocates, scientists, lawyers, supporters of health care, minorities—a raft of new organizations emerged in opposition to the new administration, as Hahrie Han and Michelle Oyakawa show in their chapter.

- Even moderate nonprofit groups like the American Civil Liberties Union (ACLU), whose efforts have historically centered on lobbying and litigation, were pushed to launch "people power" campaigns that lent financial strength and organizational experience to the Resistance.[9] Lawyers, whose activism is normally limited to the courtroom, emerged as prime actors in defense of refugees at airports around the country, as Michael Dorf and Michael Chu's contribution shows.
- Given the high degree of polarization in American politics (Heaney 2017; McAdam and Kloos 2014), new forms of "crossover" activism—such as "Indivisible"—linked classical movement organizations to more institutional forms of political participation. Indivisible, started by former Democratic congressional staffers,[10] became an important broker among the broad spectrum of groups opposing Trump's agenda, as Megan Brooker shows in her chapter.

Whatever emerges from the Resistance, we are in the middle of a major cycle of contention, with intersecting institutional and noninstitutional facets (Tarrow 2011). This dual character gives the movement great potential power, but it also threatens to create a left–liberal divide that may weaken its appeal to a broader constituency. To make sense of all this, we will need to bridge the gaps between approaches that focus on social movements and those that center on institutional politics. This is one of the major goals of this book. Among other things, it will involve trying to understand the effects of this historic movement on the American Left.

A Challenge to the Left

Donald Trump won the presidency despite suffering a substantial deficit in the popular vote; small margins in three traditionally Democratic states (Wisconsin, Pennsylvania, and Michigan) carried him to a victory in the electoral college. The shift of just 120,000 votes, out of more than 125 million cast, would have changed the outcome. Thus, virtually any theory of alternative outcomes is plausible.

Critics on the Left blamed Hillary Clinton for both her tactical mistakes and a strategic decision to deemphasize policy and a programmatic liberal agenda; others castigated FBI director James Comey for reinserting Clinton's private email server into the closing days of the campaign; still others were outraged by the Russian government for its apparent hacking of the Democratic National Committee.[11] Deeper analyses pointed to the Democratic Party's distance from the needs of lower-income white voters who have paid the price for deindustrialization—especially after the financial crisis of 2008—and the distortions of the electoral college, which allowed the GOP to claim victory in the presidential election with fewer popular votes than the Democrats. Pundits argued over whether white working-class anxiety, often expressed in terms of a culture war, could be redressed with economic policies. This has exposed a cleavage between liberals who want to defend America's traditional political institutions and those who consider them beyond repair, as David Meyer argues in his contribution.[12]

Although these were important factors in the faltering of the Democratic Party in the 2016 election, our approach leads us to look further back in America's political history, and more deeply at the relations between social movements and electoral politics in that history. Drawing on the contributions of one of our authors, Doug McAdam,[13] we are inclined to look to the recent past of American history and to the key role of race in shaping today's political polarization. Briefly, because many of these issues are taken up more thoroughly in the chapters that follow:

In the 1950s and 1960s, the Civil Rights movement reached wide public visibility, setting an agenda for mainstream politics. Like the current Resistance, it featured institutional (i.e., going to court) and noninstitutional (e.g., the sit-in movement) efforts. Although much of the literature focused on the successes of that movement, it also triggered a countermovement of segregationists—some of them quite violent—and the broader "southern strategy" of the Republican Party in national politics. The adjective "southern" in that strategy is partly a misnomer because Richard Nixon, who was responsible for its invention, exploited and promoted racial resentment to seek conservative white support throughout the country.

In both the Democratic and the Republican Parties, these developments led to a "movementization" in the parties' bases and laid the groundwork for the current polarization of American politics. As McAdam and Kloos put it,

> By revitalizing and legitimating the social movement form, the civil rights movement of the early 1960s reintroduced . . . centrifugal pressures to American politics. Or more accurately, it was one movement—civil rights—and one powerful countermovement— white resistance . . . that began to force the parties to weigh the costs and benefits of appealing to the median voter against the strategic imperative of responding to mobilized movement elements at the ideological margins. (2014: 10–11)

But there was an important difference in how the two parties responded to this growing polarization: While the Democratic Party remained a coalition of interest groups, the Republicans were drawn together by an increasingly focused conservative ideology (Grossman and Hopkins 2016). This asymmetry meant that while the Democrats continued to try to build alliances across interest group lines, the Republicans relied increasingly on resentment toward government in general and to those who might benefit from government initiatives. This included both domestic minorities, suspected of taking advantage of government largesse, and immigrants and refugees. Ideological groups with a coherent ideology had a greater chance to take over the Republican Party than a corresponding movement could effect in the more diverse and decentralized Democratic Party.

Barack Obama's election in 2008 expanded the ideologization of the Republican Party. Almost immediately, the Tea Party rebellion and then its insertion into the Republican Party vigorously offered the promise of mobilized concern, and initially carried both traditional economic conservative and white populist messages, unified by opposition to the new president and to his race. In addition to putting an African American in the White House, that election produced both an ambitious Affordable Care Act, reforming health insurance, and an explicitly activist approach to domestic policy, presiding over new consumer protections, increased regulation of the financial sector, and, to varying degrees, support for women, and ethnic, racial, and sexual minorities.

The faces of the Democratic leadership reflected these policies: In overseeing financial reform, for example, President Obama worked with Nancy Pelosi, the first woman to serve as speaker of the House, and Representative Barney Frank, openly gay, Jewish, and chair of the House Financial Services Committee. Obama also appointed record numbers of women and minorities to visible positions. Additionally, he offered a vision of international engagement that differed from his predecessor's, but still included committed engagement to international institutions, the deployment of military forces abroad in the service of national interests and human rights, and a commitment to free trade.

Even before Trump entered the scene, Republicans found that they could benefit from the mobilized anger of people who were driven by racial resentment and who had deeper differences with the administration than they themselves did. Starting in 2010, the Republican Party began to play to a populist base that would prove dangerous, first to Democrats, but then to the Republican Party and ultimately to the Republic itself.

Many factors converged to bring about the election of Donald Trump in 2016, but we think that its background was the reciprocal movementization of the party system, the ideological form it took at the base of the Republican Party, and the increasingly open role of race in getting out the vote for that party. None of this was inevitable, but it seems to us to have opened the opportunity for a populist, antiminority, antifeminist, antiregulation, and anti-internationalist demagogue to win, first, the nomination of a major political party, and then election to the presidency. This takes us to the third challenge we see for the Resistance in the Trump administration: the challenge to democracy and the rule of law.

A Challenge to Democratic Norms and Institutions

Even more than a challenge to the Left, the Trump campaign represented a challenge to the norms and institutions of a pluralist democracy, one that offered eerie echoes of historical authoritarian movements and regimes, both in the United States and abroad, as Roberts argues in his comparative chapter. In his historical study, *American Demagogues* (1954), Reinhart Luthin offers a laundry list of characteristics that he found in the public careers of selected American demagogues of the 20th century—those "masters of the masses" who, in their aspirations for political place and power, pandered to the passions and prejudices, rather than the reason, of the populace, and performed all manner of crowd-captivating tricks, only to betray the people who had supported them. Luthin did not compare his list of American demagogues with those of other countries; but there are striking similarities between the behavior of figures like Juan Perón and Benito Mussolini and the behavior of Donald Trump in his first year in office. These figures also came to power in countries fractured by splits between Left and Right, church and state, and weak institutions, not identical to, but evocative of the polarization and "negative partisanship" in the American body politic today.[14]

In the creation and evolution of the Resistance we see the embodiment of all three of the challenges we have sketched in this part of our introduction: a challenge to the central canon of social movement theory; a challenge to the Left that may be shifting the Democratic Party from the centrism of its Clinton–Obama wing to something more progressive; and the challenge to American democracy. All of these challenges were foreshadowed by three of the movements that preceded the election of Donald Trump—the Latino movement for immigrant rights, the Occupy movement, and Black Lives Matter.

Origins of the Resistance

Social movements rarely have the distinct beginnings and endings that make for compelling narratives. Historians and activists edit events to construct those more riveting stories. What Verta Taylor (1989) called a "spontaneous genera-tion myth" haunts our histories of effective social movements. But civil rights ac-tivism didn't start with Rosa Parks in Montgomery, Alabama, in 1955, nor did gay rights activism start with the Stonewall Rebellion in 1969 (Armstrong and Crage 2007). Activism and ideas simmer in legislatures, elections, and the streets, some-times bubbling up to public recognition and sometimes reaching a sustained boil. The anti-Trump Resistance finds roots in both organizations and individuals en-gaged in political action on a range of issues from long before Donald Trump took office. In this section we briefly survey three important predecessors that would intensify against the provocations represented by the Trump presidency.

The Latino Movement for Immigration Reform

Like the Resistance today, the Latino-led movement for immigrant rights was born in opposition to a threat—in this case, the threat of the "Border Protection, Antiterrorism, and Illegal Immigration Control Act of 2005," generally known as "the Sensenbrenner Bill" after the congressman who proposed it.[15] Among other things, the bill criminalized violations of federal immigration law, ex-panded the definition of "aggravated felony" to include smuggling offenses and illegal entry and reentry crimes, reduced the maximum period of voluntary de-parture of illegal immigrants from 120 to 60 days, and required the Department of Homeland Security (DHS) to provide a training manual and "pocket guide" relating to enforcement of immigration laws to state and local law enforcement authorities, and provided grants to state and local law enforcement for equip-ment and other products to enforce harsh immigration laws.[16] In the latter two clauses, it foreshadowed the demand that state and local police forces collabo-rate with federal agents in turning over arrested illegal immigrants for prosecu-tion and deportation.

Immigrant rights groups immediately saw in the Sensenbrenner Bill a threat, not only to the large number of undocumented immigrants in the country but also to the large and growing immigrant populations who feared being stigmatized and criminalized from Washington. In response, writes Chris Zepeda-Millán, "The spring of 2006 exploded with a historic wave of protests across the United States" (2017: 1). There were mass demonstrations and other forms of dissent, "ranging from school walkouts and hunger strikes to boycotts and candlelight prayer vigils. Seas of people chanted '*Si se puede*' ["Yes we can"] and carried homemade signs that read 'Today we march. Tomorrow we vote!'" (Zepeda-Millán 2017: 1).

Of course, turnouts for these protests were highest in centers of immigrant populations like Houston, Los Angeles, Chicago, and New York, where they were led by established immigrant rights groups. More surprising was that protests erupted in rural and unexpected places like Siler City, North Carolina, and Fort Myers, Florida. "Members of labor unions, religious groups, hometown associations, and community organizations joined in the protests," but "the preponderance of protesters were people who did not belong to any of these groups and had never participated in political activism" (Zepeda-Millán 2017: 2). By the end of the protest wave, an estimated five-million people had taken part in close to 400 demonstrations across the country (Wallace, Zepeda-Millán, and Jones-Correa 2016).

In policy terms, these demonstrations didn't produce a victory so much as a stalemate, effectively stopping the bill—but not the conservative movement that it reflected. Perhaps more important, they demonstrated that Latinos—despite their typically low levels of political engagement—were capable of high levels of mobilization when they felt themselves threatened. Subsequent studies have shown that both Latino voting and participation in contentious politics increase in hostile political contexts (Barreto and Woods 2005). Although lacking many of the resources traditionally associated with political participation, Latino electoral engagement can increase in times of serious political threat (Zepeda-Millán 2017: 5).

No one in 2006 could have imagined that six years after the immigrant marches, a candidate for the American presidency would launch his campaign with a racist meme by stating that among Mexican immigrants there were "people bringing drugs . . . bringing crime . . . rapists." Soon after, Donald Trump doubled down on this provocative statement by claiming that the Mexican government was "sending" these bad people.[17] The combination of anti-immigrant and xenophobic nationalist rhetoric almost made the Sensenbrenner Bill seem tame by comparison, turning the Latino electorate into an important force in the anti-Trump resistance. We see its heritage and its underlying logic in the "sanctuary cities" movement today that Zepeda-Millán and Wallace examine in their chapter.

Occupy Wall Street

The Occupy campaign was a second antecedent of the anti-Trump Resistance. Fed by several streams of inspiration and provocation, it appeared in lower Manhattan in September 2011. Democrats had suffered severe electoral losses in the 2010 Congressional elections, losing control of the House of Representatives and many state legislatures. The center of gravity in public discourse shifted sharply to the right. Although the presence of a Democratic president and Senate majority preserved some of the policy victories of the previous two years, discussion from the White House and in mainstream politics focused squarely on the budget deficit, overshadowing any ambition for addressing political and economic inequality.

Occupy grew out of the efforts of an anarchist collective in New York, which had previously focused on challenging the policies of Mayor Michael Bloomberg, even staging an encampment outside City Hill in protest of local budget cuts. It followed both a long history of public space protests through occupation (e.g., "Bloombergville" deliberately evoking the "Hoovervilles" of the Great Depression), and far more recent protests around the globe. In particular, activists cited the mass protests in Tahrir Square (in Cairo) that helped bring down Egyptian President Hosni Mubarak, and the Arab Spring more generally, as inspirations. But 2011 also saw an Israeli summer occupation focused on the welfare of the middle class, and an occupation of the Wisconsin state capitol building protesting the newly elected Republican governor's proposals to limit collective bargaining severely. Oddly, the more distant inspirations received more attention.[18]

A small contingent arrived on September 17, 2011, and began to camp out at tiny Zuccotti Park in lower Manhattan. What began as an encampment intended to stage protests against corporate capitalism grew quickly to comprise hundreds of encampments around the United States broadly focused on inequality. Map I.1 represents the extraordinary diffusion of the Occupy encampments during the first few weeks after the original encampment.

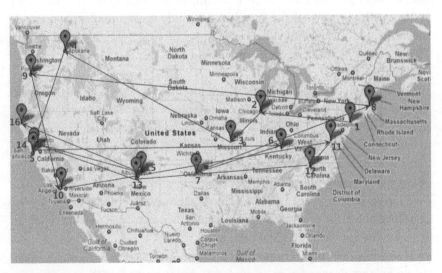

Map I.1 The Spread of Occupy Wall Street, September 17–October 1, 2011.
Source: Occupy Together website (www.occupytogether.org), from Tilly and Tarrow, 2015: 218.

In part, the rapid growth and diffusion of the movement were the result of blunders in social control, most notably the entrapment and arrest of hundreds of marchers crossing the Brooklyn Bridge and the pepper-spraying of students sitting down on the campus of the University of California in Davis. In part, the growth reflected activists reaching out to allies in large cities seeking to spread the movement. And, probably most significantly, local groups self-recruited, emulating the one approach that seemed to generate both mobilization and attention for causes on the left (McAdam et al. 2001). The Occupations offered a place and a tactic to gather and hold public concerns, particularly among young people, on many issues.

The Occupations varied a great deal in terms of their constituencies and their causes, which included different mixes of concerns about the environment, health care, taxation, banking regulation, student loans, and police brutality. All, however, were organized along some sort of hyperdemocratic model, in which General Assemblies, comprising whomever was in attendance, made decisions about both political strategies and governance of the camp by consensus—or didn't make decisions. Ultimately, Occupy became a set of holders for all kinds of grievances about the political climate.

None of the Occupations ever found the single demand that activists consensually found worth negotiating for, and efforts to focus on consensual goals really produced agreement only on the necessity of continuing the occupations and the discussions. Some local authorities tried to negotiate noncontentious ends to the Occupations, with very little success. On November 15, 2011, two months after the Zuccotti Park encampment had begun, New York City police forcibly evacuated the site, then vigilantly spent months making sure activists could not return with camping gear or reestablish any kind of continuing presence. In fairly short order police cleared out hundreds of other encampments.

Occupy disappeared, though, as an unprotected trademark, all sorts of political entrepreneurs tried to appropriate the name. Under this rubric, Occupiers spilled out into many other causes. Occupiers who had activist backgrounds before the campaign returned to the sorts of activities they were doing previously, but now equipped with somewhat more extensive networks of contacts (Brooker 2017). But Occupy was also the first experience for many young people who were now primed and politicized for future action. Many of them—somewhat chastened about the potential of the hyperdemocracy it tried to foster—would appear in the anti-Trump resistance.

Meanwhile, although Occupy itself disappeared, it left a mark on mainstream politics. Responsive politicians, seeking to appropriate the energy of the movement, offered legislation to regulate big money in elections or toughen regulation of big banks. President Obama, in a highly publicized speech delivered in a high school in Osawatomie, Kansas, pivoted from a fixation on the budget deficit to a focus on economic inequality in the United States.[19] Obama wrote the words, but the music came from Occupy.

Other politicians also took up the themes initiated by Occupy, most notably Elizabeth Warren, who ran for the US Senate from Massachusetts, largely on the issue of economic inequality. To be sure, Warren had a long record of scholarship and advocacy on exactly these issues, but Occupy provided an anti-institutional assault that opened political space for her candidacy within institutional politics. Occupy marked an important resurrection of core Democratic Party issues and constituencies, carried by an extremely decentralized and loosely organized movement without ties to that party.

Black Lives Matter

If the immigrant marches organized Latino populations and Occupy drew heavily on mostly white insurgents, Black Lives Matter helped to produce a new, post–civil rights generation of African American activists. The term first appeared as a hashtag (#) on Twitter in 2012, after the acquittal of a Neighborhood Watch volunteer who had shot and killed 17-year-old Trayvon Martin, a black high school student visiting relatives in a gated community in Florida. The police booked the killer, who said that he shot Martin in self-defense, but released him after 5 hours of questioning. When it emerged that Martin's murderer would not be charged with any kind of crime, Martin's parents started an Internet petition demanding criminal prosecution that improbably gathered national attention and more than two-million signatures.[20]

Again, institutional politics picked up on an issue that had emerged at the grassroots, when President Obama, noting that he could have had a son who looked like Martin, expressed his concern. In sympathy and outrage, supporters—including dozens of professional basketball players—posed for photographs wearing hooded sweatshirts, the ostensibly suspicious attire that had led to the shooting. High school students staged walkouts, and activists organized protests across the United States. Over the course of a few months, the case was taken up by a special prosecutor for the state and the US Department of Justice, while the local police chief and state's attorney, who had declined to prosecute, resigned their positions. More than a year later, in July of 2013, Martin's killer was acquitted of second-degree murder as well as a lesser charge of manslaughter. In the wake of the acquittal, three young women started a hashtag on Twitter, #BlackLivesMatter, as a basis for organizing.

Subsequent police killings reached broader activist and public concerns, and these protest demonstrations were larger and more visible than in the past.

Importantly, this was not a new issue to communities of color: The names of young men brutalized or killed by police were well known in their own cities, often appearing on placards at local protests; moreover, Black and Latino parents had long become accustomed to having "the talk" with their children, particularly sons, about how to behave when in sight of police to try to avoid brutal overreaction.[21] What was different was that the Martin story alerted both media and larger audiences to the recognition of a national problem, as additional cases of police killings of young black men drew national attention—but seldom criminal prosecutions.

The conflict exploded when a police officer in Ferguson, Missouri, a small city outside St. Louis, fired 11 shots at unarmed 18-year-old Michael Brown. Cell phone videos of police violence and abusive treatment of young men injured or killed by police circulated around the Internet. Brown's death was followed by large protests in Ferguson, which grew larger and more disruptive in the face of aggressive militarized policing. The protests also drew national attention, but again, there were no criminal indictments.

Black Lives Matter provided an overarching identity to numerous campaigns and demonstrations that started in cities but soon spread to college campuses. The movement was united in identifying a set of problems, especially police violence, but was notably slow in coming up with a clear program of redress. Campaigns generally focused on demanding punishment for the officers who committed racist violence; although some implicated officers lost their jobs, the overwhelming majority were not indicted or tried, much less convicted, of crimes. Besides, activists had identified a general pattern of discrimination, and punishing an individual would do little to redress larger injustices. Sympathetic politicians offered incremental steps, including equipping police with body cameras and better training, but most of the policy responses to a growing national movement occurred at the local level.

Meanwhile, young activists took an even more broadly defined campaign to their college campuses. The first large protests took place at the University of Missouri in 2015, in response to both specific incidents of racist behavior and a larger campus climate that underrepresented minority students found hostile. Students generally demanded a more visible presence and more support for students and faculty of color, as well as the resignation of the removal of the president of the University of Missouri system.[22] Both the campus chancellor and the system president resigned in response, but progress on other demands has been much slower.

More significant, the events at the University of Missouri served as inspiration for a wide range of antiracist campaigns on at least 80 other public and private college campuses. Protests focused on particular incidents of violence, underrepresentation, and inadequate support of Black and Latino students and faculty, provocative speakers, and institutional histories of racism—often represented by statues. Some of the campaigns claimed victories, most visibly the resignation of some administrators, but mobilized grievances remained largely unaddressed.

Taken together, the street protests of Black Lives Matter and the campus protests loosely grouped under "The Demands" that followed raised difficult issues of racial justice. Overwhelmingly, they were characterized by extreme decentralization, in which local concerns were most visible.[23] Both campaigns were met with a backlash, which would soon prove helpful to the mobilization of the Trump campaign, for in a system as polarized as the American one, virtually every movement triggers a countermovement.

The larger point we want to make is that first the Latino movement, then Occupy, and finally Black Lives Matter, offered broad and decentralized challenges to institutionalized inequality in the United States, challenges that were met with mobilized and mobilizable opposition. By the time Donald Trump announced his candidacy for the presidency in June 2016, the politics of race and inequality were more visible and more polarized than they had been for a generation. Both of these themes would come to dominate the 2016 election.

The Dilemmas of the 2016 Election

In the United States, routine elections present activists with regularly scheduled dilemmas about strategies of influence; effective engagement in campaigns promises a chance at touching the levers of power, rather than simply yelling at them. At the same time, electoral participation requires a blurring of issues, a building of broad coalitions, and the inevitable disappointments in signing onto a candidate rather than onto an agenda.[24]

The heritage of the immigrant rights movement, Occupy, and Black Lives Matter was present in the campaign in very different ways, and they mattered.

The dramatic campaign against the Sensenbrenner Bill receded when the bill died in the Senate in 2006. Nonetheless, it triggered a heritage of Latino resentment and sympathetic mobilizing among non-Latinos that emerged rapidly even before the 2016 election when the "Sanctuary" movement arose in hundreds of cities and several states to defend undocumented immigrants from Immigration and Customs Enforcement (ICE). This in turn led to threats from the Trump administration to withhold federal subsidies for local and state programs in cities and states that refused to collaborate with ICE agents attempting to arrest and deport undocumented immigrants.

Similarly, although Occupy has largely vanished as a distinct political concern, its claims, or at least some of them, had been embraced within the left end of the political mainstream. In focusing on political and economic inequality and targeting the privileges of the 1%, Occupy unleashed a left populism that would prove to have substantial appeal. Bernie Sanders, an independent US senator from Vermont, had been using the same language and making the same claims for decades. Sanders challenged Hillary Clinton, the presumptive Democratic nominee, for the party's nomination from the Left. Finding that Occupy had prepared a large audience, many young and new to electoral politics, Sanders ran a campaign based on broad and ambitious politics that, he promised, made for a "political revolution." Sanders called for campaign finance reform, universal health care financed by taxes skewed to weigh most heavily on the rich, free public college tuition, and substantial regulation of finance. Even more modest versions of such claims had been anathema in the Democratic Party for decades. The lineaments of the youthful Occupy movement could be seen in the person of a 74-year-old formerly marginal true believer.

Unlike Occupy, Black Lives Matter was present directly in the 2016 election, appearing at campaign events, and even seizing the stage from Senator Sanders at one event and driving him out.[25] Activists challenged the Democratic candidates to address racial injustice directly, questioning Sanders's assumption that addressing economic inequality would ultimately address the problems of race. Sanders tried to adapt but was largely unsuccessful in reaching Black voters. In contrast, Hillary Clinton, who enjoyed overwhelming, if not always enthusiastic, support from Black primary voters, was an even more attractive target for Black Lives Matter demonstrators. She was routinely challenged at campaign events, as activists asked her to answer for the language and policies of her husband's administration 20 years earlier. Mostly, she said that times had changed.

Although Clinton carried the overwhelming support of Black voters during the general election, Black voter turnout was notably lower than in the elections when Barack Obama was on the ballot. In conjunction with the narrow Trump victory in a few states, lower turnout among African Americans was a contributing factor for the outcome, and some analysts blamed Black Lives Matter for undermining enthusiasm for the Clinton candidacy.[26]

Initially, most of the activist challenges focused on the Democratic primaries. Donald Trump, the most polemical and provocative of the Republican candidates, wasn't generally viewed as having a realistic chance at the nomination. As he began to win primaries, however, Black Lives Matter activists started showing up at his rallies. Unlike other candidates, Trump tried to restrict attendance at his events to only those who already supported him. Protest challengers were removed, often forcibly, and the theatrical Trump rallies became sites for physical confrontation, which Trump encouraged. Rhetorically, Trump emphasized his support for the police and explicitly evoked an earlier time of American greatness, in which America was whiter.

When Hillary Clinton claimed the Democratic nomination, she tried to unite the nonwhite constituencies that Trump had alienated, and this included reaching out to Black Lives Matter. At the Democratic National Convention, she arranged an extended and visible speaking slot for Rev. William Barber, president of North Carolina's chapter of the NAACP (National Association for the Advancement of Colored People), and coordinator of Moral Monday protests in North Carolina for the past two years. She later gave podium space to the Mothers of the Movement, women who had lost children to police violence. Candidate Hillary Clinton reached out to Black Lives Matter, proposing a fainter version of Sanders's Occupy-like proposals. To a large extent, she won the support, but not the enthusiasm of these voters. Although she did well with Black voters, turnout was smaller than that for Barack Obama (Frey 2017).

By the time Donald Trump had claimed a narrow upset victory on the evening of November 8, disappointed voters were even more disaffected than usual. The overwhelming consensus of expert projections had predicted a Clinton victory, albeit with varying degrees of confidence. Trump had failed to win mainstream elite support, garnering, for example, 27 newspaper endorsements in comparison with 500 for Clinton.[27] Moreover, experts opined that Trump's poor performance in debates, demonstrable ignorance on issues, and offensive personal conduct had disqualified him from office. Disaffected and disappointed Sanders and Clinton voters were ready to take to the streets as soon as Trump was elected. This was the background for the construction of what came to be called the Resistance.

Organizing the Resistance

What we describe as the Resistance appeared as soon as Trump claimed victory. The first expressions of alarm were visible in street demonstrations that swept a few large cities in the days after the election. Activists were determined not to accept the impending Trump presidency as normal, declaring that the winner of the electoral college was "Not Our President." In Oakland, California, the marchers were animated by experienced left activists, who clashed with the police.[28] In New York City, demonstrators massed at Trump Tower, determined to show opposition. Far-left organizers tried to take advantage of broader anger against Trump to build an ambitious antisystemic movement. On inauguration day, anarchists marched in Washington, DC, some breaking windows of storefronts and cars and battling police.

A much larger and potentially more effective movement came on its heels. As we have seen, the Women's March followed the day after the inauguration, mobilizing millions nonviolently and adhering to a more conventional demonstration script: negotiating routes and routines with local police. Marie Berry and Erica Chenoweth detail this process in their chapter. The broad Women's March agenda, endorsed by scores of existing organizations, animated massive demonstrations, followed by a series of more narrowly focused events, as Dana Fisher's chapter shows.

The following week, in essentially spontaneous response to the instant and confused implementation of a hastily drafted version of the "Muslim ban" candidate Trump had promised, activists, many of them practicing attorneys, massed at international airports around the country. In addition to large unpermitted demonstrations announced on social media, the lawyers offered free services to people caught in transit, as Dorf and Chu describe in their chapter. Demonstrators sported signs announcing not only opposition to Trump, but support for a multiracial, multiethnic, and religiously diverse America. In the pictures that circulated in mainstream media and social media feeds, pussyhats, the homemade symbol of the women's march, were sported by demonstrators everywhere. The activists found institutional support immediately. President Trump fired acting Attorney General Sally Yates, who refused to defend the travel ban in court, and several federal district judges issued injunctions against its implementation. The Resistance was provoked, and the Trump administration was frustrated in coming up against institutional obstacles amplified by protest in the streets.

The airport protests were followed by large demonstrations organized for racial unity, for science, for climate change, for immigrant rights, for tax justice, to preserve the Affordable Care Act, and for truth about Russian influence in the election. The large demonstrations, organized by coalitions of groups that overlapped across events, followed the pattern of sympathy actions in large cities across the United States. Coupled with local events directed against elements of the Trump agenda and more immediate actions against new provocations (the nomination of Neil Gorsuch to the Supreme Court, for example, or the announcement of a withdrawal from the Paris Climate Accords), the Resistance mobilized extensively, even as Trump's core support remained largely untouched.[29]

The new efforts built on the well-established activist organizations from the center to the left of the American political spectrum, filled with indignation about the president and animated by an intensified urgency for action. In the context of Republican control of most state legislatures as well as the House, Senate, and presidency, activists across the political spectrum took up demonstrations. People who wanted to retain the Affordable Health Care Act called members of Congress and turned up at town hall meetings, while CODEPINK pacifists[30] turned up at the confirmation hearings of Trump's appointees to heckle and ridicule their opponents. Many new groups rapidly appeared to organize the new activists while established groups, flush with money raised in urgent anger, stepped up their activities, all the while promoting a very broad spectrum of grievances and activities, as the chapter by Han and Oyakawa shows. The breadth of the opposition ranged from formerly mainstream Republicans, now defined as "Never Trumpers," to frustrated civil servants leaving the government in protest, to business leaders resigning from presidential commissions, to Occupy and Black Lives Matter–inspired proponents of direct action. This created a sense of both confusion and possibility, one that the truly radical but poorly organized Trump administration made possible.

But this was an inherently unstable situation. The American political system provides for routine elections at all levels of government, affording those with grievances repeated opportunities to turn toward more conventional politics. Special elections to the House of Representatives, mostly to replace Republicans who had been appointed to the administration, drew extraordinary attention, and massive infusions of Democratic and Republican money. Although most of these electoral outcomes were far closer than electoral history would have predicted, Republicans retained all the initial contests, testifying to the strength of the Trumpian movement, or at least of a very polarized politics, in many parts of the country.

The point we wish to emphasize is that the opposition to Trump included both groups concerned with making a broadside attack on American political institutions and others that were desperately concerned with defending those very institutions. Trump faced opposition from generally marginal pacifists and anarchists and from federal judges trying to protect constitutional rights. Some of Trump's opponents broke windows, but a much larger share wrote letters to Congress, talked to neighbors, and donated money to candidates and to the broad spectrum of groups who opposed his administration. Trump's inconsistent and often erratic behavior, his lack of deference to well-established norms, and his savage attacks on opponents made it possible for those in the Resistance to downplay their differences on tactics and ultimate goals—at least during the first year of his presidency. We want to understand how activists define these moments, how the inherent tension about goals and strategies and political instability develops, and how movement activism and the electoral process affect each other. In the pages that follow, we offer an early look at the dynamics of a cycle of contention that may define much of American politics for a long time to come.

The Dynamics of Contention

Before turning to the Resistance, it is important to place it in the dynamics of American politics more generally. Today's American politics provides a notable contrast with older models offered by political scientists decades ago in which the pursuit of the "median voter" defined both politics and policies. Instead we see an exceptionally polarized politics in which each party is increasingly captive to its most passionate and ideological supporters. We also see a fundamental shift in the relationship between activism and the party system. Whereas, in the cycle of contention of the 1960s, the two parties overlapped in their policy positions, forcing movement activists to work largely outside the party system, partisan polarization has now allowed movement activists to enter each of the two main parties, and indeed given them the opportunity to increase it (McAdam and Kloos 2014).

This does not mean that all movement activists have found a home within the party system, but it does mean that movements are more likely to assert their positions in relation to the party that is closest to their interests than they did in the past. The most important example on the Left was the movement against the Iraq War, in which many of the activists in the street were Democrats (Heaney and Rojas 2015). The most successful example on the Right was the Tea Party movement, which was so successful in advancing its ideas that it became a powerful interest group within the Republican Party (van Dyke and Meyer 2014).

The "movementization" of the party system has had another important effect on the dynamics of American politics: It led to fierce sequences of movement–countermovement interaction. As Tarrow argues in his chapter, all cycles of contention produce reactions among those who oppose the "early risers" in these cycles (Meyer and Staggenborg 1996). To the degree that Donald Trump is the figurehead of a movement, the Resistance against his government has taken on the character of a countermovement. But that resistance has itself produced a spiral of countermovement-like reaction in the form of a white nationalist fringe that—encouraged by Trump's rhetoric—has been willing to adopt violent rhetoric and physical violence against opponents. The upsurge in antiminority violence that followed Trump's election is both the expression of traditional white racial resentment (Abramowitz 2017) and a response to the political opportunity offered by Trump's racist rhetoric, now with the imprimatur of the White House. Just as the Tea Party became an integral movement wing of the Republican Party in the early part of the decade, the racist Right has become a critical part of that party's corona today, albeit one that some institutional Republicans accept only reluctantly.

Meanwhile, Black Lives Matter, whose efforts often included nonviolent civil disobedience, spurred a political backlash that presaged the Trump campaign. Although the movement gained support among ethnic minorities and young people, it became a focal point for opposition from older whites. The response was easily visible on cable television, as conservative hosts identified the movement as racist or a hate group, rather than as a response to such problems.

Competing hashtags, including "bluelivesmatter" (expressing support for police) and "alllivesmatter" emerged in public debate, largely obscuring the issue of differential policing. Heightened attention from advocates on multiple sides of this issue meant that each subsequent event, usually a shooting of a young black man, drew an unusual degree of national attention.

This takes us to the loosely connected spectrum of groups that our book will examine under the rubric of the Resistance. Its components share an abhorrence of Donald Trump and his government, but it is far from a unified movement, with recognized leaders, cohesive organizations, and a generally accepted ideological message. The Resistance also bridges the fuzzy line between institutional and noninstitutional politics. Whereas groups like Move-on and Indivisible have loose links to the Democratic Party, many others—like Black Lives Matter—see the party as part of the problem they face in attempting to transform the American polity. In parallel to these policy differences, some groups use performances that work within the boundaries of system—for example, in the organized use of mass visits to congressional offices and town meetings—whereas others employ a repertoire of contention that leans more heavily toward street politics and—at the margins—uses violence against the extreme elements on the Right.

These internal differences of viewpoint and repertoire make it difficult to predict a cohesive "intersectional" unity among the varying components of the Resistance. As Dana Fisher's contribution shows, on some issues, the components of the Resistance find it easy to make common cause, whereas on others, there are differences of perspective that may make it difficult to effectively oppose the (thus far) solid ranks of the Trumpian movement. Although Trump offers these groups a single highly visible focal point, his tendency to shift his policy targets and identify new enemies on an almost-daily basis leaves his opponents off-balance and makes it difficult for them to formulate a common program and common collective forms of action.

Our Book

In this Introduction, we have done no more than provide the background and a broad framework for the chapters that follow:

In Part One, Doug McAdam and Kenneth Roberts provide, respectively, a historical and a comparative perspective on the Trump presidency and on the resistance to it. McAdam elaborates on a point we made earlier: that although Trump is an unusual figure and has brought his movement into the heart of the American state, his excesses must be seen in the context of the more general movementization of American politics and of the role of racial resentment in the Republican appeal that goes back to the civil rights era. Similarly, Roberts's chapter shows how—despite his unique characteristics, Trump can be seen as an American version of the right-wing populism that has spread across Latin America and Europe in recent decades. These two chapters embed the book in both a historical and a comparative framework.

Part Two of the book surveys some of the main actors who initiated the anti-Trump resistance. Marie Berry and Erica Chenoweth's chapter begins where the Resistance began—with the organizational tributaries that produced a tidal wave of support for the Women's March on January 21, 2017. Ostensibly the result of a new organization, the Women's March actually represented the sustained work of many well-established interest groups that spread the word and supported the political mobilization, as Berry and Chenoweth show.

The next two chapters analyze two highly visible facets of the early phase of the Resistance. In "Mobilizing for Immigrant Rights," Chris Zepeda-Millán and Sophia Wallace draw on the Latino-based movement that grew out of the 2006 struggle against the Sensenbrenner Bill to analyze today's immigrant rights movement. Then, using three on-site protester surveys, Dana Fisher shows how the climate movement expanded over the 3-year period of her research. She also shows how it intersected with other parts of the Resistance through joint participation in the climate and women's marches.

Part Three of the book turns to actors and organizations that powered the Resistance during its first year. In their chapter, Michael Dorf and Michael Chu show how a lawyers' movement rapidly arose to contest the Trump administration's abrupt and savage ban on trying to come to the United States. In his chapter, David Karpf shows how the media—both new and old—transmitted the messages of resistance both to decision-makers and to the various sectors of the resistance. Karpf shows how social media tools—particularly Facebook and Twitter—have become the new town square through which activist messages are shared and protest participants are recruited. In her chapter, Megan Brooker focuses on the Indivisible movement, showing how its founders went from institutional to noninstitutional contention by modeling a campaign for town hall meetings after the campaign of the Tea Party.

Part Four of our book turns to the dynamics of this rapidly changing movement. In his chapter, Sidney Tarrow sees the Resistance as part of complex movement–countermovement interaction whose beginnings go back well before the 2016 election and that ripened into a cycle of contention that has put American democracy to the test. In her chapter, "Generational Dynamics in the Resistance," Nancy Whittier explores the emerging generational dynamics in the Resistance, with special attention to points of generational transmission (particularly the recruitment and framing efforts of long-standing organizations) and generational conflict (particularly differences of collective identity and culture).

In their chapter, Hahrie Han and Michelle Oyakawa show how two different organizations—a traditional church-based grassroots organization and a new organization that began in Washington—the Indivisible movement—proposed two different solutions to the challenges of the Resistance.

The book concludes with two chapters: David Meyer draws on the experiences of Year One of the Resistance to speculate on what we have learned about the dilemmas of coalition-building, focusing on the tensions between tactics and ultimate aims; and, in his Afterword, Jacob Hacker draws on the chapters in the book to reflect on the prospects for American democracy.

PART ONE

TRUMPISM IN COMPARATIVE-HISTORICAL PERSPECTIVE

Putting Donald Trump in Historical Perspective

Racial Politics and Social Movements from the 1960s to Today

DOUG MCADAM

The tumultuous onset of Donald Trump's administration, to say nothing of the president's oversize presence, has so riveted our attention in the moment that we're in danger of losing critically important historical perspectives. Trump's rhetoric and behavior are so unprecedented and extreme that the tendency is to see him and the divisions he embodies as something wholly new in American politics. They are not, nor in broad relief, is the president. Instead, Trump is only the most extreme expression and product of a brand of racial politics practiced ever-more brazenly by the Republican Party since its origins in the 1960s. His unexpected rise to power was also aided by a number of illiberal institutional developments in American politics that also have older roots. It is critically important that we understand these historical forces and the ways in which they shaped and facilitated his rise, lest we come to see Trump as the source of all of our problems. If we so conclude and Trump winds up being ousted from power without the underlying structural and institutional threats being addressed, ours will be a hollow victory and America will remain a flawed and fragile democracy. Motivated by this worry, I use this chapter to (a) detail the origins and evolution of the exclusionary brand of racial politics characteristic of the Republican Party since the mid to late 1960s, and (b) to describe three flawed institutions that not only aided Trump's rise to power, but that will continue to threaten the long-term survival of American democracy if left unchanged.

The Decisive Shift in the Racial Geography of American Politics

As one of the two or three most significant movements in US history, the modern civil rights struggle is routinely credited with any number of specific effects. Arguably the most important legacy of the movement, however, is one whose significance is only now starting to be recognized. By setting in motion a fundamental transformation of the racial geography of American politics, the movement brought to a close the most sustained period of progressive policymaking in federal history (1932–1968) and ushered in the era of rising inequality and political polarization in which we remain firmly mired.

The pivot point of this transformation comes in the early to mid 1960s as a result of the relentless pressure that civil rights forces brought to bear on the American state and the Democratic administrations who were serving as its stewards at the time. But to really grasp the decisive effect the movement had on the two major parties, the New Deal coalition, and American politics more generally, it is necessary to go back even further in time and describe in some detail the distinctive racial geography that structured politics in this country from the close of the Civil War (1865) to the onset of the 1960s. Only by putting the events of that pivotal decade in broader historical context can we appreciate the seismic shift in the political landscape set in motion by the civil rights revolution.

The standard narrative account of the relationship between the civil rights movement and the Democratic Party tends to depict the two as allies in the struggle. To be sure, the celebrated legislative achievements that marked the struggle—the Civil Rights Act of 1965 and the 1964 Voting Rights Act—could not have been achieved without the contributions of both. But to see the movement and the party as allies is to ignore the enduring and deep antipathy that marked the relationship between civil rights forces and the Democratic Party until well into the 1930s. In truth, the relationship evolved through three distinct phases. The first lasts from the close of the Civil War until the election of Franklin Delano Roosevelt (FDR) in 1932. This is the period of intense, sustained enmity between the Democratic Party and civil rights forces who, in truth, are a small and beleaguered group during this, the heyday of Jim Crow. The antagonism is rooted in history. It is hard to overstate the lasting hatred that southern whites felt toward a Republican Party that, from their point of view, had inflicted the "war of northern aggression" on the region. With southern blacks denied the franchise during this period, white elites transform the region into a one-party racial autocracy—for example, the "Solid South"—that serves as the electoral cornerstone of the national Democratic Party.

Roosevelt's election in 1932 marked the onset of a second, much more complicated, contradictory period in the relationship between the Democratic Party and civil rights forces. For besides reclaiming the White House after a 12-year hiatus, FDR's victory also served to fundamentally remake the party itself. Although the South remained solidly Democratic in 1932, Roosevelt's resounding victory essentially marked the birth of the modern Democratic Party with its dominant northern, liberal, labor wing. In the 1960s this wing would, indeed, ally itself and the broader party with the civil rights movement, ushering in the third and final period in that evolving relationship. From 1932 until the early 1960s, however, the party remained fundamentally divided on the issue of race, though by default committed to accommodating the regional "sensibilities" of the Dixiecrats. No one was more adept at this accommodation than FDR during his long tenure in office. Given his patrician background, his clear liberal views, and the even more radical sensibilities of some of his key advisers—especially those of his wife, Eleanor—you would have thought that southern whites would have abandoned the party in droves during the Roosevelt years. To the contrary, Roosevelt was wildly popular in the South, carrying every single state of the former Confederacy in all four of his electoral victories.

Some of this popularity was due to the fact that, unlike today, social programs then had considerable appeal in the South, the nation's poorest region, struggling as it was under the added burden of the Great Depression. But make no mistake about it; had Roosevelt openly espoused pro–civil rights views, his stance on any other issue would have mattered little to the white South. The fact of the matter is, FDR took great care during his 13 years in office to give the white South—and especially the region's powerful Congressional delegations—no reason to doubt his commitment to the long-standing federal–southern "understanding" with respect to race. With the close of Reconstruction in 1877, federal involvement in racial policy came to an abrupt end. Control over matters of race reverted to the states. Roosevelt was not about to violate this tacit "hands-off" policy. Even on as morally a compelling issue as lynching, "Roosevelt remained silent on racial matters throughout his four-term presidency, refusing to come out in favor of anti-lynching legislation on the numerous occasions such bills were brought before Congress" (McAdam 1999: xx).

The important point is that as long as the progressive racial views of northern liberal Democrats were held in check and tacit support for Jim Crow remained the guiding—if unofficial—policy of the party, the South remained solidly and reliably in the Democratic column. This status quo held throughout FDR's tenure in office and, indeed, was still in place as the 1960s dawned. Owing to the South's critical electoral significance to the party, the Democrats remained, as late as 1960, far more conservative on racial matters than the GOP. Consider Congressional voting on the 1957 Civil Rights Act. Notwithstanding its

Table 1.1 **Congressional Voting on 1957**
Civil Rights Act

	House		Senate	
	Yes	No	Yes	No
Democrats	118	107	29	18
Republicans	167	19	43	0

substantive weakness, the bill's status as the first piece of federal civil rights leg-islation since Reconstruction made it symbolically highly significant. Table 1.1 reports the partisan breakdown in support for the bill.

For those conditioned by today's stark partisan divisions to think of Republicans as extreme racial conservatives, the results of the 1957 vote will come as a revelation. Whereas Senate Republicans backed the bill by a 2 to 1 margin, 22 of their 29 Democratic colleagues opposed the measure. In the House, a stunning 90% of GOP representatives cast their votes in favor of the Act, whereas Democrats favored the bill by the slimmest of margins (52% to 48%). Quite simply, this important piece of breakthrough legislation was the work of Republican, not Democratic, lawmakers.

Nothing much had changed in regard to race and region heading into the 1960 presidential election. Indeed, the Republican candidate, Richard Nixon, had amassed an impeccable civil rights voting record while in Congress and, as vice president, had been tasked by Eisenhower with steering the aforemen-tioned Civil Rights Act through Congress. By contrast, the Democratic can-didate, John F. Kennedy (JFK), had shown little interest in civil rights during his brief tenure in the Senate. In the end, the election turned out to be one of the closest in US history. Out of better than 68 million ballots cast, JFK won by just over 112,000 votes. The demography of JFK's win, however, had disqui-eting implications for the future of his party. Reflecting the strategic dilemma that would roil the Democrats in the decade to come, the votes of both African Americans and southern whites were crucial to JFK's razor-thin victory. These electoral cross pressures meant that the new president began his term in a serious strategic straightjacket. If, on the one hand, he remained silent on racial matters, as FDR had done, JFK risked alienating the large and strategically positioned black vote so key to his victory against Nixon. If, on the other hand, he sought to solidify black support by aggressively promoting new civil rights measures, he risked the wrath of the Solid South. As bad as this strategic dilemma was, two developments in the early 1960s were to make it even worse. The first was the heyday of the modern civil rights movement. Which brings us to the second di-lemma: Kennedy had to contend with the intense bottom-up pressure of the civil rights movement during an especially "hot" phase of the Cold War (Dudziak 2000; Layton 2000; McAdam 1999, 2009). In his celebrated 1,000 days in office, JFK confronted no fewer than four major Cold War episodes: the erection of the Berlin Wall by East German authorities; the collapse of the Diem regime in South Vietnam; the disastrous Bay of Pigs invasion in Cuba; and the single most dangerous confrontation with the Soviet Union in the history of the superpower competition. This refers, of course, to the Cuban Missile Crisis in October of 1962.

Nor should these two dilemmas be regarded as separate sources of pressure on the administration. Instead, there was a close connection between the two. For their part, the Soviets monitored racial tensions and conflict in the United States very closely, launching major propaganda attacks in the wake of every celebrated attack or atrocity. And central to movement strategy during this period was a savvy understanding of just how vulnerable the US state was to criticism on racial grounds, as a result of the Cold War. Publicized instances of American-style racism constituted an enormous liability when it came to countering Soviet influence in the world, especially among "peoples of color" in the emerging nations of Asia and Africa. The central tactical dynamic at the heart of the movement during these years reflects this understanding. "Lacking sufficient power to defeat the segregationists at the state or local level [in the South], movement forces sought to broaden the conflict by inducing opponents to disrupt public order to the point where sympathetic media coverage and broad public support—international no less than domestic—for the movement could be mobilized. In turn, the media coverage and public [outrage] virtually compelled federal officials to intervene in ways supportive of the movement" (McAdam 2009: 67–68).

The picture is of the Kennedy administration and, by extension, the Democrats, being inexorably pushed off-center by the centrifugal force of a national movement operating at the peak of its extraordinary mobilizing powers. Like Truman and Roosevelt before him, Kennedy had taken office determined to mollify the southern wing of his party, without whom he knew he would never be returned to office in 1964. Ultimately, however, the pressure brought to bear on him by the movement—compounded by the Cold War dynamic just described—forced him to move sharply left in policy terms

There was, of course, a price to be paid for so direct a challenge to the southern wing of Kennedy's own party. As much as he had hoped, at the time of his election, to be able to balance the demands of Dixiecrats and civil rights forces, by the time of his death (1963), Kennedy was clearly perceived as siding with the movement. While doing fieldwork in Mississippi more than 20 years after JFK's assassination, it was not uncommon to find framed pictures of JFK and Martin Luther King, Jr. on the walls of the homes of black interview subjects. Kennedy remained a revered figure to many in the black community, especially those old enough to have experienced his presidency. On the other side of the political ledger, it seems clear that most Dixiecrats, outraged by what they saw as federal complicity in the attack on "the southern way of life," were poised to abandon JFK and the Democrats in 1964. In the end, though, his death meant that the revolt, if it were to come, would be on someone else's watch. That someone would be a native southerner, Lyndon Baines Johnson (LBJ).

Correctly divining the mood of the country, LBJ hitched his own electoral prospects to the fallen president, in essence dedicating the balance of his term to the realization of JFK's legislative program. The most immediate, high-profile manifestation of this stance was LBJ's sustained and effective advocacy of what would become the Civil Rights Act of 1964. In his own words, "No memorial oration or eulogy could more eloquently honor President Kennedy's memory than the earliest possible passage of the civil rights bill for which he fought so long." Johnson's embrace of his predecessor's civil rights agenda did not, however, mean that he was blind to the serious political risks posed by this stance. Indeed, as both a white southerner and one of the consummate majority leaders in the history of the Senate, LBJ understood the contradictions inherent in his party better than almost anyone. As he headed into the election year of 1964, he was determined to manage those contradictions and retain the loyalties of both civil rights forces and his fellow Dixiecrats. He assumed—rightly in the end—that his support for the aforementioned bill would mollify those civil rights leaders who were initially deeply skeptical of Johnson's commitment to the cause. The bigger trick, he knew, would be avoiding another rebellion by the southern wing of his party. The bill was bad enough. The threat of more Birminghams, with armies of civil rights protestors descending on southern cities, was worse still.

Johnson did what he could to avert this threat, indirectly calling on civil rights leaders to effectively suspend disruptive demonstrations in the run-up to the fall election (McAdam 1999: 168). With the Republican presidential candidate, Barry Goldwater, voicing strong opposition to the civil rights bill, LBJ argued that additional demonstrations could further alienate the white South and drive Dixiecrats into the GOP fold in November. In the end, virtually all of the major civil rights groups acceded to Johnson's call for a suspension of direct action during this period. Notwithstanding his mastery of consensus politics, Johnson's efforts to hold his fractious party together came to naught. In 1964 disaffected white southerners did the unthinkable and cast their votes for the once-despised Republican Party. For the first time ever, the electoral votes of the Deep South went to the GOP. The magnitude of LBJ's landslide win in 1964 may have obscured the revolution for most Americans, but the full implications of the electoral realignment evident in the 1964 returns were not lost on everyone.

Even as the Democratic Party was being pushed sharply left by the civil rights movement, the GOP was moving in the opposite direction. Numerous commentators have, in fact, noted the significance of the Republican shift, attributing it largely to Nixon's aggressive courtship of the white South in his successful 1968 run for the White House (Carmines and Stimson 1989; Edsall and Edsall 1992). But without denying the significance of Nixon's win, the conventional account obscures two key points. First, the GOP shift to the right began earlier than the 1968 contest. Second, at least in part, we see the same movement–party dynamic at work in the Republican shift that motivated the leftward movement of the Democrats. That is, the GOP also shifted its ideological center of gravity in response to the force of social movement activity; this time on the right. The movement in question is the "white backlash" that develops in response to the civil rights struggle, and in particular the electoral embodiment of that movement in the form of the presidential challenges mounted by Alabama Governor George Wallace in 1964 and 1968.

Given its intensity at the time and, more important, its significant long-term political and electoral consequences, it is remarkable that this movement is largely forgotten today and certainly not invoked as an important factor by those seeking to understand the racialized, partisan divisions in the contemporary United States. Bottom line: If it was the civil rights struggle that largely pushed the Democrats left in the early to mid 1960s, it was the mobilized force of this amorphous white resistance movement that encouraged the sharp shift to the right by the Republicans in the mid to late 1960s and, of course, beyond. Indeed, one of the central sources of continuity linking the Republican Party that emerged under Nixon in the late 1960s and early 1970s with the GOP of today is a sustained politics of racial reaction. I will subsequently have much more to say about this. For now, I am simply trying to highlight the origins of the distinctive, if thinly veiled, racial conservatism that has now defined the GOP for better than a half-century. Its origins are bound up with the aforementioned white resistance movement and especially with its spread to the North in the mid to late 1960s.

It began, however, as a strictly southern segregationist response to the resurgent civil rights movement. To be sure, this regional struggle has *not* been forgotten. What commentators have almost entirely missed, however, is the extent to which the southern segregationist countermovement morphed into and inspired the more generalized nationwide "white backlash" of the mid to late 1960s. But make no mistake about it; these two forms of resistance were definitely linked, if not organizationally then in intent—resistance to integration—and underlying racial antipathy. And no figure was more crucial to this linkage than the South's most celebrated defender of "segregation now, segregation tomorrow, segregation forever," Alabama Governor George Wallace.

Wallace burst onto the national scene in 1963, first by issuing the aforementioned rallying cry during his inaugural address as governor in January of that year. That was nothing, however, compared with his follow-up of June 11 when he "stood in the school house door"—actually the entrance to Foster Auditorium on the campus of the University of Alabama—to bar the admission of the first two African American students in school history. The act was, of course, futile, with the students admitted to campus with little fanfare the following day. Wallace, however, had achieved his political aim; not only enhancing his popularity as governor, but emerging overnight as the most potent symbol of racial resistance in the country. He showed just how "potent" when he shocked both parties and mainstream political analysts by successfully challenging the popular sitting president of his own party in three northern primaries in the run up to the 1964 general election. Wallace's surprising showing sent shock waves through both parties. Partly in response, many Republicans—including Barry Goldwater, the party's surprise nominee in 1964—began to openly call for a shift to the right to capture the Wallace vote and make inroads in the no longer "Solid South." In the wake of Wallace's surprising showing in the North and Goldwater's capture of the Deep South in the general election, GOP calls to look south and move right grew louder and more frequent, especially as the "white backlash" took hold in the rest of the country.

Events between 1966 and 1968 did nothing to reverse the general trend previously discussed. If anything, the increased frequency and destructiveness of the riots in 1967 and 1968, the full flowering of the black power movement in these years, combined on the other side with the growing use of an inflammatory "law-and-order" rhetoric by white politicians, accelerated the racial polarization already evident in the 1966 elections. As the 1968 presidential contest drew near, two candidates moved aggressively to exploit this dramatic shift in the political landscape. Both would have been seen as wildly improbable candidates just a few years earlier, but their shrewd understanding of the changing nature of American racial politics gave them a significant strategic edge heading into the 1968 race.

The Republican nominee, Richard Nixon, was thought to have been washed up as a serious contender when he was soundly beaten by Pat Brown in the 1962 California gubernatorial race. And yet, here he was 6 years later, running for president on the basis of what he termed his "southern strategy." Although the Democrats had lost the Deep South in 1964, Nixon now believed that increasing racial polarization in the country rendered the entire region up for grabs. By distancing himself from the civil rights struggle and reminding voters of the close connection between blacks and the Democratic Party, Nixon hoped to make big inroads in the region while capitalizing on traditional Republican strength in the West and Midwest.

If Nixon's candidacy was surprising, George Wallace's third-party challenge was anything but. First and foremost, there was his surprising showing in the 1964 Democratic primaries. Beyond that, however, the deepening divisions within the country, increasing anger at urban riots, court-ordered busing, and general lawlessness made Wallace a more formidable candidate in 1968 than he had been 4 years earlier. Although still a hero to the white South, Wallace now enjoyed considerable support throughout the country and especially among the embattled white working class of the cities of the industrial North. Like Nixon, Wallace too had taken notice of the deepening racial divisions nationwide, but especially the loss of the once Solid South by the Democrats 4 years earlier. As a Dixiecrat himself, Wallace aimed to appeal to his regional base while reaching out to disaffected whites elsewhere in the country.

Standing in the way of these two men was the Democratic nominee, Hubert Humphrey. It would be difficult, however, to think of any presidential candidate from the incumbent party in American history who went into the election burdened by more "negatives" than did Humphrey in 1968. For starters, it took the assassination of Robert Kennedy to open the door for Humphrey's nomination in the first place. As a consequence, many in Humphrey's own party saw him as an illegitimate candidate, as effectively usurping a nomination that, by rights, should have gone to Kennedy, or even the early antiwar candidate, Eugene McCarthy. More important, as Johnson's VP, Humphrey was tainted both by the administration's prosecution of the war in Vietnam and its increasingly unpopular social programs, including its association with the civil rights movement. Finally, as if Humphrey needed anything else to overcome, there was the almost-surreal spectacle of the violence and mass unrest that accompanied that year's Democratic Convention in Chicago. On the eve of the election, it seemed as if Humphrey's best chance might come from Nixon and Wallace splitting the white southern vote, allowing the Democrat to squeak by with the slimmest electoral plurality. It didn't quite work out that way.

Nixon and Wallace did indeed wind up splitting the South, with Wallace prevailing in the Deep South and Nixon capturing most of the border states.

In the end, though, the division was not enough to give Wallace the electoral votes needed to deny the outright victory to the two major parties and to force, as he had hoped, the House of Representatives to resolve the matter. Nixon edged out Humphrey by the narrowest of margins, 43.4% to 42.7%. As both parties looked to the future, however, it wasn't the slim gap between Nixon and Humphrey on which they were focused, but rather the overwhelming majority represented by the combined votes cast for Nixon and Wallace. The significance of the Wallace candidacy (and the broader white resistance movement he represented) for the future electoral prospects of both parties was clear on the face of the 1968 election returns. With the two major parties evenly dividing

86% of the popular vote, the remaining 14% who had supported Wallace clearly emerged as the balance of power in future elections. As Converse and his associates noted in the wake of the election, "it is obvious to any 'rational' politician hoping to maximize votes in 1970 or 1972 that there are several times more votes to be gained by leaning toward Wallace than by leaning toward [Eugene] McCarthy" (Converse et al. 1969: 1105).

The Evolving Rhetoric of Racial Reaction

Wholeheartedly embracing this strategy, after winning in 1968, Nixon was to spend much of his first term in office perfecting a politics of racial reaction to cement his appeal with white southerners and racial conservatives elsewhere in the country. In their 1991 book, *Chain Reaction*, the Edsalls succinctly describe the racial politics that animated the Republican "brand" pioneered by Nixon. In their words:

> Race was central, Nixon and key Republican strategists began to recognize, to the fundamental conservative strategy of establishing a new polarization of the electorate, a polarization isolating a liberal, activist, culturally permissive, rights oriented, and pro-black Democratic Party against those unwilling to pay the financial costs of this reconfigured social order.

The strategy was to depict the GOP as the party of the law-abiding, tax-paying, "silent (mostly white) majority" and demonize the Democrats as the party of liberals and the undeserving (disproportionately minority) poor whose dependence on social programs was taking money out of the pockets of hard-working, overtaxed (white) Americans. Sound familiar? It should, because in its broad outlines, it echoes the thinly veiled, racialized rhetoric that is now virtually consensual in the Republican Party. But it was Nixon who set the basic template 60 years ago.

In his 1969 book, *The Emerging Republican Majority*, Nixon adviser Kevin Phillips nicely captured the critique of Democratic social programs that informed much of Nixon's rhetoric and policy pronouncements as candidate and president. Wrote Phillips, "The Democratic Party fell victim to the ideological impetus of a liberalism which had carried it beyond programs taxing the few for the benefit of the many to programs taxing the many on behalf of the few." In the coded language of the emerging racial politics of the GOP, the "many" were understood to be white and the "few" were black (or other minorities) and undeserving. I could offer countless examples of essentially the same thinly veiled, racialized attack on liberal social programs, unfair taxes, big government, and the undeserving, dependent poor offered up by prominent Republicans spanning the last five decades, but I will confine myself to just a few of the "greatest hits."

One of the highlights of Ronald Reagan's standard stump speech during his 1976 primary challenge to Gerald Ford was an outrageous story about an unnamed "welfare queen" from Chicago who had amassed a small fortune by using multiple Social Security cards to fraudulently collect welfare and other government benefits. Here was Reagan's actual description of the woman: "There's a woman in Chicago . . . . She has 80 names, 30 addresses, 12 Social Security cards . . . . She's got Medicaid, getting food stamps and she is collecting welfare under each of their names. Her tax-free cash income alone is over $150,000."[1]

It was a great story and one perfectly calibrated to curry the support of outraged white voters; too bad it wasn't really true. There was a woman in Chicago whose circumstances vaguely resembled Reagan's foil, but only if you wildly exaggerated her behavior. In the end, though, it didn't matter what the truth was; the story of the welfare queen quickly attained the status of an urban legend, believed to be true by nearly everyone. Why did the story survive if it wasn't really true? Probably because it played on the racial stereotypes and prejudice of many white voters. Although Reagan did not mention the race of the culprit, the colorful details with which he embellished the story—the woman lived on the South Side of Chicago, drove a Cadillac, and so on—left little doubt in the listener's mind that the woman was black.

In 1988, Ronald Reagan's vice president, George H. W. Bush, squared off against Massachusetts Governor Michael Dukakis in the general election. Dukakis maintained a sizable lead in the polls throughout the summer, but one of the most famous attack ads in presidential history helped turn the tide when first aired in September. The ad, titled "Weekend Pass," opens with side-by-side photos of the two candidates, over a header reading "Bush and Dukakis on Crime."[2] A narrator then tells us that "Bush supports the death penalty for first-degree murderers. Dukakis not only opposes the death penalty, he allowed first-degree murderers to have weekend passes from prison. One was Willie Horton who murdered a boy during a robbery, stabbing him 19 times. Despite a life sentence, Horton received 10 weekend passes from prison. Horton fled, kidnapped a young couple, stabbing the man, and repeatedly raping his girlfriend. Weekend passes: Dukakis on crime." The narrator makes no mention of race, but with two pictures of Mr. Horton filling the screen for most of the ad, he doesn't need to. If the candidates' positions on crime are the nominal text of the spot, the subtext is race, with the ad underscoring the close association between the Democratic Party and African Americans.

Space constraints make it impossible to provide similar examples of thinly veiled Republican racial rhetoric from every election cycle, but I would be remiss if I did not take up the especially charged racial dynamics of the Obama years. For all the consistency of the GOP's racialized rhetoric over the past four to five decades, a significant body of evidence supports the conclusion that the party's racial politics grew that much more extreme during the Obama years. Analyzing data from the American National Election Studies, Tesler and Sears show that the racial attitudes of those who identify with the two major parties are now more polarized than ever. Consistent with that finding, a host of analyses of the 2008 election results suggest that a nontrivial number of white voters, who otherwise would have probably voted for President Obama, cast ballots for John McCain. Using various statistical models, one analyst estimated that Obama would have received anywhere from 2 to 12 additional percentage points of the vote had the racial attitudes of the American electorate been "neutral." For all the evidence showing the influence of antiblack attitudes on voting behavior and party identification in 2008, those attitudes strengthened and polarized even more over the course of Obama's first term in office. Most tellingly, Pasek and his colleagues show that Republican identifiers in 2012 expressed significantly greater antiblack attitudes than their counterparts did in 2008.

The question is this: Where did this upsurge in "old-fashioned racism" come from? Based on the best survey data on support for the Tea Party, it seems reasonable to credit the movement for at least some of the infusion of more extreme racial views and actions into American politics. We begin by considering the racial attitudes of Tea Party supporters and what that suggests about the animating racial politics of the movement wing of the Republican Party. In this, we rely on two sources of data: the multistate surveys of support for the Tea Party conducted by Parker and Barreto in 2010 and 2011 and Abramowitz's analysis of the October 2010 wave of the American National Election Studies.

We start with a key finding from the Parker and Barreto study. Fifty-six percent of those survey respondents who identified as Republicans in their study were also Tea Party supporters. In and of itself, this is a remarkable figure, suggesting that Tea Party views are close to being modal among rank-and-file Republicans. But given what we know about the tendency of party activists to embrace more extreme views, we can be sure that even this figure understates the influence of Tea Party attitudes in the Republican Party. That is, if Tea Party adherents and sympathizers constitute 56% of all Republicans, it's almost certain—given the typically more extreme views of party activists—that a higher proportion of party activists were aligned with the movement. Given the disproportionate influence of the Tea Party within the GOP, it becomes all the more important to understand the attitudes that motivate those who identify with and support the movement. To date, no one has studied this issue as systematically as Abramowitz and Parker and Barreto. Their findings are especially important for the strong, consistent support they afford of the central role that race appears to play in shaping the views of movement adherents and the Republican base more generally.

Tea Party defenders have been understandably sensitive to charges that the movement is fueled by racist attitudes. Supporters typically rebut such charges by arguing that the movement is simply animated by traditional conservative values, conventional partisanship, or both. And to be sure, these factors do differentiate Tea Party supporters from all other respondents in both the Parker and Barreto and the Abramowitz studies. But when the explanatory power of those factors is assessed simultaneously with a host of other independent variables, their influence tends to wane in comparison with a few key variables with clear racial implications. We begin with the Parker and Barreto study. In their analyses three variables with clear racial implications emerge as especially important in explaining variation in support for, and active engagement in, the movement. These are "fear of Obama," "racism," and what Parker and Barreto term a "social dominance orientation." The first two variables should be clear on their face. Tea Party supporters are far more likely than all other respondents to express fear and antipathy toward Obama and what Parker and Barreto refer to as "racial resentment" (i.e., "racism") toward blacks. The concept of social dominance orientation (SDO), however, requires some explanation. Developed by psychologist Jim Sidanius, the concept has been defined as a "preference for inequality among social groups." Social dominance orientation is essentially the opposite of egalitarianism. Those who embrace SDO deny that "all men are created equal" and instead see some groups as clearly superior to, and more deserving than, others. Although not exclusively racial in emphasis, the concept nonetheless has clear racial implications, especially when it occurs in combination with the two previous variables. No doubt, race is one of the dimensions along which proponents of social dominance believe society should be structured. Given this racial dimension, it is hardly surprising, then, that SDO also bears a strong predictive relationship with support for the Tea Party. It is worth noting, though, that of all the variables included in the Parker and Barreto study, the strongest single predictor of Tea Party support is fear and antipathy toward the first African American president in US history.

The 2012 election did nothing to damp down this "fear and loathing." Indeed, the 2012 Republican primary offered an especially rich array of quotes in this vein. For his part, Newt Gingrich accused President Obama of being a "food-stamp president," adding that "poor people should want paychecks, not handouts." Rick Santorum offered up the most racially explicit quote when he said, "I don't want to make black peoples' lives better by giving them someone else's money." And even though he chose not to enter the 2012 race, let's not forget Donald Trump's steady drumbeat of "birther" accusations in the midst of the campaign (Parker and Eder 2016). But no candidate in 2012 received more attention for his remarks than did the eventual nominee, Mitt Romney, for his famous—or infamous—disputation on the "47 percent" at a fund-raising event during the campaign. Romney's intent, in making the remark, was to stress what a difficult challenge he faced in the election, given the "dependence" of large segments of the American electorate on "big government." As he saw it, "there are 47 percent of the people who will vote for the president no matter what . . . . [They] are dependent upon government [and] believe that they are victims, who believe that government has a responsibility to care for them, who believe they are entitled to health care, to food, to housing . . . . you name it."[3]

Interestingly, although Romney apologized and sought to distance himself from his remarks when they first became public, he returned—even more explicitly—to the same themes in his first press appearance following the election. In fact, if anything, his postmortem comments on his defeat were much more explicitly racial than his original remarks had been. Eschewing the normal practice of congratulating his opponent for the win and commending him for a campaign well run, Romney instead blamed his defeat on the policy "gifts" that Obama had bestowed on the very "dependent" segments of the population to whom he had alluded in his initial "47 percent" commentary. But this time he named those groups, "especially the African American community, the Hispanic community, and young people," going into considerable detail about how specific policies benefited each group, thus effectively "buying" their votes.

For all the rhetorical consistency reflected in the preceding remarks, however, nothing quite prepared us for the blatant racism of Donald Trump. If Nixon, Reagan, and others had perfected a form of dog-whistle racial politics, Trump traded in the whistle for a bullhorn. In the wake of Romney's defeat in 2012, pragmatic Republican strategists called on the party to moderate its rhetoric and make a concerted effort to broaden its appeal by reaching out to racial and ethnic minorities, especially the rapidly growing Hispanic segment of the electorate. Among the early entrants into the 2016 presidential race, Marco Rubio and Jeb Bush clearly "got the memo," speaking out in favor of comprehensive immigration reform. By contrast, Donald Trump doubled down on the appeal to white racial conservatives by using his speech announcing his presidential candidacy to oppose immigration reform and attack the character of Mexican immigrants. In the most widely quoted of lines from that speech, Trump asserted that, "when Mexico sends its people, they're not sending their best. They're sending people that have lots of problems. They're bringing drugs. They're bringing crime. They're rapists" (New York Times, June 17, 2015). And that was just the beginning, with Trump, over the course of the campaign, attacking Muslims, doubling down in his characterization of Mexican immigrants, and cozying up to David Duke and, by extension, to other white supremacists.

Mitt Romney and many other mainstream Republicans criticized Trump for his racist remarks, but it was the brand of dog-whistle politics perfected by the likes of Romney that set the stage and created the audience for Trump. It is in this sense that Trump, I contend, is simply the most extreme expression or product of a brand of exclusionary, stigmatizing racial politics practiced by the GOP for nearly 60 years. But although stressing the continuity between Trump and what came before, there is no denying that the extreme nature of his rhetoric and behavior is without precedent in presidential history. Given what we used to believe about American politics, this raises an important question. In view of the supposed power of the "median voter," how did someone as extreme as Trump get elected president?

Movements and the Marginalization of the Median Voter

It is now the norm among political commentators to lament the absence of anything resembling a bipartisan "middle" in American politics. What a difference a few decades make. Whereas it is now commonplace for analysts and older citizens alike to celebrate the strong, bipartisan consensus that prevailed in the period after World War II, there were those at the time who saw the dominance of moderates in both parties as a kind of tyranny of the middle. In 1950, the American Political Science Association issued a report titled "Toward a More Responsible Two-Party System" that identified the ideological sameness of the two parties as the central problem of American democracy. More colorfully, George Wallace explained his third-party challenge to Nixon and Humphrey in 1968 in very similar terms. Said Wallace, "there is not a dime's worth of difference between the Democrat and Republican parties!"

Whatever one's normative take on the centrist tendencies of the era, the received wisdom among scholars was that the two-party, winner-take-all structure of the American system virtually compelled presidential nominees to hew to the center if they hoped to be elected. In his influential book, *An Economic Theory of Democracy*, Anthony Downs argued that in a two-party system, candidates could be expected to "rapidly converge" on the center of the ideological spectrum "so that parties closely resemble one another." Introduced a year later in his book, *A Theory of Committees and Elections*, Duncan Black's "Median Voter Theorem" represented a highly compatible, if more formalized, version of Downs's "convergence" theory. For several decades thereafter this general model of voting was thought of as akin to a natural law when it came to US politics, especially in elections involving large numbers of voters. Because the ideological preferences of voters were assumed to be distributed normally around a moderate midpoint, any candidate adopting a comparatively extreme position on the liberal to conservative continuum would seem to be easy prey for a more centrist candidate.

Not only was the theory appealingly parsimonious, but it also seemed to accord with the available real-world "data." When Downs and Black offered their versions of the theory, Dwight Eisenhower—the quintessential moderate Republican—was in office. Both candidates in the 1960 race—Kennedy and Nixon—were moderates within their parties. The same was true in 1968, when, as Wallace complained, the general ideological positions of the nominees of the two major parties seemed largely indistinguishable. But perhaps the most powerful affirmations of the theory came in 1964 and 1972 when the decidedly conservative and liberal candidates, Barry Goldwater and George McGovern, respectively, were soundly trounced by their more moderate opponents (Lyndon Johnson in 1964 and Richard Nixon in 1972).

Ronald Reagan's victory in 1980, however, was much harder to square with this view, as was the growing body of empirical evidence attesting to increasing polarization among party elites and activists during the 1980s and, even more so, the 1990s. By the mid to late 1990s, campaign strategists and political analysts were routinely acknowledging the brave new world of extreme partisan politics. "Playing to the base" was on its way toward replacing appeals to the median voter as the dominant logic of American electoral politics. But that leaves the key question unanswered: How did we go from the seeming "natural law" of the median voter theorem to the decisive power wielded by the ideological extremists who carried Trump to the White House? In *Deeply Divided: Racial Politics and Social Movements in Postwar America*, Karina Kloos and I sought to answer the question. Here I offer a brief summary of the more complicated account featured in the book.

I begin with a stark theoretical claim: The convergence perspective of Downs and Black (and others) holds only under conditions of relative social movement quiescence. This claim carries with it important implications for an understanding of the extent of bipartisan consensus in the postwar period as well as the erosion of that consensus in the 1960s and the increasing polarization that has followed. Owing in large part to the "chilling effect" of the Cold War and McCarthyism, the immediate postwar period was largely devoid of any significant social movement activity. This spared the two parties the centrifugal pressures that often follow when mobilized movement elements seek to occupy their ideological flanks. When challenged by sustained national movements attuned to electoral politics, "playing to the base" can come to be seen as strategically more important than courting the "median voter."

By revitalizing and legitimating the social movement form, the civil rights struggle of the early 1960s reintroduced these centrifugal pressures to American politics. Or more accurately, as I previously argued, it was one movement—civil rights—and one powerful countermovement—white resistance or "white backlash"—that began to force parties to weigh the costs and benefits of appealing to the median voter against the strategic imperative of responding to the mobilized movement elements at their ideological margins. Owing in part to the tight control they exercised over national conventions and the selection of presidential candidates, the parties were able to manage these pressures for a while, but this became increasingly more difficult with the convention and primary reforms of the 1970s. In *Deeply Divided*, we devoted the better part of a chapter to the origin and impact of these reforms; here I use Trump's improbable victory to highlight the ongoing significance of the reforms for an understanding of the rising tide of extremism in American politics.

From the outset, it was clear that the Republican establishment was deeply opposed to Trump's presidential bid. What was rarely, if ever, mentioned during the race was that, under then-prevailing party rules, the Trump revolution would have posed little or no threat to "the establishment," had it bubbled up any time before the mid 1970s. Consider the instructive case of Eugene McCarthy's doomed bid to secure the Democratic nomination for president in 1968. The general outline of the story is well known. Little known outside the Senate, McCarthy, an avowed opponent of the Vietnam War, decided to challenge the sitting president of his own party, Lyndon Johnson, for the nomination. Virtually no one gave him a ghost of a chance to pull off the upset, but after a strong showing in the New Hampshire primary, Johnson stunned the country by announcing he was withdrawing from the race. Robert Kennedy's decision to enter the fray complicated McCarthy's path forward, but after Kennedy was assassinated following his victory in that year's California primary, McCarthy remained the lone declared candidate in the race. Under today's rules he would have breezed to the nomination. But today's rules did not apply in 1968, when many fewer primaries were contested and, more important, the results were "nonbinding." Disdainful of McCarthy's brazen bid for the nomination, the Democratic establishment simply closed ranks at the party's convention in Chicago and anointed Johnson's vice president, Hubert Humphrey, as the nominee, despite the fact that he had contested not a one of that year's 17 primaries.

But today's Republican establishment did not have the ability to summarily dismiss Mr. Trump in this fashion. Why not? Answer: because of a little-known, but critically important, "silent revolution" that took place between 1968 and 1972. That revolution, orchestrated by antiwar activists operating semicovertly within the Democratic party, effectively stripped party bosses of control over the nomination process. But if, as a result of this revolution, parties or, more accurately, party elites were no longer able to control the nominating process as they once had, where did the control now reside? It was increasingly vested in those party activists who chose to participate in the new primary (or caucus) process. What we have learned since the implementation of the 1972 reforms, however, is that only a small percentage of registered voters actually take part in the primaries. *And* that this minority tends to be more ideologically extreme in its views than the typical member of the party. In short, although reformers had sought to democratize the nomination process, the resulting system has proved to be the perfect vehicle for empowering the movement wings of the two parties. Whether this is the same as democratizing the process is left for you to decide. Which brings us to the institutional threats that preceded and aided Trump's rise. Without an understanding of the ways in which these threats have already severely weakened American democracy, resistance to Trump will do little to restore the health and well-being of that system.

Institutional Threats to the Principle of Political Equality

Equality is fundamental to the theory of democratic governance. Here, however, I refer not to any notion of economic equality, but rather equality of voice in civic life. Dahl (1971: 1) cuts to the heart of the matter when he asserts, "that a key characteristic of democracy is the continued responsiveness of the government to the preferences of its citizens, considered as *political equals*" (emphasis added). Our normative disdain for autocratic forms of government stems from the fact that "the consent of the governed" counts for so little compared with the power wielded by the select few. When we proudly proclaim that democracy flows from "the will of the people," we don't mean some of the people, or that the will of some counts for more than others. And although we acknowledge that this ideal has never been perfectly realized in the United States, we would like, and are generally taught to believe, that our history represents an inexorable, progressive march toward that goal. Among the most troubling aspects of the present political moment in the United States is the accumulating evidence that we have been moving rapidly *away* from this ideal for some time.

Nor is this trend only an attitudinal matter of increasing support for "old fashioned racism" (Parker and Barreto 2009; Pasek et al. 2012; Tesler and Sears 2010) or various forms of nationalist populism. As troubling as these ideational trends may be, the more serious threat comes from a host of illiberal institutions that have been put in place over the past few decades, eroding the principle of political equality in the process. In bringing the chapter to a close, I focus on just three of these flawed institutions, beginning with more detail on our current system of presidential primaries and caucuses.

The Tyranny of Primaries and Caucuses

It is deeply ironic that our current system of presidential primaries and caucuses was born of the very principle of political equality that serves as our normative touchstone here. The institutional reform movement of 1968–1972 that birthed the present system was motivated by the desire to democratize the selection of convention delegates, wrest control of the presidential nomination process from party elites, and "let the people decide" by means of binding primaries and caucuses. It is simply beyond dispute that the widespread use of primaries is far more democratic—far more in keeping with the principle of political equality—than the old system, at least as measured by the number of citizens who take part in the process. And yet, it seems increasingly clear that this "more democratic" system is implicated in a host of illiberal effects, including the election of a president openly disdainful of democratic norms and institutions. The problem results from two features of primary elections and caucuses previously touched on: low turnout and the more ideologically extreme character of primary and caucus voters.

These features are ideally suited to magnify the influence of the ideologically extreme, movement wing of a party. The New Left took advantage of the primaries to secure the Democratic Party nomination for George McGovern in 1972, an "extreme" liberal. Since then, however, it is the movement wing of the GOP that has been the most consistently active, pushing the party to the right through the strategic exploitation of the primary system. And no group of activists has been more strategically savvy in taking advantage of the "movement bias" of the primaries, caucuses, and other low-turnout elections than Tea Party forces. By recruiting and backing Tea Party candidates for elective office at all levels of the system and mounting primary challenges to targeting "suspect" GOP moderates, the movement has succeeded in moving the party and a host of legislative bodies—most notably the House of Representatives—sharply to the right since it burst on the scene in 2009. The net effect of this rightward lunge has been to sharply increase partisan polarization, amplify the "voice" of the mobilized movement wings of the two parties, and further marginalize the median voter.

What is more, the ideological bias inherent in the nominating process has grown more pronounced over time and threatens to grow even more so in the future. That is because the proportion of primaries to caucuses has been shifting, with the number of caucuses steadily increasing. In 1980, for example, the GOP nominating process included 35 primaries and just 3 caucuses. In 2016 the balance had shifted to 38 primaries and 11 caucuses. In the same year, the Democrats held 37 primaries and 14 caucuses. Why should the increasing shift toward caucuses concern us? Answer: because if primaries are low-turnout elections, caucuses are the lowest-turnout formats of all; and by a large margin. Voter turnout in primaries varies widely, but typically falls between 10% and 20% percent of registered voters. Caucuses, on the other hand, rarely draw more than 1% of all voters, making them especially ripe for "capture" by mobilized movements operating within the party system. Consider the success rate of the Sanders "movement" versus the more conventional party-based candidacy of Hillary Clinton across the two nominating formats. Sanders prevailed in 11 of the 14 caucuses, while losing 27 of the 37 primary contests. And all indications are that the trend toward more caucuses will continue. This is partly because caucuses are much less expensive for state party organizations to stage than primaries. More important, the shift toward caucuses is occurring precisely because movement activists recognize the unique opportunity the format affords them to exercise influence far beyond their numbers.

The nondemocratic implications of the current nominating system pose a tricky normative challenge for reformers. At first blush, it might seem tempting to blame the mobilized movement wings of the two parties for exploiting the biases inherent in the primary system to promote nonrepresentative ideological views. Nonsense. Movements, of whatever ideological stripe, are *not* the problem. Quite the opposite; throughout American history, social movements have been a critical vehicle for safeguarding or advancing the rights and views of all manner of minorities, ethnic, racial, religious, or ideological. As such, they have generally served to promote, rather than undermine, the principle of political equality. More pragmatically, progressive and conservative activists can hardly be faulted for taking advantage of the unique opportunities afforded movements by the primary system. No, the problem lies with the anemic turnout typical of primaries and, indeed, all too many elections in the United States. What can be done to address this endemic problem? For starters, it is incumbent on more moderate segments of the electorate who are especially exercised by the alleged bias of the primary system to recognize that the system is in fact ideologically neutral and affords them the same opportunities for amplified voice as it does movements on the Left and the Right. They simply have to do a much better job of getting their own supporters to turn out for primaries and other low-turnout elections.

In general, how much better things would be if we could achieve much higher voting rates across the board. And we certainly could, if we were willing to follow Australia's lead and make voting in specified elections compulsory. Concerned that declining rates of voter turnout were beginning to undermine the principle of representative democracy, in 1924 Australia enacted a law requiring all citizens 18 years and older to participate in federal and state elections. Just to be clear, the law does not actually require citizens to vote, only to register to vote, appear at a polling station, and deposit a ballot in a secret ballot box. Still, the change in the law increased voter turnout in Australia from around 55% to over 90%. More important, as Mann and Ornstein (2013: 22), point out, the new law "changed campaign discourse. Politicians of all stripes have told us that when they know that their own base will turn out en masse, and will be balanced by the other party's base, they shift their efforts to persuading voters in the middle." This would have the positive effect of reducing the felt powerlessness and frustration of the median voter, without in any way suppressing minority views. But quite apart from its immediate salutary effects on the ideological tenor of American electoral politics, it is simply hard to imagine a normative objection to a reform that would so clearly advance the goal of political equality.

Restricting Electoral Voice

For nearly 60 years, Republican presidential candidates have based their campaigns squarely on appeals to white racial conservatives. But this strategic continuity has been played out against a backdrop of demographic discontinuity. When Nixon first succeeded in transforming the GOP into a party composed disproportionately of white racial conservatives, the white share of the country's population stood at just under 85%. Hispanics, by contrast, were but 4.5% of the population. When Reagan solidified the racial cast of his party by completing the electoral realignment of the white South, whites still constituted better than three-quarters of the nation's population. By the time Americans cast their ballots in 2040, whites are expected to constitute a minority of all voters. Quite simply, the demographic noose is tightening on the GOP. And yet, in the wake of Trump's victory, the demographic and ideological make-up of today's GOP will make it very hard to "turn" the Republican ship around anytime soon. Having painted themselves into this particular demographic corner, Republicans have little choice but to do all they can to limit the votes of racial minorities. And indeed, that is what they have been systematically doing for a decade or more. More specifically, the GOP has sought to restrict Democratic electoral voice through two general strategies pursued on a systematic, nationwide basis. The two strategies have involved the passage of new, restrictive state voting laws that effectively target presumptive Democratic constituents, and extreme gerrymandering by Republican-controlled state legislatures to concentrate and thereby dilute the "urban" (read: Democratic) vote, while distributing the rural and suburban (read: Republican) vote to maximize electoral effect. Of the two approaches, the former has received the most attention, but the latter has probably had the greatest aggregate effect. But make no mistake, the intent is the same in both cases: altering the rules and geographic structure of voting to suppress or mute the electoral voice of traditional Democratic voters (e.g., racial minorities, the poor, and young people). We take up each approach in turn, beginning with the epidemic of proposed new voting laws since 2010.

The Brennan Center at the New York University School of Law has been especially vigilant in tracking proposed changes to electoral laws around the country. According to data reported on the Center's website, in just the 4 months between October 2010 and January 2011, "at least 180 bills were introduced in 41 states. Ultimately, 25 new laws and two executive actions were adopted in 19 states. These states represented 231 electoral votes, or 85 percent of the total needed to win the presidency. *This amounted to the biggest threat to voting rights in decades*" (emphasis added).[4]

The most common of the new laws were statutes requiring voters to obtain new identification cards in order to cast ballots in the 2012 general election. Drew (2012: 26) reports that, by the time Americans went to the polls that November, "more than thirty states had passed laws requiring voters to present some form of identification, often a government-issued photo ID that they didn't possess and couldn't obtain easily, in many cases not at all." The nominal justification offered for the ID requirement was the prevention of voter fraud, though, as many commentators noted, there was something inherently fraudulent in the rationale itself. Many of the states seeking to implement these laws had no reported cases of voter fraud in the past few decades. In general, voter fraud had been a nonissue in the United States until it was conveniently seized on by Republican lawmakers as cover for the new laws.

On occasion, however, even they—in moments of carelessness or bravado—went "off message" and owned up to the transparent aim of the new ID laws or restrictions on voting. After orchestrating the passage of Pennsylvania's especially restrictive voter ID law, Mike Turzai, the GOP leader of the state's House of Representatives, couldn't help but boast a bit. Said Turzai, "Voter ID, which is going to allow Governor Romney to win the state of Pennsylvania. Done" (quoted in Toobin 2013: 17). And then there was the adviser to Ohio's Republican Governor John Kasich, who defended the governor's decree drastically limiting early voting by saying that "we shouldn't contort the voting process to accommodate the urban—read African American—voter turnout machine" (quote in Gourevitch 2012: 18). And then there was the case of the Republican official in North Carolina who was forced to resign after touting ID cards as a way to reduce voting by "a bunch of blacks that wants [*sic*] the government to give them everything." But these rare admissions merely confirmed what was already clear to any neutral observer. "The point," as Drew (2012: 26) noted, was simply "to make it more difficult for constituent groups of the Democratic Party—blacks, Hispanics, low-income elderly, and students—to exercise their constitutionally guaranteed right to vote."

Nor did the movement to restrict the franchise stop with the 2012 election. Instead the effort has continued unabated and with a major assist, in 2013, from the Supreme Court. In June of that year, the high court, in *Shelby County (Ala.) v. Holder*, invalidated the crucial "preclearance" provision of the Voting Rights Act of 1965. To be more precise, the Court left the preclearance section in place but declared that the formula used to determine which jurisdictions were required to secure federal approval before they could make changes in voting laws was "based on decades-old data and eradicated practices." So even as the Court left Section 5 intact, it effectively terminated the preclearance requirement by invalidating the formula used to trigger a preclearance review.

The practical implications of the ruling were made all the more evident the very day the ruling for *Shelby County (Ala.) v. Holder* was handed down. Within hours of the ruling, Texas Attorney General Greg Abbott announced that the state's controversial voter ID law, which had been struck down as unconstitutional by a federal court panel, authorized under the preclearance section of the Act, would be immediately implemented. Let that sink in for a moment. A law that had been declared unconstitutional was quickly reinstated following the Supreme Court ruling. If the nationwide voter suppression campaign in the run-up to the 2012 election proved less effective than many had feared (or hoped), among the main reasons for this was the fact that several of the most restrictive proposed laws—including the Texas ID law—had been struck down under preclearance review. With the threat of judicial review now removed, those motivated to make it that much harder for minorities, the poor, and young voters—Democratic constituencies all—to cast ballots will have a freer hand to operate.

They will also have a powerful ally in the White House aiding and abetting their efforts. Having captured the White House, one might have thought that Donald Trump would soften his claims of widespread voter fraud echoed often during the 2016 campaign. Instead he made ridding the system of "fraud" one of the first acts of his presidency. On May 11, 2017, he issued an executive order creating the Presidential Advisory Commission on Election Integrity (since closed down), urging the new body to "bring him the dirt" he "knew" was out there. The fact that Commission Chair Mike Pence and Vice-Chair Kris Kobach were also on record as fully convinced that electoral fraud is rampant in the United States supported the worry voiced by those at the Brennan Center that the Commission would simply be a vehicle for imposing even greater restrictions on voting rights in the United States. As the editors of the Center's website put it: "there is strong reason to suspect this Commission is not a legitimate attempt to study elections, but rather a tool for enabling voter suppression."[5]

Gerrymandering

Whereas Republican efforts to restrict the voting rights have drawn lots of critical comment, much less attention has been focused on the epidemic of extreme gerrymandering that has characterized the last 15–20 years and the nondemocratic implications of the same. Redrawing electoral boundaries to advantage the party in power is, of course, a time-honored American political tradition. That may help explain why these most recent efforts have received scant attention relative to the GOP's transparent vote-suppression tactics, but the truth of the matter is, we should be much more concerned about the former than the latter. Although the impact of the new restrictive laws remains disputed, it is absolutely clear that the restructuring of House districts since roughly 2000 has had the effect of making the entire system much less competitive, essentially rendering the issue of political voice meaningless in the great majority of locales. The trend is shown all too clearly in Figure 1.1.[6]

If we define districts in which one party routinely prevails over the other by at least 5%, nearly 40% of all House races remained competitive in 1992 (188 of 435). As of 2014, that number was just 20% (90 of 435). But even these numbers underestimate the drop in true "swing" districts. Of the 90 districts depicted as

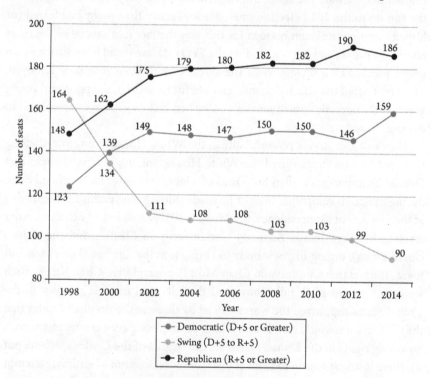

Figure 1.1 Distribution of House Districts, 1998–2014.
Source: Cook's Report: http://cookpolitical.com/story/5604.

competitive in Figure 1.1, the well-respected Cook Political Report defines 55 as "moderately Democratic" or "moderately Republican," leaving only a scant 8% (35 of 435) as true swing districts. For all intents and purposes, the great majority of Americans now exercise little electoral voice when it comes to those who represent them in the House. But this dramatic increase in the number of "safe districts" has done more than simply mute the electoral voice; it has also served to greatly enhance the power wielded by the Tea Party wing of the Republican Party. The point is, in noncompetitive districts, the only election that really matters is the primary. In safe Republican districts, whoever wins the GOP primary is virtually assured of going to Washington. And given the exceedingly low-turnout characteristic of primaries, this greatly favors the Tea Party–backed candidates who appeal to the nonrepresentative, ideologically motivated voters who tend to turn out for such contests. In turn, this dynamic is key to understanding how the House has become the central impediment to Congressional action in recent years. With so many movement conservatives coming to the House from safe Republican districts in and after 2010, there is simply no electoral incentive for them to moderate their views once in office. Facing no electoral threat, they are subject neither to party discipline nor to general public opprobrium. As a result, they remain free to hold firm to their narrow ideological agenda, rendering Congress increasingly irrelevant and dysfunctional in the process.

Nor is the absence of any real choice in most House districts the only cost of gerrymandering. In a recent article in *Daedalus*, former Republican House member Mickey Edwards highlights two other nondemocratic consequences of the practice. The first reflects his own experience of gerrymandering as a first-term Republican House member in a state still very much under the control of the Democrats. Ironically, the opposition's transparent efforts to redraw House districts to preserve their advantage also benefited Edwards. Nonetheless he came away from the experience with a very jaundiced view of the practice. Writes Edwards (2013: 91),

> After I won a congressional seat that had been held for nearly a half-century by the other party . . . my district was redrawn from a single square-shaped county in the middle of the state to a large upside-down "L" stretching from central Oklahoma to the Kansas border and halfway over to Arkansas, the only purpose being to put as many fellow Republicans into my district and thus make the other districts safer for Democrats. The result was to place tens of thousands of wheat farmers, cattle ranchers, and small-town merchants in a new district where they would be represented by an urban congressman, familiar with big-city issues and unfamiliar with the economic interests of his new constituents. So much for the founders' intended representativeness.

Unfortunately, the kind of willful disregard of geographic integrity described by Edwards has become increasingly the norm among the partisan legislators charged with redrawing district boundaries. The game is simple enough: Using ever-more sophisticated sources of geographic data, seek out and concentrate your voters in several "safe" districts while conceding one large noncompetitive district to "their" side. The results are districts that, like Edwards's, lack any kind of social, geographic integrity or coherence.

Besides reducing the competitiveness of districts, redrawing boundaries also tends to powerfully reinforce partisan polarization, further reducing prospects for the kind of minimal bipartisanship so crucial to and sadly so rare in today's legislative process. Again, Edwards (2013: 88) explains:

> Running in a district with no serious likelihood of losing to a member of an opposing party, a [representative] becomes even more dependent on remaining in the good graces of members of his or her own party.... Compelled by the pressures of partisan redistricting to stick to the party line, elected officials are further discouraged from reaching across the aisle to find common ground or forging compromises with members of another party.

Increased polarization, diminished electoral voice, and freakish district boundaries that undermine the concept of representative government; can anything be done to redress these distortions of democratic ideals and practice? Yes, indeed the answer is simple, straightforward and already in place in 13 states. It is only fitting that we give the last word to Edwards. These 13 states, he writes (2013: 91) "have taken this power away from their state legislatures, either entirely or to some degree, and placed much of the redistricting authority in the hands of independent, nonpartisan redistricting commissions. Every state should do the same: drawing district lines should be about able representation, not partisan advantage."

Conclusion

The current volume takes contemporary resistance to the Trump presidency as its principal focus. It is an important topic, in both its scholarly and real-world implications. But, as I noted at the outset, the narrow focus on the here and now carries risks. I have sought to highlight two such risks in this chapter. Both risks follow from variants of what might be thought of as "Trump Exceptionalism." The first has to do with a view of Trump as a *sui generis* figure in American politics; as demarcating a clear break with the past. To be sure, lots of "data" can be offered up in support of this view, starting with rhetoric and behavior so extreme and erratic as to stand alone in the annals of the American presidency. Then there are his wildly inconsistent policy positions, which make it hard to locate him on any conventional Left or Right ideological continuum. Finally, his strained, adversarial relationship with his own party reinforces the conviction that he is an N of 1, with no ties or loyalty to anything that came before.

I actually think there is much truth to the *sui generis* view, at least when it comes to Trump himself. When it comes to the Republican Party, however, and the exclusionary racial politics that have largely defined the GOP for nearly 60 years, the links between Trump and the past become all too clear. Even as many in the party have sought to distance themselves from Trump, the fact remains that by embracing an increasingly extreme form of exclusionary racial politics during Obama's presidency, the GOP—and especially its Tea Party wing—created a party structure and culture ideally suited to capture and exploitation by Trump and his allies. In recounting the crucial shift, in the mid 1960s, in the "racial geography" of American politics, I was simply using the first half of the chapter to recall the origins of today's overwhelming white, conservative, southern-based Republican Party. Whatever else he might be, Donald Trump must be counted as the product of that party and its sustained shift to the far right over the past 60 years.

In the last section of the chapter, I describe three trends that, along with a good many others, had already badly eroded the legal and institutional basis of American democracy before the 2016 election. These "threats" to the health and well-being of American democracy contradict another version of Trump exceptionalism, which holds that he alone is the source of the crisis we now confront. Although agreeing that Trump and the policies he has pursued since gaining office have immeasurably deepened the crisis, the truth, once again, is that his rise was greatly aided and abetted by the already weakened state of our Democratic institutions. In recounting the origins of three of the most flawed of these institutions, I have sought, once again, to place Trump in historical and institutional context. Whatever aided his rise to power, however, there is no gainsaying the stark threat that he, in combination with the already weakened state of our political institutions, poses to the survival of American democracy. Just because we were born a democracy does not guarantee we will always remain one. For at least two decades, the evolution of our political institutions has rendered our democracy increasingly flawed and fragile. Removing Donald Trump from office, will not, in and of itself, alter this trajectory.

Populism, Democracy, and Resistance

The United States in Comparative Perspective

KENNETH M. ROBERTS

The election of Donald Trump to the presidency of the United States in 2016 was widely interpreted around the world as a shocking victory for a particular brand of right-wing populism that had been on the political ascendance, in Europe and elsewhere, over much of the previous decade. As Doug McAdam argues in his contribution to this volume (see Chapter 1), Trump's rise represented an "extreme expression" of an "exclusionary brand of racial politics," one that had been practiced "ever more brazenly by the Republican Party since its origins in the 1960s." Similar forms of exclusionary politics based on racially or ethnically coded national identities have long been the hallmark of right-wing populism in Europe (Art 2011; Bornscheir 2010; Mudde 2007). These cross-regional parallels suggest that the rise of Trump is not a national aberration, but a high-profile case of a larger and more generalizable political phenomenon. As such, it calls for a comparative analysis to contextualize Trump's electoral victory, identify how it is similar to or different from other cases of populist ascendance, and better understand "the Resistance" it has spawned.

A comparative perspective clearly demonstrates that the United States is not alone in providing the breeding grounds for exclusionary populist politics. What sets the United States apart, however, at least in comparison with its long-standing democratic counterparts in Western Europe, is (1) the steady infusion of varied right-wing social movements into a mainstream conservative party, rather than a smaller far-right ethno-nationalist "niche" party, and (2) the *de facto* transformation of that mainstream party into a vehicle for the election of an antiestablishment populist outsider who is openly contemptuous of democratic norms and procedures. Although right-wing populist parties have come to power in post-Communist East European countries like Hungary, Poland, and Slovakia, they did so in contexts in which democratic regimes were fairly recent creations and party systems were highly unstable. In comparative terms, then, the election of a far-right populist figure like Trump as head of state in a highly institutionalized democracy is certainly a rare, if not *sui generis*, political phenomenon. So also is the rise of a populist outsider in a context of acute partisan and ideological polarization of the type found in contemporary American politics.

Indeed, resistance to Trump has been heavily conditioned by the grafting of his autocratic populist leadership onto the partisan and ideological agenda of a Republican Party that has moved steadily rightward, along multiple dimensions, in recent decades. As Meyer and Tarrow argue in their Introduction to this volume, the Resistance is best understood as a countermovement in a cycle of contention that reflects the "reciprocal movementization" of the party system at large. On the Republican side, movementization transformed a mainstream conservative party into a confluence of right-wing movements—or, perhaps better put, movement currents—of varied and even disparate ideological predispositions, ranging from market fundamentalism to Christian evangelicalism and white ethno-nationalism. As subsequently explained, the convergence of these movement currents behind the insurgent, antiestablishment populist leadership of Donald Trump accentuated the polarization of US politics that had been underway since the 1960s (McAdam and Kloos 2014). From a comparative perspective, it was also the most distinctive feature of the contemporary populist eruption in American democracy.

A comparative perspective also demonstrates that resistance can take a variety of forms and occur along a number of different fronts. Most basically, perhaps, resistance occurs in the electoral arena when voters and social groups mobilize to support electoral challengers to populist leaders or parties. Resistance may also occur in various institutional arenas—such as legislatures, courts, and investigative agencies—that uphold the rule of law, defend minority political rights, and enforce democratic checks and balances against unwarranted concentrations of power by populist autocrats. The media and various civic organizations may express resistance in their oversight, monitoring, investigative, and communicative roles, and social movements may take to the streets in protest or practice other forms of "contentious politics" (McAdam, Tarrow, and Tilly 2001). Some of the most controversial measures adopted by populist rulers are expressly designed to curtail such forms of resistance—for example, by criminalizing social protest, censoring or muzzling the media, asserting partisan control over the courts, government agencies, and civic organizations, and manipulating or suppressing the right to vote.

Societal pushback against such measures virtually ensures that resistance to exclusionary populism will unfold in a multilayered process. On one level, it entails opposition to specific policy initiatives, particularly those that are exclusionary in their treatment of certain interests or groups in society. At another level, it involves resistance to the efforts of populist rulers to whittle away at democratic checks and balances that restrain their autocratic proclivities. This latter defense of democratic institutions is perhaps best understood as a form of metaresistance aimed at protecting essential freedoms and safeguarding the exercise of democratic rights. In short, metaresistance seeks to buttress an institutional edifice that not only allows societal actors to have input in the policymaking process, but also one that recognizes their very right to resist.

Such forms of multilayered resistance are best understood through a comparative analysis of contemporary populisms and the challenges they pose to democratic institutions.

Populism's Political Logic and Programmatic Space

Populism is one of the most slippery and contested concepts in the social science lexicon, but it is an inescapable starting point for understanding the Trump phenomenon and the Resistance it has spawned. At the most basic level, populism is widely understood to be a way of structuring the political field along an antagonistic divide between a virtuous "people," however defined, and a morally bankrupt dominant elite or political establishment (Laclau 2005). For exclusionary far-right populisms, this dominant elite or establishment is typically alleged to favor and protect "undeserving" or "superfluous" (Snow 2018) social groups—such as racial and ethnic minorities or immigrant populations—that are not seen as properly belonging to "the people." Populism, then, is a mode of antielite and antiestablishment politics par excellence, as it entails a transgressive invocation and assertion (or reassertion, in its most redemptive forms) of popular sovereignty. Although the populist label is often adopted in US politics to refer to specific types of economic policies—typically redistributive ones, making "populism" one of many euphemisms for "Left" in a national political discourse truncated by Cold War antagonisms—scholars of comparative politics overwhelmingly locate populism in the political domain (Laclau 2005; Roberts 2016) and treat economic policies as incidental or instrumental to populism's essential political logic. Populists of the Left may attempt to mobilize "the people" by challenging economic elites and promising redistributive policies; those on the Right, on the other hand, may rebel against state taxation and regulatory policies. Indeed, the latter may politicize ethno-national cultural identities that are capable of being mapped onto a wide range of economic platforms, whether of statist or free-market inspiration.

When conceived in terms of this central political logic, populist leaders, movements, and parties have clearly been on the rise in global politics in recent decades (Kriesi and Pappas 2015; Moffitt 2016; Rovira Kaltwasser et al. 2017). From Latin America to Europe, Asia, and the United States, they have capitalized on widespread discontent with traditional parties and political establishments. Populist eruptions therefore are widely understood to reflect—and also to deepen—crises of democratic representation and of party systems in particular. Because populism thrives where institutionalized forms of representation are seriously flawed or discredited, the varied subtypes of populism are at least partially conditioned by the kinds of representational failures to which they respond.

As such, populism can map onto party systems in strikingly diverse ways, and it is capable of fundamentally transforming or realigning political representation. In some countries, for example, populism is characterized almost entirely by its antiestablishment political logic and the invocation of popular sovereignty that accompanies it; any programmatic or ideological positioning beyond this central cleavage is minimal, as populist figures draw from an ill-defined or eclectic mix of policy options. A paradigmatic example is contemporary Italy's Five Star Movement (M5S) begun by the comedian and political blogger Beppe Grillo. The M5S is staunchly antiestablishment, but it defies conventional ideological positioning by advocating an eclectic mix of probusiness, environmental, redistributive, nationalistic, and cyber-participatory stands (della Porta et al. 2017; Tronconi 2015).

More typically, however, populist movements can be readily located in programmatic space, even when they self-consciously eschew ideological labels (as many do). Nonetheless, the conventional Left–Right labels are potentially misleading, as the programmatic space of populism is clearly multidimensional. Indeed, this space is largely structured by two orthogonal competitive axes defined by conflicts over economic interests and sociocultural identities (see Figure 2.1). Populisms of the Left and the Right exist, then, but they are not necessarily located on the polar ends of the same competitive axis. Those on the Left politicize the statist and redistributive poles of a horizontal axis defined by economic interests and preferences. They define "the people" and "the elite" in terms of socioeconomic stratification, though not strictly in terms of social class; the people are understood to be less fortunate, or at least nonprivileged, members of the national community, whereas the elite refers to economically privileged groups and a political establishment that is beholden to them. Populisms of the Right may politicize the opposite, promarket pole of that same economic axis by appealing to the people—hardworking, tax-paying citizens—allegedly

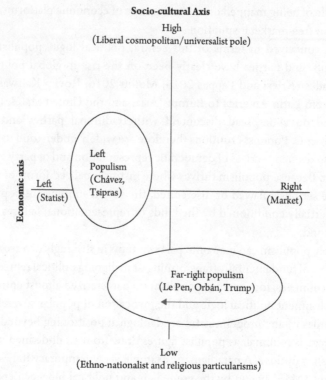

Figure 2.1 Economic and Sociocultural Axes of Competition.

oppressed by a spendthrift state that favors other (putatively "less-deserving" or "superfluous") societal groups.

More consistently, however, populisms of the Right locate near the lower pole on the orthogonal, vertical axis of sociocultural contestation in Figure 2.1. This spatial location entails a politicization of the ethno-national, religious, or both particularisms of a given people and their "heartland" identities (Taggart 2000), in opposition to more liberal universalist and cosmopolitan values on the upper pole of the competitive axis. Neither pole on this vertical axis necessarily inclines toward the Left or the Right on the horizontal axis of economic contestation; nothing requires, for example, that staunch nationalists, immigration opponents, and religious conservatives on the lower pole also favor free trade and open markets on the right pole of the economic axis. As Kitschelt (1997) argued, many of Europe's far-right populist parties started out—much like the US Republican Party—with avowedly promarket, antitaxation planks, largely reflecting their broader opposition to political elites entrenched in state institutions. Over time, however, a number of these parties abandoned or softened the free-market component of their ideological profile, prioritizing instead the sociocultural dimensions, in particular issues related to immigration and national identities (Art 2011; Mudde 2007).

In so doing, parties like the National Front of Marine Le Pen in France became proponents of economic statism, nationalism, and so-called "welfare chauvinism." They opposed free trade, economic globalization, and transnational European institutions while supporting traditional welfare states that protected members of the national community. This community, however, was defined in exclusionary ethno-nationalist terms, leaving aside "less-deserving" immigrant "others," especially Muslims, who were alleged to overburden state capacities and threaten national cultural identities (Filc 2015; Mudde and Rovira Kaltwasser 2013; Snow 2018). In short, some of these parties shifted from the lower-right to the lower-left quadrant in Figure 2.1, as depicted by the arrow in the figure.

Party Politics and the Conditions for Populism

These different expressions of populism are not randomly distributed across the globe. Instead, they cluster in regions where established patterns of democratic representation and partisan competition leave party systems susceptible to populist outflanking on one or another of the aforementioned poles of contestation. In particular, populism has thrived in contexts in which citizens become detached from mainstream parties that have progressively converged in their platforms and policies or otherwise failed to represent one of the salient poles on the two central axes of competition (Mudde and Rovira Kaltwasser 2017: 104–106). Left-wing populists in Southern Europe and Latin America, for example, have repoliticized the statist and redistributive pole on the left side of the economic axis in the aftermath to recent financial crises that induced mainstream parties to converge around austerity measures and market-based (or "neoliberal") structural adjustment policies. Populist outflanking on the left was especially common where traditional center-left parties played a major role in the adoption of austerity measures and market reforms that converged on the policy platforms of their conservative rivals. This left-populist pattern was seen in Latin America's so-called "Bolivarian" cases—Venezuela under Hugo Chávez, Bolivia under Evo Morales, and Ecuador under Rafael Correa (Roberts 2014)—as well as Greece (SYRIZA) and Spain (*Podemos*) in Southern Europe (Aslinidis 2016). Conversely, ethno-national populists in Northern and Central Europe have politicized the lower pole on the sociocultural axis that mainstream parties largely neglected, especially in countries where traditional conservative and social democratic parties converged in their support for international integration, free trade, and relatively liberal immigration policies.

Trump's variant of populism in the United States has clear parallels to this latter European ethno-national form in its politicization of the lower pole on the vertical sociocultural axis. With his harsh criticisms of immigrants, Islam, and free trade accords, his thinly veiled appeals to white identity and nativist circles, and his strident assertion of national interests shorn of entangling international obligations, Trump's discourse is strikingly reminiscent of that of prominent European far-right populists like Jean-Marie and Marine Le Pen of the French National Front, Geert Wilders of the Party for Freedom in the Netherlands, Umberto Bossi of the Northern League in Italy, and the late Jörg Haidar of the Austrian Freedom Party. Like Trump, many of these populist figures made explicit appeals to blue-collar and less-educated middle-class sectors of society, playing on fears that national cultural identities as well as economic livelihoods were threatened by the pressures of globalization, immigration, and multiculturalism (Kriesi 2008).

In contrast to Trump, however, these West European counterparts built new right-wing populist parties out of nationalist subcultures or movements on the fringes of mainstream party systems (Art 2011; Berezin 2009; Mudde 2007). The growth of these far-right populist parties inevitably had a polarizing effect on national party systems, given the long-standing dominance of mainstream party organizations that were only weakly differentiated in their programmatic appeals. Fearing that new populist challengers would resurrect fascist and authoritarian tendencies on the political Right, mainstream parties often tried to erect a *cordon sanitaire* to isolate and marginalize far-right populists, excluding them from consideration as potential alliance partners in governing coalitions (Art 2011).

Nevertheless, growing competition from far-right populist challengers arguably exerted a "radical flank effect" (Haines 2013) on mainstream party systems. This competition politicized immigration issues as well as the process of European integration, inducing many parties—especially, but not exclusively, conservative parties—to toughen their own stands on immigration issues. The radical flank effect thus reshaped the policymaking agenda (Schain 2017) and pulled mainstream parties toward the lower pole on the sociocultural axis of competition. As policy differences between far-right populist and mainstream conservative parties narrowed and national immigration policies became more restrictive, the *cordon sanitaire* broke down in a number of countries, and right-populist parties became junior partners in governing coalitions in Finland, Austria, the Netherlands, Italy, Switzerland, and Greece.

At least in Western Europe, however, the impact of these far-right populist parties on democratic regimes and public policies has been restrained by their electoral limitations and their secondary role in governing coalitions (Mudde 2013). To be sure, far-right populist parties have become serious contenders for power in a number of countries, most notably France, where Marine Le Pen made it to the second round of the presidential election in 2017 and earned over one-third of the vote; the Netherlands, where Geert Wilders' Party for Freedom finished second in the 2017 parliamentary elections; and Austria, where the Freedom Party received over one-fourth of the vote in 2017 parliamentary elections and over 46% of the second-round presidential vote in 2016. Nowhere in Western Europe, however, has a far-right populist party won a national election and taken the lead in forming a national government. As Schain (2017: 470) argues, "In virtually every case where there has been an electoral breakthrough of the extreme-right, established parties have reacted by co-opting some aspects of their programme in an attempt to undermine their support." Mainstream actors have also forged broad multiparty electoral and/or governing alliances to relegate far-right populists to the political sidelines—as in France—or to contain their influence as junior coalition partners.

Indeed, patterns of institutionalized participation have arguably had a "taming effect" (Minkenberg 2017: 443) or "a moderating impact on the radicalism" of far-right populist parties (Schain 2017: 460). In contrast to interwar Germany and Italy, "the new radical right . . . continues to play the democratic game" (Minkenberg 2017: 455), one in which its political agenda has been resisted and contained by electoral majorities, parliamentary safeguards, and, at times, the courts. This institutional containment, however, has entailed forms of issue cooptation and cabinet participation that have allowed far-right populist parties to exert some influence on public policies. Consequently, as Minkenberg (2017: 455) states, "government of the people, by the people, for the people" may not be at stake, "but the concept of 'the people' is," with the *demos* being increasingly redefined in more exclusionary terms of the *ethnos*. Furthermore, "populists in all cases kept putting forward proposals and championing initiatives that repeatedly, consistently and purposely clashed with the fundamental tents of liberal democracy," producing an "unrelenting erosion of the liberal consensus that has provided one of the foundations of the European project from its very start" (Albertazzi and Mueller 2017: 508, 520). Paradoxically, far-right populists consistently used parliamentary institutions and procedures to contest liberal democratic norms, at times leaving it largely to the courts "to safeguard the rule of law, freedom of information and fundamental human rights" (Albertazzi and Mueller 2017: 520).

Altogether, the design of parliamentary institutions in Western Europe has provided far-right populists with access to democratic channels of representation and policymaking, while largely containing their political impact. Under proportional representation electoral rules, populists—whether of the Right or the Left—can win parliamentary seats and even cabinet positions with a modest share of the vote, but their electoral niche is typically limited to a relatively small set of voters located near one or another of the ideological poles. The rise of populist challengers, therefore, may increase fragmentation in multiparty systems, but barring a major crisis, mainstream parties have generally been able to maintain their hold over the bulk of voters in the broad center of the political spectrum. Likewise, so long as mainstream parties remain electorally dominant, the election of prime ministers by party legislative blocs—that is, by career politicians—rather than by a direct popular vote discourages the ascendance of antiestablishment figures to high-level executive office. Under parliamentary rules, the Republican Party Congressional delegation would have selected Jeb Bush, or perhaps Marco Rubio, as the party's candidate in 2016—never Donald Trump.

Not surprisingly, then, antiestablishment populist figures have been elected prime minister in only two West European countries—Italy and Greece—where mainstream party systems had broken down in contexts of severe representational crises. Moreover, in neither of these countries was the populist figure a representative of the far-right ethno-nationalist brand of populism. In Italy, on the one hand, business and media tycoon Silvio Berlusconi capitalized on the crisis and eventual implosion of the Italian party system in a massive corruption scandal in the early 1990s. Although neither Berlusconi nor his personal partisan vehicle, the *Forza Italia*, belonged to the family of far-right ethno-nationalist parties, he forged a coalition with two smaller far-right parties and was elected prime minister on four different occasions in the 1990s and early 2000s (see subsequent discussion). In Greece, on the other hand, the leader of the radical left-populist party SYRIZA, Alexis Tsipras, was elected prime minister in 2015—ironically, in coalition with a smaller far-right populist party. Tsipras was elected on an anti-austerity platform in a context of acute economic crisis that seriously weakened the mainstream parties responsible for the adoption of austerity measures.

What makes the US case different from those of Western Europe is that an exclusionary, ethno-nationalist brand of populism emerged within—and eventually came to dominate—a mainstream conservative party in a stable but highly polarized two-party system. Paradoxically, a mainstream party, in part inadvertently, brokered Trump's rise to power as an insurgent, antiestablishment populist outsider. According to conventional theorizing, this never should have happened. The US system of winner-take-all plurality elections is expected to produce two large, ideologically eclectic "catch-all" parties that compete for support around the "median voter" in the center of the electorate (Downs 1957). The electoral rules therefore create centripetal competitive dynamics that induce parties to nominate moderate figures with support from "party insiders" (Cohen et al. 2008) as presidential candidates. In the seminal work of Juan Linz (1990: 53), US presidentialism was historically different from other, less-stable presidential regimes—such as those in Latin America—because of the moderation and "unusually diffuse character" of American political parties. These traits fostered the construction of flexible bipartisan policymaking coalitions and allowed American democracy to avoid the extreme types of ideological polarization that destabilized presidential systems in other parts of the world. They also made it possible for a wide array of institutions—such as the US Supreme Court and the federal judiciary, the IRS, the FBI, and state-level electoral agencies—to operate in a manner that was "above," or at least relatively independent of, partisan politics.

As McAdam and Kloos (2014) demonstrate, however, this centripetal logic gave way to more polarizing centrifugal dynamics in response to two critical changes starting in the 1960s: (1) the conservative backlash and countermobilization to the Civil Rights movement and other progressive movements of the 1960s and 1970s, and (2) the introduction of primary elections in the 1970s, which loosened the controls that party elites traditionally exercised over presidential nomination contests. The Civil Rights movement and its sequels in the student, antiwar, feminist, Lesbian, Gay, Bisexual, and Transgender (LGBT), and environmental movements were all located near the upper pole of the vertical axis in Figure 2.1. Not surprisingly, these movements triggered a countermobilization on the right with both economic and cultural components, including antitaxation movements, religious mobilization against abortion and gay rights, various militia and gun rights movements, and nativist currents that opposed immigration and, in some cases, asserted "white identities." The Tea Party movement of the Obama era wove together many of these conservative strands, which were often critical of both the Republican and the Democratic Party establishments (Parker and Barreto 2013; Schlozman 2015; Skocpol and Williamson 2013). Rather than creating a new niche party on the far right, however, as they might have done in a system of proportional representation, these movement currents largely remained within the Republican orbit, given the winner-take-all logic of US elections. The infusion of these currents into the GOP strengthened its grassroots networks and pushed the party even farther toward the right pole (on the economic axis) and the lower pole (on the cultural axis) in Figure 2.1.

Crucially, this mobilization at the grassroots interacted with the second key change previously mentioned—the spread of primary elections and statewide caucuses—to shatter the Republican establishment's control over the presidential nomination process. Given generally low voter turnout, primaries and caucuses empower the most active, and often the most ideological, sectors of a party in the selection of a presidential candidate. Although the Republican establishment contained the populist and Tea Party currents to nominate Mitt Romney as a presidential candidate in 2012, by 2016 an activated and agitated grassroots base swamped the establishment in the primary campaigns. The movement currents delivered the nomination to Trump, a vintage populist outsider whose vitriolic rhetoric assailed political elites from both sides of the partisan divide.[1] Once Trump had secured the party's nomination, the vast majority of Republican voters fell in line behind his candidacy, as acute partisan polarization and the antipathies associated with "negative partisanship" (Abramowitz and Webster 2015b) prevented voters from crossing over to the other side.

In short, the *sui generis* character of Trump's victory was made possible by the interaction between American electoral institutions and a process of partisan polarization driven by the reciprocal mobilization and countermobilization of social movements on the left and right flanks of the party system. Trump's ascendance to the presidency ensured that the Resistance to his exclusionary populism would not be limited to the electoral arena; indeed, it quickly shifted to a wide range of institutional venues, civil society, and social protest outlets. As explained in the next section, a comparative analysis of populism in power in other international settings provides useful insights into the character and content of this resistance.

Populism in Power: Autocracy and Resistance

As Mudde and Rovira Kaltwasser (2012) argue, populism can sometimes offer a corrective to flawed or failed forms of political representation, but it typically is in tension with liberal democratic norms and procedures. Populism may entail, as Laclau (2005) suggests, an antagonistic division of the political sphere between a corrupt elite and a virtuous "people," but many forms of populism rest on a conception of the popular will that is unitary and essentialist, rather than pluralistic; they express that popular will in a majoritarian and plebiscitary manner that pays little heed to minority rights; and they endow a leader with the authority to divine that popular will and act on its behalf, if necessary by circumventing the institutional constraints of "politics as usual." Populism, then, is naturally antithetical to established institutions, understanding that these are inhabited by and biased toward incumbent elites. Indeed, it typically emerges where established institutions are in crisis and incapable of providing effective representation for broad, popular constituencies (Laclau 2005). And it is especially averse to institutionalized checks and balances, which serve largely to block, distort, or water down the expression of the popular will as enacted by the leader.

So conceived, populism in power has powerful autocratic tendencies, and it is intrinsically polarizing. This polarization breeds resistance not only among social and political groups opposed to specific policy initiatives, but also among those threatened by potential institutional changes, an autocratic concentration of power, or both. Such resistance is readily apparent in the comparative political landscape where populist leaders and parties have taken the reins of state power.

Latin America's left-leaning "Bolivarian" populisms in Venezuela, Bolivia, and Ecuador provide illustrative examples. In all three countries, populist figures arose in contexts in which mainstream party systems were experiencing acute representational crises after converging around neoliberal programs of market reform. In each case, widespread social protest was eventually translated into mass electoral protest when voters rejected traditional parties and elected left-populist figures who had promised to sweep aside the established order (Roberts 2014). Indeed, all three leaders had campaigned on pledges to convoke a constituent assembly and "refound" the democratic regime—pledges that they quickly implemented through a series of popular referendums upon taking office. In short, they employed plebiscitary means of popular sovereignty to circumvent the inherited constraints of established legislative and judicial institutions. The Venezuelan case, in particular, culminated in a highly autocratic form of populist authority, as Chávez and his party proceeded to purge and pack the judiciary, elect a new legislature with a *Chavista* majority, and assert hegemonic partisan control over electoral institutions and other state agencies (Hawkins 2010).

This concentration of autocratic authority in Venezuela was clearly facilitated by the virtual collapse of traditional political parties. So long as Chávez's charismatic leadership was available, his political reforms were generally backed by broad, popular majorities in plebiscitary and electoral arenas, reflecting in part the "inclusionary" character of a populist project that launched new social programs for low-income constituencies, enjoyed ample oil revenues, and promoted various forms of community-based popular participation (Rhodes-Purdy 2017). Nevertheless, Chávez's Manichean populist rhetoric and his autocratic authority were intensely polarizing, provoking widespread resistance, particularly among middle- and upper-class citizens. This resistance was expressed in a wide range of political and institutional settings, ranging from mass social protest to a short-lived military coup, a massive strike in the state-owned oil company, a failed recall referendum, and both electoral boycotts and electoral contestation. The Bolivian and Ecuadorean cases, for which the concentration of autocratic authority was less complete, demonstrate that electoral contestation remains an important check on executive power, as does the capacity for autonomous forms of social mobilization by popular constituencies (Anria forthcoming; Madrid 2012).

Clearly these inclusionary leftist populisms in Latin America have different patterns of societal support and opposition from the exclusionary populism of a leader like Trump, and their eruption in contexts of acute crisis and party system collapse created unique opportunities for regime-level institutional change.

The United States is not on the precipice of a plebiscitary refounding of regime institutions, Trump's incendiary antisystem rhetoric aside. Closer parallels to the United States under Trump are thus to be found in Europe, where conservative and far-right populisms with exclusionary tendencies have also gained access to state power, operating within established institutions to challenge liberal democratic principles.

Italy under Belusconi provides the closest parallel in Western Europe, even if Berlusconi created his own partisan vehicle and was not, properly speaking, an exclusionary, far-right ethno-national populist. Like Trump, Berlusconi parlayed a business and media empire along with a tabloid celebrity persona into a maverick assault on the political establishment, while thoroughly conflating his private business interests with the institutions of public office. Also like Trump, he embodied a style of populist leadership that engaged in flagrant patterns of norm-breaking, coarseness, and incivility, what Ostiguy (2017) characterizes as a "flaunting of the low" and what Moffitt (2016: 57–63) simply calls "bad manners."

Berlusconi governed in alliance with two more radical far-right parties— the regionalist and ethno-nationalist Northern League and the National Alliance, a descendant of interwar Italian fascism—as well as, at times, splinters of the former Christian Democratic Party. Berlusconi's allies from the Northern League pushed through a number of anti-immigration measures that ran afoul of European human rights conventions (Albertazzi and Mueller 2017: 513–514). Arguably, however, the most important challenges that Berlusconi posed to liberal democratic institutions were related to his flagrant efforts to protect and promote his private business interests while ensconced in public office. Facing repeated judicial proceedings for corruption and financial improprieties, the Berlusconi governments passed a series of so-called *ad personam* laws that "appeared to be designed primarily to resolve Berlusconi's personal and business problems" (Ruzza and Fella 2009: 32). The government sought constitutional reforms to strengthen the executive and passed a law—subsequently thrown out by the Constitutional Court—to shield the prime minister from judicial trials. Berlusconi clashed repeatedly with the courts and challenged the right of "unelected" judicial bodies to restrain executive power. He also manipulated both public and private media to ensure favorable coverage of his party, remove critical journalists, and bring libel suits against independent newspapers. Consequently, the Berlusconi governments "attracted fierce criticism from organizations monitoring media freedom," and they induced Freedom House (an independent monitoring group) to downgrade Italy to "partly free" status in its 2009 report (Albertazzi and Mueller 2017: 514).

Ultimately, the fractious nature of Berlusconi's governing coalition limited the damage it could do, while the courts and the media performed critical watchdog roles. Electoral institutions remained resilient enough to contest the populist figure and preserve opportunities for alternation in office. Such democratic checks and balances have been less effective, however, in a number of post-Communist East European countries. The Hungarian case is especially instructive, as it demonstrates how an ethno-nationalist populist leader and his party can operate within established democratic institutions to dismantle checks and balances and move in the direction of a hybrid regime or "competitive authoritarianism" (Levitsky and Way 2010). Hungary also demonstrates that a mainstream, democratic political party—Viktor Orbán's Fidesz—can be transformed over time into an instrument of an autocratic and exclusionary populist project.

Fidesz traces its roots to the democratic student movement that emerged under Communism in the late 1980s. The party was founded in 1988 on a platform that supported political and economic liberalism, but it began a drift toward more conservative and nationalist positions in the mid 1990s following Hungary's transition to democracy. Fidesz elected Orbán to a term as prime minister in 1998 and proceeded to shift its international affiliation from the Liberal International to the Christian Democratic-led European People's Party. A narrow victory by Fidesz's principal rival, the Hungarian Socialist Party (MSZP), pushed Orbán back into opposition in 2002, but the MSZP was severely damaged politically by its mishandling of a deepening economic crisis after being reelected in 2006. A steep decline in the socialist vote allowed Orbán and Fidesz to return to power in 2010, when Hungary's mixed electoral system translated 52.7% percent of the vote into a crushing supermajority (68%) of parliamentary seats for Fidesz and its smaller Christian Democracy ally.

The Fidesz that returned to power in 2010 was not the same party that dutifully left office after being electorally defeated in 2002. As stated by Stanley (2017: 148), Fidesz "embarked on an increasingly radical shift in programmatic priorities" after losing power in 2002, competing for support "on the terrain of ethnic nationalism while openly rejecting liberal constitutionalism." This terrain, it should be noted, was also occupied by an even more radical ethno-nationalist party, Jobbik (or the Movement for a Better Hungary), whose emergence and strengthening after the early 2000s exerted radical flank effects on more mainstream parties. Increasingly, then, Orbán became a champion of an exclusionary vision of Hungarian national identity that had little place for Muslim immigrants, gays, and ethnic minorities like the Roma, and he became increasingly critical of supranational European institutions that limited national sovereignty, especially on immigration issues. As Europe's immigration crisis intensified in the summer of 2015—what Orbán characterized as an "invasion" of Europe—Hungary built a fence along its southern border to keep immigrants out, and it joined neighboring states in rejecting the European Union's proposed refugee quota system (Rupnik 2016: 82).

By that point Hungary had advanced well along the path toward creating what Orbán himself characterized as an "illiberal democracy." Upon its return to power in 2010, Fidesz employed its parliamentary supermajority to unilaterally write a new constitution, invalidate judicial precedents, control court appointments, impose favorable electoral laws, and subject the media, universities, and religious groups to new forms of state regulation. Although the vote for Fidesz dropped below 50% in 2014 elections, the party retained a large majority of parliamentary seats and generally remained broadly popular. As Rupnik (2016: 81) states, the party followed a pragmatic mix of "economic nationalism and social welfarism," positioning itself toward the "left" economically while staunchly located on the "right" culturally.

Ultimately, Hungary's democratic institutions largely failed to block the concentration of power by Orbán and Fidesz after 2010. Indeed, Orbán used democratic institutions as instruments to weaken independent and opposition actors, concentrate authority, and legally transform the rules of the game. Societal resistance, however, provided at least some measure of restraint on the exercise of autocratic power. In particular, domestic and international protests induced Orbán to back away from a proposal that threatened to close an internationally acclaimed independent university, the Central European University in Budapest.

Social protest was even more widespread in neighboring Poland, where the right-populist Law and Justice (PiS) party followed much of the Fidesz playbook in trying to weaken democratic checks and balances. With roots traceable to the anti–Communist Solidarity trade union movement, the PiS—like Fidesz in Hungary—began as a mainstream party but moved progressively rightward over time (Stanley 2017: 147), embracing Catholic and ethno-nationalist forms of exclusionary right-wing populism. The PiS led a short-lived parliamentary government from 2005 to 2007, then returned to power in 2015 and quickly took steps to undermine the independence of the Constitutional Court, the public media, and the Polish civil service (Rupnik 2016: 79). Although massive street protests in 2016 forced the government to withdraw proposed legislation banning all abortions, another cycle of protests in 2017 failed to block a government plan to force Constitutional Court judges into early retirement and to subject the judiciary to executive and legislative branch controls. These challenges to judicial independence and the rule of law evoked a rare threat from the European Union to suspend Poland's voting rights as a member of the regional bloc.

The Polish case demonstrates how societal resistance to exclusionary populism may combine opposition to specific policy initiatives—such as a ban on abortions— with mobilization aimed at the defense of basic, regime-level democratic checks and balances. In the United States, the grafting of Donald Trump's autocratic populist leadership onto the ideological agenda of the Republican Party virtually ensured that both policy-based and regime-level metaresistance would emerge. Early mobilizations by women, immigrant rights groups, environmentalists, and health care advocates articulated a wide range of policy grievances following Trump's assumption of the presidency, but they did not necessarily, at least directly, "problematize" the democratic regime itself. Indeed, social movements in the United States generally presume regime continuity as an overarching "opportunity structure" for varied forms of societal contestation (see McAdam 1996; Tarrow 2011: 157–180). This political and institutional opportunity structure, however, is under serious strain, and it cannot be taken for granted in the contemporary political context. The stakes involved in controlling regime institutions have been readily exposed by Trump's willful flouting of democratic norms and procedures, but this flouting is only the tip of the iceberg; below the surface, less-visible but potentially more-enduring and insidious challenges to democratic checks and balances have been spawned by decades of accentuated partisan polarization, and in particular by the radicalization of the Republican Party along both the economic and cultural axes of competition (Mann and Ornstein 2012; Mickey, Levitsky, and Way 2017).

Acute partisan and ideological polarization raises the stakes of democratic competition, and it can induce actors to transform regime institutions into instruments of partisan advantage and control. The comparative research on authoritarian backsliding in countries like Hungary and Venezuela has identified myriad ways in which partisans in the executive and legislative branches can use their appointment powers to pack the courts and place personal or partisan loyalists at the head of other agencies where they can whittle away at institutional checks and balances. Courts can interpret and enforce the rule of law in a selective or partisan manner; libel laws or efforts to stem the "leaking" of information can be used to muzzle the press or impose self-censorship; investigative agencies and commissions can shield incumbents from oversight and target political opponents; taxation authorities can use political criteria for enforcing regulations; electoral procedures can screen out certain voters and candidates or otherwise skew representation; and social protest can be criminalized. In essence, temporary competitive advantages provide access to, and potentially control over, crucial institutional nodes that can then be used to tilt the democratic playing field in ways that create durable imbalances (Levitsky and Way 2010).

Democratic institutions in the United States were explicitly designed to fragment and disperse power. They include multiple "veto points' (Tsebelis 2002) in which policy change can be blocked or frustrated, along with a complex web of institutional checks and balances to guard against efforts to concentrate or abuse power. These safeguards, however, rest upon a delicate equilibrium;

they are not fixed, self-enforcing, or independent of the partisan balance of power. Where partisan competition is fierce and democratic norms are increasingly contested, institutions that are designed to restrain and disperse power can be repurposed for partisan advantage. Indeed, political actors may openly challenge the legitimacy of rivals to occupy institutional spaces, and they can manipulate the rules to limit their influence where they do.

This is not the place to catalogue such forms of democratic backsliding in contemporary US politics, but the warning signs are easily recognizable. Electoral outcomes—already seriously distorted by the Electoral College and legislative malapportionment—are increasingly subject to thinly veiled partisan manipulation through district gerrymandering and voter identification laws that suppress turnout among blacks, minorities, and the poor. Trump claimed that national elections were "rigged" and alleged massive electoral fraud, both before and after he won the presidency. Republicans in Congress refused to consider a Supreme Court nominee of President Obama, choosing to leave a seat vacant until they were positioned to control the nomination process. They have also repeatedly used the threat of a government shutdown and a debt default as political leverage in policy disputes. Trump has maintained a running battle with the mainstream media, which he has labeled the "enemy of the people" and accused of spreading "fake news." Pro-Trump media outlets like Fox News, Breitbart, and conservative talk radio have sought to discredit the special counsel investigation of Russian involvement in the 2016 elections, characterizing it as a partisan witch hunt, and Trump sacked the FBI director and threatened to fire the special counsel as the investigation encroached upon his inner circle. Trump demanded personal loyalty from such officials and suggested that investigations be redirected at Hillary Clinton instead. From the racially coded "birther campaign" against Obama to anti-Hillary chants of "lock her up" and calls for the rough treatment for protestors, Trump has challenged the democratic legitimacy of his rivals. Indeed, Trump has advocated waterboarding and "a hell of a lot worse" in the war against terrorism.

Metaresistance targets these and other authoritarian tendencies in US politics (Hetherington and Weiler 2009). It is aimed at safeguarding civil rights and liberties and keeping democratic channels of institutional access open—in short, protecting the right to dissent and the ability of societal actors to shape public policy. This layer of resistance necessarily involves political contention in institutional sites—in Congress, the courts, investigative and electoral agencies, etc.—as well as the media, civil society, and, potentially, on the streets.

What remains to be seen in the United States is whether this metaresistance maps onto (and deepens) the existing partisan cleavage, such that the defense of democracy is transformed de facto into a partisan project, or whether it instead cuts across the Republican Party and splits the latter into rival democratic and populist-authoritarian camps. On the one hand, the former scenario would entail a vigorous effort by the Republican Party to use its existing control of institutional levers[2] to protect Trump from legal scrutiny and accentuate its partisan advantages. It is most likely to unfold if Trump is able to retain popular support among grassroots Republicans, capitalize on a domestic or international crisis to rally the party behind his leadership, or both. The second scenario, on the other hand, would require that a significant bloc of the Republican leadership join Democrats in upholding democratic norms and enforcing institutional checks and balances on the populist autocrat. It would, in essence, construct a transpartisan "regime cleavage" to cut across and supplant the existing partisan divide. Such a scenario is more likely to emerge if Trump's popularity sharply declines and he becomes a clear electoral liability to the Republican Party.

Needless to say, these alternative scenarios depict radically different trajectories for US democracy in the years ahead, as well as a very high degree of political uncertainty. It is not clear, for example, whether anti-Trump social protest will drive a wedge between the Republican Party's democratic and populist currents or accentuate interparty polarization in ways that induce Republicans to close ranks behind the president. Even if Republicans close ranks, however, extra-electoral social mobilization is arguably essential to contest potential erosions of democratic checks and balances, given the autocratic tendencies of a populist president and a movement-based party that is increasingly in control of critical institutional levers in American politics.

Conclusion

Societal resistance to Donald Trump's presidency has been heavily conditioned by the grafting of autocratic populist leadership onto the ideological agenda of the Republican Party in a context of acute partisan polarization. As we will see in the chapters that follow, this grafting spawned complex, multilayered forms of resistance that mobilized diverse social actors across a wide range of political and institutional sites. Although much of this resistance took aim at the exclusionary policy initiatives of the Trump administration, his Republican Party sponsors, or both, others were designed to safeguard basic democratic rights and the institutional checks and balances of the democratic regime itself.

These latter types of regime-level resistance, which I have characterized as metaresistance, are sure to loom large if the Republican Party continues to close ranks behind the Trump administration. Over the course of Trump's electoral campaign and his first year in office, the party's multiple strands largely fell in line behind the populist figure, and remarkably few high-level party leaders—namely, a handful of senators who declined to run for reelection—broke ranks.

This partisan cohesion can be attributed to a number of different factors, including the intrinsic political tribalism associated with acute partisan polarization, the political opportunism of disparate ideological currents that seek to use executive power to advance their programmatic goals, and the fear that Trump and sometimes allied hardliners like Steve Bannon will support grassroots primary challenges to any incumbent legislators who defect from the populist bandwagon. The character, scope, and focal points of metaresistance will be heavily conditioned by the relative cohesion of the Republican Party and the inclination—or disinclination—of prominent party figures to safeguard democratic checks and balances against unwarranted concentrations or abuses of power.

Patterns of metaresistance are not without precedent in the US political context. They are, however, surely unfamiliar to most contemporary social movement activists. Modern social movements in the United States are accustomed to mobilizing to gain recognition and amplify citizenship rights within an "opportunity structure" afforded by democratic institutions; they are not accustomed to mobilization aimed at the defense of those very institutions. The national political field has thus shifted to a new set of coordinates in which the continuity of the regime itself is in play. These coordinates are well known in other parts of the world where populist leadership is a reflexive response to flawed or failed forms of democratic representation. The comparative record suggests that social actors in the United States are likely to play a crucial role in activating democratic checks and balances and holding institutions accountable to a plurality of societal interests. Such challenges are sure to outlive the Trump administration, whatever its eventual denouement, as they are deeply embedded in longer-term patterns of contention, mobilization, and counter-mobilization over the character and reach of citizenship rights in American democracy.

PART TWO

THE BIRTH OF THE RESISTANCE

Who Made the Women's March?

MARIE BERRY AND ERICA CHENOWETH

Introduction: The Women's March in Context

In part because of women's historical marginalization in institutionalized politics, women's activism and organizing have often happened in the streets, outside of formal political spaces (Ferree 2006; King and Codur 2015; Molyneux 1998; Principe 2017). Women have featured prominently in movements mobilized around broader issues, including civil rights, labor rights, prison reform, land reform, peace, security, community safety, and food security. For instance, in 1905, Russian women organized marches against the price of bread, which launched the first Russian Revolution. In the decades since, women have marched on Pretoria during Apartheid in South Africa, against the disappearance of loved ones in La Plaza de Mayo during the "Dirty War" in Argentina, and, most recently, to insist resolutely that Black Lives Matter and to defend indigenous land and resources in Standing Rock. Beyond their participation in broader movements for social change, women have also mobilized around claims specifically related to women's rights, such as women's suffrage, reproductive rights, campaigns against women's sexual exploitation, and campaigns against female genital mutilation (King and Codur 2015; Principe 2017: 4). From the abolitionist movement to the labor movement that preceded the suffragist parades in the United States and Britain in the early 20th century, to recent mass protests in Poland against abortion restrictions, such women-led and women-centered movements have been instrumental in advancing human rights and women's rights in particular.

The Women's March of January 2017 built on this legacy of women's organizing. The loss by Hillary Clinton, the first female candidate for president of a major political party, to Donald Trump, a man widely accused of misogyny and sexual harassment, generated shock and dismay among many in the United States and across the world. This mammoth event had its unlikely origins in a conversation in the pro–Hillary Clinton group Pantsuit Nation on Facebook, where member Teresa Shook posted that she thought the election of Donald Trump on November 8, 2017, necessitated a women's march in Washington. When other Pantsuit Nation members responded to her post favorably, Shook, who is from Maui, Hawaii, created an event on Facebook that called for a prowomen march in Washington, DC, the day after the inauguration. Overnight, the originally billed "Million Women March" had 10,000 RSVPs, even though Shook initially shared it only with friends (Stein 2017). Several other New York–based organizers started similar Facebook event pages. Within the first few days after the election, hundreds of thousands of people—mostly white, cis-gender, and upper-middle-class women—purchased tickets to fly, train, or bus to Washington, DC, with the aim of protesting Trump's inauguration. These efforts were eventually consolidated into the Women's March on Washington and co-organized by National Cochairs Bob Bland, Tamika Mallory, Carmen Perez, and Linda Sarsour (Kearney 2016). The resulting Women's March on Washington of January 21, 2017, was probably the largest single-day demonstration in contemporary US history (Broomfield 2017).

This chapter examines how and why the Women's March evolved from a mostly white, elite liberal feminist movement to a broader-based, intersectional march through various framing techniques and a process of coalition-building. We explore how this ability to draw in various organizations and interest groups under a single coalition expanded the participation of the Women's March and potential for its staying power as a broader movement with considerably more political leverage than recent social movements in the United States, such as Occupy Wall Street. This chapter concludes with a discussion of the tactical and strategic effects of the Women's March so far, as well as its position in the overall landscape of social movements in the United States.

Organizational Tributaries

How did anti-Trump sentiment in the American polity channel itself into a massive, coordinated, nationwide event in just 9 weeks' time? We argue that the collective action of the Women's March did not emerge suddenly out of nothing; instead, the convergence of these preexisting organizational tributaries greatly facilitated collective action. We identify six major organizational tributaries, although of course there is overlap across them.

The first organizational tributary involved progressive organizations and political action committees who had been focused on electing Hillary Clinton during the 2016 presidential election. Although such groups represented both centrist and progressive wings of the Democratic Party, they were quick to back

Hillary Clinton after she gained the Democratic Party's nomination for president in July 2016. These organizations were largely engaged in electoral politics and institutional actions—especially those whose work had largely centered around get-out-the-vote campaigns among women and minority voters, like MoveOn.org, the League of Women Voters, and Black Youth Vote!—rather than community organizing and noninstitutional or extra-institutional action, per se.

The second organizational tributary involved the various feminist organizations that have been active in the United States for decades. Such organizations include groups like Planned Parenthood, CODEPINK, UltraViolet, Emily's List, and the National Organization for Women, all of whom have actively fought for women's equality in political, economic, social, and cultural life. It is certainly the case that such groups were poised for action in the wake of Trump's election, both because of their decades-long work in promoting women's equality, but also because of the fact that many of them actively mobilized against Trump's candidacy—particularly once women began claiming that Trump had sexually assaulted them and an "Access Hollywood" video was released that caught Trump bragging to host Billy Bush about his sexually assaulting women.

A third and related tributary that developed during the election campaign was a digital one. In particular, the establishment of the secret[1] Facebook group Pantsuit Nation on October 20, 2016, was an important precursor to the Women's March. Libby Chamberlain of Brooklin, Maine, initially started the page after the third presidential debate between Hillary Clinton and Donald Trump as a way to encourage her women Facebook friends to wear pantsuits to the polls on November 8 in support of and solidarity with Hillary Clinton. The page quickly went viral; by November 8, it had nearly three million members who shared stories, photos, encouragement, and resources. It was in the Pantsuit Nation group that Theresa Shook posted on November 9 the idea of holding a Women's March on Washington—an idea that immediately elicited thousands of affirmative responses in a way that would be difficult to imagine outside of the context of digital activism. The quickly assembled website, www.womensmarch. com, became a clearinghouse for information, news, sister march registration and guidance, messaging and protest art, and other announcements. The Women's March's social media presence on Facebook, Twitter, and Instagram facilitated the diffusion of information coming from the national hub (see also Karpf, Chapter 7 in this volume).

The fourth organizational tributary involved different progressive organizations that had supported Bernie Sanders as the Democratic nominee during the primary process and were frustrated at the Democratic National Convention, which their members saw as sidelining leftists and radicals in the party and elevating Hillary Clinton, a centrist candidate. These groups included various labor organizations, like the National Union of Healthcare Workers and the

Vermont and South Carolina divisions of the American Federation of Labor and Congress of Industrial Organizations (AFL-CIO), as well as social movement organizations like Occupy Wall Street, all of which had formally endorsed Sanders. It is important to distinguish this organizational tributary from those supporting Clinton as well as established advocacy organizations like the American Civil Liberties Union (ACLU), because of their prioritization of economic inequality, corruption and climate change as the key issues animating their mobilization. Sanders's populist platform was more appealing to such groups, who were seeking transformative reforms for economic justice, fairness and accountability, and debt relief—three areas for which Hillary Clinton's establishment record failed to inspire their support. Yet most Sanders's supporters, who represented more radical elements on the Left, were not attracted to Trump's brand of populism either, leaving many of them ready to recommit to their core policy agendas rather than to a particular party or elected candidate. Democracy Spring was one such group; it emerged from a group of former Occupy Wall Street activists whose primary goal was to overturn the Supreme Court's decision on Citizens United and get money out of politics as a way to begin to address economic inequality.

The fifth organizational tributary involved less-institutionalized, grassroots groups whose members had been organizing campaigns for social justice over the past few years. Certainly since Occupy Wall Street in 2011, the United States has seen a higher level of mobilization and activism across many different issue areas. But most grassroots community organizing since 2012 has involved black-led mobilization demanding transformational reforms triggered by police killings of unarmed black people (e.g., Black Lives Matter, Freedom Side, and the Movement for Black Lives), immigrant justice campaigns (e.g., United We Dream), labor and wage rights (e.g., Fight for $15), indigenous rights (e.g., the Standing Rock Sioux), and climate action (e.g., Greenpeace). A growing consciousness has emerged that these struggles are interrelated; that racial justice is related to economic justice and climate justice, for instance. Indeed, the national cochairs of the Women's March cut their teeth in community organizing in related campaigns, bringing with them decades of collective experience in forming coalitions and solidarity networks across their organizational affiliations, from the National Action Network (a national civil rights group), the Arab American Association of New York, and the Gathering for Justice, a criminal justice reform network. In the end, it was this tributary that provided the national leadership of the March, whereas the other five tributaries provided the mass participation and, for many of the sister marchers, the local-level organizational work.

Sixth, the United States has long featured a broad-based web of existing legal and civic advocacy organizations, like the ACLU, Human Rights Campaign (HRC), the National Association for the Advancement of Colored People

(NAACP), the Southern Poverty Law Center (SPLC), and others. Upon Trump's election on November 8, such organizations, though ostensibly non-partisan, were poised to mobilize their members and capital resources to resist many of Trump's stated policy proposals. Many women sitting on local civic organizations, associations, and governing boards—such as school boards, chambers of commerce, and neighborhood associations—also provided organizing capacity and experience that would prove crucial in organizing sister marches in the coming weeks.

Because many gender-inclusive progressive groups threw their weight behind the March, the event was able to elicit the participation of many men and broaden its focus to more general political and social issues. Interestingly, this may be a case of "general" social and political issue interest groups throwing their weight behind a "women's" cause, rather than the historical trend of women providing often-invisible political and organizing labor for broad-based causes—an essential task in coalition-building.

The fact that these tributaries combined to form into a larger umbrella structure speaks to several important literatures in social movement theory. First, the early recruitment of veteran organizers and activists into the leadership of the March provided the ability to recruit other experienced activists and organizers on a nationwide level. This formal recruitment capacity is consistent with the findings of McAdam and Paulson (1993), Passy (2003), and Saunders et al. (2012), who argue that experienced activists tend to be recruited through organizational channels. Second, the incredibly active social media environment during the 2016 presidential election allowed for more informal and nonhierarchical recruitment from first-time activists, consistent with Klandermans et al.'s (2014) finding that inexperienced activists tend to mobilize by means of friendship networks, mass media, and social media channels. Third, the intersectional and intergenerational nature of the organizational and participant base meant that the frames and mobilization tactics available to the March were likewise incredibly diverse (see Fisher's and Whittier's contributions [Chapters 5 and 10, respectively]), providing the movement with considerable organizational resources. Thus the character of the emergent movement was one in which the coalition had access to both national and local-level organizational capacities without necessarily requiring a hierarchical, formalized structure that might have infused heightened conflict into the organization prior to the March itself. Fourth, we can see that the six tributaries were able to overcome collective action problems—at least temporarily—by organizing around a singular focal point (although there were many frames expressed related to this claim). This ability to overcome collective action problems may be explained by (1) the fact that this swift mobilization occurred at the beginning of a new protest cycle, when intramovement tensions and conflicts are not always visible or operative

(Tarrow 2011); and (2) a mutual sense of emergency, which allowed the various organizations to temporarily set aside their parochial interests in favor of a shared claim in the short term.[2]

From Election Day to Inauguration Day

Evidence of the confluence and convergence of these organizational tributaries was clear in the aftermath of November 8. In the days following the election, many of these groups—and the voters they had mobilized—participated in quickly organized "Not My President!" protests around the country.[3] Formal efforts emerged to contest the election outcome through the mobilization or support of recount efforts in Michigan and Wisconsin, the claim that there was voter suppression in key swing states, and claims of direct Russian interference and collusion with the Trump campaign. Online petitions at Change.org and MoveOn.org (Warner 2016) obtained millions of signatures to demand that the electoral college break with its standard practice and install Hillary Clinton into the presidency on January 21. As it became obvious that such efforts would amount to nothing except dashed hopes among Clinton supporters, such groups turned to calls for collective action to express that Trump did not represent the majority of American voters.

As the call for a women's march on Washington began to spread, so too did criticisms of the proposed event. The initial, viral Facebook invite had taken the name of the "Million Women March." A 1997 march of the same name was organized by and for black women in solidarity with the 1995 "Million Man March," organized by black men to protest the discrimination and marginalization of black communities. When the predominantly white organizers of the 2017 March were confronted about their appropriation of this name, they changed the name to the "Women's March on Washington"—the name of the historic civil rights march led by Martin Luther King, Jr. This did not sit well with many activists from communities of color, who began to write blog and social media posts objecting to the overwhelming whiteness of the organizing committee and the fact that white women had little authority to lead such a movement given that 53% of white women voted to elect Trump (Malone 2016).

Other critiques emerged around the framing of the March as exclusive to women. With many men, and especially men from historically marginalized communities, also opposed to Trump's election and values, some felt excluded from the protest's organization. Further, organizers were criticized for focusing on gender difference and not including the many different identity groups that Trump and his administration had attacked—from queer communities to Muslims and communities of color. In general, many questioned what the

March's primary goal was and whether its organizers had a long-term plan for sustaining momentum and catalyzing progressive social change.

In reaction to this criticism, a more formal structure of the March emerged. Vanessa Wruble, cofounder of the online media platform OkayAfrica, was appointed to serve as head of campaign operations. Committed to ensuring that the March was inclusive, diverse, and centered around the leadership of women of color, she brought in four cochairs of the March: Bob Bland, a fashion designer who had been among the first organizers; Carmen Perez, executive director of Gathering for Justice; Linda Sarsour, executive director of the Arab American Association of New York; and Tamika Mallory, a political organizer and former executive director of the National Action Network. Perez, Sarsour, and Mallory had collaborated before in organizing marches against police brutality and were widely known in activist circles (Felsenthal 2017). The four national cochairs were supported by a team of other creative directors and honorary cochairs, including Gloria Steinem and Harry Belafonte, in addition to a national (and, before long, global) network of local organizing teams.

A third set of critiques related to failure to articulate goals that could galvanize alternatives to Trump and Trumpism. On the one hand, during the Civil Rights movement, for example, Martin Luther King's famed "I Have a Dream Speech" came during the 1963 March on Washington for Jobs and Freedom. The Women's March, on the other hand, was billed simply as the Women's March on Washington. Some argued that organizers missed an opportunity to express what the Women's March was *for* rather than just signaling frustration and resistance to Trump's presence in the White House.[4]

Although people broadly debated whether the goal of the March was to protest Clinton's loss, Trump's election, or commence to focus on a different set of goals all together, among the national organizing structure that emerged, the goal was more clear: to galvanize women to resist the surge and visibility of hate, racism, and misogyny in the country as a whole, which Trump's campaign fed and helped reveal. Intersectionality, and women's intersectional oppression, became the central frame of the March, alongside the need for disciplined nonviolent approaches to social change. The March organizers were insistent that the March was about more than protesting Clinton's election loss; indeed, Clinton's name was conspicuously omitted from the list of 28 women who had inspired American feminists, and she did not attend the March herself (Cooney 2017). Thus the March aimed to bring progressive people together around a shared inclusive vision for the country.

With about 9 weeks to organize and plan the March, the organizers moved quickly to placate critics and bring together many of the organizational tributaries previously mentioned. National organizing committees in charge of sponsorship, logistics, the program, and so forth emerged, which, given the tight timeframe, oftentimes comprised people with direct ties to the national organizers. Beyond the four national cochairs, it is remarkable how few members of the national organizing committee actually had ties to organized activism before. Many of them had personal connections or came from within networks of people in more central leadership positions. For instance, OkayAfrica, a media platform for "New African music, culture, fashion, art, and politics" that was not particularly well known among national organizing circles, sent several of its senior executives to coordinate social media and production for the event (Cusumano 2017). As momentum grew and communities planned "sister marches" outside of Washington, DC, the national march organizers relied heavily on a nonhierarchical organizational structure with rotating and fluid coalitions in charge of particular parts of the event. Compared with Occupy Wall Street, which was nonhierarchical by design, the Women's March was nonhierarchical by necessity, although several key organizers also possessed ideological attachments to nonhierarchical, horizontal, and cooperative decision structures (Felsenthal 2017).

This fluid structure, combined with the tight timeframe, often resulted in conflicting messaging between the national and local organizers. As cities announced local solidarity marches, there was a resurgence of concerns about the degree of inclusive and intersectional messaging coming from march organizers. This was particularly the case in cities where white women took on leadership roles, often without organizing experience or networks among local activists. As women of color became the central organizers of the national March, local chapters faced internal battles over leadership and messaging; debates emerged about whether to elevate seasoned activists—who were often from communities of color—to leadership positions or whether to remain reliant on the predominantly white women who had taken the initial lead.

At the national level, the organizers were committed to employing intersectionality as the dominant frame of the March (see Benford and Snow 2000 on the importance of framing). Intersectional approaches explore how race, class, gender, ability, sexual orientation, and other forms of difference combine to produce different situations of advantage or disadvantage (Fisher et al. 2017). For example, women who have children but who wish to engage in political activism may require childcare in order to participate fully, but childcare may be more accessible to women with sufficient financial resources compared with women who live paycheck to paycheck. Here the intersection between childcare responsibilities and class produces a possible cleavage within the movement, particularly if organizers are tone deaf to such differences and the needs they produce for participants. Although such "intersections" can allow for mobilization and organization within particular groups (silos), they can also be a framework for bringing people together. Because people are also likely to participate in marches and movements that speak to particular forms of their identities, the organizers faced the risk of fracturing women and others interested in coming by alienating one group and privileging another. Some Jewish groups, for instance, felt that the March was hostile toward Israel (Fox-Bevilacqua 2017); likewise, some black women declined to participate because they felt the March demanded a sense of sisterhood with white women when they felt none (Lemieux 2017).

Nevertheless, the use of intersectionality as the dominant frame of the March had a particular resonance for many people—even for those not previously familiar with intersectionality as a concept or frame—because of Trump's dismissal of multiple groups, from women to Latino communities to Muslims. The March organizers, drawing from Audre Lorde's work, explicitly emphasized that the liberation of one group is bound up with the liberation of all oppressed groups. This framing set the stage for a march and movement that explicitly (and unapologetically) centered the experiences and knowledge and leadership of people of color, queer people, differently abled, immigrants, undocumented, and those with any other marginalized identity. The March also clearly situated itself as committed to nonviolent principles of social change, emphasizing the importance of pursuing King's legacy of "the Beloved Community."

The Women's March organizers also distinguished themselves among many national-level coalitions by explicitly and forthrightly committing to nonviolent action as the path the March would follow. Carmen Perez, one of the national codirectors, suggested that she adhered to "Kingian nonviolence" as her primary guide for action, both morally and strategically, because nonviolent action held the constructive potential to transform existing structures and create new and just outcomes rather than simply destroying and antagonizing existing structures (Perez 2017).

The organizers then secured the partnership of over 400 organizations to join the March in solidarity as sponsors of the broader movement.[5] These included smaller, regionally based organizations like the YWCA from Central Maine or the Virginia Democratic Women's Caucus, together with larger, national or international organizations like Democracy Spring, Occupy Wall Street, the ACLU, the AFL-CIO, the SPLC, the NAACP, the National Resources Defense Council (NRDC), and American Jewish World Service. In this way the centralized March became an umbrella movement, drawing together the organizational tributaries previously identified. By determining which organizations and platforms could be included as official "partners" of the March and which excluded, the national organizing team shaped the movement's platform.

About a week prior to Inauguration Day, the organizers released a staunchly progressive, feminist platform of "unity principles" that affirmed the values of the March. This list of unity principles was expansive, ranging from broad statements

that women's rights are human rights and that gender justice is economic justice is racial justice, to more concrete policy values like the right to paid family
leave and clean water.[6] The principles moreover situated the March in a history
of women's organizing, citing movements from the suffragists to Black Lives
Matter as those that have paved the way for the current movement. Although
many progressive feminists embraced this platform, there were rumblings of discontent and public disagreements that broke out, often in online forums and on
social media.

The exclusion of prolife women's groups—and the inclusion of statements
supporting sex-workers' rights—were particularly contentious. Prolife women's
groups, some of which had supported Hillary Clinton's candidacy and found
Trump's comments toward women particularly egregious, initially intended to
attend the March. A prolife group from Texas, New Wave Feminists, was briefly
listed alongside hundreds of other organizations as a partner to the march. After
Planned Parenthood became a core sponsor of the March and a prochoice
stance was included in the platform, the New Wave Feminists group was un-
listed as a sponsor, setting off a round of criticism about the "intolerance" of liberal feminists (Riddell 2017). With abortion rights and access centrally included
in the platform, some prolife women's groups announced they would withdraw
their plans to attend the March.

Moreover, the unity principles affirmed that the March stood "in full solidarity with the sex workers' rights movement." After this statement generated
a flood of protest, the statement was briefly deleted before being reinstated
(Breiner 2017). The conflicted signaling of including and excluding particular
tenets of the platform revealed the evolving and fluid nature of the movement's
priorities during the short timeframe between its conception and Inauguration
weekend.

The decision to remove prolife groups from the umbrella coalition—and
the inclusion of a radical, intersectional, and progressive agenda—eventually
mollified some of the March's early critics, although it is not clear whether this
act motivated others to join the March. Black feminists concerned about the initial dominance of white women within the organizing structure were relieved
(Ruiz-Grossman 2016) when the cochairs were announced and when prominent Black intellectuals like Angela Davis became officially involved. Some still
disagreed, arguing that white people needed to take responsibility for Trump
and the white supremacy that pervades American society, and that attending the
March as a person of color and feigning an inauthentic sisterhood with white
women would be exhausting. At the same time, some white women lamented
what they felt to be their silencing within the movement: They did not appreciate being told to check their privilege and lashed out when others within the
movement emphasized the need to foreground race over gender. Debates testing

the usefulness and resonance of intersectionality as the dominant movement frame continued throughout the run-up to the March, although it was unclear the degree to which such conversation affected the ultimate level of participation.

The broader-based resistance to Trump's impending presidency manifested as various coordinated protests leading up to and including Inauguration Day on January 20. Thousands of protesters descended on the National Mall in Washington to demonstrate against and disrupt inaugural events. Black Lives Matter activists formed human barricades around Inauguration celebration entry points. Democracy Spring protesters audibly interrupted the presidential oath of office from the stands, as did CODEPINK activists at various remote viewing locations. An anarchist collective, J20, also engaged in various actions including protests, human blockades, and some vandalism resulting in injuries and arrests. Several of these groups—such as Democracy Spring and CODEPINK—were listed as partner organizations with the Women's March. And although these Inauguration Day efforts were not directly connected to the Women's March, many of those who participated in these events stayed on for the Women's March the next day.

January 21, 2017

The following morning, after merely 9 weeks of organizing, an estimated 4.5 million people gathered in a mass demonstration across the world. In Washington, DC, the primary site of the March, between 750,000 people and 1 million people turned out. Los Angeles turned out an enormous crowd as well, with perhaps 750,000 marchers. Marches occurred in 654 cities within the United States, and another 261 locations globally, in locations as far flung as Antarctica and Utqiaġvik (formerly Barrow), Alaska. After the number of marchers was tallied, observers speculated that the Women's Marches of January 21, 2017, constituted the largest single-day protest in US history. Incredibly, there were no reported injuries or arrests among marchers.

Participants in the Women's Marches in the United States were disproportionately white, middle aged, highly educated, and female (Shulevitz 2017). Their median age ranged from 37 to 42, although this varied substantially across the different marches. At the March in Washington, 53% had graduate or professional degrees (Fisher, Chapter 5 in this volume). Although most marchers associated themselves with the Democratic Party, others were independents or Republicans who opposed Trump's agenda. A staggering proportion were first-time protesters: According to a crowd study by Dana Fisher, one-third of the participants reported never participating in a protest before (Shulevitz 2017). According to Michael Heaney's (2017) research, 5% of protesters admitted to having previously participated in prolife rallies, suggesting that, despite the platform offered by the March organizers, many still participated without aligning fully with the March's agenda.

From March to Movement?

As Tarrow argues in this volume, the Women's March is, in some ways, best understood as a countermovement to Trumpism. Certainly it is easier to mobilize against a target than to mobilize for an alternative political project. This may explain why many unlikely bedfellows—including pro-Hillary groups, established progressive advocacy organizations, grassroots social justice groups, anticapitalist groups like Occupy, and first-time activists—were able to unify under the banner of the Women's March in January 2017.

But has the Women's March turned a single-day demonstration into a larger movement for social justice? As Tarrow suggests in his chapter, three organizational tasks are required for a major protest to transition into a broader cycle of mobilization: amplification, scale shift, and spillover.

The Women's March performed exceedingly well on all three counts. First, with regard to amplification, the Women's March national cochairs drew on their own organizational resources and experiences to establish a cross-cutting, broad-based coalition. This has resulted in support among establishment politicians, progressive grassroots groups, and more radical groups as well. A key technique in securing and maintaining such support has been mobilizing on behalf of such groups when asked. For example, Women's March organizers and staff have participated in and endorsed many other events organized by their partners. These include actions in solidarity with Muslim immigrants, Deferred Action for Childhood Arrivals (DACA) individuals, indigenous rights related to the KeystoneXL pipeline's proposed project in Standing Rock, LGBTQIA Pride (LGBTQIA indicates Lesbian, Gay, Bisexual, Transgender, Queer, Intersexual, Asexual), and racial justice in the wake of white supremacist mobilization in Charlottesville, Virginia, in August 2017. Women's March organizers have also visibly supported the A Day Without an Immigrant on February 21, 2017, a Day Without a Woman on March 8, 2017, the Tax Day protests of April 15, 2017, and the Science March on April 22, 2017, among others. On January 20, 2018—the 1-year anniversary of Trump's inauguration—Women's Marches once again mobilized impressive numbers of people into the streets, with between 1.8 and 2.6 million people marching in 407 locations in the United States alone (Chenoweth and Pressman 2018).

Second, with regard to scale shift, the Women's March on Washington developed a number of connections with local organizers in the United States and abroad who organized sister marches for local participants. This translated into hundreds of distinct march locations in the United States, ranging from a single participant in a Colorado mountain town to a million participants in Washington, DC (Chenoweth and Pressman 2017). Because of the extensive donor base available to them from these various organizational tributaries, they had considerable resources to devote to online communication, which also assisted in achieving international scale. In an attempt to maintain stamina and engagement, the Women's March has rolled out several programs, including a call for women to take 10 actions in Trump's first 100 days in office, as well as a call for women to hold "huddles" (i.e., small gatherings in which they could continue discussions on local levels about their struggles, solutions, and strategies). Women's March organizers say that over 5,600 huddles have taken place since January 2017. They also released a resource toolkit to support their Daring Discussions initiative, which encourages women to break their silence and engage in difficult discussions with family members and friends regarding progressive values.

Third, the March has also seen some spillover. After the Women's March in January 2017, many marchers wondered how they could continue to remain engaged and have visible impacts on the polity. The Women's March national organization did not anticipate such mass participation and did not have a well-developed strategy for maintaining mass engagement after the March. As a result, many Women's March participants found their way into Indivisible, a progressive organization developed by former congressional staffers that provided a tactical manual about how best to pester and influence elected officials. By early February 2017, over 3,800 local chapters of Indivisible had sprung up, largely collecting the hundreds of thousands of newly activated people in the United States whom grassroots groups had limited capacity to organize.

Nevertheless, this transference of supporters to other local-level political organizations has not diminished the awakenings that many women experienced on January 21, 2017. For example, some credit the Women's March with increased awareness of gender-based grievances, such as women's relative exclusion from public office, sexual harassment, wage gaps, and workplace discrimination. The #MeToo campaign, for instance, which emerged on the heels of a number of high-profile sexual harassment and sexual assault cases later in 2017, is emblematic of the sense of widespread outrage about the status of women in the United States. It also reflects a renewed and widespread sense of solidarity among women, which has encouraged women to speak out against such injustices and crimes at unprecedented levels. Such responses are wholly consistent with the concept of cognitive liberation—a collective recognition of an injustice along with an enduring commitment to engage in action to set it right

(McAdam 1983). As such, we should expect considerable engagement to continue, even as it transforms into other forms of advocacy.

Conclusion

The 2017 Women's March was likely the largest single-day demonstration in US history. Yet, some skeptics suggest that staging a massive march is easier now than in the past because of social media's ability to facilitate short-term coalition-building and broad-based mobilization. Large participant numbers do not necessarily reflect high levels of organizational strength and durability that previous events of this size required. For instance, Tufekci (2017) suggests it is easier to stage a march—a short-term event—than to build a movement, particularly one representing diverse communities with varied interests and diverging approaches to formal and informal advocacy. However, what the Women's March demonstrates is the ability of an organization to mobilize for a political protest event that has the potential to catalyze a durable coalition-based movement. Moreover, the size of the 2018 Women's Marches suggest a certain durability and continued momentum to the movement.

Indeed, the question of what comes next for those who marched on January 21, 2017, remains a topic of ongoing discussion among national-level organizers and participants alike. More important, the "what's next" debate has maintained active electronic and social media communication channels. It has been the linchpin for whether the event of the March can become a durable movement, and as a result has generated various opportunities for mobilization that continue to draw in many of the Women's March leaders and participants. Ten months after the initial march, for example, the Women's March held a National Convention in Detroit from October 27 to October 29, 2017, which gathered about 4,000 women to rally around local organizing in preparation for the 2018 midterm elections (Davey 2017). And excitement around the 2018 Women's March, particularly in locations like Los Angeles, Seattle, New York, Chicago, and Denver, suggests the possibility of a major annual event going forward.

This focus on running women candidates and contesting the 2018 elections speaks to a broader trend in the anti-Trump resistance: that of turning away from extra-institutional grassroots mobilization and toward institutionalized electoral politics. This partly reflects a third example of spillover as leading organizers seek to turn event-based mobilization into a long-term movement and coalition strategy. Their emphasis on formal politics also illustrates an important tactical and ideological tension in social movement organizing. On the one hand, organizers seek a foothold through the inside game, in which they aim to work for change within existing institutions, systems, and structures to achieve their goals. And, on the other hand, they aim to play an outside game, maintaining a credible mobilization and disruption capacity, and putting popular pressure on institutionalized elites and officials (see, for instance, Raeburn 2004). The channeling of many participants of different Sister Marches into Indivisible chapters while national cochairs of the March continue to issue calls for solidarity mobilization is emblematic of this embrace of a dual-track approach.

These are common processes in social movement coalitions, and they can often produce coalitional instability, particularly among those whose interests and preferences are not identical to those of the core leadership. This can be evident in the changing composition of the coalition over time. For instance, whereas at the outset, Planned Parenthood and the ACLU were anchors for the coalition, the ACLU quietly reduced its centrality over time, likely because its interests were gender inclusive and included broader civil rights issues as opposed to women's issues alone. At times, coalition dynamics tend to produce continual challenges in their members' ability to agree upon proximate and ultimate goals, methods and tactics, and framing.

That said, to a large extent, Trump and Trumpism continue to function as powerful unifying and mobilizing factors since the Women's March. For example, many link Trump's sexual abuses to the vitality of the #MeToo social media campaign, the speed and resonance of which builds on the mobilization capacity and solidarity evident on January 21 (Redden and Siddiqui 2017). And, although the Women's March has spawned and evolved into several new— and renewed—campaigns linked to broader issues, its intersectional approach to progressive politics continues to provide a powerful reference point for organizers. Intersectional frames and organizing structures or principles can make movements more resilient and adept at addressing both tensions and mutual concerns (Crenshaw 1991).

Ultimately, several features of the Women's March may hold the key to its long-term coalitional prospects, compared with other contemporary major social movement organizations. Its umbrella structure as both an organization and coalition, its intersectional approach, its unmatched mobilization capacity, and the persistent sense of urgency felt among millions of feminists in the United States continue to resonate and provide both latent and active political power. What remains to be seen is whether the coalition will be able to consolidate local gains and capitalize on unprecedented levels of engagement to translate the momentum from the streets into substantive policy and electoral change.

Acknowledgments: We are grateful to Zoe Marks, David Meyer, and Sidney Tarrow for their helpful and constructive comments on this chapter. All errors remain our own.

4

Mobilizing for Immigrant and Latino Rights under Trump

CHRIS ZEPEDA-MILLÁN AND SOPHIA J. WALLACE

On the heels of the historic 2006 immigrant rights protest wave, the US immigrant rights movement and Latino voters were part of the coalition that helped defeat a nativist Republican Party in two consecutive presidential elections (Barreto and Segura 2014; Zepeda-Millán 2017). Accordingly, when, in 2015, Donald Trump decided to run for president by "starting off his campaign calling Mexican immigrants rapists and criminals," he "sent shockwaves through the immigrant community and the immigrant rights movement."[1] Since then, no other segment of the Resistance has been targeted as openly, directly, or as often by the president as the Latino immigrant community. Among other attacks, Trump has signed executive actions targeting them, promised to build a border wall to keep them out, pardoned a sheriff convicted of racially profiling them, and ended a popular program that legalized hundreds of thousands of undocumented youth[2]—all actions that negatively and disproportionately affected the Latino community and the nation's immigrant rights movement.

Given that President Trump's assaults against Latino immigrants show no signs of abating a year into his presidency, in this chapter we examine some of the ways the 2016 presidential election has impacted immigrant rights activism. In addition, because nativist actions in this country have a disparate effect on both US- and foreign-born Latinos (Abrajano and Hajnal 2015; Chavez 2008; Masuoka and Junn 2013; Sampaio 2015), we pay particular attention to this community's current support for contentious politics on behalf of the foreign born. However, as the other chapters in this book illustrate, because Latino immigrants have not been the only group targeted by the Trump administration, we also assess the degree to which Latinos support the activism of other segments of the Resistance, specifically the Black Lives Matter and lesbian, gay, and bisexual (LGB) movements.

In the first two parts of our chapter, we draw on a series of personal interviews we have carried out with activists in the immigrant rights community. In the third part, we draw on survey evidence to reflect on the actual and the potential participation of Latinos in the Resistance. In the fourth part, we address a question that lies at the heart of this book: that of the Latino movement's potential role in the broader Resistance through both intersectionality and cross-movement connections between Latinos and other sectors of the movement.

In line with Goldstone and Tilly's landmark article (2001), we find that threats and opportunities can coincide and "combine to shape contentious action" (181) in different ways and at different levels. On the one hand, the immigrant rights movement has been put on the defensive by having to operate under a context of increased threats and limited political opportunities at the national level. On the other hand, in some cities and states, activists are taking advantage of an unexpected opening of opportunities that, in many respects, are greater than those found under the previous Democratic administration. In locales where organizers are operating in an environment of high levels of threat and closed political opportunity structures the immigrant rights movement seems to be in a state of "abeyance" (Taylor 1989) in which activists are focusing their efforts on less-overt forms of political action, such as base-building and base-movement strengthening. But in some other cities and states—like much of California—the movement has found surprising resonance as activists of all kinds rally to the cause of the so-called "Dreamers" and support what has become a vigorous "sanctuary" movement.

Fighting for Immigrant Rights Under Trump

Almost no one thought that Donald Trump would become president of the United States. On June 16, 2015, when he announced his desire to be his party's nominee, Reuters reported that "Republican strategists and officials cringed at the thought" of the reality TV star and real estate mogul "grabbing attention away from the party's more serious candidates," as it tried "to win back the White House after defeats in 2008 and 2012."[3] Even subsequent to surprising everyone by winning the Republican primaries, few believed that such an outlandish and openly racist candidate could have a chance of succeeding our nation's first—and twice-elected—African American president. Indeed, just days before Americans went to the polls to cast their ballots in November 2016, the popular survey website *FiveThirtyEight* reported, "Top public election pollsters are almost unanimous in their belief that Hillary Clinton will be the next president."[4] Political forecasters had "put Clinton's chance of winning at anywhere from 70% to as high as 99%."[5] Yet, "When Election Day dawned," although "almost all the pollsters, analytics nerds and political insiders in the country had Hilary Clinton waltzing into the White House," *Politico* noted that, "By the time polls had closed nationwide on Tuesday night, those projections had been left in shambles."[6]

Dashed Hopes, Devastating Realities

Trump's victory was particularly devastating for the immigrant rights movement in general and for Latino activists in particular. Not only had an openly anti-immigrant and anti-Latino candidate just won the White House, but news headlines had also projected Latinos would have played a central role in Trump's expected electoral defeat. For instance, leading up to Election Day, national media outlets proclaimed that, "Early voting by Latinos may help Clinton in several states,"[7] that a "Latino voting surge" was rattling the "Trump campaign,"[8] and that "Latino support for Clinton" was "set to hit a record high for a presidential candidate."[9] Thus, if Hillary had been victorious, political pundits would have undoubtedly boasted about the new electoral power of Latinos and how Trump's defeat was a national referendum against racist nativism. As Laurence Benenson of the National Immigration Forum, a centrist immigration policy coalition, put it, "Had Clinton won, as most of us expected, I think a lot of the narrative would have been that the position Trump took on immigration was the primary reason" he lost.

Immigrant rights advocates had anticipated making major gains under a Hillary Clinton presidency. According to several national movement leaders, they were preparing to push for a host of progressive legislative changes, given the fact that, from the start of her campaign, Clinton had promised to use her administrative authority as president to enact pro-immigrant policies. Chris Newman of the National Day Laborer Organizing Network (NDLON) explained,

> We were ready to try to get whistle blower visas for immigrant victims of workplace rights violations. Some people thought a version of CIR [comprehensive immigration reform] was possible. Some people thought smaller bills were possible and that expanding deferred action was going to be possible. A further rolling back of Secure Communities was possible, winning the Texas vs. U.S.-DAPA [Supreme Court] case was possible, the list goes on and on and on.

Another activist added, "You probably would have also seen advocates pressing her on some of Obama's policies that weren't popular, like some of his family detention policies and some of his administration's work with private prisons."[10] The chances of any of these goals being accomplished were crushed as a result of

Clinton's electoral defeat. Consequently, the general feeling among movement interviewees was that, "Today, under a Trump administration, passing any national legislation is a pipe-dream."[11]

Notwithstanding Obama's stringent interior immigration enforcement measures (Gonzales 2014; Macias-Rojas 2016), the national immigrant rights leaders we interviewed for this chapter asserted that under a Democratic president, at a minimum, they would have "had a seat at the table." As one organizer described it, "Despite the fact that it deported hundreds of thousands of people," in response to their protests the Obama administration "would at least open the door to the immigrant rights movement to have conversations about the administration's practices and to make sure that they were held accountable."[12] Whereas now, another activists clarified, "the groups that the Trump people reach out to are those more aligned with his campaign, which are outwardly hostile" toward the immigrant community and the immigrant rights movement.[13]

Summing up the overall impacts of the election on the movement's national policy goals, one activist admitted,

> Almost all of our plans were changed because no one had anticipated the possibility that Trump would win. The shift that occurred overnight was that we went from all kinds of incredibly ambitious things we thought were going to be possible at the federal level, legislatively, administratively, and even through the courts, to after the election feeling that nothing is possible at the federal level.[14]

As another pro-immigrant national policy leader expounded, "From an advocacy standpoint, it's a different world we're in than just a couple years ago. Now we're playing a lot more defense on all sorts of different fronts."[15]

Widespread Fear, Ineffective Tactics

Although after a year of his presidency Donald Trump had suffered a string of administrative and policy defeats and had only one legislative victory to his name—the tax bill—he did keep his promise to aggressively attack immigrants. Upon taking office, on top of explicitly targeting places where the immigrant rights movement had successfully helped pass local "sanctuary city" ordinances, the new president increased arrests of undocumented people across the country by close to 40%.[16] What is more, going beyond the Obama administration's record number of expulsions, his "White House issued clear policy memos that directed ICE [Immigration and Customs Enforcement] agents to prioritize criminals when sifting through the mountains of files of people facing deportation." But according to *Newsweek,* Trump "effectively overturned Obama's policy" by directing immigration officers to go after and deport any undocumented person they come across, even for minor violations.[17] As the *Miami Herald* put it, "The big accomplishment of Trump's first 100 days" in office was his "Terrorizing [of] undocumented immigrants."[18]

This "terrorizing" has had a chilling effect on the immigrant rights movement. According to activists, although there had been fear of deportation under Obama, after Trump's election those anxieties increased exponentially. Mario Carrillo of America's Voice explained, "There's been a considerable uptick of deportations among people without any criminal record," which "has certainly led to a lot of confusion and a lot of fear and a lot of panic" because of "not knowing how the administration will come down on any given day."[19] Laurence Benenson of the National Immigration Forum pointed out that, "People think, with good reason, that they're at risk of getting swept up and them or their loved ones being deported. There's always been some sense of fear but it's gotten much more extensive since January," when Trump took office.

Elizabeth Cuna of United We Dream (UWD), the leading cross-country network of undocumented youth, agreed, adding that many Deferred Action for Childhood Arrivals (DACA) recipients who are in college or have jobs are now "scared of losing everything" they've worked so hard to accomplish. These fears, however, aren't limited to young activists. As another organizer described, "I think there was a time when parents of undocumented youth started shedding the fear that was associated with being undocumented." Under the Obama administration, "They saw their kids being able to come out and express in public who they were" and, as a result, began to have the desire to do the same. But now, according to the activist, when they try to hold public events, "the vast majority" of undocumented youth they work with "say that if there's going to be media involved, their parents will not come out and try to defy this administration by being so outspoken about their status."[20]

Contentious politics scholars have long asserted that the opening of political opportunity structures, which include the presence of sympathetic allies in key positions of power, are crucial for the success of social movements (McAdam 1982; Tarrow 2011). In this respect, it is important to note that, for the most part, the undocumented youth movement emerged and reached its peak accomplishments during the Obama administration (Nicholls 2013). Unfortunately, today, as one activist argued, "there's a lot more risk and a lot more at stake when DACA recipients and Dreamers decide to go through with acts of civil disobedience."[21] Despite the fact that there are still a number of activists willing to protest against the Trump administration, a UWD organizer explained, "there's a huge amount of youth who think it's crazy to risk getting arrested and deported now."[22]

Chris Newman of NDLON shared a concrete illustration of the difficulties of fighting for immigrant rights under Trump. He said, "The great innovation that occurred during the Obama administration was organizing to stop individual deportations, which then had an upward impact on administrative policies." Regrettably, Newman lamented, "None of the old strategies and tactics of shaming the administration in order to compel administrative reforms work anymore" (see Patler and Gonzales 2015). He confessed that "no one has figured out how to organize and stop a deportation yet," and held that "the idea of left-side pressure as a tactic no longer works."

Operating in a political environment in which the federal government is overtly threatening their social movement and constituencies has had an especially adverse impact on the younger generation of immigrant rights activists. As Newman noted, "A lot of the younger folks don't know what it's like to do advocacy under a Republican administration, much less the type of Republican administration we have now." The "recently woke crowd who are super hip to things like the deserving and undeserving immigrant dichotomy and intersectionality, and who formed these intellectual insights under the Obama administration, don't have the intellectual or tactical considerations for the world we're in right now." As a result, "we're left with much more ambitious intellectual aspirations but a complete brick wall in terms of what can be done . . . . It's f*****g bleak, like really bleak, there's no point in sugarcoating it."[23] Carrillo of America's Voice concurred and declared, "We're dealing with something completely different, something completely hostile compared to the previous administration." Consequently, "we're doing a lot of soul searching now about what advocacy looks like in the time of Trump, and I don't think moving forward it will look the same" as it did in the past.

Responding to the Now; Building for the Future

There is a consensus among activists on the need to immediately resist and respond to the Trump administration's attacks in an attempt to limit, as much as possible, the negative ramifications of the president's actions. However, although all of the national advocates we interviewed were "on high alert" and "on the defensive," depending on their specific foci, constituencies, and local political dynamics, different segments of the movement are responding differently to what they think is achievable "in the time of Trump."

For instance, in addition to publicly stating their opposition to the president's anti-immigrant actions, some of the more politically moderate groups in the movement are trying to identify policies that may not be as partisan as comprehensive immigration reform and can, they hope, possibly lay the foundation for more expansive legislative discussions in the future. As an example, the National Immigration Forum is a coalition of faith leaders, law enforcement agents, and members of the business community—or, as they put it, "Bibles, Badges, and Businesses"—who are supportive of comprehensive immigration reform. Whereas their religious partners have been worried about the moral implications of Trump's policies, their law enforcement members have reported that immigrant communities are rapidly losing trust in local police officers, which makes it harder for the police to do their jobs.

Moreover, the coalition's business partners are concerned about the new administration's plans to cut legal immigration, which they believe would have an extremely negative effect on their labor force needs and on the general economy. Nonetheless, one of the organization's main policy strategies at the moment is trying to push for what its leaders call "skills and workforce issues," which include things like "jobs training, vocational, and language skills training" for immigrants. They believe that these "are areas that are less controversial" and that "you don't have the parties fighting with each other." Their hopes are that if they "get some traction on these policies, maybe it could open some doors with members of the administration for what we think of as more general immigration policies."[24]

Shifting Scale Downward

Writing about the Civil Rights Movement in the 1960s, Sidney Tarrow and Doug McAdam pointed out that cycles of contention frequently shift upward as they diffuse, a move that can offer new targets, different tactics, and greater threats and opportunities (Tarrow and McAdam 2005). What Tarrow and McAdam failed to investigate, however, was that when opportunities close at the national level, movements often shift their attention downward, closer to the grassroots, where there may be opportunities that are closed off at the national level. This was the case for the immigrant rights movement after 2006.

But there is a complication in shifting a movement's scale downward: as Edelina Burciaga and Lisa Martinez have argued, the opportunity structure for the immigrant rights movement—like much else in American politics—varies from place to place (2017). From data collected between 2006 and 2011, Burciaga and Martinez argue that "contexts of varying levels of antagonism or accommodation . . . shape both the emergence and character of undocumented youth movements" (Burciaga and Martinez 2017: 452). In Los Angles, activists took advantage of California's generally welcoming context for undocumented immigrants; for example, the state has offered in-state tuition and financial aid at public colleges since 2001 and financial aid to students since 2013 (Burciaga and Martinez 2017: 458). This helped to shape a new "socially acceptable identity" and invigorated activists "to continue to push for state-level changes within a rapidly shifting and unstable federal context" (460).

In contrast, in antagonistic contexts like Atlanta, Georgia, undocumented youth were on the defensive after 2006, mobilizing to oppose a ban barring them from accessing institutions of higher education and focusing on students, rather than on the broader issue of immigrant rights, In summary, America's variegated political landscape has generated different degrees of activism and different strategies on the undocumented youth movement, influencing "the claims they made, the target of their claims, and the strategies and tactics they employed in each city" (Burciaga and Martinez 2017: 466).

In our research, we found that although the more progressive and grassroots groups in the movement do not believe that even minimal national legislative gains are possible under Trump, they are shifting scale downward—concentrating their efforts on building local power and expanding their membership bases. As Cuna of UWD explained,

> The truth is that when we started in the movement we took advantage of the political moment that existed [under Obama] .... But the reality is that we didn't have a 10-year strategy of how we would sustain and cultivate our youth leadership, or how we would retain the distinct generations that entered our movement .... This has definitely changed. Today we know we have to deal with the urgent issues that come up, but we also need a long-term strategy that includes us maintaining strength in the places where we already have a presence, but also includes more rural places and new places.

She continued, "The tactic of growing our membership in locations where Trump won is essential now. We realized we're not changing the narratives and local policies in these places, so right now our focus is on cultivating as much local power as possible." Cuna illustrated, "If there's a school board election in these places, if there's a mayoral election, whatever it is, our focus now is on local elections and influence because that's the only way we could" continue to build our movement "over the next ten years." Thus, in response to the results of the 2016 presidential race, UWD has renewed their efforts to target specific districts in Texas, New Mexico, and Florida, where they are "running civic engagement programs" in which they are attempting to influence local candidates' platforms, doing educational phone-banking, canvasing, and even plan to eventually "cultivate" their immigrant youth "leadership to run for school board, for city council, etc."

Chris Newman of NDLON also put forward the idea of having the "dual goal" of "on the one hand, having meaningful interventions that help people on immediate stuff like self-defense, preparing for more scapegoating, criminalization, and attacks on our institutions." On the other hand, he elaborated, "we have to also try to build a more longer-term" political agenda, which includes taking advantage of the opportunities that have arisen in some more politically progressive locations. For example, "California is the one place where the inverse of the political dynamic of what occurred in D.C. took place." In the Golden State, Trump's electoral victory "created all these weird dynamics where left-side politicians are feeling more incentivized to show their pro-immigrant credentials." According to Newman, local California politicians are now willing to take public stances they were unwilling to adopt under the Obama administration. This seems to be especially true among Latino elected officials.

For instance, similar to the vital role lawyers played in challenging Trump's discriminatory travel ban (see Dorf and Chu's chapter in this volume, Chapter 6), California's Latino attorney general, former Los Angeles Congressman Xavier Becerra, has taken the lead in suing to stop the president from building his controversial border wall with Mexico and over his plan to end the popular DACA program, which "protects young immigrants from deportation."[25] California legislators' recent passage of a "sanctuary state" bill "to protect immigrants without legal residency in the U.S" is another example. According to the *Los Angeles Times*, this law was "part of a broader push by Democrats" in the state "to counter expanded deportation orders under the Trump administration."[26] Newman believes that Latino State Senator Kevin de Leon, the legislator who led the efforts to pass the new law, "wouldn't have run a bill that was antagonizing to the Clinton administration." He recalled that "in the shock and awe moment of Trump winning and facing the reality of it," de Leon contacted several immigrant rights organizations across the state and "said every idea that we've rejected as politically unfeasible for the last 8 years because Barack Obama was president, we want all of those ideas back on the table so that we could maximize every possible thing we could do under California law to protect immigrants." Hence, at least in some locations, it seems that elected officials—particularly Latino ones—are seeing the current moment as one in which it may be politically expedient to work with movement activists on passing progressive immigration policies at the local level.

That said, it shouldn't surprise us that in a state where Latino elected officials wield considerable political influence, "California has become a model" for liberal immigration legislation.

These dynamics, of course, are premised on the fact that Latino politicians find it politically beneficial to flaunt their "pro-immigrant credentials" to their pro-immigrant Latino voting bases. But why would both Latino elected officials and immigrant rights activists believe they could count on the backing of the Latino electorate? Part of the reason is simply because Latinos are dispropor- tionately impacted by immigration issues because the vast majority of them are either foreign born themselves or "are children, spouses, in-laws, and neighbors" of immigrants (Pedraza, Segura, and Bowler 2011: 2).

In addition, as Cuna of UWD bluntly stated, "At the end of the day, over 70% of the 11 million undocumented immigrants are Latino, that's the dem- ographic reality." But although most people without papers are in fact Latino, not all Latinos are immigrants, let alone undocumented ones. There is another key factor explaining why this community would be especially supportive of immigrant rights today. According to Newman of NDLON, because of Trump, "There's been an unmasking of the institutional white supremacy involved in the evolution of U.S. immigration policies." As a result, "Now there's an opportu- nity to talk about how immigration policies are both racist and racializing," espe- cially toward Latinos—US and foreign born. This matters politically because, as a representative of the National Immigration Forum explained, demographically "you have growing Latino populations that are building up electoral strength" across the country, and "I think that in the medium term its gonna really hurt the Republican Party." He added, "Texas and Arizona are seen as red states right now, but if you look at their demographics and this administration's rhetoric and policies, they could be like California after 1994 with Prop. 187."[27]

In sum, in response to a president as adverse to their movement as Trump is, some immigrant rights activists have taken to base-building and expanding their membership to new locations, especially in places that helped put Trump in office. In addition, at least some elected officials in liberal states seem emboldened by Trump's anti-Latino and anti-immigrant rhetoric and are more willing to push for local policies they were hesitant to pursue under a Democratic president. In other words, Trump's draconian attacks against immigrants have created local opportunities in some progressive locations where activists could take advantage of Democratic lawmakers' new will- ingness to publicly oppose and defy the White House. Consequently, some organizers are capitalizing on the political moment in these locales by pushing for policies that can help protect immigrants from the federal government and expand their rights at the local and state levels.

Nonetheless, although these long-term goals are undoubtedly essential to the future of the nation's immigrant rights movement, and despite the limits of using contentious politics to help pass liberal immigration policies under this administration, all of the national advocates we spoke to for this study agreed on the need to publicly protest against Trump's actions. As such, be- cause issues related to immigration in the United States have been racialized as distinctively Latino, and because this community is increasingly influential in national politics, it is essential for us to explore the degree to which Latinos currently support not only immigrant rights, but also other types of activism given the diversity of movements that comprise the Resistance against President Donald Trump.

Latino Support for Political Activism

Thus far, we have used our interview data to map the contours of the struggle for immigrant rights in the Trump Era. We have focused on how movement strategies have shifted and have been redirected from the national to local levels and on the unique role Latinos play in the US immigrant rights movement. We now turn to an examination of current Latino support for various types of activism. We do this for several reasons. First, because of the numerous ways contentious politics can impact policymaking (Gillion 2013), we believe it is also important to investigate if Latinos today are supportive of immigrant rights and other high-profile types of activism. Second, in the current political climate under the Trump administration, multiple groups feel under attack from rhetoric, policies, and laws targeting them. Accordingly, by taking the pulse of Latino support for contentious politics across a range of topics in 2016, we can draw inferences about whether they see activism as a vehicle for political change, as well as the potential for other social movements in the Resistance to seek their backing.

To investigate Latino support for political activism, we drew upon the 2016 Collaborative Multi-Racial Post-Election Survey (CMPS) (Barreto et al. 2017).[28] In this collaborative survey, researchers from various institutions designed their own questions and then purchased time on the instrument to field their survey items. The poll was fielded between mid November 2016 and February 2017. Similar to most observational research, our survey data provide a snapshot of Latino support for activism in late 2016–early 2017.

We fielded a series of questions related to support for activism among the survey's sample of approximately 3,000 Latino respondents and utilize several of these items for our analysis in this chapter. The survey also included a battery of various common sociodemographic variables, including political party affiliation, nativity, citizenship, and national origin group. Specifically, in three separate questions we asked respondents how much they support or oppose immigrant rights and LGB activism,[29] as well as the Black Lives Matter (BLM) movement. Respondents were presented with the following answer choices: "Strongly Support," "Somewhat Support," "Neither Support nor Oppose," "Somewhat Oppose," and "Strongly Oppose." We intentionally asked about activism beyond immigrant rights because we suspected Latinos would be most supportive of

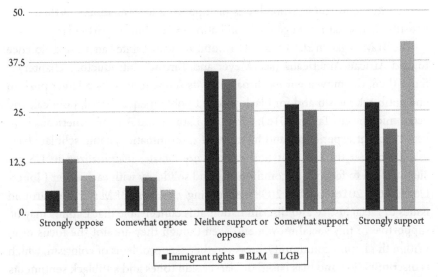

Figure 4.1 Latino Support for Activism.
Source: CMPS 2016.

contentious politics on behalf of the foreign born, given the personal nature of immigration to the Latino community (Sanchez et al. 2015; Wallace 2012). The overall survey results demonstrate that Latinos overwhelmingly support polit-ical activism across all three issue areas. Figure 4.1 displays the raw percentages of levels of support and opposition for each movement. Opposition, either strongly or somewhat, in any of these areas is quite low in comparison with support. This provides strong evidence that Latinos have a considerable amount of faith in activism as a form of political expression.

Latinos have a long history of participating in protests, marches, and rallies in support of immigrant rights (Zepeda-Millán 2017). Immigration is also con-sistently ranked as a highly important and personal issue for Latinos (Casellas 2010; Sanchez et al. 2015; Wallace 2013). Thus it is not surprising that Latinos overwhelmingly back immigrant rights activism, with the majority (nearly 54%) indicating some level of support. Latino opposition to this type of activism is also quite minimal. Across the three issue areas we examine, Latinos expressed the lowest levels of opposition (less than 12%) to immigrant rights activism. In fact, even a third (32%) of Latino Republicans support contentious politics on behalf of immigrants, though nothing close to the amount of backing (59%) expressed by Latinos who do not identify with the GOP. With regard to nativity, we were also not surprised to find that, given the direct impact on their lives, foreign-born Latinos support immigrant rights activism at an even higher de-gree (63%) than Latinos born in the United States (50%). Hence, in the time of Trump, immigrant rights activists should find some comfort in knowing that they continue to enjoy strong levels of support among members of their core constituencies, Latinos in general and Latino immigrants in particular.

The BLM began in 2013 as a call to mobilize against state-sanctioned violence toward African Americans (see Meyer and Tarrow's introductory chapter).[30] Since then, the movement has broadened its scope to include a larger push to end antiblack racism and for black people to obtain equal social, political, and economic power (Taylor 2016). Although Latinos and African Americans have very different experiences and histories of discrimination, some scholars have asked whether the fact that both groups are racially marginalized in US society has led to feelings of commonality and solidarity with each other (Jones-Correa et al. 2016; Sanchez 2008). Accordingly, because BLM is framed around issues of racial justice and discrimination, it is conceivable that Latinos may be supportive of this social movement, even though they are not the focus of it. Within the Latino community, however, there are problems of colorism, which is discrimination and bias based on darker skin tones and antiblack sentiments (Hunter 2007; Oboler and Dzidzienyo 2005); thus it is far from a certainty that they would back the BLM movement. In fact, some previous research has argued that rather than working in coalition, black and brown relations are riddled with conflict and competition (see Marrow, 2011; McClain et al. 2006; Morin et al., 2011).

Notwithstanding the latter body of literature, our results provide some evidence to be more optimistic about black and brown solidarity. Only about 22% of Latinos expressed opposition to the BLM movement, compared with the large plurality (45%) who somewhat to strongly support BLM. Contrary to our findings on greater support of immigrant rights activism by foreign-born respondents, when nativity is considered, a larger percentage (53%) of US-born Latinos support BLM, compared with a still-solid 41% of Latino immigrants whose backing BLM garners. Matched with the other two movements we examined, Latino Republicans expressed the highest degree of opposition to BLM, with about 50% being somewhat to strongly opposed to this movement. Nevertheless, despite BLM's not primarily focusing on what are often considered to be Latino-specific issues (e.g., immigration, bilingual education), a large number of Latinos do in fact support the movement for black lives. Thus, if BLM desires to expand its base and work in coalition with groups beyond the African American community, it seems to have a potential ally in Latinos.

National attitudes toward lesbian, gay, and bisexual people have shifted considerably over time to be more positive and more supportive of policies that expand their rights (Markel and Josyln 2008). Yet, after the momentous 2008 presidential elections, despite voting overwhelming for Barack Obama, the Latino electorate was criticized for voting in favor of the passage of California's infamous Proposition 8, which repealed gay marriage in the Golden State.[31] Prior research has found that their socially conservative politics and the conservative values associated with their religiosity have traditionally decreased Latino support of LGBT rights (Ellison et al. 2011). In light of this prior scholarship, we did not expect Latinos to express high levels of approval of lesbian, gay, and bisexual rights activism. Our survey results, however, show that they are actually quite supportive of contentious politics on behalf of the LGB community.

Only 14% of Latinos expressed any level of opposition to LGB rights activism, in contrast to 42% who said they strongly supported activism in this area. An additional 16% of Latinos indicated they somewhat supported LGB activism. In total then, 58% of Latinos in our sample expressed that they somewhat to strongly support activism for the rights of LGB people. Even more surprising was the degree to which Republican Latinos support this type of contentious politics. Indeed, more Latinos (35%) who identify as Republican support LGB activism than oppose it (31%). In distinction, Latinos who do not identify with the GOP support contentious politics on behalf of the LGB community at over 64%, whereas Latinos born in the United States back this type of activism at a higher rate (62%) compared with a still-solid nearly 46% of foreign-born Latinos.

To summarize, if activists fighting for immigrant, black, and LGB rights in the Trump Era are to be successful, then it is of the utmost importance that they find ways to get the support of politically relevant constituencies, such as Latinos—the nation's largest racial minority group. The results of our survey questions show signs for hope and suggest that this community is strongly supportive of progressive political activism. These findings are important to note not only because they imply that all three of the aforementioned segments of the Resistance —BLM, LGB, and immigrant rights organizers—should invest in seeking the support of Latinos, but also because they suggest that this politically vital community may be open to backing cross-movement and intersectional forms of activism. In the next section we highlight some specific examples of how these types of organizing are already occurring and are all the more vital during this presidency.

Intersectionality and Cross-Movement Solidarity

Because of the Trump administration's simultaneous attacks on various marginalized groups, the president may be creating opportunities for the immigrant rights movement to forge more productive and meaningful intersectional and cross-movement alliances. As such, it is critical to explore the ways in which the immigrant rights movement has engaged in these types of organizing, because they will become all the more important as long as Trump is in the Oval Office.

Before we discuss these concepts in relation to the immigrant rights movement, it will be useful to distinguish intersectionality, or intersectional activism, from cross-movement solidarity (Ayoub forthcoming). Cross-movement solidarity occurs when independent groups have an overlapping shared interest or grievance that leads these respective groups to work together to achieve a common goal. Examples range from women suffrage and Christian temperance activists uniting in the late 18th and early 20th centuries, to contemporary unions and environmental groups working against corporations (McCammon and Campbell 2002; Rose 1999). The critical component here is that these coalitions stem from a shared interest, not shared identities or group membership.

In contrast, intersectionality theory contends that individuals have multiple identities that can produce marginalization, often simultaneously, as in the case of gender and race (Crenshaw 1991; Hancock 2007). In movements, this implies that groups share not only interests, but also identities. As one national activist illustrated, "When Trump won, it became very clear that we were all being attacked by an agenda whose goal was to eliminate difference." Therefore, "As people of color in the U.S., we began to understand that aside from our immigration status, our youth also have to fight against criminalization, the school-to-prison pipeline, in addition to poverty, in addition to neighborhood segregation, etc." Thus, "At the moment our network is facing an organic and real challenge of how to merge all of our other identities with our realities as immigrants."[32]

Preceding the election of Donald Trump, the immigrant rights movement already had elements that were intersectional (Terriquez 2015). For example, UWD frames and contextualizes much of its organizing through an explicitly queer lens. They estimate that 86% of their leadership and 43% of their membership identifies as Lesbian, Gay, Bisexual, Transsexual, and Queer (LGBTQ). As Cuna explained, "We're all very queer, which is good and beautiful so we can't separate" immigrant from LGBTQ rights. "It's totally an overlap," so "we've created a message about being 'UndocuQueer.'"[33]

One of the major components of UWD's organization is their Queer Undocumented Immigrant Project (QUIP). QUIP aims to "transform the immigrant and LGBTQ movements, to adopt an intersectional analysis in their efforts to advance and build power for the rights of both communities."[34] The broader UndocuQueer movement, which includes activists across a host of organizations, has specifically centered the intersection of the fight for LGBTQ rights with the struggle for the broader protection of immigrants (Seif 2014). Looking to the future of the movement, it is likely that a major part of its organizing will continue to center on issues that intersect both legal status and sexuality.

Another potential area for both intersectional and cross-movement solidarity is with organizations that focus on racial justice for African Americans. Although immigrant rights activism has traditionally been heavily Latino focused in terms of for whom advocacy is organized and who is involved in it (Zepeda-Millán 2017), there is an increasing broadening of the immigrant rights movement to include other racial and ethnic groups. For instance, the number of black immigrants in the United States is on the rise (Greer 2013), and there may be more mobilization on immigration issues among this community as a result. Groups already organizing on behalf of the rights of black people in the United States, such as BLM and the National Association for the Advancement of Colored People (NAACP), have also increasingly discussed and advocated for immigrant rights. As an example, the NAACP recently filed a lawsuit in response to President Trump's ending of the DACA program.[35] In addition, BLM also added immigration reform, deportations, and immigrant detention centers to its recent platform, with a specific emphasis on black immigrants.[36] BLM may be particularly interested in these issues because one of its co-founders, Opal Tometi, the daughter of Nigerian immigrants, is also a cofounder of the Black Alliance for Just Immigration (BAJI) and has a long history of activism in the immigrant rights community (Ramshaw 2017). Hence, it may be possible for black and brown organizations to work together in the fight for immigrant rights and that both groups will see not only overlapping interests, but also shared struggles, given the impending risks they face under Trump. Again, our survey data point to the potential of this scenario becoming a reality.

There are also some important opportunities and examples of cross-movement solidarity between women's groups and immigrant rights advocates. For instance, draconian immigration enforcement strategies in the Trump Era, such as ICE agents appearing in court to arrest undocumented women who are the victims of domestic violence (Mettler 2017), place immigrant women and their rights in peril. As a result, these activities have led to more frequent calls by women's rights activists and organizations—such as the National Organization for Women—to frame immigration as a feminist issue.[37] Groups such as the National Women's Law Center have also developed resources and called for actions to protect the rights of immigrant women (including their reproductive rights) and have criticized harsh immigration policies for their detrimental effects on foreign-born women's health.[38] Moreover, not only did organizers of the historic 2017 Women's March also explicitly declare their oppositions to the federal government's deportation practices, but as Fisher's chapter in this volume (Chapter 5) shows, many of the participants in the national mobilization were also supportive of immigrant rights.[39] Thus there may be rich possibilities to bring together a coalition between activism rooted in gender justice and activism on behalf of the rights of the foreign born.

Key bridges to these types of coalitions will undoubtedly be intersectional organizations, such as the National Domestic Workers Alliance, which advocates for domestic workers who are more often than not immigrant women. Both types of groups—mainstream women's organizations and immigrant women organizations—might see the opportunity, for example, to joining the fight against detention centers, given the fact that Trump plans to expand these forms of prisons where documented cases of rape, sexual assault, and sexual harassment against women chronically occur.[40] In Chapter 5, Fisher demonstrates that some participants in the Women's March and the People's Climate March not only reported participation in marches on racial justice and immigration, but also in some instances cited these issues as the main motivator for their participation in the Women's March and the People's Climate March. This offers further evidence of how multiple elements of the resistance are rooted in intersectionality and cross-movement solidarity.

The potential political power of coalitions among progressive groups is considerable (Phillips 2016; Van Dyke and McCammon 2010). Nevertheless, this has consequently led some political elites to try to create conflict and schisms between various groups in order to reduce their ability to create robust and productive alliances. For example, President Trump's rhetoric has intentionally pitted Latino immigrants against African Americans by signaling that restrictive immigration policies will benefit the latter group who he claims has been negatively impacted by immigrant labor competition (Lockhart 2017). Accordingly, one hurdle moving forward will be for segments of the Resistance to withstand external efforts to frame its various members as in direct competition with one another. However, although our interviews with activists suggest that intersectional framing was already a key component of immigrant rights activism before Trump, we did not find evidence—as a result of the 2016 election—of current cross-sectional or intersectional organizing with groups that are not explicitly linked to immigrant rights activism. Nonetheless, as one of our interviewees stated, "Among the emerging cadre of leaders" in the immigrant rights movement today, "there's a heightened sensibility of the need to have an intersectional approach to our work."[41]

Conclusions

Our overall goal in this chapter was to take the initial pulse of the immigrant rights movement during the first year of an administration that has shown itself to be both overtly and covertly nativist. One of the difficulties of taking on such a challenge is the fact that by the time this book is published, there will undoubtedly have been further developments in the movement's strategic and tactical responses to both the president's attacks, as well as additional ones that—unfortunately—will surely have followed. In particular, the fate of the Dreamers is still—at this writing—uncertain, between a president who has both revealed nakedly racist views and expressed sympathy for Dreamers, and a movement of undocumented young people that has shown growing political sophistication.[42] Nevertheless, we believe our contribution to this volume provides some valuable empirical and theoretical insights.

To begin with, our study goes beyond the often-rudimentary understanding of political opportunities as being merely the "flipside" of political threats, in which an increase in the latter results in the reduction of the former (Goldstone and Tilly 2001:181). Our examination of the state of the US immigrant rights movement in the early days of the Trump administration suggests that opportunities and threats interact in dynamic ways, often varying by level of government and by geographic location. Trump's attacking of immigrants through executive actions and his party's control of every branch of the federal government have created a highly threatening context and closed the legislative political opportunity structure at the national level. Moreover, some evidence indicates that the president's hostility toward the foreign born has had local ramifications as well. Indeed, Trump's rhetoric and actions seem to have emboldened Republican elected officials "who favor stricter immigration enforcement at the local level."[43] Thus, in some places throughout the nation, the immigrant rights movement finds itself operating in an environment of high degrees of national and local threats that have led to closed legislative opportunity structures at these same governing levels. The result is, as one of the activists we quoted earlier put it, that any hope for liberal immigration reform by the federal and many local and state governments is a "pipedream."

These dim prospects for progressive policy change, however, do not mean that activists have retreated, given up, or both. The state of the immigrant rights movement in several of the previously mentioned types of locations is best described as one of "abeyance." According to Taylor and Crossley (2013), "hostile political and cultural environments" often create periods of abeyance during which movements sustain themselves by developing "distinct repertoires of contention" that provide "continuity from one stage of mobilization to another" (1). For instance, on top of directly responding to and resisting the president's immediate attacks against its members, the immigrant rights movement is attempting to expand its base by building its membership in new locations, including traditionally conservative places such as the rural Midwest and the US South.

In contrast, in cities and states with different political and demographic dynamics, the national threat of Trump has created an unexpected opening of political opportunities for activists to push for pro-immigrant local policy reforms

In places like California, for example, immigrant rights organizers are taking advantage of the current political moment to lobby for progressive immigration legislation at the state and local levels for which Democrats are now willing to prove their "pro-immigrant credentials" by directly challenging the federal government (Burciaga and Martinez 2017).

The president's draconian agenda to "eliminate difference" also seems to have alerted Latinos to the fact that their struggles are intertwined with those of other marginalized segments of American society. As a consequence, our original survey data suggest that Latinos are quite supportive of not only immigrant rights in general, but also of activism on behalf of African Americans and LGB people. This is important to note not only because our findings signal possibilities for cross-movement and intersectional coalition-building, but also because today Latinos are the nation's largest minority group, and more than 800,000 (more than 66,000 a month) of them turn 18 each year and become potential voters.[44] Moreover, millennials made up almost half (44%) of the over 27 million Latinos eligible to cast a ballot in 2016 (Krogstad et al. 2016), and the vast majority of Latino millennials backed an openly socialist candidate— Bernie Sanders—during the Democratic primaries.[45] This means that the largest minority group in the country will become an increasingly progressive and important electoral force to be reckoned with in American politics. Consequently, given the high levels of support for activism of various sorts among immigrant and US-born Latinos, the Resistance against Donald Trump would be wise to invest in reaching out to and working in alliance with this politically critical constituency.

5

Climate of Resistance

How the Climate Movement Connected to the Resistance

DANA R. FISHER

On President Donald Trump's 100th day in office, Americans took to the streets once again to protest the policies of his administration. This time, participants joined the 2017 People's Climate March to express their concerns about the environmental agenda of the Trump Administration. This event marked the second People's Climate March. The previous event took place on the Sunday before the United Nations held talks on the issue of climate change in New York City in September 2014.

Although this event was explicitly intended to build on the momentum of the People's Climate March, it got folded into the resurgence of public forms of social expression such as protests and street demonstrations that have taken place since the inauguration of Donald Trump. Because the Women's March mobilized almost three-million people across the country (see Chapter 3), large-scale protest events have taken place around a variety of causes including racial justice; Lesbian, Gay, Bisexual, Transsexual, and Queer (LGBTQ) rights; the Trump Administration's perceived stance on science, and climate change.[1] This chapter looks at how the climate movement has connected to the Resistance.

As Meyer and Tarrow note in their Introduction, demonstrations are part of a much larger repertoire of contention employed by social movements.[2] Large-scale events mobilize substantial numbers of people to participate and, as such, have been the focus of much scholarly inquiry. Accordingly, this chapter builds on the research that compares large-scale protest events,[3] studying how the climate movement has connected with the Resistance. First, I compare the 2017 People's Climate March (PCM17), which was held on President Trump's 100th day in office, with the 2014 People's Climate March (PCM14) to assess how the movement has changed in the past 3 years. Then, I compare the PCM17 with the

Women's March to demonstrate the ways that the climate movement has joined the Resistance.

I begin this chapter by reviewing the scholarship on social movement mobilization and participation in protest events, focusing specifically on the ways researchers have understood participant mobilization by means of social networks and differential participation. I also discuss the studies that look at how participants with intersectional interests that cross racial, class, gender, and sexual identities are mobilized to protest. Then, I present the results of analysis of survey data from the PCM14 in New York City and the PCM17 in Washington, DC, as well as from the Women's March in 2017. I conclude this chapter by discussing how my findings help us understand the ways in which the climate movement has joined the Resistance.

Channels of Mobilization

An extensive body of research focuses on mobilization processes and participation to understand the growth of social movements.[4] In particular, researchers have focused on the role of social networks and intersectional interests in mobilizing participants. In the pages that follow, I review these relatively unrelated strands of research to highlight how both processes are seen as playing a role in bringing people out to participate in social protest.

Personal and Organizational Networks and Mobilization

The facilitating role of social networks is a central theme of research on participation in collective action.[5] Scholars have explored how different types of social ties assist in social movement recruitment, with much of the research focusing on the role of individual and organizational ties. In some cases, research also looks at the push and pull of social networks.

Many studies have focused specifically on how personal ties with friends, family members, and colleagues can lead to participation in a variety of forms of collective action. Studying the East German Revolution of 1989, for example, Opp and Gern find a specific type of ties with individuals whom they call "critical friends" to be one of the two main variables that explain participation in protests against the regime.[6] In their research on the Dutch Peace Movement, Klandermans and Oegema also look at the role of personal connections, concluding that social networks—particularly informal recruitment networks—helped activists to overcome barriers to participation in the movement.[7] Similarly, Rochford finds that nearly half of the devotees to the

International Society for Krishna Consciousness in his sample were recruited through their personal ties.[8]

Other research, however, has found that individuals' formal ties to organizations play a more powerful role than personal connections.[9] McAdam and Paulson, for example, conclude that organizational ties were more significant than interpersonal channels in mobilizing activists to participate in Freedom Summer.[10] Similarly, when studying the mobilization against low-flying military jets in West Germany, Ohlemacher explains that organizations and associations acted as brokers, unifying individuals to protest as part of the movement.[11]

At the same time, studies of participation in large-scale protest events have noted that different types of networks mobilize different types of participants. Klandermans and colleagues look at unaffiliated participants at 69 demonstrations in seven Western European countries, finding that protesters who were not members of organizations were more likely to hear about demonstrations by means of what they categorize as "open" communication channels, which include personal networks, along with the mass media and social media.[12] Protesters listing organizational affiliations, in contrast, were more likely to hear about protest events by means of "closed" channels, which include fellow members of organizations or organizational magazines, websites, or mailing lists.[13] Similarly, Saunders and colleagues assess the role of closed mobilization channels in their survey of protest participants. The authors find that the most experienced protesters were the most likely to have heard about protests by means of organizational communication channels.[14]

This finding is consistent with the broader literature that looks at levels of participation in protest.[15] Comparing across 18 different demonstrations in eight countries, Verhulst and Walgrave find that nonorganizational members tend to be first timers (i.e., less engaged in protest than organizational members).[16] In other words, organizational ties have been found to bring in joiners who are more actively engaged in protest.

Expanding Mobilization Through Intersectional Interests

A handful of studies of collective action have focused their attention on the ways that intersectional interests and identities—across race, class, gender, sexual orientation, legal status, and other categories of identity—can be used to build coalitions within and across social movements.[17] This strategy increases the number and diversity of activists. In contrast to claims that intersectionality leads to silos that work in isolation,[18] Kimberle Crenshaw suggests that it can promote coalitions rather than divisions.[19] Looking specifically at what they call "movement intersectionality," Roberts and Jesudason conclude that "attention to intersecting identities has the potential to create solidarity and cohesion" across identity categories.[20]

Within this limited body of work, some research has specifically explored intersectional mobilization processes and how shared grievances play a role. For example, Terriquez finds that "LGBTQ undocumented youth exhibited an intersectional consciousness regarding the multiple forms of oppression they experienced," which, in turn, intensified their individual activism.[21] In her work exploring how organizations cross movement boundaries, Van Dyke comes to similar conclusions without explicitly discussing intersectionality. Studying protest on college campuses, the author concludes that larger political threats that have implications for multiple constituencies inspire cross-movement coalitions that involve women's, black, student, and gay student organizations, along with other less–intersectionally focused groups.[22] In their recent study of the 2017 Women's March, Fisher and colleagues look specifically at what motivated participants to turn out for the event.[23] They find that "individuals' motivations to participate [in the Women's March] represented an intersectional set of issues" showing explicitly "how coalitions of issues emerge."

In this chapter, I look at the climate movement in the United States, focusing on what mobilizes participants to join large-scale marches, how participation has changed, and how it relates to the broader Resistance. Specifically, I look at the role that social networks have played in mobilizing individuals with a diversity of motivations and previous protesting experiences to participate in the People's Climate Marches.

Studying Large-Scale Protest Events in the United States

This chapter compares participation at two of the largest climate mobilizations ever held in the United States: The People's Climate March in New York City in 2014 and the People's Climate March in Washington, DC, in 2017. Both People's Climate Marches were organized by the People's Climate Movement, a coalition of organizations focused on climate change. Both events had over 500 organizations registered as "partnering organizations." I also compare the data collected from the PCM17 with data collected at the Women's March, which was held the day after the Inauguration. Using data collected from field notes, media accounts, and materials provided by the organizations involved with the protests studied, I provide a brief summary of the three events. The Marches are introduced in the order in which they took place.

People's Climate March 2014

On September 21, 2014, the Sunday before the United Nations held talks on the issue of climate change, hundreds of thousands of people took part in the People's Climate March in New York City. This event coincided with over 2,600 coordinated protests across 162 countries calling for action on climate change.[24] The march highlighted communities affected by the consequences of climate change, demonstrated public support for climate action, and called for international and national policies to combat the causes of climate change. It included members of the more professionalized organizations that are regularly associated with the climate movement, members of the movement for climate justice, as well as members of other types of social movement organizations, political parties, and unions.[25] The march was framed broadly, calling for climate action that recognizes that those who are most likely to feel the effects of climate change first—the so-called front lines—tend to be less privileged and less capable of responding.[26]

The organizers projected that the event would be the "largest climate march in history," and turnout far exceeded expectations.[27] After the march, organizers estimated that 400,000 people had participated,[28] and media sources called it the "largest-ever climate change march."[29] A 12-member research team entered the crowd at the entrances designated by the organizers along Central Park West in New York City. March participants were sampled throughout the morning and early afternoon as they lined up and then waited to march (it took more than 5 hours for the end of the crowd to begin walking).[30] Researchers completed 468 surveys. Ninety-one people refused to participate in the study, representing a refusal rate of 16%.

The Women's March

As Marie Berry and Erica Chenoweth write (see Chapter 3), the Women's March was initiated by a white grandmother in Hawaii who posted a call to action on Facebook on the day after the 2016 election. However, it soon transitioned into a broader, intersectional coalition of seasoned activists. The four national cochairs of the March were a racially diverse group of women who were already engaged in a range of political activism and social mobilization. Together, these activists aimed to create an inclusive event that responded to Donald Trump's rhetoric, which seemed to encourage women's marginalization and social inequality. By the day of the event, the March's website listed over 400 organizational partners,[31] which sent a clear signal that the Women's March intended to appeal to participants across social categories of race, class, gender, sexual orientation, and legal status.

The day after average-sized crowds came out for Donald Trump's Inauguration, much larger numbers of people, estimated in the hundreds of thousands, descended on Washington, DC, to participate in the Women's March. The March in the nation's capital was part of a broader day of action that took place in other cities across the United States and around the globe. As participants flooded the same streets that had hosted the inaugural parade only 24 hours beforehand, chants opposing the new administration reverberated through the air. An eight-member research team entered the crowd at the entrances designated by the organizers. March participants were sampled throughout the morning and early afternoon of the January 21 as they listened to speeches and performances during the rally. Researchers completed 528 surveys. Forty-three people refused to participate in the study, representing a refusal rate of 7.5%

People's Climate March 2017

On April 29, 2017, hundreds of thousands of people took part in the second People's Climate March, which was held in Washington, DC. This event coincided with over 370 coordinated protests across the United States.[32] Participants marched to express their concerns about the environmental agenda of the Trump administration, particularly as the president had signed an executive order in March rescinding the Clean Power Plan,[33] which was designed to regulate the emissions of utilities in the United States, and was threatening to pull out of the Paris Agreement on climate change, which he did in June.[34] The 2017 March was originally scheduled as a follow-up to the first People's Climate March in 2014. Although this march was unique in that it was connected to a broader effort to draw attention to the issue of climate change in the United States and was not a direct response to the Trump administration and its policies, participants had a lot to protest by late April. Like the 2014 March, the 2017 March included members of the more professionalized organizations that are regularly associated with the climate movement, members of the movement for climate justice, as well as members of other types of social movement organizations, political parties, and unions. Protesters marched to the White House and circled it to show that the world was watching as President Trump passed his 100th day in office.

Turnout for this event was half the size of that of the PCM14. Although this decrease could be interpreted as a sign that the movement is abating, as I discuss in more detail later in this chapter, environmentally concerned individuals attended numerous protest events during this period of time. In fact, the week before the PCM17 took place, the March for Science turned out over 100,000 people in Washington, DC. Even though there were many opportunities to express concerns about the environment through anti-Trump activities, organizers estimated that 200,000 people participated in the event in Washington, DC.[35] A ten-member research team entered the crowd in the designated areas around the National Mall.[36] March participants were sampled throughout the morning and early afternoon as they lined up to march. Researchers completed 348 surveys. Forty-three people refused to participate in the study, representing a refusal rate of 11%.

Data and Methods

To understand how the outcome of the 2016 election changed the dynamic of the climate movement and how it connects to the broader Resistance that has emerged since Donald Trump took office, this chapter draws on survey data collected from a random sample of protest participants at the PCM14 in New York City, the PCM17 in Washington, DC, and the 2017 Women's March in Washington, DC. Participants at all three events were selected using a sampling methodology consistent with other studies of street demonstrations in the United States and abroad,[37] which uses a field approximation of random selection at the march. Snaking through the crowd as people gathered, researchers "counted off" protesters while participants were lining up, selecting every fifth person as determined by researchers working in a particular block section to participate. This method avoids the potential of selection bias by preventing researchers from selecting only "approachable peers."[38] Given the large size of the crowds and the labor-intensive nature of the survey methodology, the samples presented here represent small, randomized portions of the overall participant populations at each demonstration.

The survey was designed to be short and noninvasive, so as to encourage the highest level of participation possible and facilitate data collection in the field: It took about 10 minutes for participants to complete it. Although the 2014 and 2017 versions of the survey were almost identical, questions were added in 2017 about the race of participants and to learn participants' motivations for attending the marches. All data were collected in accordance with the relevant Institutional Review Board Protocols.[39] As such, only individuals over the age of 18 were eligible to participate in the study. It is worth noting that the refusal rates previously noted are consistent with other studies that use this methodology and are substantially lower than those studies that rely on mailed-back questionnaires, which can suffer from delayed refusal bias.[40] Table 5.1 presents the reported attendance at the three Marches compared in this chapter, the number of survey participants, and the refusal rates for each of the protests.

Table 5.1 **Overview of Marches Studied**

	People's Climate March 2014 New York City	Women's March 2017 Washington, DC	People's Climate March 2017 Washington, DC
Estimated Attendance	400,000	500,000	200,000
Total Completed Surveys	468	528	348
Response Rate	84%	93%	89%

This chapter focuses specifically on questions about participant mobilization in terms of how participants heard about the event, with whom they came to the March, as well as their previous protest experiences. Then, as in my previous research on the Women's March,[41] I examine the relationships among the issues that motivated protesters to participate in the PCM17 in Washington, DC. Specifically, by using logistic regression analysis, I examine the relationship among each of the motivating issues to determine if patterns emerge among individuals with certain motivations for participating.

Findings

I begin my analysis by presenting a comparison of the turnout for the People's Climate Marches in 2014 and 2017. Then, I present results comparing the more recent PCM17 with the Women's March, which was held in January 2017 and is seen as the "trigger" for the beginning of the Resistance (see the Introduction).

Comparing the People's Climate Marches

Overall, there is remarkable similarity among the two climate marches in terms of the demographics of the participants and the channels through which they mobilized. Turning first to the demographics of the crowd, when I compare participants at the 2014 and 2017 People's Climate Marches, the demographics are relatively consistent. More women turned out at each event than men (55% in 2014 vs. 57% in 2017). This finding is consistent with the broader research that finds that more women than men participate in environmental stewardship activities.[42] The average age at both the 2014 and the 2017 Marches was 42 years old. Protest participants at the two events were also highly educated: 80%

Table 5.2 **Demographics of Climate March Participants**

	2014 (N = 468) (%)	2017 (N = 348) (%)
Gender		
Women	55	57
Men	44	41
Other	1	2
Education		
Some High School	0	0
High School Degree	4	7
Some College/University	15	16
Bachelor's Degree	36	35
Graduate or Professional Degree	44	42

percent of participants at the PCM14 reported holding a bachelor's degree or higher versus 77% at the PCM17. Table 5.2 presents the demographics of participants. Across all of these measures, the demographic characteristics are consistent with those of the broader resistance, which is found to be made up of "highly educated women who are around 40 years old."[43]

There is also remarkable similarity in how participants were mobilized to participate in the two climate marches. Consistent with the research that finds social networks play a significant role in mobilization,[44] the majority of participants at both events attended the event with people, organizations, or both, in their social networks. However, in contrast to the research that finds formal ties to organizations play a more powerful role than personal connections in mobilizing people to participate, organizations played a smaller role in mobilizing participants at both climate marches. More participants attended the marches with individuals from their personal networks than from their organizational or professional networks (85% vs. 24% in 2014 and 82% vs. 22% in 2017).[45] Similarly, more than 70% of respondents at each event reported hearing about these marches through their social networks. Although the numbers are more similar here, more participants reported hearing about the event from personal networks rather than from organizational networks. Tables 5.3 and 5.4 present these findings.

There are two big differences worth noting in the ways participants heard about the two events. First, many more participants reported learning about the 2014 event from flyers or posters than in 2017 (22% vs. 9% respectively). Second, many more participants reported hearing about the event through

Table 5.3 **With Whom did Climate March Participants Attend?**
          (Check all that apply)

	PCM14 (%)	PCM17 (%)
Alone	12	12
Personal Network (Partner/Family, Friends/Neighbors)	85	82
Organizational or Professional Network (Members of an Organization, Colleagues/Costudents)	24	22

Table 5.4 **How Did Climate March Participants Hear**
          About the Event? (Check all that apply)

	PCM14 (%)	PCM17 (%)
Family/Friends	42	40
People From an Organization	33	38
Flyers or Posters	22	9
Social Media	21	46
Website	18	12
School/Work	16	11
Email/Mailing list	15	13
Radio/TV	12	11
Newspaper	9	10
Other	6	7

social media in 2017 (21% in 2014 vs. 46% in 2017). In both cases, these results are not particularly surprising. Organizers for the 2014 event in New York City invested in a poster design competition that drew a lot of attention as the top two designs were placed in "one out of every 10 train cars on the New York City subway from August 25 until the People's Climate March."[46] Also, from 2014 to 2017 social media usage in the United States continued to grow among the American population.[47] In other words, investment in local outreach efforts such as a poster competition is a very effective way to gain local attention for protest events. Moreover, social media use has become a very important tool for mobilizing activism of all sorts.

Beyond their mobilization channels, the two People's Climate Marches were also very similar in terms of the protesting experience of the participants. About

Table 5.5 **How Experienced Were Climate March Participants?**

	PCM14 (%)	PCM17 (%)
First Time or First Time in 5 Years	38	37
Between 2 and 5 Times	45	42
Between 6 and 10 Times	7	16
Between 11 and 20 Times	4	2
More than 20 Times	6	3

a third of participants at each event reported no protest participation in the past 5 years, and almost half of the participants at each event reported participating in two to five protests in the past 5 years. More participants in the 2017 event reported attending 6–10 events in the past 5 years (7% vs. 16% in 2017). Since the PCM17 took place roughly 3 months after the Women's March during this "major cycle of contention" (see Tarrow's Chapter 9), it makes sense that the percentage of participants who were highly engaged had gone up. Table 5.5 presents these findings.

Even though there was a lot of similarity among participants at the PCM14 and PCM17 events, when we look at the focus of participants' previous protesting experience, there were some interesting differences. As we might expect, the percentage of climate march participants with previous experience protesting the environment went up over the 3-year period (from 39% in 2014 to 51% in 2017). This finding suggests that the PCM17 drew, in part, people who had first participated in protest at the PCM14. It also shows that participants' commitment to climate and other environmental issues, as measured by participation in protests around the same issue, had grown over this period. At the same time, participants also reported much more experience protesting other more identity-focused issues. Specifically, the percentage of participants who had participated in protests around racial justice and immigration went up from 15% and 11% in 2014 to 23% and 22%, respectively, in 2017. These changes suggest that, in addition to increased involvement in environmental activism during this 3-year period, participants in the more recent event had been more involved in other movements than other participants had in 2014. To restate claims by Meyer and Tarrow in the Introduction, immigration reform and Black Lives Matter, which focus on racial justice, are two of what the authors call "origins" of the Resistance. It is also worth noting that the percentage of climate march participants who reported previously participating in protests around peace and labor issues went down between 2014 and 2017. Table 5.6 presents the previous protesting experiences of climate march participants.

Table 5.6 **Focus of Climate March Participants'**
Previous Protesting Experience

	PCM14 (%)	PCM17 (%)
The Environment	39	51
Racial Justice	15	23
Immigration	11	22
Peace	30	19
Labor	13	10

The People's Climate March as Part of The Resistance

Next, I compare the participants at the PCM17, which was held in April 2017, to those who participated in the Women's March, which took place the day after Donald Trump's Inauguration and has been called the "trigger" to the Resistance. In addition to participants' previous protesting experiences focusing on more identity-based issues, such as racial justice and immigration, participants at the PCM17 (70% of whom reported also attending the Women's March in January) reported being motivated by a diversity of issues to attend the event.

As previously noted, the demographics of the climate marches are consistent with those of other marches in the Resistance including the Women's March, which had a majority of educated women.[48] However, the racial make-up of the PCM17 was quite different from that of the Women's March. Although both marches turned out a predominantly white crowd (77% for each march), the PCM17 turned out more Latinos and more Native Americans whereas the Women's March turned out more Blacks and more people who identified as mixed race. Table 5.7 compares the racial and ethnic breakdowns of these two marches.

Table 5.8 compares the motivations of participants at the Women's March and the PCM17. As expected, Women's Rights was the most common motivation for participants at the Women's March (61%), and the Environment was the most common motivation for participants at the PCM17 (97%). Participants at both events also reported being motivated by a number of other issues. Over a third of participants in the Women's March also reported being motivated by the Environment (36%), Racial Justice (35%), LGBTQ Issues (35%), and Reproductive Rights (33%). Participants at the PCM17 3 months later reported higher percentages of motivations overall. Over half of the PCM17 participants reported being motivated by President Trump (56%). Almost half reported being motivated by Equality (47%). Forty-three percent reported being motivated by Peace, and 40% reported being motivated by Women's Rights.

Table 5.7 **Race and Ethnicity of Participants in the Two Marches**

Race/Ethnicity	Women's March (%)	PCM17 (%)
White	77	77
Hispanic/Latino	4	6
Black	7	3
Native American	0	2
Asian	4	6
Multiracial/Other	8	6

Table 5.8 **Motivations for Participants at the Women's March and PCM17**

	Women's March (N = 528) (%)	PCM 2017 (N = 337) (%)
Environment	35.5	96.8
Trump	25	55.5
Equality	25.1	47.4
Peace	19.5	43.1
Women's Rights	60.6	39.7
Politics/Voting	15.9	39.4
Social Welfare	23.1	37.1
Racial Justice	35.1	35.9
Immigration	21.6	33.6
Police Brutality/Black Lives Matter	18.0	29.3
Reproductive Rights	32.6	28.2
LGBTQ	34.7	27.9
Labor	12.2	25.3
Religion	9.2	16.7

Table 5.9 presents a regression graph for the associations among the different issues that motivated participants to attend the PCM17. These models control for the number of protests attended in the past 5 years, gender, race, and age. Like previous analyses of participants at the Women's March,[49] these models

Table 5.9 Intersectionality of Motivations for People's Climate March

People's Climate March 2017 Regression Models by Motivation for Attending (N = 337)

Dependent Variables / Ind. Variables:	Equality	Immigration	Labor	LGBTQ	Peace	Police Brutality	Politics	Racial Justice	Religion	Reprod. Rights	Social Welfare	Trump	Women's Rights
Environment	░					░		░		░	░		░
Equality	■												
Immigration		■		░									
Labor			■										
LGBTQ Issues				■									
Peace					■								
Police Brutality						■		░					░
Politics						░	■	░					░
Racial Justice	░							■					
Religion									■				
Reprod. Rights	░									■	░		░
Social Welfare										░	■		
Trump												■	
Women's Rights													■

Note: ░ means significant association ($p < .05$)

make it possible to examine the extent to which individuals reported intersectional motivations for participating in the March. As can be seen clearly in this table, some motivations overlap more than others. Because of the high percentage of participants who mentioned the environment (97%), models would not converge with this motivation as the dependent variable. Looking at the other motivations, however, we are able to see varying levels of intersectional motivations. Participants who mentioned President Trump as a motivation were statistically more likely to mention Politics. Participants who mentioned Equality were statistically more likely to mention Peace, along with a number of identity-based issues: Immigration, Racial Justice, and Reproductive Rights. Those participants who mentioned Peace were less likely to mention identity-based motivations and were statistically more likely to mention Equality, Labor, and Social Welfare. Participants who mentioned Women's Rights were more likely to mention Police Brutality and Reproductive Rights and were statistically less likely to mention the Environment. Overall, these findings suggest that the PCM17 mobilized a crowd of participants with very diverse reasons for joining.

Discussion and Conclusion

Many of the people who turned out for the PCM17 had also been involved in other marches that were not climate focused but were part of the broader Resistance. Moreover, many more participants in the PCM17 reported having previous protesting experience in identity-based movements. Although some people were more motivated by identity-focused issues than others, this analysis shows clear clusters among the motivations. In terms of the motivations that mobilized participants to join the March, these data provide evidence regarding the ways that the climate movement is connected to the Resistance through both more and less identity-based motivations.

The findings from this study of the PCM17 are consistent with previous research that finds that social networks play an important role in mobilization. Unlike these previous studies,[50] however, personal networks, and not organizational ties, played a bigger role in mobilizing participants for the PCM17. In a period of such heightened contention, it is likely that friends and family members play a substantial role in keeping people mobilized to participate.

Also, like previous research on participants at the Women's March,[51] this analysis of the PCM17 shows that a large proportion of the participants demonstrated intersectional motivations. To restate, from 2014 to 2017, the climate movement continued and the two climate-focused marches turned out very similar crowds. Although the march was smaller in 2017, it took place within the context of the huge wave of contention of the Resistance against the Trump administration and its policies. In fact, as of this writing in December

2017, the People's Climate March has been the second-largest protest event to take place since the Inauguration of Donald Trump.

Although data from the PCM17 show that many participants were motivated by identity-based issues, it is important to point out that the overlapping motivations found among participants at the climate march are not the same as those found at the Women's March 3 months earlier. Because the majority of participants at the PCM17 reported also attending the Women's March, this finding suggests that participants' motivations shifted over the 3-month period. Participants seem to have listed the issues that motivated them on that specific day. Given the ways that the Trump administration has been eliciting moral shocks to progressive Americans on a regular basis,[52] it is not surprising that expressed motivations would shift.

More generally, the findings presented here suggest that although the climate movement is continuing to engage people motivated by environmental issues (50% of the participants at the most recent People's Climate March reported previous environmental protest experience), it is also mobilizing people who have been engaged in other movements and are now coming together to participate in the Resistance. Environmental issues have clearly emerged as one of the areas of concern that connects participants in interesting ways during the current cycle of contention. The presence of more-experienced protesters who are engaged in other issues means that climate concerns are appearing in a range of other movements, thereby broadening a movement coalition.

Future research needs to focus more attention on the similarities and differences among the overlapping motivations of protest participants to understand what the changes mean to specific movements as well as to the broader Resistance. At the same time, although the Resistance has mobilized progressive people (including many of who were motivated by climate-related issues and the environment) to march in the streets throughout 2017, by the end of the year the marches had decreased in frequency and size. Time will tell if the cycle of contention that is the Resistance is dying down for good or just transitioning to other forms of politics as it evolves.

Acknowledgments: I would like to thank the members of the research teams that helped collect data at all three events plus. Direct all correspondence to drfisher@umd.edu.

PART THREE

ACTORS AND ORGANIZATIONS

6

Lawyers as Activists

From the Airport to the Courtroom

MICHAEL C. DORF AND MICHAEL S. CHU

Introduction

On December 2, 2015, a US citizen and his Pakistani-born, permanent resident wife killed 14 people and seriously injured 22 others in San Bernardino,
California, in an attack that was apparently inspired by the Islamic State. Days
later, Republican presidential candidate Donald Trump responded by calling
for a "a total and complete shutdown of Muslims entering the United States
until our country's representatives can figure out what the hell is going on."[1]
Trump's proposal was widely condemned by elected officials of both parties.
Over the course of the ensuing campaign, Trump's plan for a Muslim Travel
Ban appeared to morph into a planned ban on entry into the United States of
persons coming from countries posing a high risk of terrorism,[2] even though
Trump never renounced his implicit claim that religious affiliation created a risk
of terrorism. Within a week of his Inauguration as president, Trump signed an
Executive Order that imposed restrictions on entry into the United States of
nationals of seven overwhelmingly Muslim countries, capped and suspended
refugee admissions, and initiated a review of screening procedures.[3] This chapter
tells the story of the resistance that was galvanized around Trump's Travel Ban
and the role played by lawyers and judges in that resistance.

The key events occurred in somewhat distinct phases. First, in the immediate
chaos that followed the announcement of the Trump policy, lawyers provided
direct services to foreigners detained at airports. Although these services may
have been instrumental in securing entry for particular individuals, they also
operated as a form of protest, continuous with the Women's March that occurred
the day after Trump's Inauguration and the broader Resistance to Trump that
was emerging. Lawyers *inside* the airport were working to secure the admission

of foreign travelers, while lawyers who could not find clients to assist directly joined street protests *outside* the airport. Some such protests were already in progress. For example, the New York Taxi Workers Alliance organized a boycott at New York's John F. Kennedy International Airport (hereafter designated as JFK) that quickly spread by means of social media. By refusing to pick up any travelers, taxi drivers (many of whom were foreign born themselves) expressed solidarity with the people caught in the Ban's web.[4] The lawyers who joined them and other airport protesters may have come to the airport to vindicate the constitutional rights of travelers to the privilege of the writ of habeas corpus, but they found themselves exercising their own First Amendment rights.

This first phase of lawyer participation in the resistance to Trump's Travel Ban was highly successful. It dramatized the cruelty of the Ban as rolled out. On its face the Ban applied to *all* nationals of the seven countries, including permanent residents of the United States (that is, green card holders), and the administration at first appeared to apply it to bar even such permanent residents. However, within a few days and partly as a result of the lawyer-led protests, Trump's official spokesman "clarified" that green card holders could enter the country,[5] although no formal action changing the order occurred at that time.

Phase one was triumphant but brief. In phase two of the legal resistance to the Travel Ban, civil liberties nongovernmental organizations (NGOs) and state governments sued the administration in federal courts around the country. These lawsuits claimed that Trump lacked the statutory authority for the Executive Order and that it was substantively unconstitutional because it discriminated against Muslims. The plaintiffs won nearly all of these cases, leading the administration to back down. A little over a month after issuing the first version of the Travel Ban, President Trump signed a second, superseding Travel Ban with modifications that left it somewhat less vulnerable to legal challenge.[6]

Nevertheless, the revised Travel Ban retained key features of the original. It relied on the same questionable statutory authority, and, like its predecessor, it applied chiefly to Muslims, a disproportionate impact that was hardly coincidental, given the expressed policy of Trump and his supporters during and after the campaign. In phase three, the lawyers who had contested the original ban returned to court to challenge the revised version. They again met with success, resulting in injunctions against the Ban in its entirety. These victories were mostly affirmed in the federal appeals courts.[7]

The legal resistance to the Travel Ban then suffered a partial setback in the US Supreme Court. Without ruling on the merits, the high court partially granted a government request to lift the injunctions against the Ban's enforcement. In an unsigned opinion that spoke for six justices, the Court allowed the government to enforce the Ban against "foreign nationals who lack any bona fide relationship with a person or entity in the United States."[8]

Soon confusion once again reigned, as the Trump administration (pre-dictably) construed the term "bona fide relationship" narrowly, excluding grandparents, aunts, and cousins from the injunction's protection. Further litigation clarified the scope of the term, but even after that clarification, the Ban was in effect as to substantial numbers of foreigners (mostly prospective refugees) over the summer and into the fall of 2017, when the Supreme Court was scheduled to hear full argument in the case.

Then the Ban morphed again. On the same weekend that President Trump called for the firing of professional football players who silently protested racist policing by kneeling during the national anthem, he released a presidential proc-lamation replacing the expiring Travel Ban with a permanent one.[9] This third version of the ban—which was followed a few days later by a revised refugee policy—still had a disparate impact on Muslims, but it also appeared to be based on an actual country-by-country review of immigration screening policies. In November 2017, a federal appeals court permitted this third Ban to go into effect "except as to 'foreign nationals who have a credible claim of a bona fide relationship with a person or entity in the United States.'"[10] That limitation was dissolved by the Supreme Court in early December 2017,[11] whereupon the same federal appeals court reaffirmed its view that the Ban was unlawful but stayed its ruling pending further Supreme Court review.[12] Oral argument was held in April 2018, and at this writing, the Ban is in effect.

The rulings in the Travel Ban case will be studied by legal scholars and may play a role as precedent for lawyers in future cases. However, the court rulings should not obscure what came before. Court cases often have consequences be-yond their ultimate outcomes. Accordingly, in the balance of this chapter, we focus on the role of lawyers in challenging the Travel Ban. We look for lessons that might be drawn from characterizing lawyers as part of the Resistance to the Trump administration.

The first section briefly canvasses a long-standing debate about the efficacy of litigation as a strategy for social reform.

The second section fills in details about how the lawyers who flooded the airports in the immediate wake of the Travel Ban's announcement were organ-ized and what they did. We interviewed Henrike Dessaules, communications manager for the International Refugee Assistance Project, about the role formal public service organizations played in the story. We also interviewed Camille Mackler, the director of Immigration Legal Policy for the New York Immigration Coalition and leader of the lawyers on the ground at JFK, for a view from the trenches. We subsequently explain that after the mass mobilization, the lawyers' resistance was carried out by a smaller group of core activists.

The third part locates the lawyers' resistance to Trump in the debate about the efficacy of litigation as a strategy for social reform. We argue in this section that the lawyers' activism in responding to the initial version of the Travel Ban dramatized its cruelty, which led the administration to soften it and contributed to the broader anti-Trump resistance. We also point out what should be, but often is not, obvious: Even when courts cannot bring about social change, they can bring about legal change, which can itself be quite valuable.

We conclude this chapter by suggesting that the nature of the threat to constitutional democracy posed by the Trump administration may make lawyers (and journalists) especially effective actors in the anti-Trump Resistance, but that this very fact may limit the generalizability of our conclusions in the event that future presidents are, for lack of a better term, more normal.

Litigation as a Vehicle for Achieving Social Change

The lawyers who responded to the Travel Ban were hardly the first members of their profession to try to use the law to pursue the greater good as they saw it. Lawyers have long been active in social justice movements. National Association for the Advancement of Colored People (NAACP) lawyers brought cases challenging Jim Crow, and their success in court spawned like efforts by lawyers working for the rights of other ethnic groups, for women, and for Lesbian, Gay, Bisexual, Transsexual, and Queer (LGBTQ) persons. Thus, when President Clinton nominated Ruth Bader Ginsburg to the Supreme Court in 1993, he observed that "admirers of her work say that she is to the women's movement what former Supreme Court Justice Thurgood Marshall was to the movement for the rights of African-Americans."[13] The comparison was widely understood as a high compliment, because Marshall was regarded as the advocate most responsible for *Brown v. Board of Education*.[14]

Yet even as the legal establishment lionizes advocates like Marshall and Ginsburg, an undercurrent of skepticism persists. As David Meyer and Steven Boutcher have observed, the promise of *Brown* led activists to devote resources and time to litigation rather than to other activities that might have served their respective causes better.[15] A more radical challenge—one that targeted *Brown* itself—was set forth in Gerald Rosenberg's 1991 book *The Hollow Hope*. Subtitled "Can Courts Bring About Social Change?," Rosenberg's answer was "no." Cases like *Brown*—and especially *Brown* itself—may change the formal legal rules, he argued, but real social change does not come from courts. Rosenberg pointed to evidence that Southern schools remained segregated for over a decade after *Brown*, with real change coming only after the enactment of the Civil Rights Act of 1964 committed the resources of the federal government to desegregation. Anticipating a counterargument that would be offered by his critics, Rosenberg also contended that *Brown* did little to "catalyze" the Civil Rights movement that led to the key national legislation.

Rosenberg's argument was and remains controversial. Indeed, relatively recent events would seem to refute his strongest claim. In the second edition of *The Hollow Hope*, published in 2008, Rosenberg argued that state court decisions finding a right to same-sex marriage in state constitutions were highly unlikely to advance the cause of marriage equality and would likely spark a backlash.[16] Although that was a plausible prediction at the time, it proved false. Less than a decade later in *Obergefell v. Hodges*, the Supreme Court recognized a federal constitutional right to same-sex marriage, based in part on the fact that public opinion had shifted in favor of same-sex marriage.[17] Since that decision, the trend has continued. Although it is possible to think that the trend in public opinion was completely independent of the court rulings, a more straightforward explanation is that just as judicial decisions can sometimes spark backlash, so they can sometimes catalyze forward movement. In this view, Rosenberg's answer to whether courts can bring about social change is too doctrinaire. In response to court-centric reformers whom he rightly regards as overestimating the efficacy of litigation as a means of social reform, Rosenberg underestimates its efficacy. Courts cannot *always* bring about social change, but neither can they *never* bring about social change; in combination with other actors, they can *sometimes* bring about social change.[18]

The foregoing argument, based on the example of same-sex marriage litigation, contests Rosenberg's thesis on its own terms. Another approach, exemplified by the work of Michael McCann, shifts the focus away from courts as ultimate decision-makers and to the litigation process itself. Even when litigation produces ineffective victories or outright defeats, McCann explains, it can serve as a vehicle for organizing social and political action or shine a spotlight on injustice that leads to a more effective political response.[19] The lawyers' movement to stop the Travel Ban did both.

Litigation can win by losing if, despite the loss in court, the process itself serves as a focal point for organization.[20] NGOs build membership lists based on public support for litigation; those members can then be enlisted in other, potentially more successful efforts, in other venues. In other words, lawsuits can win by losing if they provide what McCann and others have called "legal mobilization."[21]

Where does the work of lawyers who opposed the Travel Ban fit into this schema? Did they win by winning, win by losing, lose by losing, or lose by winning? Or, as we suggest in the third section, does the Travel Ban response demonstrate still other possibilities for lawyers as activists? To answer these questions, we begin by taking a closer look at the activist lawyers' response to the Travel Ban.

What Happened?

Almost immediately after the first version of the Travel Ban was announced, many organizations sprang into action: the American Civil Liberties Union (ACLU), the Southern Poverty Law Center, the New York Immigration Coalition, and surely more. The first organization to respond effectively, however, was the International Refugee Assistance Project (IRAP).[22]

In the week before the first Travel Ban Executive Order was signed, a leaked draft had circulated through the refugee advocacy community.[23] The draft order said nothing about when it would take effect. The leadership of IRAP had many theories about what that meant, including a worst-case scenario in which the order would provide no grace period and would take effect immediately when signed.[24] IRAP used its advanced warning to advise its clients to travel to the United States as quickly as possible. IRAP also emailed its pro bono contacts at various law firms, asking them to volunteer for a "legal rapid response team" to help anyone who might be detained.[25] IRAP posted this electronic sign-up sheet on its website, although it later took the list down because of the volume of the response. More than 1,400 people responded to this initial inquiry.[26] Other organizations, such as the New York Immigration Coalition, similarly used the extra time to prepare for battle, knowing that they would likely take some sort of action but not knowing precisely what form that action would be.

As IRAP feared, on Friday, January 27, President Trump signed the Executive Order, and it went into effect without any grace period. IRAP's first move was to send lawyers to defend two existing clients, Hameed Khalid Darweesh and Haider Sameer Abdulkhaleq Alshawi, both of whom were detained at JFK and both of whom would later be the named plaintiffs on the temporary restraining order against the Ban.[27] IRAP also emailed the 1,400 volunteers on its list, circulating a sign-up sheet to keep track of who was heading to airports. The volunteers distributed the sheet even further through emails and social media, causing it to "go viral" in the sense of attracting hundreds of additional volunteers.[28] By the time IRAP closed the sheet, over 9,000 people had signed up to provide assistance through IRAP. A little under half of these people were lawyers or law students; the rest were simply concerned citizens who wanted to help in any way they could.

The number of actual volunteers was likely much higher still, because many people came to airports to provide assistance without first putting their names on any list.[29] Some came simply because they saw or read news reports that other lawyers were showing up at airports.[30] Meanwhile, other organizations—such as the Urban Justice Center—also began spreading the word and arriving at the airports after IRAP's call.[31] Individual lawyers themselves spread the word through phone calls, Facebook, and Twitter, using the hashtag and twitter handle @NoBanJFK.[32]

Behind the scenes, a law professor and two of his former students created a plan to stop the chaos. IRAP Director Becca Heller reached out to her former classmate Justin Cox and their former immigration clinic professor Michael Wishnie about how to approach the litigation for IRAP's clients. Cox, a staff attorney at the National Immigration Law Center,[33] recommended filing a petition for habeas corpus, which would free IRAP's clients alone. Wishnie (who was at a Boston Celtics game) recommended filing a class action, which could potentially free every detainee at every airport. Wishnie mobilized some of his then-current students that night to research and draft papers for the lawsuit, which was later filed in conjunction with the ACLU. Heller herself pulled an all-nighter and made her way to the airport Saturday morning.[34]

Not all of the NGOs were prepared for the immediate implementation of the Travel Ban. Some organizations had expected Customs and Border Protection (CBP) to take at least a few weeks to create guidance documents. The surprise instantaneous implementation thus caught many organizations and individuals off guard. For some civic-minded lawyers, going to the airport was not so much part of an organized plan as a gut reaction that they needed to help however they could. The haphazard nature of much of the initial resistance left IRAP in the lead somewhat by default.[35]

Besides being first on the ground and putting out the first call to action, IRAP also acted as an important organizational broker coordinating efforts in the initial hours of the Travel Ban. Once Heller arrived at JFK, she organized volunteer lawyers, liaised with members of Congress, and spoke to the press about what was happening.[36] IRAP also operated a help line and emergency email address to answer refugees' questions; this address was CC'd in much of the lawyer-to-lawyer email correspondence, keeping IRAP abreast of where people were going and what was happening in the various airports. At one point, IRAP had a list of over 20 airports at which its volunteers were present. Even when lawyers began organizing themselves, they apparently continued to report back to or keep in contact with IRAP.[37]

Where IRAP's advanced planning was insufficient, spontaneity prevailed. Once at the airports, many lawyers organized themselves as needed, using their tenacity and ingenuity to solve problems that few (if any) of them had seen in their previous practice. For example, at the Los Angeles International Airport (LAX), the CBP briefly shut out lawyers from seeing the refugee detainees. In response, lawyers searched the airport for families of detainees (holding signs promoting free legal services) and communicated with the detainees through phone calls with family members. The information thus acquired was then relayed to the lawyers at the central command post in the airport as well as to lawyers at the ACLU; both groups were busily writing habeas corpus petitions and briefs for the detainees. Nonlawyers lent their support by sending free food to the lawyers through the weekend.[38]

Meanwhile, at JFK, chaos reigned for most of Saturday, January 28. Lawyers—many of whom had no experience in immigration or asylum matters—were scattered across the terminals, some sitting on the floor with their laptops writing petitions for habeas corpus for their clients.[39] Procedures were necessarily more informal than ideal. For instance, people were signing in and sharing information on a GoogleDoc, thereby putting confidential client information at risk. Camille Mackler of the Urban Justice Center attempted to control the chaos by coordinating with a few other lawyers to make Terminal 4 the unofficial base of operations. By Sunday morning, most lawyers had coalesced in the Central Diner restaurant in Terminal 4, a sprawling mass of laptops, printers, and lawyers with little or no coherent organization.[40]

When she returned from home on Sunday, Mackler and the volunteers took steps to bring order. Stations were assigned at the diner, clearly demarcating where to sign in, where to do client intake, and where to work on habeas petitions. This "makeshift office" was complete with multilanguage signage and a check-in booth. Mackler used the GoogleDoc—which had the names of lawyers, incoming flights, interpreters, and "other volunteers"—to assign people to tasks based on their skills.[41] Some manned the stations at the diner, while others were sent to find families of detainees.[42]

At first, the lawyers worked on habeas petitions for their clients.[43] Then, on Saturday, a federal district judge in Brooklyn issued the first order halting the Ban. That order did not end the effort, but it did allow some of the lawyers at JFK to transition to a support and watchdog role. Some of their time was spent simply explaining what was happening to detainees and their families. They also spent time trying to ensure that the CBP complied with the temporary restraining order. Many lawyers spoke directly to CBP agents to try to obtain the release of detainees from custody, although they were met with frustratingly vague answers and little action.

The lawyer–activists worked in concert with other activists, as people found ways to be helpful even without using legal skill or knowledge. For example, a tech-savvy volunteer helped the group switch from a Google group to a listserv, and then to a professional account on the app Slack.[44] Another helped set up a website and hotlines for families of detainees to call for legal help. A former journalist stepped off a plane and almost immediately jumped in to help manage the media and to set up a system for issuing press releases. Through these efforts, Mackler and the JFK lawyers successfully created an impromptu law firm with a public relations wing right in the terminal.

Even those unable to get to the airport found ways to lend support. A partner at the law firm Simpson Thacher compiled a daily round-up of litigation from his office. Other big law firms donated laptops, printers, and mobile hotspots. A ride-share company donated free rides for lawyers to and from the airport. The tech company Slack donated the aforementioned professional account, which made communication easier and more secure. People did whatever they could to help, even if it was merely donating donuts.[45]

Resistance by the Numbers

The initial phase of the lawyer-led opposition to Trump's Travel Ban surely counts as an important part of the anti-Trump Resistance, but it was not quite a mass protest on the scale of the Women's March. How many lawyers and others participated? No precise headcount exists, but we can estimate how many lawyers showed up at airports across the nation. By the time IRAP closed its sign-up sheet, about 9,470 people had signed. Roughly 4,570 of these people identified themselves on the sheet as attorneys, and 29 more identified themselves as law students. The number of both may be higher, because not all attorneys or law students may have identified themselves as such on the sign-up sheet. And as mentioned earlier, the number of actual volunteers was likely to have been much higher, as not everyone who went to the airports signed up for a formal assignment either before or after arriving.[46]

The volunteers were at airports throughout the country; at one point, IRAP leadership had a list of over 20 airports where it had volunteers. At JFK, different accounts say anywhere from 30 to 100 lawyers had set up shop by nightfall on Saturday the 28th. There were also more than 1,000 outside the airport protesting the ban.[47] At LAX, there were more than 100 attorneys volunteering by Monday morning.[48] The rest of IRAP's volunteers either were at JFK or LAX later in the week or were scattered at other airports across the nation.

Litigation and Symbols

Even after the first few chaotic days of the Travel Ban, the work at the airports remained relevant. One clear connection to the later Travel Ban litigation was the original judicial ruling blocking the first Travel Ban. As previously noted, the named plaintiffs in the case giving rise to the temporary restraining order were two IRAP clients, Hameed Khalid Darweesh and Haider Sameer Abdulkhaleq Alshawi.[49] Besides that, it appears that the people receiving legal services would be considered part of the "nationwide class of people" on whose behalf that original case was filed.[50] Admittedly, the litigation that eventually reached the

Supreme Court did not spring directly from the airport lawyering, because it challenged the second and third Travel Bans, rather than the first one. However, the chief arguments made against the second and third Travel Bans—that they were thinly disguised versions of Trump's original Muslim Ban and exceeded the statutory authority he had been delegated by Congress—were continuous with the chief arguments against the first Travel Ban. Moreover, the Trump policy and the litigation continued to unfold against a backdrop that was shaped by the original Travel Ban and the resistance it sparked.

The long-term effect of the airport drama on lawyers' participation in the anti-Trump Resistance is unclear. Very few of the volunteer lawyers have stayed involved in the detainees' habeas cases; IRAP and other organizations took over what was left of them after the airport phase, and, in any event, the lawyers' main job after the Travel Ban was halted was to make sure that the CBP released detainees.

Similarly, the organizational infrastructure created during the drama—once predicted to be a powerful tool to respond to other immigration emergencies[51]—has yet to find a substantially wider use. To be sure, a lawsuit challenging the president's cancellation of the Deferred Action for Childhood Arrivals (DACA) program relied in part on one of the legal theories (discriminatory animus) that was used to attack the Travel Ban; and in early January 2018 a federal judge granted a preliminary injunction against DACA rescission.[52] However, this and other lawsuits challenging DACA rescission were more of an outgrowth of the mobilization of Latinos against Trump that began during the campaign (as described in greater detail by Zepeda-Millán and Wallace in Chapter 4) than a direct consequence of the anti–Travel Ban activism. And of course, the ruling invalidating DACA rescission might not survive on appeal or, more favorably for the so-called Dreamers, might be superseded by legislation granting them a more permanent status.

Yet even if the mobilization against the Travel Ban ends up making no tangible contribution to the well-being of the Dreamers, that would not mean that there has been no lasting effect from the drama at the airports. Although we discuss the effect on lawyer activism in the next section, there is something to be said for the airport drama purely as a symbol.

Events can be symbolic of a feeling, idea, or movement beyond the sum of their parts. Woodstock, for example, was at base a concert in a muddy field, but it became a powerful symbol of, initially, antiwar activism and, ultimately, the entire counterculture associated with the late 1960s. To this day it resonates with Baby Boomers and their successors, regardless of whether they view it in positive or negative terms. The Travel Ban reaction may likewise come to be remembered as an important symbol. Whether it leads to an actual increase in *lawyer* activism, it is symbolic of the greater resistance movement against the

Trump administration. Indeed, the lawyer-led resistance to the Travel Ban may be partly responsible for some of the early failures of the Trump administration both with respect to immigration itself and perhaps even with respect to other issues, such as the unsuccessful efforts to persuade Congress to fully repeal the Affordable Care Act.

Furthermore, the legal resistance at the airports showed the world, in Mackler's words, "extreme lawyering"—a rush to defend people by any means necessary, even if it meant sitting on the dirty tile floor of an airport or using the WiFi at a nearby Pinkberry frozen yogurt shop to submit a petition for habeas corpus. The news media inundated the public with human interest stories about the lawyers who leaped at the chance to do their civic duty, of the protests outside of JFK, and of the victories that the law won over the Trump administration.[53] The last of these is probably the most meaningful: The airport drama was the first high-profile display of effective collective action—not just protest—in the Resistance to the president. It provides evidence that the Resistance can succeed, even if success proves only partial.

The lawyer-led resistance to the Travel Ban was also a shot in the arm for both the public and for a long-beleaguered profession. Whether that will translate into greater prestige for lawyers over the long run remains to be seen. Lawyers have, from time to time, been cast as heroes for noble causes in popular culture. Yet notwithstanding the boost the profession has received from the likes of (the fictional) Atticus Finch in Harper Lee's book *To Kill a Mockingbird*, lawyers remain, as Jerome Frank aptly described in 1930, the object of the public's contradictory "respect and derision."[54] At best, the leading role played by lawyers in standing up for the rights of those most vulnerable to Trumpism could lead to a somewhat greater emphasis on the respect side of the balance, at least for a time.

If it is too much to ask that the self-sacrifice of the lawyers who went to the barricades at JFK and LAX be rewarded with garlands for the profession as a whole, it nonetheless warrants asking whether the lawyers' response to the Travel Ban ought to inform our picture of whether, and if so how, lawyers and the law affect social change. We next turn to that question.

A New Model of Lawyer Activism

As we explained in the first section, litigation sometimes brings about social change. Lawyers thus have a role to play in activist movements. But what role? The lawyers' resistance to the Travel Ban differs in one notable way from most other stories of legal mobilization. In the typical account, social actors—such as workers, members of a minority group facing prejudice, or activists for a cause such as the environment—use litigation as a tool for mobilizing; lawyers and lawsuits are the instruments of these other actors. By contrast, in the Travel Ban litigation, lawyers themselves were primary actors.

To be sure, the lawyers represented (and many continue to represent) the interests of clients, but even more than in typical impact litigation (in which clients can be an afterthought), the Travel Ban featured lawyers front and center. As we explained in the second section, there were an insufficient number of clients for all of the lawyers who came to airports to provide legal services. Consequently, lawyers took to the streets, at least in the short run.

Movement lawyers acting as citizens sometimes engage in street protest and other forms of activism, but lawyers *qua* lawyers are rarely on the front lines of contentious politics. Instead, the typical division of labor has activists marching, protesting, and perhaps getting arrested, whereas lawyers go to court to secure the right to march and protest or to argue for the activists' release. Lawyer activism—as distinguished from activism by people who just happen also to be lawyers—is characteristically a matter of supporting frontline activists. What, then, are we to make of lawyers as activists *in their capacity as lawyers*?

Part of the answer may be that extraordinary times call for an extraordinary response. On the day after Trump's Inauguration, women (and sympathetic men) filled the streets of Washington, DC, to protest, among other things, Trump's misogyny. That sort of march—members of a disadvantaged group asserting their rights—fits a familiar paradigm. But the Trump administration also spawned a day of marches for science (see Chapter 5),[55] in which ordinary citizens and scientists protested Trump's environmental (and other) policies. Scientists have turned activist before, of course, typically to warn of the dangers of some weapons or looming ecological disaster, but, like lawyers, scientists do not typically engage in street protests. Thus, lawyers in the streets may be part of a broader shift in public consciousness, which may, in turn, reflect the extremism of Trumpism.

That is not to say that public demonstrations by lawyers protesting *as* lawyers are unprecedented. A decade before Trump's Inauguration, business-suit-wearing lawyers in Pakistan took to the streets to protest the removal of that country's chief justice by its president (and army chief), Pervez Musharraf. The Pakistani lawyers' actions "triggered a broader movement for democracy and constitutionalism. Musharraf's subsequent crackdown failed, and although neither the regime's legal and institutional edifice nor the military's entrenched power was entirely dislodged, the movement prompted elections that repudiated Musharraf and ultimately forced him from power."[56]

Unlike Pakistan, the United States is a mature democracy with a long tradition of constitutionalism, but lawyers in the anti-Trump resistance aim to promote the same values as their predecessors in Pakistan. Rather than seeking to replace autocracy with democracy and constitutionalism, American lawyer activists hope to preserve democracy and constitutionalism by blocking auto-cratic rule by Trump.

Also as in Pakistan, anti-Trump lawyers did not remain in the streets for long. The movement for democracy, constitutionalism, and human rights relatively quickly reverted to its usual form, even as a small army of volunteer lawyers remained (and as this book goes to press, remains) ready to mobilize off the sidelines.

Has lawyer activism sparked a wider movement for the sorts of values that lawyers distinctively serve? It is difficult to answer that question.

There is certainly plenty of activity by lawyers opposing Trump. For example, numerous lawsuits have been filed charging Trump with an array of misdeeds, including three separate lawsuits arguing that by continuing to profit from businesses directly associated with his name, Trump violates two constitutional provisions barring the receipt of various "emoluments." Meanwhile, law blogs like *Lawfare* and *TakeCare* (so-named to imply that Trump has violated his con-stitutional duty to "take Care that the Laws be faithfully executed") have come to prominence by featuring legal commentary by liberal, progressive, and even a fair number of conservative Trump critics.

Additionally, the *Stanford Journal of Civil Rights and Civil Liberties* released a special issue in February 2017 focusing on what lawyers can do to resist Trump.[57] In July 2017, the website "WeTheAction.org" launched to connect civic-minded attorneys with progressive nonprofit organizations in need of legal elbow grease.[58] And rising directly from the work at JFK is the Immigrant Advocates Response Collaborative (Immigrant ARC), a network of almost 60 immigrant advocacy organizations that will share their information, contacts, and other resources to better protect immigrants and refugees.[59] Much anti-Trump Resistance has a distinctly legalist flavor.

Yet tracing a causal path from the airport activism to the legalist opposi-tion to Trump poses challenges. With the exception of Immigrant ARC, there is no clear link between the airport drama and these actions. In fact, both "WeTheAction.org" and the *Stanford Journal of Civil Rights and Civil Liberties* cited the Inauguration, not the airport drama, as the reason for their existence.[60] And maybe these are not such extraordinary events; after all, even in normal times, activist lawyers file lawsuits while public intellectuals with legal training pitch arguments to the rest of the public. Trump may indeed have galvanized extraordinary opposition from lawyers, but it is hard to say that any substantial fraction of that opposition was due to the lawyers' detour into the airports and streets.

Nor is it clear that Trump *differentially* inspired opposition from lawyers. Perhaps Trump is simply such a polarizing figure that he has inspired increased opposition across the board, including lawyers, but in no way *especially* including lawyers. After all, even as we have seen the emergence of opposition in a distinctly legal register, we have also seen the emergence—or at least the coming to greater prominence of—forms of opposition that eschew legalism. Although anti-globalization anarchists and hacker activists existed before Trump's rise to power, his rise has apparently galvanized a counterreaction from anti-fascists (or *antifa*), whose tactics include confrontations with Trump's most vocal (and potentially violent) supporters. They are not taking orders from lawyers.

Yet even if we cannot trace a direct path from lawyers in airports and on the streets to lawyers as leaders of the anti-Trump movement, we can nonetheless note the efficacy of lawyers in the anti-Trump movement. Focusing on the Travel Ban, we can identify two dynamics.

First, the lawyers who showed up at airports to contest the initial Travel Ban played a crucial role in calling attention to the hardship it would cause. Movement lawyers and government lawyers in the blue states of Washington and Hawaii won quick court victories, but even if they had lost those battles they would have won by losing. The rollout and substance of the initial Travel Ban created a public relations disaster for the administration.

Second, the lawyers who continued the fight in court won by winning. The very framing of Rosenberg's question—can lawyers bring about social change?—necessarily shortchanges the impact of lawyers. Even though successful litigation does not always lead directly to social change, it typically results in *legal* change. The students, refugees, and families seeking medical treatment for their young children who were subject to Trump's Travel Ban but then granted entry to the United States by means of court order benefited from the litigation undertaken on their behalf. What's more, as Eric Posner has argued, they may have benefited from the activism of lawyers and others who painted a picture of the cruelty and chaotic rollout of the Travel Ban, which, in turn, led judges to grant the Trump administration less deference than courts typically give to the national executive in matters of immigration and national security.[61]

Conclusion

Despite the difficulty in defining and applying measures of the relative contribution of lawyers to the anti-Trump movement, there is reason to think that it has been and will continue to be greater than the typical contribution of lawyers to protest movements, because of the nature of the Trumpian threat. The anti-Trump coalition no doubt includes many liberal and progressive activists who oppose conventional conservative policies on matters like taxes, environmental regulation, and health insurance. Liberal and progressive *lawyers* may be active on such issues but not disproportionately more active than other actors. By contrast, lawyers appear particularly well suited to take part in or lead the opposition to Trump with respect to some key aspects of his political style that distinguish him from most other prominent Republican politicians.

Among the key factors that distinguish Trump from conventional Republicans are his willingness to challenge the institutional legitimacy of the courts and the press and his overt racism. (Trump also differs from some establishment Republicans in his support for protectionist trade policies and his disdain for the niceties of international diplomacy, but these differences do not necessarily agitate lawyers more than others.)

Trump challenged the legitimacy of courts when, as a candidate, he claimed that a US-born federal judge could not fairly adjudicate a civil case against him because of the judge's Mexican ancestry and again, as president, when he denounced a Republican appointee to the federal bench who enjoined the first version of the Travel Ban as a "so-called judge." Trump has repeatedly attacked the legitimacy of the press, subjecting individual reporters to hostile crowds at his rallies and labeling thoroughly mainstream institutions such as *The New York Times* and CNN "fake news" when they report facts that show him or his administration in a negative light. Trump's campaign was launched with a group libel against Mexicans and fueled by anti-Muslim bias; since taking office, he has soft-pedaled criticism of white supremacists and neo-Nazis, while reserving his harshest criticism for African American professional athletes protesting racist policing, whom he termed "sons of bitches." And he has objected to immigrants coming to the United States from the global South, or what he reportedly called "shithole countries," rather than from Northern Europe.

That lawyers in particular would respond to Trump's threat to an independent judiciary needs no elaboration. Courts are to lawyers as temples are to high priests. Even Trump's extremely conservative nominee to the Supreme Court—Neil Gorsuch—felt obliged to distance himself from Trump's attack on judicial independence.

Although less obvious, American lawyers also have a distinctively lawyerly stake in opposing racism and protecting press freedom. These are practically the twin pillars of the modern American lawyer's creed, celebrated in the most famous footnote in American constitutional law[62] and the most influential book ever written in defense of the role of courts in American life.[63] Even as they might disagree fiercely about abortion, guns, or campaign finance, American lawyers learn from early in their careers to venerate *Brown v. Board of Education* and *New York Times v. Sullivan* (a civil rights–era case that established protection for journalists against state libel law, which, not coincidentally, Trump has threatened to "open up"). Within American law, liberty and equality mean, first and foremost, freedom of speech and the press and opposition to blatant racism.

The Travel Ban brought together Trump's (anti-Muslim) racism with his disrespect for the courts and the press (which he falsely accused of deliberately failing to report on terrorism[64]) in a perfect storm that outraged a wide swath of American lawyers. Given Trump's personality, one can expect additional outrages that will spur lawyers to further action.

Whether lawyers continue to stay engaged as primary actors in contentious politics after Trump departs the scene remains to be seen. Partly the answer will turn on whether Trump proves to be an exceptional figure or a harbinger of a new form of politics. Whatever the answer, the successful participation of lawyers in opposition to Trump's Travel Ban shows that, in the right circumstances, lawyers, law, and courts can be highly relevant actors in contentious politics, rather than merely facilitators of activism by others.

The Many Faces of Resistance Media

DAVID KARPF

There is no understanding Donald Trump without reference to the contemporary hybrid media system. His improbable victories in the Republican primary and 2016 general election were premised on radical departures from how electoral campaigns use communications media to engage journalists, supporters, and opponents. The first year of his presidency has continued this trend of redefining presidential communications. Trump's reality-TV flair for picking dramatic fights that consume and divide our public attention is simultaneously his unique strength and greatest vulnerability. He has recast news reporters as enemies of the state, deployed partisan media and digital media to further galvanize his supporter base, and remained obsessively fixated on how he is portrayed on television. Trump's actions and motivations, more than those of any past president, must be read through the prism of their media portrayal.

For the Resistance, countering Trump has required tactical and strategic innovations in the media realm. Indivisible.org began as a GoogleDoc, was spread through Twitter and Facebook sharing, then converted waves of media coverage into a membership base that has yielded over 6,000 local groups across the country. The Women's March was framed as a powerful rejection of the Trump agenda and positioned to siphon media attention from him in an otherwise triumphant moment. Organizations like Sleeping Giants and ColorOfChange.org have leveraged social media to build consumer pressure on conservative partisan media.[1] And new progressive media organizations like Crooked Media have built a participatory progressive audience through podcasting, building new progressive media institutions to compete against the conservative media ecosystem.[2]

The term "media" is itself a boundary object. It refers to a set of established institutions (mainstream media and journalism) with well-known norms and processes, a set of competing institutions (partisan media and advocacy journalism) that challenge those norms and processes, and a set of communications technologies (communications media) that activists use to challenge their opponents and connect with one another. The Resistance's interaction with and use of media has many faces, specifically because "media" itself has so many referents.

And over the past two decades, the boundaries among established media, partisan media, and communications media have become increasingly porous, fluid, and unstable. Mainstream media organizations are still fixtures of the broader social system, but the ways that they produce the news, the ways that readers and viewers access the news, and the ways that advertisers and subscribers pay for that news have become a chaotic mess. The old John Birch Society newsletter (prime media real estate for the distribution of conservative conspiracy theories in its heyday) has been replaced by Breitbart.com and Infowars.com. Instead of reaching a small, stigmatized audience through the mail, stories from these sites are spread through social media to a mass public who is unfamiliar with the credibility of these sources. The marketplace for news now rewards a cacophony of partisan voices and rarely penalizes outright lies.

Movement power has always been interwoven with media power, and the media system exerts an almost-gravitational force on the daily conduct of the Trump presidency. Resistance groups have sought to combat Trump through the media while simultaneously building their own media and challenging Trump's partisan media supporters. This chapter discusses how the Resistance has leveraged communications media to expand the reach of their protest tactics. It explores how Resistance networks have exploited the affordances of social media to combat the worst excesses of partisan conservative media. And it discusses how Resistance leaders are building their own new media institutions to challenge the political power of the conservative media ecosystem.

The chapter begins by elaborating on Trump's own unique media footing. It then lays out a theoretical framework for understanding the interaction of media systems and movement tactics in the digital age. It then delves into three case examples—MoveOn's MediaLab, Sleeping Giants, and Crooked Media—to animate how Resistance networks and organizations are deploying digital media strategies to build power and compete with their opponents. The chapter concludes by returning to the theme of the particular opportunities and challenges the Resistance faces when trying to challenge Trump in an age of hybrid media.

Trump and the Media

Throughout both his candidacy and the first year of his residency, it has often appeared as though Donald Trump simply is not governed by the same rules of political gravity that apply to all other politicians. He was almost universally opposed by Republican elected officials during the primaries, and many conservative media organizations formally or informally opposed him. His general election campaign was rife with gaffes, contradictions, and misstatements. The first week of his presidency featured a press conference where Sean Spicer insisted, in the face of photographic evidence to the contrary, that the crowd at Trump's inauguration was the largest in history, and also included Trump embracing a bizarre conspiracy theory that three-million people had illegally voted for Hillary Clinton. Mass opposition to Trump's policy agenda has been waved away as "fake news," and a long string of embarrassing international and domestic incidents have seemed to barely faze his administration. President Trump reportedly watches between 4 and 8 hours of cable television per day (Haberman, Thrush, and Baker 2017), while simultaneously embracing some of the deepest, darkest corners of white nationalist and conspiracy theorist websites. This is not how we are accustomed to presidents (or presidential candidates) behaving.

The roots of Donald Trump's approach to the media can be traced back to his 1987 book, *The Art of the Deal*. In that book, he (and his cowriter Tony Schwartz) remarked, "If I take a full-page ad in the *New York Times* to publicize a project, it might cost $40,000 and in any case, people tend to be skeptical about advertising. But if the *New York Times* writes even a moderately positive one-column story about one of my deals, it doesn't cost me anything, and it's worth a lot more than $40,000" (Trump and Schwartz 1987). This media philosophy made him a fixture of tabloid gossip columns in the 1980s and 1990s. It later translated into his starring role in the reality-TV series "The Apprentice" (and spinoff "The Celebrity Apprentice"). Trump was, in a sense, a forerunner of the reality-TV aesthetic: What matters is not the substance of coverage; what matters is the sheer quantity of screen time.

Upon launching his presidential campaign, this media philosophy translated into three tangible assets. First, it let Trump begin with practically universal name recognition, a rarity when compared with the crowded field of 17 candidates pursuing the Republican nomination. Second, it gave him a healthy social media following, with over three-million Twitter followers before he announced his candidacy in the summer of 2015. Third, and most important, it let Trump bypass costly expenditures on television advertising. Trump deftly used his Twitter account and his press conferences to monopolize media attention and keep the national conversation focused on him and his campaign. The result was a widely remarked-on advantage in media coverage, in which Trump consistently dominated news coverage of the Republican primary (Patterson 2016). Trump received approximately six times as much media attention as his closest Republican rival, Ted Cruz, an advantage that was worth an estimated $2 billion in free advertising (Confessore and Yourish 2016).

Although his media philosophy can be traced back decades, Trump's surprising electoral success was also a particularly digital phenomenon. Trump can be helpfully understood as the first "clickbait candidate" of the digital age (Karpf 2016b). As former Gawker CEO Nick Denton once proclaimed, "Probably the biggest change in Internet media isn't the immediacy of it, or the low costs, but the measurability" (Petre 2015). Newsrooms now rely on sophisticated analytics to track and monitor audience interest. Analytics dashboards provided real-time feedback that Trump stories were more popular than stories about any other candidate. And these newsroom analytics informed editorial decisions (people seem to want more Trump, so let's give it to them!). CBS Chairman Les Moonves suggested during the primaries that Trump's candidacy "may not be good for America, but it's damn good for CBS" (Collins 2016).

The critical insight here is that, in years past, CBS would not have had the same granular, operational awareness of how "good" Trump was for the media conglomerate's ratings. The act of measuring a process also changes that process. Newsrooms have long incorporated overnight ratings reports into their editorial choices, but the breadth of audience data has grown tremendously in the past few years, and this in turn has affected how the media agenda is set. In a pre-analytics media environment, Trump would have been the same showman. He would have the same reality show flair, the same press conference antics, the same social media bravado. But without real-time analytics, journalists and their editors would have been less *aware* of Trump's impact on readership.

These changes in the underlying mechanics of the news media matter for how power operates elsewhere in the political system. In past elections, party networks have routinely exercised soft power over the presidential nomination through a combination of candidate endorsements and donor networks. The standard finding from political science research is that across the chaos of primary elections, "the party decides" (Cohen et al 2008). Trump's outsider candidacy did not obey the same laws of political gravity to which previous outsider candidacies have been vulnerable (Sides and Vavreck 2012). He had little need for Republican endorsements or Republican mega-donors, because he eschewed expensive television advertisements and never relinquished the media spotlight.

Success in television or in real estate has always required a far different skill set than success in electoral politics. Particularly in the post–broadcast era, a "hit" TV show does not need to attract a majority of the public; it needs to cultivate a loyal following among an audience that will tune in regularly and is demographically appealing to marketers. Real estate tycoons need to attract small numbers of investors, buyers, and tenants; they do not need to build broad coalitions to fix potholes or public schools. Successful politicians, by contrast, have needed to cobble together governing majorities, reaching beyond their natural base of enthusiastic supporters. Part of what made Trump's electoral victory so surprising was that he never deviated from the approach he had developed in real estate and reality television.

Trump's media strategy during the campaign continued during the first year of the Trump presidency. It can best be understood as an example of political campaigning in the hybrid media system (Chadwick 2013). Trump rarely uses social media to *bypass* the mainstream media. Instead, he uses social media to set the agenda for the mainstream media. If the spotlight drifts away from Trump, he uses Twitter to launch some fresh outrage, attacking foreign leaders (Kim Jong Un), former electoral opponents (Hillary Clinton), media outlets (CNN as "fake news"), or even members of his own party or administration (Mitch McConnell [senator, R-KY], Jeff Sessions [US attorney general], and various FBI officials). The persistent theme is that Trump cannot be out of the news headlines for long and that he will engage in erratic behavior that distracts from his policy agenda if morning news programs ignore him or cast him in an unfavorable light.

Donald Trump is a media hyperconsumer. This is both his defining strength and his egregious weakness. His instincts as a performer, honed during his decade on reality television, keep him in the center of the national conversation and inspire a devoted fan base. But his media obsession also makes him especially vulnerable to attacks on his competence and qualifications. Past presidents have looked to pollsters, consultants, subject-matter experts, and party officials to determine their policy priorities. Activists who could effectively demonstrate that public opinion opposed a course of action, or who could effectively ridicule a policy proposal, often were rewarded with a victory. Trump labels bad polling "fake news." He has little allegiance to the Republican Party network and has staffed his administration from top to bottom with people with zero policy expertise. But he routinely calls television host Sean Hannity to ask his advice, his (now former) chief strategist Steve Bannon is also the publisher of Breitbart. com, and unflattering portrayals in the *New York Times* or on "Saturday Night Live" can throw him into a multiday tailspin.

The rules of press–government interactions are virtually all informal in nature. Victory in the primary and general elections has engendered a dangerous positive feedback loop: Because Trump broke the unwritten rules of how presidents interact with the press and the public, and he still won, Trump and his supporters reason that none of those unwritten rules apply to him. Bad polls, bad media coverage, and vocal public outrage can all be dismissed as fake news generated by a hostile press. The levers of power that mass movements normally attempt to activate when targeting the Executive Branch simply don't function if the Executive Branch pretends that poll numbers, press coverage, and people in the streets are all imaginary.

Media stand at the center of Trump's self-perception. Changes to the media system are central to Trump's unlikely success. So the Trump Resistance has necessarily embraced media innovation as well. And, indeed, it is at the intersection of media and movement innovation that we are seeing some of the Resistance's most promising tactical and strategic developments. The following section will help explain why this is the case.

The Hybrid Media System: A Media Theory of Movement Power

Many of the Resistance's most iconic tactics seem timeless in nature: Mass marches through the streets with creative signs and call-and-response chants, airport protests challenging government overreach, Congressional town hall events filled with angry constituents, volunteers canvassing neighborhoods in the days before a special election. But the strategic rationale underlying these tactics—the planning and design that helped make them a success—is intertwined with a clear understanding of today's digital media affordances.

Indeed, the power of any social movement's tactics is partially based on how they are designed to align with the contemporary media system (Karpf 2016a). A press release is just a piece of paper in the absence of media organizations. A march or a rally in the absence of media coverage is largely indistinguishable from a long, crowded walk or a noisy day in the park with friends. This is hardly a novel observation—Charles Tilly's work analyzing movement tactics as displays of worthiness, unity, numbers, and commitment (WUNC) implicitly assumes a set of news intermediaries that act as the judges and arbiters to whom these displays are aimed (Tilly and Wood 2012). Taeku Lee's work on the Civil Rights movement notes how actions like the famed "Bloody Sunday" March were strategically positioned with an eye toward amplification through broadcast media (Lee 2002). The power of that March came not solely from the protesters' courage and convictions, nor from the violent overreaction from government officials. It came from the interaction of the protesters' action, their opponents' response, and the presence of broadcast media outlets that piped the conflict into living rooms across the nation, heightening and amplifying the protest event. Remove or replace the media system and you are left with a far less powerful tactic. (see Figure 7.1)

The classic treatment of social movements and media is a 25-year-old article, "Movements and Media as Interacting Systems," by William Gamson and Gadi Wolfsfeld (Gamson and Wolfsfeld 1993). Those two scholars observed how the interests of social movements and mainstream news organizations interacted and conflicted. They found substantial mutualism, while also arguing that "social movements need the media far more than the media need them" (117). But this

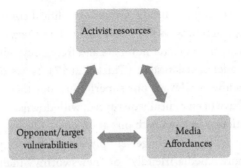

Figure 7.1 A Model of the Media Theory of Movement Power.

piece, anchored as it is in the early 1990s, treats the media system as a singular, static, and observable object of analysis. "The Media" for US movements in the industrial broadcast era comprised a small set of corporate-owned television stations, radio stations, newspapers, and magazines. The industrial broadcast media system amplified and rewarded specific forms of activist spectacle while dampening or ignoring others. Activists learned and adapted to the routines and incentives of the news system; they learned to speak in sound bites, recognizing that their access to mass audiences were filtered through an editorial process outside of their control (Ryan 1991).

In the decades since their article was published, the media system has been destabilized. First we had the rise of the 24-hour news cycle and the growth of cable television that catered to a wider range of media preferences. This made it easier for members of the public who had never particularly sought out political news to avoid it (Prior 2007). Then digital media undercut the classified advertising that was an important revenue source for local newspapers (McChesney and Pickard 2011). The rise of political blogs and social media further altered the traditional gatekeeping role of broadcast media outlets, and advances in digital advertising changed the economics of the news business. The result has been a media system that is neither solely digital nor narrowly broadcast. We have a plethora of media outlets, some of which maintain a privileged social position. News cycles still determine the political agenda, but those news cycles are shaped through alternative processes. Contentious politics remains an interactive performance with media observers, but those observers are invited to participate in different ways.

Andrew Chadwick (2013) characterizes the resulting chaos as a "hybrid media system," in which the logics of broadcast and digital media interact in new and productive ways. Media organizations remain a fixture of the broader social system, but the ways that they produce the news, the ways that readers and viewers access the news, and the ways that advertisers and subscribers pay for the news are constantly shifting. Cycles of political contestation begin, extend, and conclude in new ways in the hybrid media system. Digitally mediated protest actions happen in greater numbers and frequency, but imply less significance in the broader social system (Tufekci 2017). News organizations have been rendered neither irrelevant nor superfluous, but their internal organizational processes have been radically disrupted, with downstream effects for how activists and politicians interact with one another.

It follows that we can no longer simply assert that some protest actions are inherently more "media friendly" or "newsworthy" than others. We now must specify *which* media and *which* news. Protest tactics that were designed to flourish in the industrial broadcast media system a half-century ago often founder in today's hybrid media system. Protest tactics are rendered media friendly through alignment with the dominant media technologies of the day.

Furthermore, this media disruption is ongoing. The Internet of 2016 is different than the Internet of 2006 or 1996. It includes different technologies and devices, different firms and competitors, different civic uses and behaviors. In the Internet of 2006, the major challenges to news media came from "citizen journalist" bloggers and Craigslist's disruption of the classified advertising market. In the Internet of 2016, the major challenges to news media come from viral content factories and Facebook's domination of social sharing and advertising. This produces a cascade effect for social movement strategists. Not only do they need to think about how to develop tactics that perform well in the digital era, they *also* must remain vigilant in figuring out how the latest wave of digital changes can further amplify or dampen their tactics. Movements and media continue to be interacting systems, but the media system is in a state of constant flux and reinvention.

The networks and political associations that make up the Resistance are engaging in significant tactical innovation, both in response to the unique opportunities presented by Trump's abandonment of standard governing norms and practices (See Tarrow's chapter on countermovement dynamics in the Resistance, Chapter 9), and in response to the emerging opportunities for creating leverage in the evolving hybrid media system. Resistance activists are working to create leverage by seizing emerging opportunities on Facebook, on Twitter, and through new digital platforms. The following sections offer three case studies to elaborate this framework.

MoveOn's VideoLab

Social movement activities—town hall events and airport protests, for example—can reverberate or be muffled by the hybrid media system. Where past social movements primarily relied on broadcast media to amplify their messages, Resistance activists today also have an opportunity to gain significant traction through viral sharing on social media. But seizing that opportunity requires constant attention to the interests and priorities of social media companies themselves (Facebook in particular). Rather than designing tactics that play well on TV, Resistance activists are investing time and energy in producing media that are tailored to Facebook's algorithmic whims. MoveOn's VideoLab provides a powerful example of how this new media activism operates and what it can achieve.

Arguably the most important development in digital media over the past 5 years has been the emerging dominance of Facebook. In the realm of digital content distribution, this is Facebook's and Google's world; the rest of us just live here. Emily Bell, the director of the Tow Center for Digital Journalism, argues that Facebook has "swallowed journalism" (Bell 2016). The majority of news readership now comes through the "side doors" of search and social media, rather than direct visits to news organizations (Kalogeropoulos and Newman 2017). Small tweaks to Google's and Facebook's algorithms can have tidal impacts on the ability of activist organizations, political campaigns, and media companies to reach their audiences (Marshall 2017). In October 2017, when Facebook experimented with a modified newsfeed in six countries, news organizations lost between 50% and 80% of their readership overnight (Madrigal 2017). Google has a near monopoly on search; Facebook has a near monopoly on social sharing.

For advocates and activists seeking to extend their messages beyond the proverbial choir, Facebook is indispensable. And Facebook is not just a platform for content distribution; it is also a notoriously fickle gatekeeper. Success online generally means success on Facebook. And success on Facebook means figuring out what the algorithm is going to reward. Content sharing through Facebook is mitigated algorithmically through Facebook's newsfeed. You do not see every post that is created by your friends or by the groups you have joined or follow. Activist organizations can invest heavily in building a following on Facebook, only to learn that they cannot reliably communicate with those supporters unless they pay additionally to "promote" individual posts. Facebook constantly alters its algorithms in response to user behavior, to promote new Facebook products, and to improve the company's monetization strategy (Garcia Martinez 2016).

Those messages, stories, and communication tactics that fit well with the changing algorithmic whims of Facebook's newsfeed can "go viral" and reach a mass audience, setting the mainstream media agenda along the way. Those communication tactics that don't fit Facebook's algorithmic priorities are effectively doomed to digital obscurity. Hence, Resistance activists and other media makers regularly experiment with new communication tactics designed to flourish on Facebook.

MoveOn.org has been a trendsetter in this area (Karpf 2012). In 2013, MoveOn launched a pilot project called ShareMachine, designed to see whether optimizing existing content with Facebook-friendly headlines could attract larger audiences for progressive messages. The project team was led by Eli Pariser, MoveOn's former executive director and author of *The Filter Bubble* (2011). Through ShareMachine, MoveOn volunteers scoured the Internet for sharable progressive content; then staff tested the content to see which images and headlines had the most potential to spur viral growth through social media. ShareMachine showed massive potential, attracting an additional 16-million viewers to a video of a high school student giving testimony at an Iowa State Senate hearing about gay marriage. Pariser turned the pilot project into a digital media company, Upworthy.com, which quickly became synonymous with viral Facebook social sharing in 2014. (Pariser's cofounder would later apologize for their iconic headlines "breaking the internet.") Yet Upworthy's success also served as a cautionary tale: If you live by the Facebook newsfeed, you can die by the Facebook newsfeed. It appears that once Facebook took note of Upworthy's rapid growth, the company launched its own competing video product, then changed its algorithm to promote video sharing that stayed within Facebook's own walled garden. Upworthy's monthly reach fell from 80-million monthly unique visitors to 20 million per month—still a sizable audience for progressive content, but also a warning sign that advocacy innovation through Facebook is a constantly moving target (Karpf 2016a).

In June 2016, MoveOn launched another Facebook-oriented innovation: VideoLab. This was in response to Facebook Live, a new product announced by Mark Zuckerberg 2 months earlier. Facebook Live invites Facebook users to use their cell phones to record video and post it directly to Facebook. Whereas Facebook's algorithm had previously rewarded polished, high-resolution videos, the launch of Facebook Live signaled an algorithmic shift toward grainy, live video footage. MoveOn's VideoLab capitalizes on these changes in the Facebook algorithm to "create powerful, Facebook-optimized videos within the fast-paced news cycle. This ability to move from inception to posting in a few hours means that we're shaping the political conversation as news breaks, providing our audience with independent, carefully sourced, progressive content and analysis that they can share with others" (Thompson 2017).

The basic concept behind VideoLab is to produce newsfeed-algorithm-friendly videos that react to the political news cycle. Recent examples include a 44-second video of Senator Kirsten Gillibrand explaining the Republican tax plan and describing how outraged Democrats can fight back (5,300 shares, 243,000 views), a 4-minute video of former White House lawyer Norm Eisen discussing Special Counsel Robert Mueller's investigation of the Trump campaign as part of the Resistance movement's TrumpIsNotAboveTheLaw.org rapid response campaign (13,700 shares, 736,000 views), and a 49-minute live video of a rally where United We Dream activists called on Congress to pass the Dream Act (447 shares, 42,000 views). Some of the videos are edited to include visuals; others are simple live recordings or brief interviews with elected officials. All of the videos are timely and action oriented.

The results have been impressive. In 2017, the small team running MoveOn's VideoLab produced 536 videos. Those posts were shared 3.7-million times on Facebook and generated 285-million video views. Facebook analytics reveal that people spent 135-million minutes (or 257 years) watching VideoLab posts on Facebook. MoveOn's internal analysis indicates that these video posts generated 70,000 phone calls to Congress, 61,000 petition signatures, and 10,000 sign-ups for action-oriented text messages.[3]

VideoLab has been a valuable component of resistance bird-dogging and town hall tactics. In the midst of activist countermobilization against the proposed repeal of Obamacare, MoveOn partnered with Indivisible and other progressive groups to pack congressional town hall events with angry constituents who could tell stories about the ways that Obamacare had helped their lives. Where Republican Congress members decided not to hold a town hall event, the coalition encouraged constituents to hold their own. And VideoLab was present at these events, filming the crowd and uploading it to Facebook, where it could spread virally and attract follow-up media coverage. VideoLab created a total of 161 videos urging Congress to reject health care repeal, and those videos generated 53-million views, 1.2-million shares, and 48,010 calls to Congress.

Some social movement scholars have raised concerns that digital-era social movements are prone to "tactical freeze," in which the ease of amassing large numbers by means of the Internet leaves movements without the internal capacity for deep learning and strategic innovation (Tufekci 2017). Projects like MoveOn's VideoLab provide evidence to the contrary. Success on social media requires nimbleness and an approach to experimentation that is invigorating the Resistance with new ideas and tactics. Many activist organizations within the broader resistance have adopted a "culture of testing" that produces substantial opportunities for experimentation, learning, and innovation. In the first year of Resistance activism, an essential part of the movement's media success has been channeled through innovative efforts like VideoLab that help activists strategically adapt to the changing digital media landscape.

Sleeping Giants

Resistance activists haven't used social media only to amplify their Trump-response tactics. They have also used social media to actively challenge the partisan conservative media that promote Trumpism and the alt-right (racist right).

Sleeping Giants's campaign against Breitbart.com provides a useful window into how social media have now become a powerful tool for the Resistance in directly challenging the institutions that support Trumpism.

Among conservative media organizations, Breitbart stands out as virtually synonymous with Trumpism. No conservative media outlet is as emblematic of the Trump regime. The self-described "platform for the alt-right" was a long-time booster of candidate Trump. Breitbart's Executive Chairman Steve Bannon served as CEO of Trump's presidential campaign, and later served several months as White House chief strategist. The site has received heavy funding from Trump mega-donor Robert Mercer (Mayer 2017). Although "Fox News" continues to stand at the center of the conservative media empire, a major analysis of the digital media landscape in the 2016 election found that "*Breitbart* emerge[d] as the nexus of conservative media" (Faris et al. 2017: 11). Although much Resistance activism has focused on Trump and Congressional Republicans, the broader fight against Trumpism has included activist attempts to combat Breitbart itself.

Sleeping Giants, an anonymous, all-volunteer effort has been at the center of the fight against Breitbart. Founded by members of the digital marketing industry, Sleeping Giants has "no address, no organizational structure and no officers. At least none that are publicly known" (Farhi 2017). Its main strategy is simple: (1) Tweet at companies with screenshots of their ads appearing on Breitbart, (2) highlight Breitbart's racist and misogynist content, and (3) teach the companies how to blacklist the site from their programmatic ad buys. Unlike advertising on television or in newspapers, most online advertising is not purchased on a website-by-website basis. The companies that advertise on Breitbart have not made an intentional choice to associate their brand with misogyny and the alt-right, so a little online reputational pressure can be enough to convince companies to blacklist the site from future advertising.

To date, the advertiser boycott strategy has reaped impressive results, particularly in light of the organization's shoestring budget. Sleeping Giants estimates over 3,600 advertisers have ceased advertising on Breitbart, including major companies like Kellogg's, Audi, Visa, and Sephora. The group's Twitter account, @slpng_giants, has amassed 132,000 followers, and its Facebook account has over 40,000 followers. And those followers replicate Sleeping Giants's Twitter tactics, visiting Breitbart, taking screenshots, and then politely tweeting at advertisers. Breitbart is a private company, so it is impossible to know how much ad revenue the Sleeping Giants campaign has cost Breitbart. But as an anonymous spokesperson noted in an interview with *Mother Jones* magazine, "ultimately, when you remove lots of companies and especially bigger companies from the ad exchanges, that drives the price for the ad space down" (Hao 2017).

The strategy of targeting hostile media through their advertisers has become increasingly robust in recent years. A digital campaign targeting advertisers on Glenn Beck's Fox News Channel program began in 2009 after Beck declared that President Barack Obama was racist against white people. ColorofChange.org, Media Matters for America, and several coalition partners began collecting some of Beck's most outrageous quotes and targeted his advertisers, urging them both publicly through social media and privately through lobbying meetings to blacklist Beck's program. The campaign lasted 2 years, cost Beck hundreds of advertisers, and was ultimately successful in forcing the cancellation of his program. Angelo Carusone, who at the time was a Georgetown law student, spent years watching Beck's show, noting the most outrageous statements, and tweeting those quotes to advertisers from his @ stopbeck Twitter account. He went on to lead similar digital campaigns against Rush Limbaugh and Bill O'Reilly as resident of Media Matters for America (Lach 2017).

The logic of this strategy represents an inversion of the traditional corporate campaigning strategy. Corporate campaigns in the industrial broadcast era focused on direct boycotts of corporations or their suppliers. This leveraged the economic power of citizens as consumers. Some corporate campaigns also featured "buycotts," rewarding a corporation for its good behavior by actively promoting its product. And a few have focused on shareholder activism, purchasing shares in a publicly traded company, then introducing activist resolutions at board meetings. Boycotts, buycotts, and shareholder resolutions can be powerful tactics in the right setting, but they have limited reach when applied to companies that are privately held or partisan aligned. Liberal activists do not watch Fox News Channel, so boycotting is an empty threat. Fox is privately held, and Rupert Murdoch and Roger Ailes have intentionally positioned Fox News Channel to appeal to a conservative partisan audience while offending liberals.

Rather than targeting media companies with the (empty) threat of exacting a direct price as media consumers, the digital sponsor boycott targets advertisers with the indirect threat of reputational harm. As a Sleeping Giants representative explained to *Mother Jones*, "Companies have boned up their customer service on Twitter" (Hao 2017). Companies now actively monitor their social media presence and are notoriously fearful that online mobs will target their brand and turn it into a digital laughingstock or pariah. Companies that want to reach conservative consumers can nonetheless ask Fox News Channel not to air advertisements during Beck's program. Likewise, because digital advertising is not purchased on a website-by-website basis, activists can target reputation-conscious advertisers and build substantial economic pressure without directly targeting hostile media companies.

Ironically, this same advertiser-focused campaign strategy was also employed by Breitbart and conservative "men's rights activists" during the

2014 "Gamergate" controversy. Gamergate began as a controversy over game reviews by a female writer at the Gawker Media site *Kotaku*. After several rounds of vicious online trolling, which led (male) Gawker editors and writers to dismiss the movement as "nerds" who deserved some bullying, the Gamergate movement launched a massive advertiser boycott campaign. The campaign eventually cost Gawker Media "seven figures" in lost advertising revenue and played a role in the eventual bankruptcy and sale of the digital media conglomerate (Nwanevu 2016). Breitbart's technology editor Milo Yiannopoulos was a major figure in the Gamergate movement, and Steve Bannon has repeatedly remarked positively about the power of turning these digital crowds toward political ends. Breitbart.com has thus played a role in popularizing the digital strategy that is now undermining Breitbart.com.

Sleeping Giants's advertiser boycott campaign provides a window into the ways that activists now use social media and the changing economics of digital advertising to innovate entirely new tactics. The fracturing of the old broadcast media landscape has allowed partisan media outlets to discard traditional journalistic norms, rewarding hate and anger with clicks and advertising dollars. But those advertising dollars are not a necessary by-product of the digital media landscape; they are a strategic vulnerability that activists can now exploit. Whereas MoveOn's VideoLab uses social media to amplify offline Resistance tactics, Sleeping Giants uses social media to weaken the media institutions that buttress Trumpism.

"Pod Save America"

The Resistance is also building its own media organizations, relying on popular emerging communications platforms to build an audience that can challenge conservatives' partisan media dominance. Progressive activists have long looked with jealousy at the Republican media apparatus. Beginning with conservative talk radio in the 1980s and extending to the Fox News Channel in the 1990s and 2000s, conservative elites have established a media ecosystem with massive reach that effectively distributes partisan propaganda to its loyal supporters (Jamieson and Cappella 2010). The conservative media machine has demonstrated a capacity for setting the political agenda, introducing new issue frames, priming the anxieties of its audience, and mobilizing supporters to action. Several well-funded attempts to replicate this media apparatus on the Left have foundered and failed. Air America radio filed for multiple bankruptcies amid dismal ratings. Al Gore's Current TV never established its niche within the cable news spectrum and was eventually sold to Al Jazeera Media Network. MSNBC's evening lineup of progressive commentators is the closest analogue to Fox News but is far from the hermetically sealed media empire that conservatives have constructed over the past few decades.

As journalist Jason Zengerle suggests, "Part of the problem with these earlier ventures was their arms-race mentality: They offered liberals a mirror image of what conservatives had, rather than something liberals might actually want" (Zengerle 2017). In the aftermath of the 2016 election, there has been a huge increase in demand for political journalism and analysis. (Trump has been great for ratings, even if he has been a catastrophe for everything else.) Some of this demand has translated into newspaper and magazine subscriptions, some has translated into increased viewership at CNN and MSNBC. But there has also been substantial growth in podcasting. Today, a new digital media company, Crooked Media, and its flagship podcast, "Pod Save America," have become a powerful venue for connecting and uniting Resistance activists.

"Pod Save America" is hosted by four alumni of the Obama administration: speechwriters Jon Favreau and Jon Lovett, communications director Dan Pfeiffer, and National Security Council spokesperson Tommy Vietor. The four began collaborating on a 2016 election podcast, "Keeping It 1600," hosted by the sports-and-pop-culture website The Ringer. The original podcast was intended as a side project, an opportunity for the seasoned White House alums to digest and talk through various election-year absurdities. In the aftermath of Trump's surprise victory, they decided instead to get back and involved with politics full time. Rather than working for the Party or signing up for an electoral campaign, they decided to expand the podcast into a digital media venture. Today the program averages 1.5-million listeners per episode. By comparison, MSNBC averages 1.3-million viewers per day (Garofali 2017). Crooked Media has launched seven other podcasts, all featuring political conversations with an eye toward civic affairs, public discourse, cultural commentary, and political activism. Major political figures and journalists are regularly featured on the program, including interviews with Barack Obama, Hillary Clinton, and a range of sitting senators and candidates for public office. It has been repeatedly hailed as the "liberals' own version of talk radio" (Zengerle 2017).

"Pod Save America" is hardly the first podcasting success in the American Left. "Chapo Trap House" has a vibrant cult following among the self-described "dirtbag left," a mostly millennial audience that supports Bernie Sanders and the Democratic Socialists of America and is frequently hostile to the Democratic Party. Whereas the election night episode of "Keeping It 1600" featured reformist progressives struggling to come to terms with the existential threat posed by the Trump administration, "Chapo's" election night coverage "allowed people to direct [their] anger back inward at the Democratic Party they felt had betrayed them" (Shure 2017). Although "Chapo's" audience is firmly anti-Trump and frequently motivated to take political action, it primarily appeals to the more radical subset of the Resistance that is trying to unseat both Trump and the existing Democratic leadership. "Chapo" has a loyal and deeply political following, but it represents the left edge of the political spectrum, rather than a new center of gravity.

A key element of "Pod Save America's" success has been its orientation toward the broader Resistance. Resistance activists are frequent guests on Crooked Media podcasts, and the shows regularly offer calls to action and nuanced conversations about how listeners in blue states can be the most effective. Well-known Black Lives Matter activist DeRay McKesson hosts a weekly Crooked Media podcast, "Pod Save the People," which provides in-depth discussions of social movement strategic and tactical decisions. Jason Kander, a Democrat from Missouri who was nearly elected to the Senate in 2016, hosts another Crooked podcast, "Majority 54," which focuses on conversations with "the 54% of us who didn't vote for Donald Trump,"[4] establishing a sense of unity and shared struggle in these divisive times. During the health care fight, the podcast partnered with MoveOn to send 2,000 listeners to town hall meetings, worked with Indivisible to organize tens of thousands of phone calls to Republican senators, and teamed up with Swing Left to raise over $1 million for Congressional challengers to House Republicans (Zengerle 2017). Crooked Media podcasts regularly feature Democratic candidates, and its live touring show made stops in Virginia and Alabama just before high-profile elections, where they urged their audience to canvas and make phone calls for the Democratic nominees.

Political reporters are frequent guests on Crooked Media podcasts, as are the political elites who routinely appear on cable news. The hosts have long-standing relationships with the White House Press Corps, dating back to their time in the Obama White House. The sheer size of their audience puts the podcast on a similar footing as cable television programs. (If a journalist or politician has a book to promote, "Pod Save America" is a natural publicity stop.) This creates a valuable bridging point among the mainstream media, the political establishment, and the Resistance. Journalists hear and reckon with criticisms from "Pod Save America" whereas they might ignore or shake off criticisms from traditional activist organizations. And these interactions can be particularly fruitful in the midst of President Trump's antagonistic assault on the mainstream press. The normal habits and routines of the presidential press corps have been disrupted by the Trump presidency. Journalists find themselves in an awkward position as part of the story that they are reporting. Newsrooms are working through what it means to be an independent, nonpartisan press when the president himself routinely lies from the podium and attacks journalists as enemies of America. "Pod Save America's" hybrid role of bridging advocacy and media, combined with its hosts' long-standing relationships with mainstream reporters, lets the show exert a subtle pressure on news outlets as they figure out how to effectively cover politics in the Trump Era.

There is an irony to the sudden, explosive popularity of a political podcast in 2017. Podcasting is far from the cutting edge of communications technology. It has existed for roughly a decade and has become standard fare in comedy, sports, and entertainment. When we think about innovations in digital media and activism, we often fixate on what the latest wave of technological improvements might make possible. "Pod Save America's" success comes from finding an untapped market within an already robust technology. Resistance activists don't need to learn new skills or develop new habits to enjoy their favorite podcast. They just need to download it on iTunes.

The Crooked Media case shows that the Resistance is not just developing digital media-friendly tactics or engaging in pressure campaigns against Trumpism in conservative media; it is also building its own partisan media institutions. One of the likely outcomes of the Resistance movement will be a new generation of media organizations that unite progressive partisans in collective action around reformist political outcomes. Just as past social movements have left behind residual organizations that coordinated action after the marches and rallies had faded into history, activists within the Resistance are constructing media organizations that will likely sustain themselves beyond the Trump Era.

Conclusion

The Trump presidency is deeply interwoven with the hybrid media environment. His unlikely presidential campaign drew heavily upon the affordances of digital media and benefited significantly from the ways that hybrid media are changing newsroom dynamics. Partisan media sites like Breitbart play an active role in promoting Trump and Trumpism, while Trump himself remains fixated on how he is portrayed in the mainstream press. And just as the Trumpist movement has been centered around the changing media landscape, the Resistance countermovement has been aided by significant media-centric tactical innovations.

This chapter has focused on three prominent case examples that demonstrate the various ways that the Resistance is interacting with media. MoveOn's VideoLab highlights how Resistance activists are working to understand the latest changes to the Facebook algorithm to more effectively spread timely progressive messages beyond the activist choir. Sleeping Giant's advertiser boycott tactics show how Resistance activists are identifying new vulnerabilities in the digital media landscape, allowing them to create new forms of pressure on hostile partisan opponents. Crooked Media's podcasting success provides evidence of how Resistance activists are building new media institutions in the course of fighting back against Trump.

One of the persistent themes across these cases is that innovations in activist media occur at the intersection of robust communications technologies (Facebook, Twitter, and podcasting) and the political opportunity structure. This runs counter to how we often think about technological innovation. Today's cutting-edge technologies—augmented reality, virtual reality, blockchain, etc.—are still used only by small, technically specialized communities. The major activist innovations instead cluster around information and communications technologies that are already in use by the mass public. Tactical innovation on Facebook is powerful specifically because Facebook has already attained monolithic status. Reputational pressure on Twitter works only because companies care about their social media presence. Podcasts can build audiences that rival cable news only once people have incorporated podcasts into their daily routines. It is an old organizing lesson—"Meet your supporters where they are"—but one that has new relevance in a landscape within which people's media diets are rapidly evolving.

A second persistent theme is that new institutions, new tactics, and new strategies all emerge from creative thinking about (1) what the current media environment will encourage and support, (2) how activists can leverage their resources in response to political events, and (3) where their targets' and opponents' vulnerabilities lie. Most research treats the media as a static set of actors with clear interests and has thus focused attention on the movement's resources and the target's or opponent's vulnerabilities. What this chapter has sought to demonstrate is that the hybrid media system is a fast-changing environment, thus providing fertile opportunities for activist innovation.

Looking back at the media theory of movement power in Figure 7.1, it seems that media is especially important to the Resistance specifically because media is so central to Trump's own self-perception. We have seen in the first year of the Trump presidency that well-designed Resistance protests, amplified through social media and refracted through mainstream coverage, can stall the president's policy agenda for weeks at a time while he fixates on arguing over his public image. We have also seen that genuine public crises, such as Puerto Rico's hurricane recovery efforts, vanish from the public conversation if they are not repeatedly made accessible through mainstream media coverage. Trump's unique reality-TV flair was a singular asset during the presidential campaign. But his media obsession can also be his central vulnerability, one that Resistance activists have sought to exploit.

A third and final theme concerns the interaction of movements, countermovements, and the media in the digital era. The Resistance is a response to the specific threats posed by Trump's policy agenda and to the general threats posed by Trumpism's articulation of an authoritarian populist vision for America. Resistance activists have developed new tactics, new strategies, and new institutions that emulate or undermine the tactics that have supported Trump's movement. But Resistance innovation has been a response not only to Trumpist innovation. It has also been a response to the changing digital media landscape. The strategic insight underlying MoveOn's VideoLab comes not from watching Steve Bannon, but from watching Mark Zuckerberg. Both the changing media system and the changing political system yield opportunities for activist innovation.

What does this mean for the future of the Resistance? In the coming years, we should expect Trump and his supporters to remain fixated on media. Traditional broadcast outlets will continue to be Trump's personal obsession and will continue to be a fertile source of grievance politics for Trump's supporters. Partisan propaganda outlets like Breitbart will continue to bolster Trump's agenda, attacking foes ranging the ideological spectrum from Mitch McConnell to Black Lives Matter. Resistance activists will need to continue building their own media institutions, challenging Trumpist media institutions and investigating new leverage points for spreading their message through the hybrid media system. Both the US political system and the US media system are enduring a period of rapid, chaotic change. Although the most iconic protest actions in the Resistance will look much like protest actions of past eras (people in the streets, iconic images and slogans, struggles at the ballot box), Resistance activism will flourish where media innovation helps to amplify their political efforts.

Media has many faces within the Resistance. It is a set of communications technologies, the traditional "fourth estate" broadcast outlets, and an ecosystem of niche media outlets pursuing partisan ends. Far from simply emulating the tactics of past movements, Resistance activists have been nimble and creative with their tactical repertoires. They have experimented fruitfully with what social media makes possible, thought hard about the new vulnerabilities of their opponents, and endeavored to build their own partisan media institutions. Media innovation alone will not determine the success or failure of the Resistance, but it will continue to be a critical element of the movement as it builds and evolves.

8

Indivisible

Invigorating and Redirecting the Grassroots

MEGAN E. BROOKER

On January 30, 2017, local artist Jennifer Booher (2017a) posted a photo to Twitter documenting the first meeting of Indivisible MDI on Mount Desert Island in Maine. The crowd of 55, she tweeted, was "Not bad for a town of 5,000 (Booher 2017b)." The group quickly gained national attention when the photograph was featured in a broadcast of "The Rachel Maddow Show" three days later. Who were part of this group of 55 and why were they gathered in a small Maine town on a cold winter evening? Based solely on the photo, it would be easy to mistake the group for a resurgence of the Tea Party, which arose in 2009 against the Obama administration. Most in the room were white and middle aged. Half of those pictured wore green Statue of Liberty crowns, and one also held a paper torch. As Maddow noted, activists from the Tea Party and other conservative groups had worn similar crowns back in 2010.[1] The photo, however, offered one clue that the politics of this group differed from those of the Tea Party: A woman in the forefront of the photo held the sign shown in Figure 8.1.

Like the Tea Party, these budding activists paid reverence to the Constitution. In stark contrast to the Tea Party's nationalistic and often xenophobic rhetoric, however, they put forth a message centered on inclusiveness and tolerance of differences. In the days that followed, and still wearing their Statue of Liberty crowns, these citizens visited the office of Senator Susan Collins (R-ME) to protest the nomination of Betsy DeVos for secretary of education and stopped by the office of Senator Angus King (I-ME) to thank him for opposing her nomination. They also visited the office of Representative Bruce Poliquin (R-ME), urging him to oppose the first iteration of the "Muslim Ban," an Executive Order signed by President Trump that had placed travel restrictions on individuals from seven Muslim-majority countries (see Chapter 6).

Figure 8.1 Indivisible MDI Sign.

The resemblance between this new group and the Tea Party was not limited solely to headgear, but extended to the use of similar tactics targeting local members of Congress (MoCs). These similarities were not coincidental. Indivisible MDI is a local affiliate of the Indivisible Project (Indivisible). Indivisible began with the *Indivisible Guide*, a 26-page strategic action plan written by a group of former Congressional staffers seeking to organize grassroots resistance to President Trump's agenda. Self-consciously strategic, Indivisible explicitly described its strategy as inspired by the success of the Tea Party. Specifically, the *Guide* highlighted two facets of the Tea Party strategy that the authors saw as both effective and replicable: a local strategy targeting individual MoCs and a defensive strategy focused on stalling the President's agenda. Although condemning the *ideas* of the Tea Party, Indivisible unequivocally extolled its *strategy* and its success in producing noteworthy political achievements. Indivisible quickly gained the moniker "the Tea Party of the Left" (e.g., de Haldevang 2017b; Fouriezos 2017; Williamson 2017) as thousands of local groups were inspired to take action following the strategic roadmap described in the *Guide*.

In this chapter, I use content analysis and interviews with activists to explore Indivisible's empirical contributions to the anti-Trump Resistance and the theoretical lessons it offers to social movement scholars. I structure the chapter in five sections:

- First, I situate Indivisible within a broader literature by examining the relationship between social movements and political context.

- Second, I locate Indivisible within the anti-Trump Resistance and describe the features that set it apart from other organizations of the political Left.
- Third, I explain why Indivisible emerged in the way it did by highlighting the effects of the new political landscape.
- Fourth, I use the example of health care to illustrate Indivisible's strategic decision-making process and the consequences of its actions.
- Finally, I explore the dilemmas Indivisible faces moving forward.

I compiled an array of source material to inform my account, including the *Indivisible Guide*, organizational websites, firsthand records of Indivisible actions and events from social media, and secondary accounts from news articles and other published media. I also interviewed Indivisible's national policy director and two members of Indivisible MDI's steering committee.[2] Together, these data paint a picture of an organization strategically responding to an unstable and uncertain political environment by engaging protest tactics to fill conventional channels of political participation with opposition.

Indivisible is undeniably one of the key players in the anti-Trump Resistance. By the end of 2017, Indivisible's website boasted 18-million views from over 3-million unique users, 2-million downloads of the *Guide*, and at least 5,800 registered groups including at least 2 in every Congressional district in the nation ("About Us"). Media attention was substantial, particularly in progressive news sources. By February 2017, the Indivisible Project had incorporated as a 501(c)(4) nonprofit (Schor and Bade 2017), which maintained an active website offering resources on policy issues, explanations of the legislative process, and toolkits "to equip groups on the ground to resist Trump's agenda and hold their members of Congress accountable ('About Us')." The organization also made plans to expand, hiring additional staff for its Washington, DC, office and broadening its purely defensive agenda to include more proactive goals.

Indivisible worked to leverage grassroots support to influence mainstream politics, thus offering an example of the links between institutional and extrainstitutional politics. Although it implemented a strategy centered on collective action and employed protest tactics, Indivisible and its local affiliates focused narrowly on institutional targets. While the *Indivisible Guide* invigorated the grassroots opposition to Trump, it redirected its followers' energy to influence policy through conventional political channels. Indivisible, then, occupies a middle ground between a social movement organization and a nonprofit interest group. Indivisible emerged as a strategic reaction to an unfavorable political climate, in which the political access and influence of its creators and supporters were constricted. But, if political conditions shift, and Democrats regain control of Congress, the presidency, or both, Indivisible members are likely to leave protest behind and resort to more traditional forms of political engagement. Political circumstances, then, shape both the avenues of influence available to political challengers and the means of contention in which they engage at any given time.

Deinstitutionalization, Political Context, and the Repertoire of Contention

As traditionally conceived, social movements were seen as entities distinct from institutional politics. Movements were "challengers" seeking entrance to the polity (Tilly 1978) or "outsider" groups seeking acceptance from institutional actors (Gamson 1990). More recent scholarship, however, tends to assert "only a fuzzy and permeable boundary between institutionalized and noninstitutionalized politics" (Goldstone 2003: 2). The US democratic system offers varying levels and branches of governmental access through which political challengers can air their grievances (Meyer 2007; Meyer and Laschever 2016). The repertoire of contention from which challengers select strategies and tactics is limited (Tilly 1978) but includes action both within the conventional political arena and outside of it (Soule et al. 1999; Taylor and Van Dyke 2004). The political opportunity structure, including the degree of political access and the availability of allies in government, shapes both challengers' ability to mobilize as well as their strategic and tactical choices (Kitschelt 1986; Kriesi et al. 1992; McAdam 1996; Meyer 1993b; Meyer and Minkoff 2004; Soule et al. 1999; Tarrow 2011).

The United States has evolved into a "movement society," wherein social movements are a perpetual feature of democratic politics (Meyer and Tarrow 1998). Meyer and Tarrow (1998, 21) highlight three characteristics of this process of movement institutionalization: routinization, inclusion, and cooptation. During the process of institutionalization, in exchange for access to political institutions, movements follow familiar routines and work within the confines of conventional politics. In doing so, their repertoire of contention shrinks, as movements cooperate with new political allies and become less disruptive. "Rarely," Meyer (1993b: 39–40) concludes, "does one protest outside the White House when one believes that s/he has meaningful access within." On the one hand, when political access is high, movements focus their energy on insider tactics, working for change largely within the conventional political arena. In the United States, demobilization is also common in the presence of an elite ally in the White House (Heaney and Rojas 2015; Soule et al. 1999; Van Dyke 2003).

What happens, on the other hand, when challengers face a loss of political access or a new political opponent? Political threat has been shown to encourage mobilization and stimulate a shift to more disruptive tactics. In the student movement, for example, the presence of a presidential antagonist served as a boon for mobilization (Van Dyke 2003). Similarly, the nuclear freeze movement peaked in the early years of Ronald Reagan's presidency, when proponents saw little opportunity for institutional influence (Meyer 1993a). Presidential elections often alter the structure of political opportunities for movements, particularly when power shifts from one political party to another. Bill Clinton's 1992 election, for instance, diminished opportunities for the antiabortion movement, but offered a potential opening for abortion rights groups (Meyer and Staggenborg 1996). In response to an unfriendly political environment, it may be strategically advantageous for movements to deinstitutionalize.

Because political conditions mediate a movement's prospects for success (Amenta, Carruthers, and Zylan 1992), it is unsurprising that movements would alter their goals and tactics in response to political conditions. Institutionalization need not be a unidirectional or an inevitable part of a movement's trajectory. Instead, movement leaders must learn to interpret the political opportunity structure and negotiate the most effective relationship with the state at any given time (Meyer 1990). For example, Martin (2008) finds that labor unions that eschewed institutional tactics for disruptive ones found greater organizing success. Under certain conditions, then, strategically motivated deinstitutionalization offers tangible benefits. When political challengers lose access inside the White House and institutional tactics are no longer sufficient to gain attention or influence change, they may instead invoke a repertoire of disruptive protest tactics. In other words, protest becomes necessary when other avenues of political participation are blocked.

Figure 8.2 illustrates the diverging processes of institutionalization and deinstitutionalization. Movements, on the one hand, commonly seek institutionalization, tempering their disruptive activity in exchange for political access. The process of deinstitutionalization, on the other hand, occurs when challengers amplify disruptive activity in response to losing political access. Donald Trump's election changed the constellation of the political environment, limiting liberal

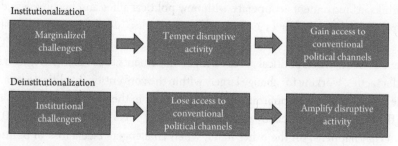

Figure 8.2 Processes of Institutionalization and Deinstitutionalization.

challengers' prospects for political influence. Facing limited political options, Indivisible deinstitutionalized and sought to overwhelm institutional political channels with grassroots opposition.

By increasing their use of contentious tactics, movements need not remove themselves from the institutional arena. In an active protest cycle, both institutional and confrontational tactics are common, so movements need not choose one or the other (Tarrow 1993). In addition, political mediation models contend that assertive tactics help movements achieve political influence, particularly in contexts that are not already supportive of their cause (Amenta, Caren, and Olasky 2005; Amenta et al. 2010). Assertive actions are those that use "increasingly strong political sanctions—those that threaten to increase or decrease the likelihood of political actors gaining or keeping something they see as valuable (their positions, acting in accordance with their beliefs)" (Amenta et al. 2005: 521). Indivisible consciously straddles this line between institutional and extra-institutional politics. The group advocates assertive action to sanction MoCs, but resorts to protest tactics when its leaders see no conventional political avenues available to influence these institutional actors.

Indivisible's Place in the Resistance

Donald Trump's election to the presidency stimulated a new wave of political resistance and protest, as detailed throughout this volume. Political challengers, ranging from moderate Democrats to the radical Left, were activated by the new political threat posed by the Trump administration. Indivisible emerged in a strategic attempt to invigorate and redirect the growing anti-Trump Resistance. Several characteristics of Indivisible set it apart from other members of the Resistance, however, and offer valuable lessons to scholars of social movements. Indivisible's distinctive qualities include its founders' preexisting political capital, its application of protest tactics directed at institutional targets, its defensive and locally focused strategy, and its rapid diffusion.

Social and Political Capital

One characteristic that demarcates Indivisible from other social movement groups is that its founders deployed already accrued social and political capital to mobilize support. Indivisible was founded not by marginalized challengers seeking political access, but by a group of well-connected political insiders seeking to manipulate conventional politics to advance a progressive agenda. Indivisible's initial contribution to the anti-Trump Resistance, the *Indivisible Guide*, names 14 individuals as "a partial list of contributors" (*Indivisible Guide*

2017). Founding contributors included Ezra Levin, Leah Greenberg, and Angel Padilla—all former Democratic Congressional staffers.[3] When I interviewed Padilla, now Indivisible's national policy director, he indicated that closer to "20 or 25 people" contributed to the *Guide*.[4]

Collectively, these contributors felt that, given their know-how as a group of political insiders, they could both inspire action and channel it based on what they'd seen work in Washington. Padilla explained:

> All of us [who contributed to the *Guide*] have come from congressional offices, and then advocacy and think tanks, definitely the sort of insider kind of world . . . . We understand the way of the world according to DCers and the way of the world according to congressional staffers. And then there's also this understanding that it doesn't need to be that way. It doesn't necessarily have to follow the same formula and we've seen that when you take a different approach, it can produce some effective and huge results.[5]

Although Indivisible's founders hoped to share their insider expertise, they never expected the rapid response that followed. Padilla opened our conversation by clarifying how the *Guide* took on a life of its own: "A lot of this wasn't planned. We put out a guide and we thought that maybe a few people would read it. It might be helpful for a certain group of people. But we never expected it to be as widely used as it has been."[6]

The *Indivisible Guide* was first posted online on December 14, 2016, and was promoted by Levin's personal Twitter account. After quickly gaining attention on social media from politicos and celebrities, the GoogleDoc crashed because of its popularity (Politico 2017). Soon thereafter, Indivisible created a website to host the *Guide* and other resources for progressive activists.[7] Attention amplified after Levin, Greenberg, and Padilla penned an op-ed, which was published in the *New York Times* on January 2, 2017. By late January, following Trump's Inauguration, local groups emerged nationwide, inspired by and prepared to implement the tactics described by the *Guide*. Previously content with institutional participation, Indivisible's founders and members adopted protest tactics to stoke political mobilization in response to a new political threat and decreased political access.

Protest Tactics Directed at Institutional Targets

A second quality that sets Indivisible apart from other Resistance groups is its unequivocal commitment to working through conventional political channels. Whereas other recent mass collective actors on the Left eschewed mainstream politics (e.g., Occupy), Indivisible explicitly advocated using existing political channels as a tool to bring about political change. The *Indivisible Guide* served as a how-to manual, outlining a thorough strategic action plan. Although the *Guide* encouraged the use of protest tactics, Indivisible's strategy centered wholly on an institutional target—MoCs.

The authors of the *Guide* relied on their political capital to justify why MoCs were an appropriate target, asserting that: "Federal policy change in the next four years doesn't depend on Mr. Trump but on whether our representatives support or oppose him. And through local pressure, we have the power to shape what they consider possible" (Levin et al. 2017a). How, then, do citizens influence the behavior of MoCs? According to the Guide, MoCs are concerned primarily with reelection and act accordingly:

> The constant reelection pressure means that MoCs are enormously sensitive to their image in the district or state, and they will work very hard to avoid signs of public dissent or disapproval. What every MoC wants—regardless of party—is for his or her constituents to agree with the following narrative: "My MoC cares about me, shares my values, and is working hard for me." (*Indivisible Guide* 2017: 8)

To avoid negative press that might damage their image, MoCs may bend to the will of constituents, making them ideal targets for challengers. The prior employment of the *Guide*'s authors as Congressional staffers shaped both their choice of target and the public reception to the *Guide*. As political insiders, they were committed to seeking political influence through conventional political channels. At the same time, given their intimate access to the Congressional venue, they came across as trustworthy sources of information about MoC decision-making. This credibility bolstered support for the Indivisible model, contributing to the viral success of the *Guide* on social media and the mass diffusion of Indivisible affiliates.

Despite its strictly institutional mission, however, Indivisible borrowed techniques from protest movements' repertoire of contention. When asked why Indivisible incorporated protest tactics, Padilla stated simply, "It's because that's where the power comes from."[8] He went on to explain that MoCs face competing pressures from their party and their constituents, but that the "pressure to keep their constituents happy, we think, is way more powerful."[9] Accordingly, Indivisible hoped to influence Congressional behavior through collective action at the local level.

Nonetheless, Indivisible's activists used protest tactics selectively. In response to the Women's March and other large events surrounding Trump's inauguration, *Guide* contributor and former Congressional staffer Jeremy Haile expressed caution: "Marches are great to bring people together, but our experience as congressional staffers had taught us that energy needed to be channeled in a smart way to make a difference on Capitol Hill" (quoted in Schor and Bade 2017). In outlining "Four Local Advocacy Tactics That Actually Work," the *Guide* promoted actions at town halls and other public events attended by MoCs, district office visits, and mass calls to Congressional offices. Instead of run-of-the mill political participation that was individualistic and unobtrusive, the *Guide* called for collective, coordinated, and even disruptive action. For each tactic, the *Guide* stressed the importance of working with fellow challengers, choosing specific and narrow goals and engaging in persistent and visible action.

In delineating its tactics, Indivisible walked the fine line between institutional and extra-institutional politics. Although its political target remained expressly institutional, the means of contention proposed by the organization more closely resembled protest than conventional political forms of action. Even so, collective action tactics were enacted principally for strategic political reasons, namely to maximize pressure on MoCs.

A Defensive, Locally Oriented Strategy

A third attribute that distinguishes Indivisible from other groups is its defensive, locally focused strategy. Although the organization's primary mission centered on influencing the national political agenda, action occurred locally through targeting individual MoCs. Indivisible also deliberately tempered its organizational goals, focusing on a defensive agenda to stall the Trump administration, rather than advocating for sweeping political change. The *Guide* asserted that acting defensively, rather than proactively, provided the best leverage given the current political environment:

> The hard truth of the next four years is that we're not going to set the agenda; Trump and congressional Republicans will, and we'll have to respond. The best way to stand up for the progressive values and policies we cherish is to stand together, indivisible—to treat an attack on one as an attack on all. (*Indivisible Guide* 2017: 7)

Through a reactive strategy, Indivisible not only acknowledged challengers' lack of political access, but also sought to avoid internal fragmentation by encouraging the Resistance to stand united against political threats rather than squabbling over alternative policy priorities that were unlikely to come to fruition.

Notably, Indivisible's strategy was modeled on that of the right-wing Tea Party movement, rather than on that of the political Left. In their *New York Times* op-ed, Indivisible leaders Levin, Greenberg, and Padilla wrote about their experience as Democratic Congressional staffers in the heyday of the Tea Party. They vehemently disagreed with the Tea Party's values, stating unequivocally, "The Tea Party's ideas were wrong, and their often racist rhetoric and physical threats were unacceptable (Levin et al. 2017a)." But they lauded the Tea Party's political accomplishments, particularly its ability to stall President Obama's agenda, stating, "Their tactics weren't fancy: They just showed up on their home turf, and they just said no. Here's the crazy thing, it worked" (Levin et al. 2017a). By mimicking the Tea Party's strategy, specifically its locally oriented defensive organizing, Indivisible hoped for comparable success in defeating the Trump agenda. "If anything," the Indivisible founders declared, "this model has greater potential now than it did for the Tea Party in 2009. Unlike President Obama, President-elect Trump has no mandate, a slim congressional majority and a slew of brewing scandals. Our incoming president is a weak president, and he can be beat" (Levin et al. 2017a). The political experience of Indivisible's founders enabled them to separate substance from strategy, modeling their organization on a successful political opponent.

Rapid and Widespread Diffusion

Indivisible also stands out because of its rapid and widespread diffusion. Activists across the country, invigorated by Indivisible's action plan, quickly established local chapters and channeled their energy into the tactics detailed in the *Guide*. With at least 5,800 local affiliates registered on its website, Indivisible boasted more than twice the number of local groups than the Tea Party Patriots at its 2010 peak (Burghart and Zeskind 2010). Indivisible also exhibited broad geographic diffusion, claiming at least two local groups in every Congressional district nationwide. A map of Indivisible's registered local affiliates is provided in Figure 8.3.

Indivisible's decentralized model helped to facilitate its swift expansion. Although relying on their political knowledge as a means of credibility, Indivisible leaders asserted early on that the fight against Trump

> won't be won by politicos in Washington, D.C. It will be won by groups in Fort Collins, Colo., Hershey, Pa., Houston and Atlanta who were organizing for justice long before a handful of former congressional staffers wrote some guide. It will be won by groups in Tucson, Madison, Wis., and St. Louis who started organizing resistance in just the last few weeks. It will be won by you, and it starts today. (Levin et al. 2017a)

The *Guide* claimed that, when targeting MoCs, a small group of local constituents has more political leverage than many nonlocal activists. Indivisible invigorated the grassroots, then, by empowering political challengers to take action and

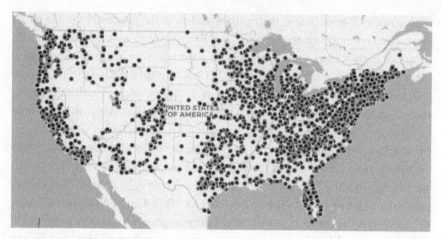

Figure 8.3 Map of Indivisible Local Affiliates.
Source: https://www.indivisible.org/act-locally/.

assuring them that even small groups of people could effect real change. This grassroots dimension enabled the rapid diffusion of the Indivisible model to an even greater effect than it had for the Tea Party.

The authors of the *Indivisible Guide* never expected the outpouring of support they received. Having initially declared that they had no intention of starting an organization (Indivisible 2016), Indivisible's founders soon established a 501(c)(4) nonprofit to keep up with the pace of growth. Levin and Greenberg quit their jobs to devote full-time attention to the organization, where they continued to serve as coexecutive directors. Padilla took on the role of policy director. He rationalized the formation of a formal organization as a necessary step to support the groups that began to organize under the Indivisible banner: "We were just trying to be responsive. We were like they need resources, they need posters, they need information, and so we were trying to do that and then we quickly became part of this like grassroots organization."[10] After a tracking component was added to the Indivisible website, thousands of local groups quickly registered as affiliates. Indivisible's plainly outlined strategy provided clear direction to both progressives and moderates who sought new outlets to resist the Trump agenda, but were unsure what to do, and facilitated its rapid growth.

Explaining Indivisible's Evolution

Indivisible solidified a unique and important place in the Trump resistance by invigorating and redirecting grassroots efforts. Leaders instrumentally appropriated protest tactics as a means of political leverage, illustrating how social movement groups can facilitate meaningful linkages between institutional and extra-institutional politics. In the case of Indivisible, this relationship grew up through a process of deliberate and calculated deinstitutionalization. Created by individuals with firm institutional roots and decisively institutional goals, Indivisible adopted tactics from protest movements' repertoire of contention. But why did Indivisible embrace extra-institutional politics, and what explains its rapid growth?

Indivisible's evolution is best explained as a reaction to shifting political circumstances. Political conditions shape both the avenues of influence available to challengers and the means of contention in which they engage at any given time. Donald Trump's election to the presidency, combined with the election of a Republican-controlled Congress, blocked conventional channels of political participation previously available to progressives under the Obama administration. Acutely aware of the new political environment, Indivisible leaders sought alternative instruments of political influence. Drawing on their insider political knowledge, they formulated a strategic model of grassroots action designed to pressure institutional targets using extra-institutional tactics. They did so not because of a lack of faith in conventional politics, but in response to a new political climate in which they lacked political access and allies.

Trump's election shaped all facets of Indivisible's strategy. Padilla rationalized Indivisible's defensive approach by highlighting the practical limitations of the new political climate: "We can't change the facts on the ground. Democrats and progressives are not in control of Congress, so we can't set the agenda. That's just a basic fact."[11] Because progressive policies were unlikely to come to fruition under the Trump administration, Indivisible aimed merely to stall the president's agenda. With access to the Executive Branch wholly closed, Indivisible's leaders instead focused their efforts on targeting MoCs. Without allies in the controlling party to disseminate their positions, however, their potential for legislative influence was also severely restricted. Conventional political engagement, such as voting and lobbying, were no longer efficient means of influence. Instead, coordinated and collective action offered a last resort to gain attention from policymakers. By redirecting political animosity and channeling it into locally organized political action, Indivisible consolidated the power of the grassroots to gain what political leverage they could within a new, unfavorable political environment.

Simply put, Indivisible would not exist had Trump lost the election. When asked what motivated their involvement in Indivisible MDI, both Meredith, an adjunct college professor, and Grace, a small-business owner, quickly and unequivocally answered "Trump."[12] National Policy Director Angel Padilla concurred, explaining that Indivisible "gave people who were angry and upset an outlet . . . [for] what they were already doing" to resist Trump. He felt that people responded strongly to the *Guide* because it offered "hope" and "promise" and showed that "if you fight back effectively, you can win."[13] By redirecting negative emotions about the president into coordinated action at the Congressional level, Indivisible provided optimism that people could make a difference.

Nonetheless, Indivisible's defensive strategy met with some hesitation in local groups. Meredith, an Indivisible MDI steering committee member, explained how she came to see its value:

> Like a lot of people, especially well-meaning white liberals, we want to be *for* something .... So, Indivisible was a little bit problematic because it was *against* everything. But the logic of it is infallible. We can't set the agenda. So, we're in the same position that the Republicans were in, you know during the Obama years. They couldn't set the agenda, so all they did . . . is prevent and tear down. So right now, the Indivisible Guide talks about just slowing down, resisting what comes out of the Trump administration, and it's actually really easy to get behind all of that.[14]

Part of the environmental shift that laid the groundwork for Indivisible predated Trump's election. Indivisible purposefully modeled its political strategy on that of the Tea Party. In addition to its political accomplishments, the Tea Party had reshaped the landscape for social movements' interactions with institutional politics. Beyond stalling the Obama agenda, the Tea Party helped loosen the centralization of power at the party level. Pressure from the Tea Party contributed to the banning of Congressional earmarks (Formisano 2012). This change restricted party control, giving more power to legislators to respond directly to their constituents. The Tea Party also provided a blueprint for future movements wanting to leverage grassroots mobilization as a tool of institutional political influence. After quickly being labeled the "Tea Party of the Left," the comparison helped Indivisible to galvanize support. Grace rationalized that Indivisible's defensive approach "made perfect sense" because of the success of the Tea Party in "doing that to Obama."[15] Indivisible, then, benefited both from the Tea Party's countermovement strategy as well as from its reputation of political success.

The Battle over Health Care

Health care provides an illustrative example of Indivisible's process for selecting strategic priorities and the magnitude of its contribution to the anti-Trump Resistance. Indivisible adapted its day-to-day strategy in response to ever-evolving political conditions. The national office had an explicit protocol for deciding where to direct its energy and resources. Indivisible prioritized issues based on four criteria: (1) those most immediately relevant in Congress; (2) those central to the Trump agenda; (3) those that would harm the most vulnerable communities; and (4) those seen as attacks on democracy (Indivisible 2017b). When asked about Indivisible's policy priorities, Padilla jumped to health care. He described the Affordable Care Act (ACA) as the "single most important" issue for Indivisible, explaining that it mattered both substantively and strategically. Saving ACA meant Indivisible could "stop harm," but would also lock Republicans into a battle over health care, making them "less likely to get some of their other priorities across the finish line."[16]

Indivisible's first major policy battle arose soon after Trump's Inauguration, as Republicans quickly moved ACA repeal to the top of the Congressional agenda. As it had for the Tea Party in 2009, health care policy rapidly mobilized Indivisible supporters. Republicans who supported dismantling the ACA (colloquially referred to as Obamacare) often bore the brunt of Indivisible's protest. As talk of Obamacare repeal ramped up in Washington, Indivisible protesters popped up at Congressional town halls and offices during the Congressional recess in February 2017. Representative Tom McClintock (R-CA), for example, met a "raucous" crowd both inside and outside his town hall event in Roseville, California, from which he eventually had to be escorted out by police (Westfall 2017). Following a "tussle" between protesters and staff in his office hallway (Wisckol 2017), Representative Dana Rohrabacher (R-CA) released a statement accusing protesters of "political thuggery, pure and simple" and calling them "enemies of American self-government and democracy" (Rohrabacher 2017).

Protest intensified as drafts of the American Health Care Act (AHCA), designed to repeal Obamacare, were introduced in Congress, beginning in March 2017. Tensions peaked in May 2017, when the bill narrowly passed the House and was forwarded to the Senate for deliberation. Representative Tom MacArthur (R-NJ), who authored an amendment that reconciled Republican disagreements and paved the way for the bill to pass the House, was then met with "sheer rage" from Indivisible protesters and other constituents at a town hall (de Haldevang 2017a). As he arrived at the event, "nearly a thousand furious protesters carrying mock-ups of their would-be gravestones were outside the town-hall venue to greet him" (de Haldevang 2017b).

Trying to avoid confrontation, some MoCs opted not to return to their districts or to avoid holding public events at all. In response, Indivisible distributed a "Missing Members of Congress Action Plan." It explained MoCs' absence by stating that "MoCs do not want to look weak or unpopular—and they know that Trump's agenda is very, very unpopular (Indivisible 2017a)." Indivisible groups were encouraged to reach out to local representatives to request a public appearance. Or, if outreach failed, groups were urged to hold a "constituents' town hall" outside their MoC's district office or at an alternative venue where constituents could air their grievances, with or without their representative present.

Despite primarily targeting Republican MoCs, Indivisible maintained that it was not a partisan organization. In a July 2017 blog post outlining Indivisible's electoral strategy, Political Director María Urbina (2017) declared in bold text: "We are not going to act as an arm of the Democratic Party." Consistent with this national messaging, Democrats did not avoid scrutiny from local Indivisible groups. For example, after Senator Dianne Feinstein (D-CA) declined to hold a town hall during the February 2017 recess, she was met with demonstrators at public events, at her office, and even outside her home (Garofoli 2017).

Further demonstrating Indivisible's commitment to avoiding partisan affiliation, some Indivisible groups have, at times, praised Republican MoCs. Indivisible MDI, the local group from Maine, visited the office of Senator Susan Collins (R-ME) and publicly thanked her for pivotal vote in defeating health care repeal legislation. Its members used imagery of Senator Collins as Wonder Woman and Rosie the Riveter to valorize her role to "Save Our Healthcare" and promoted the hashtag #CollinsStrong.[17] The group later lauded Collins's decision to remain in the Senate, after speculation that she might leave her seat to run for the state governorship (Indivisible MDI 2017). This praise came only after a months-long battle, during which Indivisible MDI visited Collins's office regularly.

Meredith and Grace both described Collins's "no" vote on health care as Indivisible MDI's greatest achievement. Meredith credits the group's persistent resistance with helping change Senator Collins's mind on health care:

> I firmly believe that the pressure groups in Maine have brought to bear on her made a huge difference . . . . We know most of the staffers now, they know us. They know that we are, as one of my favorite hymns goes: we are a gentle, angry people. And they know that . . . . So, I firmly believe, without the resistance movement, Susan Collins would have been a yes.[18]

The view that Indivisible contributed to swaying Collins's vote was not confined to activists, however. Amy Fried, professor of political science at the University of Maine, also credited Indivisible's influence. "On health care," she wrote in a political blog for the *Bangor Daily News*, "Collins did not start where she ended and she shifted after considerable grassroots action. Moreover, confronting Collins meant challenging the most popular elected official in the state, who was used to highly laudatory press" (Fried 2017). The persistence of organized pressure, she asserted, compelled Collins to respond to her constituents.

Republicans who broke with their party colleagues and voted against the Trump agenda offered Indivisible an opportunity to claim credit. Projecting a narrative of political influence can be an important tool for social movements to establish a favorable reputation and demonstrate the utility of collective action (Meyer 2006). On July 27, 2017, Senators Collins (R-ME), Lisa Murkowski (R-AK), and John McCain (R-AZ) joined their Democratic colleagues and voted against the Healthcare Freedom Act (HFA), a revised version of the original bill often referred to as "skinny repeal," preventing the ACA repeal from passing. That same day, Indivisible declared victory for its part in blocking the legislation. Executive Director Ezra Levin posted a series of tweets commending the efforts of Indivisible groups in Maine, Alaska, and Arizona for their persistent action to persuade their senators.[19] In an op-ed in the *Washington Post* a few days later, Indivisible leaders asserted the political power of the Resistance.

> The combined political might of the president of the United States, the speaker of the House of Representatives and the Senate majority leader was no match for one simple thing: people showing up. And show up they did, because constituent power is locally applied power. From town halls to "die-ins" to sit-ins to mailing protest potatoes, constituents took action not in Washington but in their home states. (Levin et al. 2017b)

In health care, then, Indivisible was able to claim its first majority victory. Building off this success the group encouraged supporters to continue the fight against the Trump agenda:

> We know that when constituents across the country rise up and apply their power, they change what is politically possible nationwide. Our task now is to build and sustain that leadership and power because we also know that if we stand together, indivisible, we will win. (Levin et al. 2017b)

When I interviewed Padilla in November 2017, he echoed this sentiment, asserting that "delaying is a win," but quickly clarifying that "we're not done."[20] The battle over health care policy will continue in Washington, as will debates over many other issues important to Indivisible and its constituents. To stay relevant and to exert substantive political influence, Indivisible would need to contend with a number of challenges after the first turbulent year of the Trump administration.

What's Next for Indivisible?

In only its first year, Indivisible established a prominent reputation within the anti-Trump Resistance, quickly mobilizing a substantial base of support and building a defensive strategy that garnered some political success despite the limitations posed by the political climate. Nonetheless, mass mobilization rarely extends over long periods of time, and social movement organizations must be prepared to adapt to ever-changing political conditions if they hope to remain influential. Moving forward, Indivisible must confront strategic, organizational, and electoral challenges that threaten its organizational longevity and effectiveness.

Strategic Challenges

First, Indivisible must face the instability of its position as antagonist and its prospects for grassroots mobilization. Although it may be easy to mobilize around opposition, this is rarely a productive long-term strategy for coalitional organizing (Brooker and Meyer 2018). Standing "Indivisible" in a unified challenge to the Trump agenda may work in the short term, but it obscures differences among supporters that may lead to strategic disagreements down the line.

In addition, Indivisible runs the risk of developing a reputation as merely an adversary rather than as an organization with its own value-driven agenda. Although the two local MDI organizers I interviewed recognized the political expediency of Indivisible's defensive agenda, both of them noted that not all members of their group agreed with this strategy. Meredith stated that many local activists "want to be for something,"[21] and Grace expressed that "some want to be proactive."[22]

Burnout is also a significant concern for grassroots Indivisible chapters, many of which are coordinated by only small groups of individuals. As members of the Indivisible MDI steering committee, Meredith and Grace had sometimes spent as much as 20–30 hours per week on organizing tasks. Endless oppositional battles do little to inspire activists to stay involved. A more proactive agenda may be necessary to appease committed activists, but it may be ineffective unless political circumstances change. In developing a long-term strategy, Indivisible must balance the ideological desires of grassroots activists with practical constraints arising from the political environment and the limited capacity of its local affiliates.

Indivisible's national office has taken steps to alleviate these concerns. When asked whether Indivisible's organizational strategy will evolve, Policy Director Angel Padilla explained:

> It will, it has to, and we want it to. But we can't change the facts on the ground . . . . In terms of this Congress and the things that it's trying to

do, all we can do is be defensive . . . . Longer term, we can't just be about defensive, we have to be about affirmative policies, boldly and unapologetically progressive.[23]

Padilla identified two distinct benefits to adopting a broader, progressive strategy. First, he recognized the importance of keeping the grassroots engaged. Through an August 2017 "listening tour" of local chapters, national Indivisible leaders sought input on developing a "common progressive political platform to fight for" (Dickinson 2017). Padilla expressed that "we have gotten the message . . . and are working on a statement of principles, that we hope will guide our work in the progressive space."[24] Second, Padilla highlighted how a more progressive agenda would aid in Indivisible's electoral goals:

> When we get to 2018, when we start talking about elections, we can't run on being against Trump. We can't run on being against Republicans. That will only get you so far. You need to be *for* things. So, part of the reason why we see the need for a progressive policy agenda of some kind is that it will help us in the process of re-taking back the House and re-taking Congress eventually.[25]

These broader and more proactive goals were also formally incorporated into Indivisible's mission statement, which was expanded in August 2017 to read "Our mission is to cultivate and lift up a grassroots movement of local groups to defeat the Trump agenda, elect progressive leaders, and realize bold progressive policies" ("About Us").

In addition to developing a long-term strategy, Indivisible must also consider its tactics. Movements that thrive over the long haul do so through continual adaptation. As political challengers, movements must stay one step ahead of their political opponents, who learn how to suppress their efforts over time. The Civil Rights movement, for example, sustained its efforts only through repeated tactical innovation, devising new protest techniques to challenge authorities (McAdam 1983). Indivisible must follow suit if its leaders hope to remain an influential force in the Trump Resistance.

Organizational Challenges

Second, Indivisible must confront its capacity to balance several competing organizational functions and establish its position vis-à-vis other groups in the Resistance. To be successful, movements must engage in a variety of tasks including acquiring resources, mobilizing a base of support, and forcing

institutional change (McCarthy and Zald 1977). When movement organizations compete for resources and external support, conflict tends to arise (Barkan
1986; Staggenborg 1986). To compensate, organizations within the same social movement industry must specialize on narrow tasks or goals to distinguish
themselves within the field (McCarthy and Zald 1977).

Certain features of Indivisible, including its focus on Congressional targets,
set it apart within the Resistance, but the organization has juggled efforts to raise
funds, to mobilize the grassroots, and to influence the policy agenda. Here, a comparison with the Tea Party reveals why balancing these tasks may pose an unsur-
mountable obstacle for a single organization. Within the Tea Party movement,
these three functions were performed by distinct organizations (Fetner and
King 2014). Resources were funneled from the top down through wealthy
donors such as the Koch brothers and their organization, FreedomWorks.
Grassroots mobilization was coordinated largely by the Tea Party Patriots and
its decentralized network of local affiliates. Meanwhile, the Tea Party Express
served as a political action committee (PAC) to raise money for Republican
Party candidates. Organizational specialization, an influx of financial resources,
and cultural support from conservative media allies all facilitated the Tea Party's
rapid growth and political success (Fetner and King 2014). In trying to carry
out all of these functions on its own, especially without resources comparable
with those of its conservative predecessor, Indivisible stretches the limits of its
organizational capacity.

Indivisible has tried to overcome this obstacle through organizational growth,
professional specialization, and partnerships with other progressive organizations. Starting with just five staff members, Indivisible soon added several more
professional staff, each specializing in a specific function. Political Director María
Urbina was brought in to map out Indivisible's electoral strategy. Organizing
Director Isaac Bloom was hired to coordinate interaction between the national
office and local chapters. As of January 2018, Indivisible was recruiting for 16
full-time positions specializing in communications, development, operations,
organizing, policy, and political tasks. By expanding the number of paid staff and
assigning each a specialized function, Indivisible has demonstrated a concerted
effort toward professionalization, a process that often promotes organizational
longevity and stability (Staggenborg 1988).

When politically expedient, Indivisible has also joined forces with other
prominent progressive organizations to amplify its influence. In May 2017,
the group teamed up with MoveOn.org, Townhall Project, and the Women's
March to launch a new initiative called the Payback Project. The project was
designed to "track local groups and events working to hold accountable the 217
House Republicans who voted for TrumpCare" (Indivisible "Statements"). In
September 2017, Indivisible joined the National Immigration Law Center and

United We Dream to encourage Democratic lawmakers to force a vote on the Dream Act after President Trump announced the elimination of the Deferred Action for Childhood Arrivals (DACA) program ("Statements"). Indivisible, then, has joined resistance coalitions, particularly when other organizations can provide issue expertise, access to larger constituencies, or both. Nonetheless, to sustain its political relevance and maintain steady funding, Indivisible will need to distinguish its contributions from those of other left organizations. Identifying opportunities for mutually beneficial coalition work while avoiding competition for resources has historically been a significant challenge within progressive movements.

Partisan and Electoral Challenges

Third, Indivisible must formalize its electoral strategy and negotiate its relationship with the Democratic Party. The organization has promoted a two-tiered electoral strategy, seeking to influence electoral politics at both the local and the national levels. At the local level, Indivisible members have run for, and sometimes won, city council seats and other local offices. Although Indivisible has not developed a formal strategy to run its own candidates, the national office has provided resources and support to affiliates whose members have run for local offices. Eight Indivisible members successfully won city-level posts in 2017, in states including Virginia, Michigan, Iowa, and Connecticut.[26]

At the national level, Indivisible played a prominent role in several 2017 Congressional elections and then began developing plans for approaching the 2018 midterm elections and beyond. In describing the group's electoral strategy, Political Director María Urbina (2017) wrote, "Congressional lobbying isn't enough—we also have to win elections . . . . We have to elect the kind of policymakers who will not only push back on this Administration, but also re-build our democratic institutions and fight for a boldly progressive future." To aid in this goal, during its first year, Indivisible devoted energy to two major projects: defining a clear policy agenda and providing resources to help get out the vote. Indivisible leaders strategically identified key races for which they felt constituent pressure was most likely to make a difference. Padilla explained where Indivisible centered its electoral involvement in 2017:

> We've already engaged, we were active on the ground in Virginia for weeks before that election [where Democrat Ralph Northam won the governorship and Democrats gained at least 15 seats in the House of Delegates[27]]. Our Indivisible groups were all over, doing stuff from like

get out the vote to just getting information out. They were actively involved organizing. And we are now in Alabama [where Democrat Doug Jones won the special Senate election]. These are in some ways like test cases for us for a larger push next year.[28]

In Indivisible's first blog post of 2018, Padilla set the stage for the new year by placing elections squarely in the center of the organization's strategy: "In 2018, we'll replace the elected officials who don't represent us with diverse, progressive, local leaders. And if we put in the work (beginning right now!), our movement will be the catalyst for the big blue wave we all hope to see on election night in just over 300 days" (Padilla 2018). House and Senate seats, as well as governorships and state houses, were all identified as priorities. In 2018, Indivisible planned to continue voter registration and outreach, while also adding a new component to its electoral strategy: candidate endorsements.

In discussing Indivisible's 435 program to promote electoral involvement in all congressional districts nationwide, Padilla explained:

> We also are issuing an endorsement guide for next year. Again, we do lightly touch on our groups. We never tell them you have to work on anything . . . . We don't tell them that you have to support this or that candidate, but what we are doing is giving them a guide that we hope will help them through the process of endorsing one of those local candidates. The way that we always view this is trying to empower the groups locally to do what they want to do, and in this case, it's getting engaged on the electoral side.[29]

Published in November 2017, the *Indivisible435 Endorsements Guide* described why local groups should consider primary endorsements and how to make an endorsement. Like in the original *Indivisible Guide*, it cited the Tea Party's successful primary challenges as evidence of the feasibility of an electoral strategy. The *Endorsements Guide* encouraged local groups in the same Congressional district to work together, to bolster strength in numbers. It also hinted that the national office was in the process of developing a strategy to coordinate national-level endorsements:

> Standing Indivisible is especially crucial for races with a national profile. We'll be working to roll out a process for national endorsements that are reflective of our grassroots movement and based on input from all members of Indivisible in early 2018. We'll keep you posted on this— we want to maintain a high level of transparency with groups as we, too, grapple with these critical endorsement decisions at the national level.

Stay tuned for more info on how we'll work with your group and others in your area to align on these key races. (*Indivisible435* 2017)

By March 2018, Indivisible had put its electoral strategy in motion and begun announcing national-level endorsements of Democratic congressional and gubernatorial candidates.

Negotiating its relationship with the Democratic Party poses an ongoing challenge for Indivisible, however, as they have endeavored to exert pressure on both parties. When I asked Policy Director Angel Padilla about Indivisible's relationship to the Democratic Party, he explained:

> We are not out to get Republicans, it's not like we are serving or an arm of the Democratic Party at all. We see that Democrats also need to be pressured, they also need to be held accountable. And that's why I think of ourselves as being non-partisan . . . . But you're right, part of what we want to do, part of our job is to move, to help move the Democratic Party to the left. And that's what the Tea Party did. The Tea Party was aggressively conservative and moved the Republican Party to the right. And we're trying to do the same thing for progressives.[30]

Maintaining a nonpartisan designation while also gaining inroads into the Democratic Party may present an uphill battle for Indivisible. To gain a formidable political foothold, as the Tea Party did, Indivisible would need to gain power *inside* the Democratic Party. Putting pressure on both parties may be a practical strategy for a movement organization, but if political conditions become more favorable with more Democrats elected in the coming years, holding power inside the party would give Indivisible greater leverage to institute its policy agenda.

Conclusion

In a movement society, strategic political challengers will utilize all available tactics (including protest tactics) to exercise influence over political outcomes. However, challengers with already-accrued social and political capital will typically engage protest tactics only as a last resort. The founders of Indivisible encouraged protest tactics only because they faced a loss of access within the realm of institutional politics. Traditional institutional strategies were no longer effective under the incoming administration; in response, Indivisible's activists expanded their repertoire to include protest tactics as a defensive strategy. They successfully mobilized a base of support to confront new threats but maintained focus on institutional targets, namely MoCs.

In response to an unfavorable political environment, Indivisible strategically deinstitutionalized. Donald Trump's election left its leaders with little opportunity to achieve political change from the inside; instead, they opted to put pressure on the administration from the outside. In its first year, Indivisible played the role of political challenger. But subsequent elections could shift the balance of power if Republicans lose Congressional seats. Through its electoral strategy, Indivisible strives to reinstitutionalize. By endorsing Democratic candidates, the group seeks to gain greater control over the policy agenda. Although Indivisible hopes to prevent cooptation by the party, staking a claim within the Democratic Party offers the most direct route to achieving its institutional goals. Indivisible can gain political leverage by claiming credit for Democratic victories and pressuring Democratic victors to adhere to its progressive agenda. Electoral involvement provides Indivisible an opportunity to take its Tea Party–inspired strategy full circle by winning elections and shifting the Democratic Party to the left.

Indivisible's long-term strategy will continue to reflect the political environment in which it operates. Indivisible grew and diffused quickly in response to the political threat posed by the Trump presidency. As the immediacy of the political threat lessens, and especially if Democrats gain back Congressional seats, the presidency, or both, grassroots mobilization will decline as political access becomes available to progressive Democrats once again. Under these new conditions, Indivisible's leaders are likely to steer the group toward reinstitutionalization. When the political climate becomes more favorable, they will redirect efforts inside Washington rather than outside it.

For Indivisible, reinstitutionalization provides the greatest opportunity for political influence should Democrats retake political control. Despite its reluctance to become an arm of the Democratic Party, doing so may offer Indivisible its greatest chance of political success. Holding institutional power offers greater potential for its constituent campaigns to lead to progressive policy change. Nonetheless, if Republicans maintain political control, Indivisible will be left with few opportunities other than to continue its outsider pressure campaigns. Political conditions, then, will perpetually dictate both the avenues of influence and the means of contention available. But, if Democratic victories permit Indivisible to move from political challenger back to the realm of political insider, reinstitutionalization will provide the group significant political leverage because it will now be backed by a grassroots movement of supporters.

Acknowledgments: I am grateful to David S. Meyer, Sidney Tarrow, Julie Kim, Alma Garza, and participants of the University of California Irvine Social Movements Social Justice Workshop for their thoughtful feedback on drafts of this chapter.

PART FOUR

DYNAMICS OF RESISTANCE

Rhythms of Resistance

The Anti-Trumpian Moment in a Cycle of Contention

SIDNEY TARROW

On November 8, 2017, CNN greeted the results of the special elections that had been held the day before with a dramatic headline:

"DEMOCRATS SWEEP VIRGINIA AND NEW JERSEY."[1]

In Virginia, a mainstream Democrat, Ralph Northam, had just defeated a mainstream-Republican-turned-Trumpite, Ed Gillespie, while, in New Jersey, a financier-turned-politician, Phil Murphy, soundly beat Republican Lt. Governor Kim Guadagno. Lower down on the balloting, the Democrats took at least 15 legislative seats in Virginia and swept local election contests in places as far apart as Seattle, Washington, Minneapolis, Minnesota, and Helena, Montana.[2] After a year in which Donald Trump and the Republican Party won nearly every House election, the Democrats had begun to take revenge for the trouncing they had received in the presidential election the year before. A month later, Trump suffered another dramatic defeat when Roy Moore—a sexually tarnished candidate whom Trump had endorsed—was defeated in a special election in the deep-red state of Alabama in the midst of the "me too" movement that saw celebrities, television and movie producers, and members of Congress accused of sexual harassment.

There was much for Democrats to be pleased about in these electoral victories, but amid the chorus of excitement in the Democratic ranks, political scientists like Larry Jacobs warned the Democrats against undue optimism: "I don't think it was a wave election or a confirmation of doom for Republicans," he said of the wins in Virginia and New Jersey. "I think Democrats are so demoralised after 2016 that any kind of good news produces elation, but it feels quite strained and forced." Jacobs added, "I don't see grounds for breaking open the champagne in 2018."[3]

As Jacobs's cautions attested, the Democrats had a long way to go before they could claim to put the Republicans on the defensive. More important, electoral shifts were not the reason why the Trump phenomenon was proving so difficult to dislodge: It was because *Trumpism was not a typical partisan coalition but a social movement that had entered partisan politics.* This meant that while he was learning how to play traditional coalition politics—a game about which he had a lot to learn—he maintained the support of his movement base, which depended less on the intricacies of policy than on his charismatic appeal.

In the current alignment in American politics, party loyalties run deep and divide Americans sharply (Abramowitz 2017). But party loyalties are permeable to changes in the political atmosphere. *Movement* loyalties, in contrast, are impervious to short-term political currents. Not every Trump supporter would go as far as Mark Lee, who appeared on a CNN panel to declare, "If Jesus Christ gets down off the cross and told me Trump is with Russia, I would tell him, 'Hold on a second. I need to check with the president if it's true.' "[4] But many members of his movement base determinedly support their leader in the face of growing evidence of his incompetence, his unreliability, and his tendency to adopt—however temporarily—the views of the last person he saw.

Social movements have infiltrated the two major parties before: From the 1960s on, as Doug McAdam shows in Chapter 1, movement activists entered both parties and initiated the growing polarization between them.[5] But this was a deeper infiltration than anyone imagined when Trump, in June 2015, announced his ambition to run for the presidency. The reason is that at the core of his constituency are many voters whose loyalty goes beyond party identification. As I and my coauthors have argued throughout our book, to defeat an insurgent movement, elections are not enough: A victorious movement must be opposed by a *countermovement* that is broad enough to respond to its challenges and deep enough to engage activists over the long haul. A European comparison displays the difficulty of defeating an insurgent populist movement in the absence of a broad opposing coalition.

Italy, 1922; America, 2016

In 1918 a wave of social protest swept across Italy, triggered in part by that country's disastrous intervention in the First World War, in part by the economic aftereffects of that war and in part by an electoral reform that had expanded the electorate to many thousands of inexperienced new voters.[6] Much of the agitation of those years came from the Left—angered at the repressive policies of the war years and inspired by the revolution that had swept the Russian tsars from power. To many on the Left, like Communist leader Antonio Gramsci, it seemed that they could do what the Bolsheviks did in Russia! To conservatives, in the wake of the occupation of the factories that marked the high point of the cycle, there was widespread fear that Gramsci's dream would become a reality.

As the protest wave from the Left declined, another movement—Benito Mussolini's Fascist movement—arose out of the war, with the support of a motley coalition of army veterans, peasants, rural thugs, wealthy landholders, and nationalists. Mussolini adopted a combination of left-wing and right-wing ideas, combining militarism with disgust at Italy's modest gains from the war, and using both violent and nonviolent tactics for which both the Left and mainstream political groups were unprepared: He was the country's—and probably the world's—original populist.

On the Left, the country was split between feuding Communists and Socialists; on the Right, conservatives and liberals were deeply divided by the war; and in the Center, a new Catholic party—the *Partito Popolare*—rejected the policies of both Left and Right. These blocs were also internally divided—the Left over what had happened in Russia and its prospects for the West; the Right over how to combat the threat of revolution; and the *popolari* between a progressive wing and those who were too wedded to the Vatican to make common cause with either bloc. The result was that although Mussolini's *Partito Nazionale Fascista* never came close to winning an election, no effective coalition arose to contest his claims, and he walked into power after staging a theatrical "March on Rome."[7]

To put this outcome in the terms I will employ in this chapter: Because the Italian party system was so internally fractured, neither the divided Left, nor the splintered Right, nor the uncertain *popolari* had an effective answer to a political adventurer with a charismatic appeal, a heterodox following, and a negative program. Although conservative elites thought they could use Mussolini to defeat their political enemies and the Left squandered the capital of revolution in an orgy of words, none of these actors had an answer to the challenge of a fundamentally new social and political movement that attacked the existing system.

Back to America

Of course, the United States in the second decade of the 21st century looks nothing like the Italy of a century ago. For one thing, Americans in 2016 had two centuries of electoral experience behind them; for another, in contrast to the fractured Italian economy of 1918–22, the American one is booming; and, for a third, there is no revolution afoot in the world to inspire some and petrify others. But we have been fighting an endless war that has drained American resources, and we are suffering increased inequality in the midst of plenty, helping to create a deeply polarized electorate and a political class striving to take advantage of it. As a result, like Italy during the 1918–1921 period of conflict, we are in the midst of a major cycle of contention.

In this chapter I employ the concept of "cycles of contention" to help us to understand the current conjuncture of American politics. I then summarize some evidence about the contours of the cycle during the first year of the Trump administration. I will argue that in a political cycle, the outcomes depend less on the initial shock than on the mechanisms it triggers.[8] Among these are three important mechanisms—*amplification, spillover,* and *scale shift*[9]—that have expanded the cycle but that have also created rifts in the Resistance. I will argue that, just as the Italian political class failed to coalesce when faced by a crude authoritarian, Americans risk the future of democracy if they fail to close ranks against the dangers of the Trumpian movement.

Before turning to these claims, let me lay out some assumptions that will help readers to interpret the burden of the chapter:

- First, as McAdam's chapter (Chapter 1) reminds us, Trump did not appear in a vacuum. His movement built on 40 years of Republican evolution, as I will argue in the second section.
- Second, though Trump has successfully infiltrated—and may be reshaping—the Republican Party, he is not a party politician in the traditional sense, but the leader of an insurgent movement, as I will argue in the third section.
- Third, this intrusion of a movement into a party—and into the heart of the state—has thrown the United States in 2016–2018 into what I call a "cycle of contention," which I define as a phase of heightened conflict across the social system, which I will summarize in the fourth section.[10]
- Fourth, a recurring tendency in such cycles is for countermovements to arise, producing both threats and opportunities for activists, expanding the range of conflicts, as I will argue in the fifth section.
- Finally, I will close with some observations about both the promise and the dangers of a spiral of movement–countermovement interaction for democracy, building both on comparative experience and on the findings of this volume.

Because it is too soon to make firm predictions about the future of the Resistance—or of the country—much of this chapter is necessarily tentative, but I will draw on evidence from the previous chapters to support my speculations.

What American History Teaches

Political scientists have not been unaware of the presence of movement-like elements in Trump's coalition. In a recent reflection, Robert Lieberman writes of Trump that "his campaign attracted the enthusiasm of a ragtag collection of groups and voices long relegated to the fringes of American politics."[11] But it is easy to exaggerate the reach of what has come to be called the "alt-right." What Lieberman leaves out—and what seems to me more important—is that Trump crystallized a broader movement that was growing out of the resentments of older white Americans since long before his appearance on the national scene. Racial appeals—which had lain beneath the surface of the Republican Party for decades—were at the core of this movement and resonated with Trump's carefully staged campaign rants on illegal immigration and urban crime. As McAdam writes in Chapter 1,

> The tumultuous onset of Donald Trump's administration, to say nothing of the president's outsize presence, has so riveted our attention that we're in danger of losing historical perspective . . . . Trump is only the most extreme expression of a brand of racial politics practiced evermore brazenly by the Republican Party since its origins in the 1960s.[12]

As is well known, the Civil Rights movement added a new voting block to the Democratic Party's "interest-group coalition" (Grossman and Hopkins 2016); what is less well understood is that the segregationist backlash that followed it blended with the religious revival that came soon after, giving Republican leaders the opportunity to build a white "Southern strategy" that reached well beyond the borders of that region.[13] The movements and countermovements of the 1960s did not produce today's polarized politics directly; but they led to a series of intraparty changes that gave activists disproportionate power in the selection of candidates.[14] As McAdam's chapter shows, with the expansion of the direct primary and the caucus, in place of state nominating conventions, the power of party activists was entrenched at the grassroots of each party.

But this was not all: As McAdam also shows, in the case of the Republicans, voter suppression and the gerrymandering of Congressional districts played a major role in moving the Republican Party to the right.[15] Polarization was not a direct outcome of racial radicalization but of the insertion of movement activists into the heart of the two parties, enhanced, in the Republican case, by the mastery of the mechanisms of electoral chicanery.

Parties and Movements

The current polarization of American politics has produced a rich and varied literature, but most political scientists have limited their gaze to the party system and the electorate. Only with the advent of the Tea Party during the Obama presidency did they begin to use movement language to describe what was happening (Parker and Barreto 2013). But we can understand the reach of polarization into American society only by seeing the relations between movements and parties as they developed earlier; as Meyer and Staggenborg summarized in their landmark study of movement–countermovement interaction:

> The civil rights and antiwar movements in the United States in the 1960s brought new actors into the Democratic party, changing substantially both the procedures and the claims of the national party. The mobilization of social conservatives in opposition to this national party led to a new Republican coalition.[16]

Although the movement of activists into the party system affected both parties, the movementization of the Democratic Party was less dramatic than that of the GOP, because, as Matt Grossman and David Hopkins argue, the Democrats remain a coalition of interest groups to which new movement actors were incrementally added, while the Republicans transformed into an ideological party.[17] Mobilized by activists on the ground and egged on by cultural figures like the Reverend Jerry Falwell, the ideologization of the GOP culminated in the Tea Party's entry into that party's Congressional delegation. It provided a model for the current infiltration of the Trump movement into the same party, producing a powerful coalition based on racial resentment, economic nationalism, neoliberalism, and nostalgia for a past in which white, male Protestants dominated the country (Parker and Barreto 2013). Rather than a sudden transformation, the Trumpian movement built on the segregationist backlash, the intraparty reforms, and the activist base that had been building in the GOP for decades.

The Trumpian Movement

Why does it seem important to insist that Trump is the leader of a social movement? The reason is that, as in the case of most populist leaders, the quality of his support is personal and not policy based, charismatic and not routinized, mobilizational and not governance oriented.[18] "More than other candidates," writes Arlie Russell Hochschild, "Donald Trump fits the classic description of a charismatic leader, as Weber defined it . . . . Trump offers himself . . . as the *personal messenger* of his followers" (Hochschild 2016: 687). This means that discordant elements in his campaign appeals are of little importance to his followers: "Followers forgive, one after another, flagrant flaws in such a 'messenger', because he is their messenger and he recognizes their suppressed, as they see it, deep story" (Hochschild 2016: 687). This means that Trump-as-movement-leader can say or do just about anything without risking the loss of his base. But it also means that Trump-as-president has to *service* his movement base. This—and not his impetuosity—is responsible for his periodic outbursts and vulgar rants against political opponents, minority groups, and foreign powers.

Although the press and the Republicans have made much of Trump's early morning tweets, these rants and outbursts are not random: As in all populist movements, they revolve around the concepts of the "pure" people and the corrupt elite (Mudde 2004; Mudde and Kaltvasser 2012). But *right-wing* populism exhibits a third cornerstone, as David Snow and Colin Bernatsky argue: Drawing on the work of John Judis (2016), they point to the populist's need for a suspect nonelite group that functions as a "negative Other, that they use to frame the obstacles to the 'pure' or 'true' peoples' interests and rightful standing" (Judis 2016:15; Snow and Bernatsky 2017: 3). As they write;

> . . . the anti-pluralism of right-wing populism takes the form of a Manichean project – that is, a dualistic worldview that provides clear contrast conceptions between "the People" and "the negative Others," and some configuration of enabling elites. (Snow and Bernatsky 2017: 4)

In Mussolini's Italy, it was the proletariat of city and countryside that served as this "negative Other" for the future Duce; in Europe today it is Muslims and immigrants from Africa and the Middle East who fill that role; and in Trump's movement it is Muslims, illegal Mexican immigrants, and nonpatriotic African-Americans. Although the first two had the greatest shock value during Trump's election campaign, his attack on the Black Lives Matter (BLM) movement during the campaign and his rants against black football players "taking the knee" in protest against police violence were the "superfluous people" in the Trump movement's eschatology.

Trump brought into the Republican coalition new actors and more radical tendencies—such as the nationalist wing led by Steven Bannon and Breitbart News.[19] Less radical are the traditional Wall Street conservatives with whom he filled his government and the military technocrats who are sometimes described as the only "adults" in the room. Unlike other authoritarian leaders who came to power with their own organizational structures (see Roberts's contribution, Chapter 2) Trump appropriated structures that others built—such as Breitbart News, which was the launching pad for the Bannon faction of his coalition. What puzzles observers was the weakness of the traditional Republican mainstream elite when faced by an intruder who was able to defeat a spectrum of its leaders in the election campaign.[20] This is a puzzle only if we forget that Trump built on a movement base that was already embedded at the grassroots of the Republican party and only needed a charismatic leader to become weaponized.

If Trump can be usefully seen as a movement leader who has mobilized a mass following with charismatic appeals that elide specific policy proposals, what does this mean for the Resistance? The argument of this chapter is that the Resistance has many of the properties of a "countermovement," using that term as David Meyer and Suzanne Staggenborg employed it in their landmark 1996 article. As I will argue in the fourth section, a countermovement has properties that are isomorphic with the characteristics of the movement it opposes, which both offers it political opportunities but also leaves it susceptible to major risks. Both opportunities and risks expand in periods of generalized disruption, which takes us to the cycle of contention that the Trump presidency triggered.

Cycles of Contention

An extraordinary wave of activism greeted the election of Donald Trump. In the Introduction, we already traced the enormous turnout for the Women's March the day after his Inauguration, and many of the chapters in this book demonstrate how widely his presidency has been contested. But is what we have seen since Trump's election a number of distinct streams of protest or has it cumulated into a "*cycle of contention*?"[21] After responding to that question, I examine three mechanisms that the Resistance has triggered, before turning to it as a countermovement, and to the costs and benefits of this status against the Trumpian movement.

As we learned from Hahrie Han and Michelle Oyakawa's chapter (Chapter 11), the Resistance is an aggregate of a number of different streams of contention. As they write,

> The Women's March on Washington was just one of many new resist-
> ance groups that emerged in the wake of the 2016 election . . . . From
> groups like Swing Left to Flippable, Wall of Us to Indivisible, and
> People Power to Daily Action, the countermobilization spawned a host
> of new networks, apps, and organizations.[22]

Trump's election also galvanized *existing* organizations into action, increasing their donor and membership bases and—in some cases, like the American Civil Liberties Union (ACLU)—leading them to shift into more grassroots forms of activity.[23] The combination of newly formed and energized existing organizations is typical of cycles of contention, like the Italian one that emerged in the 1960s (della Porta and Tarrow 1986) or the American Civil Rights movement in the same decade (McAdam 1999 [1981]).

There have been other cycles of contention in the United States in the past. Think of the anti–Vietnam War movement, when a loosely organized coalitional movement zeroed in from many directions on an administration that continued—and indeed, intensified—an unpopular war in the face of widespread opposition. There were internal differences and even conflicts in that movement, but the war making of the Johnson and then the Nixon administration provided a focal point that overcame differences of ideology and tactics among the various branches of the movement.

But the new maelstrom of movement activity against the Trump administration raises a fundamental question: Given the vast range and diversity of the Resistance, is it simply an archipelago of loosely progressive groups or is it an integrated cycle of contention? I use this term to indicate a sequence of heightened conflict across the social system, with a rapid diffusion of collective action from more-mobilized to less-mobilized sectors, a rapid pace of innovation in the forms of contention employed, the creation of new or transformed collective action frames, and a combination of organized and unorganized participation.

The anti-Trump resistance has shown all five properties of a unified cycle:

- *Heightened conflict across the social system*: Soon after Trump's election, hundreds of thousands of ordinary people went out into the cold to protest—none more dramatically than the US Army veterans who rallied to the side of the Native Americans protesting against the Dakota Access pipeline on their ancestral land. In more traditional groups, like the ACLU, both membership and donations grew rapidly, as newer groups—like Indivisible—spread rapidly across the country, as Brooker's chapter (Chapter 8) demonstrates.
- *Rapid diffusion of collective action*: A broader range of claims grew on the part of women's groups that were originally mobilized against Trump's abuse of women in the great January 21 Women's March, as we learned from Fisher's survey (see Chapter 5).[24] The exposure of the sexual abuses by producer Harvey Weinstein in late 2017 not only diffused widely to many leading figures in entertainment and politics; it was fed by the enthusiasm among many young women who had been politicized by the Resistance:
- *Innovation in the forms of contention*: When Trump was first elected, the normally slow-moving and legalistic ACLU responded as it always has: "We'll see you in court," they warned the new administration. But by early March the ACLU had launched a "People Power" network in what it called "Freedom Cities" to resist the new administration.[25]
- *The creation of new or transformed forms of protest*: Think of the former Congressional staffers who published *Indivisible, A Practical Guide for Resisting the Trump Agenda*.[26] What began as a "how-to" guide turned into a network,

which uses social media and email communications to highlight innovations and reforms in local, state, and national government.[27]

- *A combination of organized and unorganized participation:*[28] The Town Hall protests against the Republican health care repeal plans brought together experienced activists with thousands of ordinary people following a model that had been used by the Tea Party movement, as we also saw in Brooker's chapter.

The fact that the many voices in the Resistance were raised simultaneously does not mean that they created a unified movement: On the contrary, their composition and their goals were partly distinct; they varied in how they framed their messages and in the forms of contention they employed; and they ranged from those that were part of the institutional landscape to those that were outside of institutional politics. But unlike that earlier period, they responded to an insurgent movement with a charismatic—if deeply flawed—leader, his own broad support base, and the instruments of state power he had at his disposal. This led to a broad, confused and constantly shifting cycle of contention that offered both opportunities and risks to the Resistance and to American democracy.

Against these challenges, the Resistance has been accelerated by three major mechanisms—*amplification, spillover,* and *scale shift.*

Amplification

By "amplification," Meyer and Staggenborg meant efforts that "symbolize a whole set of values and behaviors" and "are likely to threaten a broader range of constituencies who will be attracted to countermovement action for different reasons."[29] Amplification can have both positive and negative effects. On the one hand, the amplification of issues into more general value-based campaigns is likely to attract the support of a broader range of constituencies and thus increase the range of the countermovement's appeals. We saw such amplification when African American, Hispanic, and Asian Pacific caucus members of Congress joined the ACLU in expressing alarm at the rise in hate crimes between 2016 and 2017.[30] Such alliances are not new, but this was the first time that they were openly linked to a President's divisive rhetoric.

On the other hand, amplification can lead to radicalization and even to mutual violence between movement and countermovement. As was argued about an earlier cycle of contention in Italy in the 1960s and 1970s,[31] a mutual spiral of radicalization—especially when it is accompanied by violence—may not help the forces of resistance, which can find themselves the "unwanted children" of the institutional Left. When politics takes the form of violence, it is the Right that usually wins because it can rally the forces of order to its side.[32]

Spillover

"Social movements," write Meyer and Whittier, "are not distinct and self-contained; rather, they grow from and give birth to other movements, work in coalition with other movements, and influence each other indirectly through their effects on the larger cultural and political environment" (1994: 277). This loose coupling means that especially in periods of heightened contention, like the current cycle of contention, movements influence one another, existing movements are influenced by new ones, and newly formed ones build on older traditions.

The Resistance was not born in a vacuum. This means that new movement organizers learned from one another, picked up on frames and forms of action demonstrated by others, and affected the practices of these existing movements. Thus, as Brooker showed in Chapter 8, despite the vast ideological gap between the two organizations, Indivisible adopted many of the practices of the Tea Party from a half-decade earlier, especially the practice of invading town halls in the districts of Republican members of Congress during the struggle over Obamacare.

One of the most vibrant movements in existence when Donald Trump was elected was the Black Lives Matter group. Founded by three black women and diffused through social media in response to George Zimmerman's acquittal for the killing of black teenager Trayvon Martin in 2012, the organization grew rapidly after the police murder of Michael Brown in Ferguson, Missouri, in 2014 and the death of other African Americans from police violence. One dramatic indicator: "In the three weeks after Brown's death, #blacklivesmatter grew from about 200,000 tweets to over 12 million tweets" (Stout, Coulter, and Edwards 2017: 7).

Black Lives Matter was born as a single-issue movement, focusing primarily on the bias against black men in the criminal justice system. But after Donald Trump's campaign, with its racially inflected rallies and its racist dog-whistles, the organization began to expand the range of its interests. On the local level, there was a natural spillover from the issue of police violence to incarceration, when Patrisse Khan-Cullors, one of the founders of BLM, joined with more than 30 other organizations in Los Angeles to launch "JusticeLA," a coalition organized to stop a proposed jail-expansion plan in Los Angeles County.[33] At the same time, at the national level, a coalition of nearly 30 BLM groups, known as the United Front, released a policy platform calling for comprehensive police and criminal justice reforms, economic investments in black communities, and the mobilization of black voters. The movement has been shifting its activities from a largely demonstration-based repertoire to one that combines public demonstrations with policy intervention.[34] Although it began with a narrow mission, BLM has begun to cooperate with cognate groups. For example, because so many refugees and Muslims are people of color, BLM has given increasing attention to the problems of immigrants under the heightened scrutiny by Immigration and Customs Enforcement (ICE) and other agencies.

Scale Shift

Closely related to amplification and spillover is the shift of scale of contention from its origins to either a higher or a lower level of the system (Tarrow and McAdam 2005). One of the major empirical features of cycles of contention is how rapidly conflicts shift from one scale to another. We saw this in the anti–Vietnam War movement when campus protests grew into a major "Moratorium" on the war in Washington, DC. Whereas ordinary diffusion moves laterally across geographic and social space, scale shift takes contention either to higher or to lower levels of the system where it can involve new groups of actors, different targets, and new performances that sometimes enter institutional politics but sometimes lead to violence.

The anti-Trump Resistance led to a downward scale shift almost immediately after the 2016 election when the President signed the refugee ban that left thousands of would-be immigrants stranded at airports around the country, as Dorf and Chu's chapter (Chapter 6) demonstrates. That threat fed into a broader movement to expand the number of "sanctuary" cities and states, in which municipal and state authorities passed measures to prevent law enforcement agencies from cooperating with federal ICE officers trying to identify and deport immigrants. Although the "airport" protests ended almost immediately, the sanctuary movement triggered a countermove by the Trump administration and Attorney General Jeff Sessions, who threatened to deprive sanctuary cities of federal block grants—thus shifting the scale of the conflict back to the national level, and ultimately to the courts.[35]

Scale shift can lead movements from contentious to more institutional forms of action—as in the case of the airport protests against the refugee ban—but it can also lead to more contentious—and even to violent—forms of action. Thus Trump's racial taunts and denigration of Muslims fed into, and encouraged, the white nationalist movement to engage in public action, like the Charlottesville rally, which in turn attracted the opposition of antiracist groups and ultimately led to the killing of an antiracist demonstrator.[36] This takes us to the relationship between the Resistance and the Trumpian movement, in a spiral of movement–countermovement interaction.

Movement–Countermovement Interaction

In their much-cited study, Meyer and Staggenborg examined the relationship between movements and countermovements during earlier cycles of contention.[37] They defined a social movement as "collective challenges by people with common purposes and solidarity in sustained interaction with elites, opponents, and authorities." A countermovement they defined, simply, as "a movement that makes contrary claims simultaneously to those of the original movement."[38]

Earlier authors regarded countermovements as essentially reactionary and directed more at state and society than at the precursor movement, and indeed, the most important work on countermovements in the United States is about conservative movements.[39] But more recently, many authors have argued that a countermovement can be either progressive or reactionary and that its defining characteristic is that it is "dynamically engaged with and related to an oppositional movement." This chapter adopts the latter view, focusing on Meyer and Staggenborg's emphasis on interaction:

> Movements . . . have a "demonstration effect" for political countermovements—showing that collective action can effect (or resist) change in particular aspects of society. Movements thus create their own opposition, which sometimes takes countermovement form. Once a countermovement is mobilized, movement and countermovement react to one another.[40]

Movement–countermovement interaction can begin in the policy realm and in the streets, but it often spreads to the cultural realm. The politicization of the media in the wake of Trump's "fake news" rants has intensified this cultural conflict, but it goes back to the "culture wars" of the 1990s and beyond (Rodgers 2011: chap. 5). The result has been an intensification of the "silo" theory of the public's media exposure: Viewers of Fox News and readers of Breitbart News would not be caught dead watching MSNBC or watching Politico on their iPads and vice versa. An example: When the *Washington Post* broke the story that Roy Moore, who was then running for the Senate, had sexually attacked teenagers, most Republican voters in Alabama were convinced that the story was "fake news."

In their article, Meyer and Staggenborg list three conditions that promote the rise of countermovements: first, that the movement [it opposes] shows signs of success; second, that the interests of some populations are threatened by movement goals; and, third, that political allies are available to aid oppositional mobilization. Let us briefly see how each of these claims applies to the current situation in the United States.

Movement Success: Trump's startling electoral success was certainly a triumph for the movement he had stimulated, although it was not an unalloyed triumph. At the end of the first year of his presidency, Trump's legislative successes were modest, although his efforts to unravel the administrative state have been quietly devastating.[41] Even the tax reform of December 2017 was not an unmixed blessing: On the one hand, Congress handed a trillion-dollar benefit to corporations and rich people in general; but, on the other hand, among the victims of the "reform" are middle-class families, many of whom voted for Trump in the illusion that he would take the burden of "big government" off their backs. As the 2018 Congressional elections approached, the Democratic Party readied its appeal to voters who had yet to see what benefits Trump's "Make America Great Again" slogan had brought them.

In terms of popular politics, the modest level of participation in Trump's Inauguration, compared with the massive turnout for the Women's March the next day, was an early sign of the limits of his popularity. Not only that: Although Republicans won a series of by-elections in the months after the election, many Republican voters outside his populist base—especially middle-class women—showed signs of falling away.[42] In Congress, despite holding a majority of seats in both houses, the GOP was able to accomplish only a few of its policy goals. Leaving aside the tax reform program, Trump's major victories have been in larding the federal court system with conservative appointees and in quietly revoking regulations that were the skeleton of the administrative state.[43] These swift changes mainly served the interests of his business base but had little or no resonance in public opinion. But as his first year in office gave way to the second, Trump's base began to ebb, even among white Evangelicals, whose support dropped from 78% in February 2017 to 61% in December, while his approval rating among the electorate as a whole remained in the mid-30s.[44]

Yet Trump's populist base remained loyal through the first year of his administration. Reasons for this are not hard to find. First, few in his base closely followed the twists and turns of national politics. Second, Trump was careful to throw them nationalist and religious bones from time to time.[45] And third, for reasons that had little to do with his policy moves, the American economy remained robust, denying the Democrats the campaign claim that Trump's economic nationalism had hurt ordinary consumers. Most important, Trump held onto much of his populist base, not because of what he had done for them, but because of racial resentment, of the vague feeling that "he means what he says," and because the Democratic Party is widely seen as a party that has been captured by identity politics—and by the interests of feminists, Hispanics, and African Americans.

Threatened Interests: During his first year in office, the Trump presidency affected the interests and values of vast sectors of the population, from African Americans to Latinos, women, businesses dependent on international trade agreements, foreign policy elites, and the lesbian, gay, bisexual, and transgender (LGBT) community. Each major policy initiative—from the refugee ban to the Affordable Care Act (e.g., "Obamacare") to tax reform has made clear that Trump's programs are a powerful threat to many Americans.

The debate over the repeal of Obamacare was archetypical in this respect. As the conflict in Congress and in the country progressed, Republicans saw an opening to demolish the signature policy success of their most hated enemy, but many Americans, who had come to the issue with instinctive antigovernment instincts, began to understand that there would be real costs to themselves if Obamacare were repealed.[46]

Less dramatic, but possibly more important in the long run, many of Trump's political moves have had the effect of splitting parts of his base from other parts of his constituency. Although the refugee ban and the attacks on African American athletes who "took a knee" to protest antiblack police violence were deeply satisfying to his base, other initiatives—like his rejection of the Pacific Trade Treaty—left important parts of his business supporters uneasy or opposed. Archetypical was the fight over tax reform in late 2017: Whereas large corporations and the richest Americans salivated at the prospect of lower tax rates, the National Association of Realtors—who stood to lose at the prospect of the loss of tax deductions on home purchases—blanketed the country with ads demanding the revision of the bill.

The most divisive issues between Trump's base and ordinary Republican voters were "cultural": When, in November 2017, a wave of exposures of sexual harassment triggered the denunciation of Alabama Senate candidate Roy Moore, who was accused by a number of women of sexual advances when they were teenagers, Trump's base was divided. The Bannon Wing of his coalition was unmoved by the claims of Moore's accusers, but Republicans in Congress were appalled and voters in Alabama defected in droves from the Republican Party. Trump's support of Moore's candidacy when he himself was being accused of unwanted sexual advances left many Republican voters repulsed.

Available Allies: The "demonstration effect" that Meyer and Staggenborg write about had contradictory results for countermovement capacity to recruit allies.

On the one hand, Trump provided a focal point for various strands of the Resistance, which helped in the formation of alliances, as many of the chapters in this book have shown. For example, his administration's reduction in the size of western national monuments brought together Native American tribes with environmental activists. His racial outbursts may have helped to advance black–brown collaborations that were already taking shape before his election.[47] The conflict over Deferred Action for Childhood Arrivals (DACA) brought together immigrant rights groups with representatives of big business who employ many of the young people who were brought to America as children.[48] His opposition to multilateralism created commonalities between principled supporters of climate change agreements with those who profit from international trade compacts.

On the other hand, Trump's propensity to leap from one issue to another at breakneck speed makes it difficult for Resistance leaders to stay focused on their central issues. Second, it sets the parameters for forms of collective action for which a countermovement may not be prepared. For example, Trump's anti-immigrant order during the first week of his presidency led to the lawyers' airport protests examined by Dorf and Chu in Chapter 6; but this was not a comfortable venue for the immigrant rights community that was unable to win in court what Trump's lieutenants had taken away through administrative decrees.[49]

A particular example of movement–countermovement interaction took place between the BLM movement and what came to be called "Blue Lives Matter"—a movement to support the police that was founded in 2016.[50] When the killing of Trayvon Martin and Michael Brown led to no significant sanctioning of those responsible for their murders, some of the responses in the black community were violent, leading to the murder of police officers in both New York and Texas. In response, the Blue Lives Matter movement was created. Rallies were held to support the police around the country, and state legislators in 45 states proposed bills designed to assure police that they had the full support of the public.[51]

In a typical sequence of movement–countermovement interaction, the ACLU stepped in to oppose these bills, arguing that hate crimes are defined as attacks on particular ethnic or racial groups and not against professional groups like the police. In response, conservative media came to the defense of the police and the issue was raised to the level of presidential politics when Trump defended the police in his acceptance speech for the Republican nomination. "An attack on law enforcement is an attack on all Americans," he said. "I have a message to every last person threatening the peace on our streets and the safety of our police: When I take the oath of office next year, I will restore law and order to our country."[52]

Will the various strands of contention we have seen in the Resistance congeal into an integrated movement? Much depends on the intersection of different forms of activism and in how new and old groups manage their relations. When Dana Fisher extended her survey from the Woman's March to the People's Climate March, the results showed hints of intersectionality. She writes that

> . . . people who were motivated by Racial Justice to participate in the March for Science reported being motivated by LGBTQ issues and Politic Brutality; and people who were motivated by Racial Justice to

participate in the People's Climate March reported being motivated by Equality, Police Brutality, Religion and Social Welfare.[53]

But despite its outsized focal point in the person of Donald Trump and the evidence of "intersectionality" that we have assembled in this book, the anti-Trump Resistance is far from integrated. The voices within it range from the often-violent anarchist fringe in places like Berkeley and Portland, to former Sanders supporters who are convinced that the Democratic Party is little better than its Republican competitors, to the new groups—many of them organized on line—described by Han and Oyakawa in Chapter 11, to more moderate groups like Move-On and Organizing For Change.

The greatest danger to the Resistance is if it splinters between its institutional and noninstitutional sectors. Much of the energy of these movements comes from young people and former Sanders supporters who find it hard to work with Democrats who are accustomed to working within the institutions of government. But the electoral successes of moderate Democrats in Virginia and Alabama suggest that the party can win only when it attracts a broad following, ranging from its solid African American base to suburban middle-class Independents turned off by the volatility of the Trump phenomenon to working-class voters disenchanted with Trump's false populism since his election.

The Dynamics of Interaction

Although cycles of contention tend to begin in the same way wherever they occur, they tend to end differently, based on the actions taken by "earlier risers," the responses of authorities, and the groups that join in after the cycle has begun. Conflicts touched off by early risers—like the activists who organized the Women's March on January 21, 2017—escalate into a cycle of contention when political opportunities are opened and when their claims resonate with those of significant others. In true cycles, coalitions form among disparate actors, leading to spirals of contention across society.[54]

But once opened up, cycles of contention do not all follow the same trajectories. Opportunities and threats that affect early risers may not look the same to those who follow, if only because the early risers change the contexts in which their successors arise. Those who follow the early risers may have different and sometimes orthogonal agendas than their predecessors and do not always have the resources to succeed—if only because authorities are now more prepared to counter their predecessors. As for the authorities themselves, they are not always unified in the mix of repression and facilitation that they employ.

In other words, such periods cannot be studied *en bloc*, as if they were single movements, and as if elites and authorities responded to all their components with identical mixtures of repression and support. Especially given the unpredictable character of the chief antagonist of the Resistance—Donald Trump—in charting the trajectory of the Resistance we can do no more than indicate possible directions, alignments, and outcomes. Here are some of these possibilities.

Conclusions

Amid the confusing clash of movements and countermovements during the year after Donald Trump came to power, one possible outcome was the emergence of a potentially new political alignment structure. Where the Republican Party after the 1960s developed an ideological project around its new conservatism and the Democrats remained a collection of disparate interests, the shoe may now be on the other foot. On the one hand, Trump inserted a new and shriller nationalist wing into the GOP, one that overlaps with the party's more traditional business constituency. But that overlap is only partial: Whereas both wings of the Trump coalition oppose illegal immigration and would like to see the size of the government shrink, the traditional GOP was anti-Communist, internationalist, and believed in free trade. The newer nationalist wing is anxious to forge an alliance with Russia, is isolationist, and is leery of free trade.

In the first year of the Trump administration, the fight to end Obamacare, tax reform, and the conflict with North Korea held these wings of the party together, but Trump's unpopularity in the electorate, his foreign policy gyrations, and the party's electoral losses produced cleavages between its nationalist and its traditional conservative wings.

Moreover, there is a third, less-visible element in the Trumpian coalition that had not yet been heard from after the first year of the Trump administration—his populist base. Donald Trump won the presidency with the votes of many lower- and middle-class white Americans who believed that his message would return them and people like them to power. As Trump's agenda tilts heavily toward the business class from which he came, will his populist base continue in its blind faith that he will represent their interests? Thus far, he has "drained" the Washington swamp of some of its elements, only to fill it with people from his own class who lack the expert knowledge of government and policy that comes with experience. The lowering of the level of political discourse and his verbal attacks on minorities have offered symbolic fuel to Trump's base, but if palpable benefits do not accrue to its members it may shrink, if not actually defect to, the opposition.

Conversely, in the wake of its momentous defeat in the 2016 elections and spurred by the challenge of the Sanders wing internally and the Resistance externally, the Democrats are trying to recapture some of their lost appeal to the white working class while convincing African Americans and Latinos to turn out in greater numbers for the party in future elections than they did for Hillary Clinton. This will not be easy, but even more difficult will be bridging the gap between the party's moderate leadership and a Resistance that is angry, militant, and mobilized.

This is a Resistance, as was argued in the Introduction to this book, that grew partly out of the insurgent Sanders campaign, partly out of the moribund Occupy movement, and partly out of a number of new groups that hover on the boundaries between institutional and noninstitutional politics. This means that acquiring the unity to mount an effective opposition will be difficult. Although some of these groups have historical ties with the Democrats, others are either too new to have forged such ties or are still smarting from the indifference of the mainstream Democratic Party to their aims. Whereas some of them focus on rule of law issues and others see Trumpism fundamentally as a capitalist take-over of American government, many are single-issue groups that mobilize only when Trump's actions seem to threaten their sectoral claims.

The Democrats have begun to make efforts to coordinate with at least the most amenable of these groups, but many of them appear to be asking, "Why co-operate with a party that allowed itself to be taken over by a centrist like Clinton, failed to give Bernie Sanders the political space he won in the primaries, and allowed important parts of the party's base to be lured away by a right-wing pop-ulist demagogue?"

There are many answers to this question, and elaborating on them would take us into the realm of ideological polemics. But there is one answer that previous studies of cycles of contention seem to offer: When the struggle is no longer over policy but over the survival of democracy, alliances are better than no alliances, and actors who would be ideological opponents in quieter times emerge as nec-essary allies in times of a danger to democracy.

Recall the cautionary tale at the beginning of this chapter: In 1919, Benito Mussolini assembled a coalition of former soldiers, rural thugs, small-farm owners, and the urban middle class who were terrified by fear of Bolshevism and angry at the excesses of the proletarian left. In opposition, liberal conservatives, centrist Catholics, Socialists, and Communists spent more energy fighting each other than holding off Mussolini. This allowed the future dictator to come to power by parliamentary means. Once in power, the future Duce immediately set about stripping away constitutional protections, corrupted the electoral system, and ultimately suborned some of his opponents, arrested others, and drove still others into exile.

We are not yet at the level of democratic fragility of Italy at the end of World War I.[55] But there are signs—for example, Trump's "attacks on the media and his indifference to the rule of law—that reveal him as a serious danger to democracy. Groups in the Resistance that focus on his outrageous tweets, on his indifference to the future of the planet, and on his giveaways to Wall Street financiers are dealing with serious—but partial—issues. The real question, as Suzanne Mettler writes, is "whether the relationship between government and ordinary citizens may be changing in ways that could undermine liberal democracy."[56] Only ordinary citizens, acting through the groups—both new and established—that make up the Resistance, can unite in defense of democracy.

Acknowledgments: I am grateful to Dana Fisher for allowing me to reproduce her original research findings, and to Eitan Alimi, Glenn Altschuler, Donatella della Porta, Mike Dorf, Doug McAdam, Steve Hellman, Jeff Isaac, David Meyer, Aziz Rana, Ken Roberts, and Susan Tarrow for commenting on a draft of this chapter.

Generational Spillover in the Resistance to Trump

NANCY WHITTIER

On January 21, 2017, I attended the Women's March in Boston with seven other people. We were three people in our 50s and one in his 30s who had been activists before the election, one in her 40s who had not, and three young teenagers. At a local sign-making party before the March, there was a similar mix of people from late childhood through their 60s, including those who had participated in protest before the election and those who had not, and signs that focused on climate change, reproductive rights, lesbian, gay, bisexual, and transgender (LGBT) issues, racism, sexual assault, the promotion of democracy, immigration, and many other issues. This is typical of the generational dynamics of the Resistance to Trump, which is diverse in its age composition and has, to an unusual degree, brought together members of different generations in the same mass protests and organizations (Fisher et al. 2017; also see Berry and Chenoweth's Chapter 3).

The anti-Trump Resistance that mushroomed after November 8, 2017, has roots in long-lived social movements around gender, class, race, and sexuality and in more recent immigrants' rights, Black Lives Matter, Occupy, Standing Rock, and anti–sexual assault movements. These organizations have also been prominent in the Resistance. These include activists who were politicized in the progressive movements of the 1960s–1970s, and individuals and organizations who sustained peace, civil liberties, antiracist, LGBT, and feminist movements throughout the slower years of the 1980s, 1990s, and 2000s.[1]

Existing organizations, such as the American Civil Liberties Union (ACLU), Southern Poverty Law Center (SPLC), League of Women Voters, MoveOn, and many others, have seen an upsurge in membership since Trump's election. At the same time, mass protests like the Women's Marches and mobilization efforts by new groups like Indivisible have drawn in people of all ages who were not previously part of social movements (see Brooker, Chapter 8).

As a result, the Resistance contains individuals from multiple generations who encounter each other at protests, in community meetings, online, and in old and new organizations. There are important differences between mostly younger activists, politicized in recent years, and older, experienced activists. However, there are also important differences between younger experienced activists and people of all ages first entering activism after the election. In other words, there are two kinds of generational differences: between older and younger participants and between veterans and newcomers.

In this chapter, I argue that the generational dynamics of the Resistance are central to the transmission of ideas and skills from prior social movements to the emerging new cycle of contention. The cross-generational mass mobilization of the Resistance provides an unusually large field for potential spillover from earlier waves of protest to this one. In addition, generational dynamics, such as turnover in leadership and conflicts between cohorts with different points of view, contribute to the rise of novel tactics, ideologies, frames, and organizational forms as social movements adapt to new political and cultural contexts. In other words, the turnover and interplay of political generations shapes movement continuity across protest cycles and influences how new protest cycles become different from prior protest. For the anti-Trump Resistance, these dynamics will shape how it resembles and differs from prior waves of protest.

There are three elements of theory on political generations that are important for understanding their impact on movements. First, political generations have different perspectives, shaped by the different contexts in which they come of age and become politicized. As cohorts turn over, change results in organizations, movements, and society more generally (Whittier 1997). Second, continuity in social movements results from how ideas, frames, tactics, organizational structure, and so forth, are transmitted across time. This spillover includes transmission across organizations, constituencies, or generations (Meyer and Whittier 1994). Third, political generations are not simply age groups, but can also form based on the time of entry into a social movement. Individuals of different ages can share a similar perspective if they first become activists in the same time and place (Whittier 1995).

This paper focuses on *generational spillover* in the context of the Resistance to Trump. I use theory about political generations and social movement spillover, in combination with emerging evidence about generational dynamics in the Resistance, to sketch out how generational spillover is proceeding and suggest likely paths for generational dynamics as it progresses over time. The influx of activists after the election brought in participants across generations and, as a result, increased opportunities for generational interaction. This was an unusual and dynamic mixture, with especially broad and robust cross-generational participation. It produced uniquely heightened possibilities for both connection and conflict across generations.

The paper proceeds as follows: First, I outline theoretical frameworks for understanding political generations and movement spillover. Second, I describe the characteristics of the major generations. Third, I show that the pre-Trump movements did not entail wide scale cross-generational participation. Fourth, I show that the anti-Trump Resistance includes unusually large amounts of cross-generational participation, both across age and among movement veterans and newcomers. Finally, I show how transmission and conflict among political generations is unfolding in the Resistance and sketch its implications for the movement going forward.

Understanding Generational Spillover

Much writing about generations focuses on broad age cohorts, such as Baby Boomers. In contrast, political generations are subsets of age cohorts that are shaped by specific historical circumstances to have a worldview that is distinct from that of other political generations (Mannheim 1952 [1928]). Mannheim argued that political generations form when external events catalyze a new worldview in the cohort coming of age in that context. New political generations form when external circumstances shift significantly. When the rate of external change is slow, the age cohorts that share a perspective are wider; when it is rapid, unified cohorts are smaller. For example, rapid change in the women's movement and the social organization of gender between the late 1960s and the 1980s produced several "micro-cohorts," distinct cohorts of only a few years' difference (Whittier 1995). The experience and worldview of the feminists who founded the movement's early organizations were quite different from the experiences and perspective of the feminists who joined those large, thriving organizations a few years later.

Individuals' membership in a political generation or micro-cohort is not defined solely by age but is also shaped by the time of politicization. For example, activists who entered the thriving and established women's movement in 1975 shared experiences with each other—and different experiences from those who entered in 1970 or 1980—regardless of age. In some ways, the politics of a 40-year-old who became a feminist in 1975 had more in common with those of a 20-year-old who became a feminist in the same year than with a 40-year-old who had become a feminist in 1965. They learned the same ideology and collective identity, experienced the same organizations and tactics as defining the movement, read the same publications, and participated in the same movement community contexts. All this contributes to a similar orientation toward the movement and the larger world.

The differences between micro-cohorts who entered the women's movement in 1970 or 1975 or 1980 were important in dynamics then. They became less salient over time as all of the cohorts had more in common with each other than with much younger generations in the 1990s and later, who had no exposure to the defining contexts of the second-wave women's movement. In addition, age matters. Experiencing, for example, the same forms of gender discrimination and life-course events (employment, marriage, childbearing, retirement) marks age cohorts. These distinctions crosscut each other. Activists of the Baby Boom generation share some commonalities with each other and differences from Millennials.

Longitudinal research on political generations consistently shows that their worldviews persist across the life course. Considerable research has documented this persistence for participants in the movements on the Left and the Right of the 1960s and 1970s (see Whittier 1997). Although the way they express them varies over time, political generations tend to remain faithful to the collective identity and political sensibilities that they form when they are initially politicized through movement participation. Because multiple generations or age cohorts coexist at any given time, their different perspectives contribute to dissent and segmentation within social movements. The goals, frames, collective identities, and other elements that one cohort takes for granted as correct, "progressive," or "feminist" are likely to differ from what other cohorts take for granted. Jo Reger (2012) has shown that local movement communities that contain more cross-generational interaction actually tend toward less generational conflict, whereas in locales with little cross-generational interaction, activists define themselves in contrast to imagined older generations.

Considering political generations helps us understand central questions about how social movements both persist and change over time. Different movements affect each other through processes of social movement spillover (Meyer and Whittier 1994). Contemporaneous movements influence each other; for example, the immigrant rights' movement may influence how Black Lives Matter conceptualizes racism (or vice versa). More important for our purposes, movements influence their successors across time: Earlier waves of activism affect later waves. They pass on their perspective and skills through direct contact among organizations, movement community, and personnel. In addition, as one wave of a movement produces social change, subsequent cohorts come of age in that new context and thus see the world and their priorities as a movement differently from their predecessors (Staggenborg 1995). As a result, goals, frames, strategy, tactics, and collective identity change over time. Spillover across generations of protest waves is thus rarely a matter of straightforward transmission, but rather a matter of both cross-generational influence and generational difference and conflict.

This process is what I am calling *generational spillover*: the interaction among coexisting and different political generations, with mutual influence, difference, and conflict. Generational spillover requires contacts across different political generations. Anti-Trump organizing is unusual in that large numbers of members of multiple political generations are participating simultaneously, often in the same protests, organizations, and social movement communities. This creates heightened possibilities for cross-generational spillover, but also for conflict. The presence of diverse generations in one movement increase the frames, tactics, and organizational experiences that activists can draw on, as Berry and Chenoweth (Chapter 3) point out regarding other kinds of movement diversity. Generational spillover has two main mechanisms: informal interaction in social movement communities, organizations, or protests; and deliberate training and mentoring. It can occur in both directions; that is, newer generations can influence older ones as well as the reverse. Generational conflict can occur in any of these contexts.

To understand generational spillover in the Resistance, I briefly answer the following questions: What ages have organized and participated in it thus far? How does this differ from the pre-Trump era? What kind of participation has emerged from novice activists of any age and from both younger and older experienced activists? What are the perspectives expressed by different political generations, and to what degree do they differ? What deliberate attempts at transmission across political generations are occurring, and what kind of generational conflict exists?

Generational Characteristics

In this section, I use the available data to outline the differences among generations. Specifically, I discuss the cultural and political contexts that shaped each political generation, their opinions about Trump and progressive issues, the key characteristics of their generational perspective, and their biographical availability for participation. I follow the Pew Center's definitions of generations, distinguishing among political generations drawn from Baby Boomers (born between 1946 and 1964), Generation X (born between 1965 and 1980), and Millennials (born between 1981 and 1996). I distinguish between older Millennials born between 1981 and 1990 and younger Millennials born between 1991 and 1998, and older Generation X (born between about 1965 and 1972) and younger Generation X (both between 1973 and 1980). These dividing years are arbitrary, of course; people born in the late 1970s and early 1980s have more in common with each other than with members of their official generation who were born much earlier or later.

Millennials

Millennials, born between 1981 and 1996, were ages 21–36 in 2017. Kotkin (2017) dubs Millennials "the screwed generation." They share a defining experience of economic precarity, including unemployment and underemployment despite high levels of education, made worse by student debt and their widespread belief in the future burden of climate change that would fall to them to address (World Economic Forum 2017). The 2008 economic downturn and foreclosure crisis were formative experiences even for those Millennials who were not personally affected by them. Even highly educated, middle-class, and white Millennials face poorer job prospects and a less economically secure future than their parents' generation did. Millennials' worldview is also marked by unique historical events. Although all generations cite the 9/11 attacks and the election of Barack Obama as among the most important historical events in their lifetime, Millennials are more likely than others to view the Iraq and Afghanistan Wars and the legalization of same-sex marriage as key events. Conversely, events that were among the most significant for older generations occurred before Millennials' births or in their early childhood, such as the end of the Cold War and the Gulf War (cited by Generation X), and the assassination of JFK, the Vietnam War, and the Apollo moon landing (cited by Baby Boomers) (Dean, Duggan, and Morin 2016). Although it is evident that Millennials could not be shaped by events they did not experience, the different significant events underscore how historical context forms political perspective.

Millennials' cultural context and upbringing also distinguish them from other generations. Widespread handwringing about Millennials as a coddled generation contradicts their economic vulnerability and worry about the future. This shapes a feeling of being unfairly denigrated and left to fix their elders' mistakes (D'Agostino 2017). A contradictory culture of social justice also shapes their perspective. They grew "up with social good embedded into their lives and school systems, thanks to boomer parents and teachers with programs such as AmeriCorps" and have become socially engaged adults (Millennial Impact Report 2017). Millennials have come of age in a time when cultural discourse downplays the ongoing significance of racism, sexism, heterosexism, and class inequality (Milkman 2017). They have seen the election of Barack Obama to the presidency, even as racial polarization grew. The legalization of same-sex marriage and declining homophobia—attitudinal shifts that began with

Generation X and intensified for Millennials—give them unique experiences with regard to sexual identity (Whittier 2016).

Given these formative experiences, it is not surprising that Millennials disapprove of President Trump's performance much more than other generations. As of June 2017, only 29% of Millennials approved, compared with 39% of Generation X, 45% of Baby Boomers, and 53% of those who were older. Patterns of party identification are similar, with Millennials having the highest percentage who identify as liberal or moderate Democrats, followed by Generation X, and then Baby Boomers (Pew 2017a).[2] Millennials' opinions on social and political issues also are to the left of other generations, with more identifying as liberal, supporting gay rights and same-sex marriage, the legalization of marijuana, immigrant rights, Black Lives Matter, and socialism.[3] Younger Millennials are also to the left of older Millennials on most opinion items.[4] In most cases, Generation X is the next most liberal generation, followed by Baby Boomers.[5] Despite criticism of college students for opposing free speech and supporting restrictions on hate speech, neither Millennial cohort had significantly higher support than other generations for restricting racist speech.[6]

Millennial activists—that is, the *political* generation drawn from Millennials—are predominantly college educated. Their level of education is similar to that of other political generations; however, some evidence suggests they are unemployed or underemployed (Milkman 2017). Twenty-seven percent of young Millennials participating in the Women's March had some university education (likely because they were still in college), and 67% of them and 91% of older Millennials had a university or graduate or professional degree. However, so did 94% of Generation X and 84% of Baby Boomers marchers.[7] Students, part-time or unemployed workers, and people without children have greater biographical availability for protest and are typically overrepresented in social movements (McAdam 1986).

What defining characteristics do Millennials as a political generation bring to the Resistance? Milkman (2017) argues that Millennial activists prior to the anti-Trump Resistance differed from other generations in their use of intersectional frames. Similarly, a small study of Millennials after the election found that they had a "distinct vernacular" and an openness to activism on "issues even when they lack a personal connection or direct benefit" (Millennial Impact Report 2017). Younger participants in the Women's March were more likely to cite women's rights, reproductive rights, and racial justice as motivations for attending.[8] It is not clear, however, how much their intersectional perspective distinguishes them from other political generations. Intersectional feminism became widespread in grassroots feminism by the 1990s, suggesting that Generation X activists are as likely to take an intersectional approach (Reger

2012, 2014a). The Women's Marches, with their intersectional approach, drew broad generational participation (Fisher et al. 2017).

Millennials are more oriented toward social media than other generations, although Generation X and Baby Boomers are also overwhelmingly engaged with social media, and Millennials' online practices vary considerably by class, gender, and race (Hargittai 2010). Millennials are more oriented toward on-line forms of activism or modes of recruitment. Their use of the micro-blogging platform Tumblr as a place to learn about and debate politics is generationally unique (Safronova 2014).

More distinctive may be Millennials' sense of political efficacy. Coming of age during Obama's presidency, while government and the law appeared to support racial, sexual, and gender equality, may have given some Millennials more trust in the state as a force for progressive change. Further, because Millennials (unlike Baby Boomers) have not participated in social movements that failed to bring about social transformation, they may have more optimism about the efficacy of activism than their elders. Unlike those of Generation X before them, Millennials' young adulthoods have been characterized by some of the largest and most militant uprisings in decades, with Occupy, Dreamers' organizing, Standing Rock protests, Black Lives Matter. Unlike Generation X, they have had extensive exposure to and opportunity to participate in social movements during their teens and young adulthoods. Since Trump's election, Millennials have been participating in more protests than they did before the election, contacting elected officials more and engaging more with local organizations around issues including reproductive health, immigration, Black Lives Matter, and Muslim rights (Millennial Impact Report 2017). They are engaging inside and outside the system and with movements whose constituencies of which they are and are not part.

Generation X

Members of Generation X, who were born between 1965 and 1980, were be-tween ages 37 and 52 in 2017. There is little research on Generation X, which is demographically smaller and falls between two larger and highly analyzed gen-erations (Pew 2014). Their perspective is shaped by the interaction of their life stage with large-scale events. The recession and foreclosure crisis of 2007–2009 hit Generation X especially hard, and they were less cushioned by savings than Baby Boomers were (Kotkin 2017). They came of age during the 1980s and 1990s in the wake of the movements of the 1960s and 1970s, with the rise of Reaganism and the neoliberal regime that followed. The historical events that they uniquely identify as important, the Gulf War, the fall of the Berlin Wall, and the end of the Cold War, occurred as they reached young adulthood (Dean, Duggan, and Morin 2016). These events underscore the dramatic shifts in the world order as they were coming of age.

As previously discussed, the attitudes of Generation X on most political issues are more liberal than those of Boomers and less liberal than those of Millennials. Generation X has less biographical availability than Millennials or Baby Boomers. They are no longer in college, are still in the workforce, and are likely to be raising children as well as caring for elderly relatives. Generation X respondents to Fisher et al.'s Women's March survey were almost all employed, at 90%; another 4% were stay-at-home parents. This contrasts with young Millennials, of whom 32% were students (and 3% unemployed); older Millennials, of whom 11% were students; and Baby Boomers, of whom 22% were retired.[9]

Not highly politicized in their youth, Generation X has long been contrasted with the Baby Boom generation that peopled the movements of the 1960s (Honan 2011). They have founded few movement organizations and were too young to participate in the 1960s–1970s protest cycle. In fact, this may be their most distinctive characteristic: They are a political generation that has historically joined, and risen to leadership in, many of the long-lived movement organizations that were founded by Baby Boomers. Many fewer members of Generation X as a whole had activist experience during their young adulthood, simply because there was little mass mobilization during the relevant years.

Participants in the anti-Trump Resistance, however, are likely disproportionately those who were activists previously, for whom one formative experience was being politically out of step with their age mates (see Whittier 1995: chap. 7). Fourteen percent of Generation X participants in the Women's March reported that their first protest experiences occurred before 1990 (when the youngest were 10 and the oldest 25) and another 33% had first protested between 1990 and 2009. Although younger Generation Xers may come to the anti-Trump Resistance from experience in the pre-Trump movements of 2008–2015, older ones came of age in the smaller and embattled Left of the 1990s and early 2000s or, as we will see, in institutional Democratic politics. Many other Generation Xers mobilizing against Trump have no previous activist experience and are distinct from their experienced age mates.

Baby Boomers

Born between 1946 and 1964, Baby Boomers were between the ages of 53 and 71 in 2017. The leaders of the civil rights, student, antiwar, antinuclear, women's, and LGBT movements of the 1960s and 1970s were almost all Boomers or older, but activists were never more than a minority of the generation (Klatch 1999). The Baby Boomer political generation includes many people who were politicized in the 1960s and 1970s and remained committed to social and political change but over time put their commitments into practice primarily through work and the ways they structured personal and family relationships (McAdam 1999; Whitter 1995). Now, as work and family responsibilities decrease, they are able to return to more direct forms of social movement participation. The biographical availability that comes with age is unique to Baby Boomers because they enjoy a longer life span in better health than previous generations.

Unlike Generation Xers, Baby Boomers had extensive exposure to mass movements in their youth and are thus less likely to be encountering left politics for the first time. The frames used by movements founded and staffed by Baby Boomers became master frames for decades of mobilization, around civil rights, feminism, peace, and other issues, and their organizations and tactical repertoires have defined progressive activism. From longitudinal studies of activists, Boomers overall likely continue to adhere to similar views of the issues (Whittier 1997). These frames remain important in the anti-Trump Resistance, with its emphasis on women's rights, reproductive rights, antiracism, and environmental protection. But as I discuss later, other frames for these issues are also emerging.

The Pre-Trump Era: Millennial Movements?

An increase in movement activity already was underway before Trump's election, with new organizations, campaigns, and frames emerging in the late 2000s. These included the Occupy movement, Black Lives Matter, Dreamers' activism around immigration, the Standing Rock pipeline protests, and activism against sexual assault and harassment on college campuses. These campaigns were organized by younger activists, mostly without prior movement experience, including substantial numbers of younger members of Generation X as well as Millennials. As Milkman (2017) points out, Dreamers and activists against sexual assault on college campuses organized specifically around a Millennial age cohort.[10] The initial organizers of Black Lives Matter were older Millennials, now in their early to mid-30s (Garza 2014).[11] Although Milkman (2017) says that Occupiers were "mostly young people," 60% of actively involved respondents to her survey of Occupy protesters were over 30. In other words, the "young" included younger Generation X members, then in their 30s, as well as older Millennials, then in their 20s (Captain 2011; Milkman, Luce, and Lewis 2013). Finally, young Millennials, many in their teens and early twenties, initiated the antipipeline protests at Standing Rock, but the movement grew to include all ages, including multiple generations of families (Elbein 2017; Enzinna 2017; Gauthier 2016).

These movements departed from long-standing social movement organizations that were energized by Baby Boomer and older Generation X movement veterans. In all of these campaigns, Millennials and young Generation X members sparked new frames and tactics, although older generations also participated. Consistent with this, Fisher et al.'s survey of the Washington, DC, Women's March shows that around half of Millennials had attended two or more protests in the past 5 years. This compares with around one-third of Generation Xers and Baby Boomers.[12]

In contrast, older, experienced activists staffed long-lived organizations, often founded in the 1960s–1970s wave of protest or even before. Some of these organizations, such as the National Organization for Women (NOW), the National Association for the Advancement of Colored People (NAACP), NARAL ProChoice America, and the National Gay and Lesbian Task Force, were professionalized, bureaucratic, and active in lobbying for state and federal policies. Others, such as local peace groups, were less professionalized, but nevertheless primarily the domain of veteran activists. Although some long-standing organizations made concerted efforts to bring in younger activists—through dedicated programming, internships, campus outreach, and the like—such efforts were not especially successful (Reger 2014a; Taylor and deLaat 2013).

The new movements were not only peopled disproportionately by younger activists; activists on both sides of the generational divide also defined them as distinct from earlier organizing. As Black Lives Matter activist Tef Poe said, "This is not your grandfather's civil rights movement" (Murphy 2015). Black Lives Matter was more confrontational and less hierarchical than institutionalized civil rights organizations had become, and it deliberately elevated the participation of women and queer people. Dreamers, too, despite closer organizational links to established immigrant rights organizations, differed in their leadership by queer youth, influencing their use of "coming out" as a strategy for change (Terriquez 2015). Occupy's nonhierarchical structure and broad focus were criticized by veterans of the Left for its lack of clear goals and statements, even as some veterans participated and helped mentor the new activists coming into Occupations (Milkman, Luce, and Lewis 2013). Although younger feminists innovated the "slutwalks" to protest rape culture, some veteran feminists criticized slutwalks for embracing objectification (Reger 2014b).[13]

In sum, in the pre-Trump Era, Millennial and younger Generation X activists animated newer campaigns, while veteran activists sustained long-lived ones. The rapid and broad surge in participation after the election changed these generational dynamics.

Cross-Generational Participation in the Resistance to Trump

After Trump's election, activism ballooned as rapidly as at any time in history (see Han and Oyakawa, Chapter 11). People of all ages organized and attended massive, numerous protests, joined new organizations founded mostly by activists in their 30s, and streamed into preexisting organizations. Astounding numbers, especially Generation Xers and Millennials, are participating in protest: Among Democrats, 27% of respondents between the ages of 18 and 49 reported attending an event or protest since the election, as did 16% of those 50 or older (Pew Research Center 2017b).[14] The Resistance brought together multiple political generations in the same protests, organizations, and social movement communities on a much larger scale than pre-Trump, heightening the potential for both generational spillover and conflict. The relevant questions for understanding the basis for generational spillover are the age make-up and previous activist experience of the protest organizers and participants. In this section, I briefly describe generational participation in the organizations and protests that grew after the election.

Social Movement Organizations

In the immediate aftermath of the election, experienced activists and progressive political operatives emerged quickly from their shock to plan actions and establish new organizations. Although the *Huffington Post* proclaimed that "Millennials are the Ones Leading the Resistance against Trump" (Mahmoud 2017), many leaders of new organizations are from Generation X. About two-thirds of the founders and leaders of these organizations are older Millennials, and most of the rest are younger members of Generation X, in their late 30s.[15] Few were politically inexperienced. Even the youngest thus are not from a post-Trump *political* generation, but rather were politicized in an earlier era. They differ from their age mates who are first entering political activism after Trump's election.

One of the most visible of the new organizations is Indivisible (see Brooker, Chapter 8). Modeling itself as a progressive analog of the Tea Party, Indivisible promoted tactics and strategies for influencing the federal government. Founded by two Democrats who had worked in Congress, Indivisible spawned loosely affiliated chapters across the country. Local groups packed town hall meetings, offices, and public appearances by members of Congress, organized calling and letter-writing campaigns, and raised the visibility of numerous policy proposals and Cabinet nominees, both online and offline. Indivisible's founders were in their early 30s, among the older micro-cohort of Millennials. Members of its paid staff, including the two founding directors and four others, are almost all in their early 30s, with one in his late 30s ("About Us" 2017). Leaders and members of local chapters appear to cover a wider age range and include both experienced activists and newcomers. For example, Indivisible Tosa (of Wauwatosa, Wisconsin) was founded by a 46-year-old man, part of Generation X, without previous activist experience, after his wife learned about Indivisible when she attended a Women's March (Dickenson 2017). Skocpol (quoted in Shulawitz 2017) characterizes the organizers of Indivisible chapters as "middle-aged white women." (Keep in mind that "middle-aged" encompasses most of Generation X as well as Baby Boomers.)

Other new organizations sought to recruit, train, and support candidates for elected office. Running for office is not in itself a form of movement activism, but organizations aimed at increasing and supporting runs for office—especially by women—are movement organizations, and they appear to be yielding results. New organizations included Sister District, which aims to recruit donors from Democratic areas to support Democratic candidates in competitive state-level races and claimed 100 local chapters in 2016; Swing Left, which focuses on mobilizing volunteers in "safe" Democratic Congressional districts to help Democratic House campaigns elsewhere; and Run for Something, which works with Millennials who want to run for office (Dickinson 2017; "What We Do" 2017). Existing organizations, such as Emerge, that train women to run for office also grew dramatically. These groups fielded large numbers of successful candidates in 2017 (Delgadillo 2017; Emerge 2017).

All were founded by younger Generation Xers or older Millennials. Sister District was founded a by 38-year-old woman who was somewhat politically savvy as a result of working as a federal public defender, but had little actual organizing experience; Swing Left was founded by a 36-year-old political neophyte with help from "seasoned political operatives" including "a former national field director for MoveOn;" and Run for Something was cofounded by two Millennials who had worked for Democratic campaigns (Dickinson 2017; "Who We Are" n.d.).

In addition, online movement communities developed in Facebook groups, such as the invitation-only Facebook group Pantsuit Nation. Formed in the run-up to the election to support Clinton's candidacy and provide a site for her supporters that was sheltered from the vitriol aimed at them from "Bernie bros" on the left and Trump supporters on the right, the group transformed into a hub for resistance after the election.[16] The founder and leaders of Pantsuit Nation were older Millennials, in their early 30s, but participants in the Facebook group included all ages ("Our Mission"). Pantsuit Nation, along with similar Facebook sites like "Nasty Women" and smaller state and local offshoots, was a source of information about the marches and other calls to action, how to lobby local officials, and where to donate money, but was also a location for conversations across race and generation about intersectionality and white privilege in feminism.

Alongside the emergence of new organizations, many preexisting liberal and progressive organizations reported a huge influx of new members after the election. These included professionalized organizations with legal and lobbying arms like the ACLU and Planned Parenthood, newer professionalized progressive organizations like MoveOn, the Democratic Socialists Alliance (DSA), and smaller local organizations from Democratic Party chapters to liberal churches, mosques, and synagogues, to small social movement organizations. For example, membership in the DSA has reportedly grown from 5,000 to 30,000 since the election, with primarily Millennials as the new members (Leonard 2017).

In sum, new and preexisting organizations that grew after the election brought together multiple political generations. New leaders came mainly from older Millennials and Generation X, but participation was cross-age. The massive protests were generationally equally broad.

Protest

Massive and numerous protests emerged in the wake of Trump's election, led by the Women's Marches in Washington, DC, and countless other cities and towns, and followed by the March for Science, People's Climate March in New York City, the Tax March, and the March for Truth. (See Berry and Chenoweth, Chapter 3; Fisher, Chapter 5; Han and Oyakawa, Chapter 11.) Demonstrations in international airports, organized on very short notice when the Trump administration placed a Travel Ban on travelers from several Muslim-majority countries, also followed a similar pattern (Dorf and Chu, Chapter 6). Countless protests occurred at Trump Tower in New York, Trump's Mar-a-Lago in Palm Beach, and Trump-branded buildings in other cities, and at local state houses and city capitols. The Day without Immigrants and Day without Women protests urged people to stay home from work and school and protest instead.

These protests were distinguished by their size, the fact that they occurred in multiple locations at a coordinated time, and atypical patterns of recruitment. Participants were recruited through online and in-person networks, as with typical marches, but there was also a surprising amount of "self- recruitment," in which previously inactive people heard about the demonstrations and (perhaps with friends or family) attended them. Social media made it possible for individuals to learn about the marches without previous network ties to others planning to attend; but the galvanizing shock of Trump's election is likely what motivated unconnected individuals to attend (Fisher 2017;

Fisher, Dow, and Ray 2017). Recruitment across and outside of multiple networks, combined with cross-generational participation, created a rare opportunity for spillover.

March organizers included both experienced leaders and many political newcomers (Berry and Chenoweth, Chapter 3). The initial spark for the Women's Marches came from a Baby Boomer woman who was not politically active, although an experienced organizing committee made up of two older Millennials, one young Generation Xer, and one older Generation Xer took over as the March gained steam. The speakers at the DC Women's March reflected this cross-generational demographic. Twenty-four percent were Millennials, all but one from the older micro-cohort; 42% were from Generation X, 26% were Baby Boomers, and 8% were older than Baby Boomers. All of the speakers, regardless of age, had some political involvement before the election.[17]

Participants similarly covered a wide age range, with all generations represented. No definitive data exist on the demographics of protesters across cities, but research by Dana Fisher and collaborators on the Women's March and the People's Climate March in Washington, DC, gives us some information. They found a mean age of 43 for participants in the Women's March and 42 for the Climate March (Fisher, Dow, and Ray 2017; Fisher Chapter 5). Attendees at the Women's March were nearly evenly divided among Millennials (36%), Gen X (29%), and Baby Boomers (33%), with the remaining attendees from the generation prior to that of the Baby Boomers. More than 13% were young Millennials, ages 18–25.[18] The sampling protocol excluded those under 18, but media reports suggest that many teenagers and children also attended. Millennials are the most numerous generation demographically (Fry 2016), so these data do not establish that they are *disproportionately* active. Given their life stage, it is notable that members of Generation X are participating in numbers equal to or greater than those of Millennials and Baby Boomers in protests and new anti-Trump organizations.

Like movement organizations, the protests included experienced activists and newcomers of all ages. More than one-third of participants in the Climate and Women's Marches were participating in their first-ever march or their first march in 5 years (Fisher 2017; Fisher, Dow, and Ray 2017; Fisher, Chapter 5). Forty-five percent of Millennial and Generation X participants in the Women's March first attended a protest in 2017, as did 27% of Baby Boomers. Most of the rest of Millennial participants had first protested between 2000 and 2016 (with young Millennials clustered between 2010 and 2016 and older Millennials between 2000 and 2009). Generation X participants had a wide range of years for their first protests, with 18% between 1990 and 1999 and 15% between 2000 and 2009. Notably, half of Baby Boomers, in contrast, first protested in the 1960s and 1970s. The point here is that the anti-Trump Resistance was generationally diverse in "movement age," that is, when people first entered activism, as well as in chronological age.

When large numbers of new participants enter an organization, previous members have the task of socializing new members into a political point of view and teaching them how to be an activist. New members often join an organization for exactly these reasons. Nevertheless, newcomers see issues differently because of their shorter activist history and because their perspective is shaped by their time of entry into activism. This is true regardless of whether the newcomers are younger or older than established members.

Movement participation contributes to the formation of political generations. For those who had not previously been activists, the experience of massive and frequent protests is likely to shape their political viewpoint. The multi-issue coalition, the use of "Women's Marches" as an umbrella for a wide range of issues, and March organizers' emphasis on intersectionality may shape the connections they draw among issues. The sheer experience of participating in an action shared by so many others in so many different locations may shape their sense of solidarity or collective identity.

The experience of the anti-Trump Resistance doubtless will shape and solidify a new political generation, but it will likely contain distinct micro-cohorts. For younger Millennials just entering activism, early resistance to Trump's election is the key formative experience, whereas slightly older Millennials with prior experience in social movements or electoral politics differ. Many older Millennials had already participated in movements like Occupy, the Dream movement, Black Lives Matter, or opposition to sexual assault, alongside younger Generation Xers. Trump's election made their goals and struggles more salient, both because of the moral shock and because of concrete policy threat. Other older Millennials with experience in electoral politics under Democrats were thrust into an unexpected political wilderness. Losing paid work in a Democratic administration and horrified at the political turn, they used their skills to found organizations to influence electoral politics. Younger Millennials (and people of all ages who were newly politicized) lacked this prior experience and will likely have a somewhat different collective identity and political viewpoint. Older Generation Xers and Baby Boomers, with experience in movements of the 1960s–1990s, bring yet another perspective.

In addition to the formation of new political generations, mass mobilization that brings together multiple political generations provides a concrete location for generational spillover. The new organizations and protests were organized mainly by older Millennials and Generation Xers but brought together participants of all ages and levels of movement experience. Given the differences among the generations, their overlapping presence and interaction in protests and organizations raised possibilities for conflict as well as mutual influence.

Generational Transmission and Conflict

Generational spillover is about how incoming activists are socialized and mentored and how they learn from preceding movements. This is occurring directly and indirectly within the Resistance to Trump. In this section, I describe cross-generational transmission through three conduits: activist training schools, formal and informal mentoring within intergenerational organizations, and indirect influence through proximity in multigeneration campaigns or groups.[19] I then show how both preexisting and novel frames, organizational structures, and tactics are emerging in the anti-Trump Resistance. Finally, I discuss conflict, both between age-based political generations and between experienced activists and novices. These dynamics are at the crux of how the anti-Trump Resistance can build on the skills and lessons of prior movements and how it can—crucially—develop new ways of confronting what is an unprecedented situation.

Formal and Informal Transmission Across Generations

Beginning shortly after the election, new and long-standing organizations sought to train the influx of newly engaged Trump opponents in activism. Activist "schools" emerged to teach new activists how to organize, but these were not necessarily founded by veteran activists. For example, the Resistance School was founded by Harvard graduate students, some of whom had taken classes with Marshall Ganz, a longtime scholar of social movements, activist, and Democratic organizer. The Resistance School billed itself as teaching "Practical Skills to Reclaim, Rebuild, and Reimagine America," with lectures by longtime organizers and younger, but experienced, activists, academics, and Democratic Party organizers (Resistance School 2017). It reportedly reached 175,000 people in its first four sessions, including face-to-face and livestreamed trainings. A photograph of an in-person session shows a multi-age audience, with many people with gray hair, along with younger organizers (Pappano 2017).[20]

In Northampton, Massachusetts, a similar effort emerged, under the name Sojourner Truth School for Social Change Leadership, to teach organizing and movement-building skills, such as how to run for office, managing group dynamics, nonviolent direct action, and cross-cultural dynamics. Founded and directed by a longtime Baby Boomer activist who described herself as "Radicalized during the Vietnam War; Lifelong Activist," the Truth School's steering committee, volunteer staff of experienced activists, and trainers span the generations (Truth School 2017). It is likely that similar efforts developed in other communities.

Efforts to teach new activists how to organize are not unique to the anti-Trump Resistance. The Highlander School was crucial in the development of the Civil Rights movement and New Left (Morris 1986.) The rapid entrance of so many new activists into the anti-Trump Resistance, along with the capacities for online instruction, made these efforts more widespread.

Less formally, veteran activists worked with younger activists interested in learning from their experience. For example, veterans of ACT UP worked with a multi-age anti-Trump group called Rise and Resist that adapted ACT UP's civil disobedience and media-focused actions. Rise and Resist's "cough-in," in which protesters went to brunch at restaurants in Trump properties, began to cough, and "held up signs saying 'Trumpcare is making us sick,'" mirrored similar actions against AIDS in the 1980s. More broadly, ACT UP veterans reported trying to help the anti-Trump Resistance think more "strategically" about how to influence a situation in which, as with AIDS in the 1980s, the Resistance felt powerless (Westervelt 2017). Generational spillover also occurs simply through proximity. The uniquely widespread cross-generational participation in the anti-Trump Resistance entailed extensive informal interaction and exposure.

Old and New Frames, Organizational Structures, and Tactics

It is too soon to know what form the Resistance will take longer term, but we can draw some preliminary conclusions about generational spillover thus far. Thus far, the Resistance shows the influence of frames from previous protest cycles, including the women's movement, antiwar movements, the smaller queer and AIDS movements of the late 1980s and 1990s, and recent Millennial-led movements around racism, economic inequality, climate change, and sexual assault. The official program of speakers at the DC Women's March reflected the strong influence of contemporary intersectional feminism, with feminists and antiracist leaders of various political generations invoking intersectional frames, albeit with slightly different emphases. For example, Angela Davis, the prominent long-term antiracism activist, said, "This women's march represents the promise of feminism as against the pernicious powers of state violence. An inclusive and intersectional feminism that calls upon all of us to join the resistance to racism, to Islamophobia, to anti-Semitism, to misogyny, to capitalist exploitation" (Lindig 2017). From the other end of the generational spectrum, Millennial actress and activist America Ferrera framed unity across issues and identities differently, proclaiming, "The president is not America. His cabinet is not America. Congress is not America. *We* are America. And we are here to stay. We will not go from being a nation of immigrants to a nation of ignorance"

(Deerwester 2017). Ferrera proclaimed a broad and inclusive collective identity, the diverse "we," the nation of immigrants, and Davis listed the issues that "all of us" should resist. Intersectional frames, by connecting multiple forms of inequality, effectively work to link issues, fostering cross-movement as well as cross-generational spillover.

Chants and signs also reflect both old and new frames. For example, chants at marches included old favorites like, "Hey hey, ho ho, Donald Trump has got to go!" alongside new ones like, "This is What Democracy Looks Like," and "Pussy Grabs Back" (Waters 2017). The endlessly adaptable "Hey hey, ho ho" has been passed from movement to movement, generation to generation. But democracy-focused chants reflect the broad ideological base and specific focus on Trump, whereas the "pussy" chants and pussyhats drew not only from Trump's own language, but from young anti–sexual assault activists' sexually confrontational approach. Signs from the Women's Marches included slogans and signs that could have applied to movements from the past 50 years; preexisting organizations with the capacity to provide preprinted signs increased their frames' circulation that way. Other signs that used slogans from pre-Trump movements like "We are the 99%" and "Black Lives Matter."

But many signs used new slogans, framing issues of sexual assault around embodied power ("Pussy Power;" "My Uterus is not up for Grabs"), emphasizing women's power more generally ("Girl Power;" "Fempire Strikes Back") and emphasizing intersectional feminism (for example, downloadable poster art by Shepard Fairey contained images of women of color and Muslim women under the phrase "We the People") (Abrams 2017; Vagianos and Dahlen 2017). The use of American flags and flag-themed apparel and signs, white dresses and sashes drawn from the women's suffrage movement, and the singing of patriotic songs alongside classics like "We Shall Overcome" further illustrate the entry of novel and repurposed frames into the Resistance. Overall, although long-standing frames remained prevalent in these protests, they were not the majority. Without further data, it is impossible to know whether members of the Baby Boomer political generation or experienced younger activists are themselves adopting new frames or simply are outnumbered by the influx of new activists with different generational perspectives. It is also too soon to know how the explosion of creativity in sign-making and sloganeering will translate into more elaborated framing projects by organizations.

Unlike frames, the organizational structures and tactical repertoires of the anti-Trump Resistance are thus far similar to those of prior decades. The Millennials and Generation Xers who cut their activist teeth in the movements of the early 2010s may have a predilection toward those groups' nonhierarchical structure and symbolic and direct-action tactics. However, these features also characterized movements staffed by Baby Boomers and Generation X throughout the 1960s, 1970s, 1980s, and 1990s. In contrast, many organizations that have sprung up since the election, also headed by younger Generation Xers and older Millennials, have a loosely hierarchical form, with national offices and local chapters that are largely free to shape their own activities. Direct-action tactics have been relatively scarce in actions targeting elected officials, but protest and disruption are common. Here, too, these organizations are following well-worn paths. This suggests cross-generational learning. Indeed, the conduits of transmission previously discussed help train activists in these tactics, as did relationships with older activists in the pre-Trump movement.

Most of the Resistance focuses on protest, chanting, planned civil disobedience, occasional direct action, and letter-writing and phone-calling campaigns to elected officials. These represent a broad and familiar tactical repertoire. The Resistance's orientation toward influencing elected officials also has spawned new tactics aimed at organizing targeting of members of Congress on a massive scale. Countless mailing lists and Facebook groups suggest daily actions such as calling lawmakers; local groups meet weekly to make calls and send postcards; and influential individuals online and in community networks summarize an overwhelming stream of information about objectionable administration actions and suggest priority targets. These are not entirely new tactics, but activists are combining them and scaling them up in a distinct way. They effectively serve to channel the participation of less-experienced activists.

Because the anti-Trump Resistance is still very young, organizations may yet evolve into more hierarchical federated structures, local chapters may split off from national headquarters, and new tactics may emerge. If the focus on elected officials wanes (in the face of either significant success or significant failure in the 2018 elections), direct-action or other forms of dramatic protest may yet come to the fore. At this point, however, there is no basis to conclude that the anti-Trump Resistance, or younger activists within it, will rely more on direct action tactics, or form less hierarchical organizations over the long haul, than other generations.

Generational Conflict

Cross-generational participation unsurprisingly entails conflict. Older activists have historically complained that younger ones don't understand their history or aren't grateful for what has been accomplished (Reger 2014b; Whittier 1995), but there is little evidence of this yet in the anti-Trump Resistance. Instead, the most visible conflict at 1 year in is between experienced younger activists, especially people of color and often-older, often-white newcomers. As one commentator suggested, "Some new members of the Resistance may have people they can turn to easily for guidance: their kids" (Leonard 2017). Illustrating these generational differences, a Millennial organizer in an Ohio group that has been mostly black-led contrasted the many new members with the perspective of its veteran organizers, saying, "Many people that become deeply discontent with the status quo have some moment in their lives when all of a sudden they realize that what they've been taught are lies," explaining that people of color experienced that insight as children but, "for a lot of middle-class people, and for a lot of white Americans, that . . . moment is actually happening right now" (quoted in Leonard 2017). In Pantsuit Nation, similarly, conversations over race and gender often entailed conflict, as political neophytes—mostly white women who had been infuriated by Trump's election and understood it as about sexism—entered into conversation with politically experienced activists, both white women and women of color, about racial and class differences in women's experiences through the analytical framework of intersectionality. Berry and Chenoweth (Chapter 3) also point to conflicts in local Women's March organizing committees between experienced activists of color and white neophytes.

The generational differences at play relate to both age and point of entry into the movement. Experienced and younger activists are more inclined to intersectional analyses than Baby Boomer veterans and newcomers of all ages. At the same time, there are emerging complaints about excessive focus on the young. As veteran activist L. A. Kauffman said, "Why chase after millennials . . . ? Why ignore the salt-and-pepper-haired folks who have deep local connections and higher levels of engagement?" (quoted in Shulevitz 2017). It is too soon to predict the long-term development of the perspectives of Generation X or Baby Boomer white women whose formative activist experiences included Hillary Clinton's loss and conversations about intersectionality online. It is safe to assume, however, that their perspectives will be different from those of their age mates who have been activists since the 1970s or 1990s. Going forward, the anti-Trump Resistance will need to balance participation and influence across chronological political generations as well as ones based on "movement age." Although this is a dilemma faced by previous movements, it is more intense for the anti-Trump Resistance because of its generational structure and explosive growth.

Conclusion

The generationally separate movements prior to Trump's election have given way to a broad multigenerational resistance. The unique circumstances of extremely rapid growth produced the entry of activists of all ages and levels of experience into new and existing organizations, protests, and movement communities. Political generations differ in basic worldviews based on both age and time of entry into activism. Generational spillover includes explicit attempts to teach organizing, to pass on the concrete skills that activists need and to suggest longer-term questions of strategy, as well as indirect influences on prevailing frames, organizational structures, tactics, ideologies, goals, which issues are prioritized and which are seen as connected to each other, and collective identity.

The anti-Trump Resistance, because it brings together large numbers of activists of all generations, has the potential for extensive generational spillover. There will nevertheless be variation across locations, organizations, and sectors of the Resistance. More face-to-face contact across generations, paradoxically, may reduce conflict because generations may be less likely to construct collective identities based on generational difference (Reger 2012).

Intergenerational conflict is not new. Scholars and activists in the women's movement have written for 30 years about divisions between second- and third-wave feminism, between a political generation who defined the women's movement of the 1960s and 1970s and multiple younger generations (Henry 2004; Reger 2012; Whittier 1995). The New Left of the 1960s had fraught relationships with older generations, including the Old Left and organizers of the 1950s Civil Rights movement (Isserman 1987; Morris 1986). Similar conflicts exist between the generation that organized the Civil Rights movement and more recent antiracist organizing (Akom 2006; Franklin 2014; Harris 2015).

The anti-Trump Resistance has temporarily submerged generational differences, but if it persists they will doubtless resurge, as new activists solidify different points of view and shift from their current position as eager mentees to shaping their own organizations, strategies, and collective identity and as older activists grow frustrated with what they see as younger ones' ingratitude, recalcitrance, or naiveté. Older Millennials and younger Generation Xers, whose skills were honed in the 1990s and 2000s, will rapidly become the old guard as activists politicized in the Resistance come into leadership. The youngest members of the anti-Trump Resistance—young Millennials and current teenagers—are coming of age at a unique historical moment, both because of the nature of the Trump administration and of the emerging mass mobilization. This is likely to mark them and give rise to a worldview that is equally unique from their predecessors. They doubtless will depart from what experienced activists take for granted. Although older and experienced activists rightly want to pass on what they have learned, these lessons can come with blinders about how circumstances change over time. Although newcomers can innovate new and changing goals and inflection points for influence, they can unnecessarily invent the wheel.

What will all this mean for the anti-Trump Resistance? That will depend on how the generational dynamics of influence, difference, and conflict play out. The movement could define itself as a continuation of the goals of the 1960s–1970s Left, Civil Rights, and feminist movements, confronting neoliberalism, inequalities of class, race, and gender, with protest and mass resistance, skeptical of government-focused solutions. It instead could define itself as a broad ideological coalition, including moderates, liberals, and radicals, targeting federal and state officials to restrain Trump and elect more liberal or moderate officials. It could define itself as one arm—or a beginning—of a movement toward a world order that would prioritize undoing intersectional oppressions culturally as well as politically, elevating the voices of people of color, women, and LGBT people. These different visions of the movement are not just political: They are generational, shaped by the taken-for-granted perspectives of those of different ages and those who came of political age in different historical and movement contexts. The processes of generational spillover and conflict are central to shaping these different possible movement paths.

Acknowledgments: Thanks to Dana Fisher for access to her data on the Women's March, and to Marc Steinberg, Mary Ann Clawson, Steve Boutcher, and the editors for comments on an earlier version of this chapter.

Constituency and Leadership in the Evolution of Resistance Organizations

HAHRIE HAN AND MICHELLE OYAKAWA

> But longtime organizers from all sets of the anti-Trump Venn diagram know the pitfalls of treating mass protest as a litmus test for potency. The question of what "changes anything" looms large. The refrain is echoed so regularly by organizers and activists that it verges on platitude: There needs to be organization; street protest is necessary but not sufficient; we need a broad-based coalition. But there's no boilerplate for what "organization" beyond mobilization means.
> —Natasha Lennard, *Esquire Magazine*, May 13, 2017[1]

A retired lawyer in Hawaii, Teresa Shook watched in disbelief as the election results rolled in on November 8, 2016. As it became clear that Donald Trump would become the 45th president of the United States, Shook searched desperately for a way to channel her anger and take action to counteract the fear she felt for the future. As Marie Berry and Erica Chenoweth describe in greater depth in Chapter 3, she turned to Pantsuit Nation, a Facebook group dedicated to supporting Hillary Clinton.[2] "We need a pro-women march," she wrote, receiving enthusiastic support from the members of the sprawling online community. Buoyed by the response, Shook asked for directions about how to create a Facebook group, and created one dedicated to a Women's March.

Much to Shook's surprise, when she woke up the next morning, over 10,000 people had RSVP'd, and the numbers only grew from there. Her Facebook page became the basis for what would eventually become a historic protest on January 21, 2017, which drew hundreds of thousands of people to Washington, DC, and an additional 3.5-million people into the streets in sister marches around the world. As the March grew with exponential speed, Shook and others realized the event was becoming too big for them to plan without greater expertise. An organization called the Women's March on Washington emerged, with a team of veteran organizers in place to harness some of the protest energy that had emerged after Trump's election into the March.[3]

Shook's experience was not isolated. The Women's March on Washington was just one of many new Resistance groups that emerged in the wake of the 2016 election. We refer to these groups as the "countermobilization" because they were a response not only to the election of Donald Trump but also to the wider phenomenon of Trumpism (as described by Sidney Tarrow in Chapter 9 of this book).[4] From groups like Swing Left to Flippable, Wall of Us to Indivisible, and People Power to Daily Action, the countermobilization spawned a host of new networks, apps, and organizations. Although some of these groups, like Indivisible, organized themselves into formal organizations that mirrored traditional federated organizational structures,[5] others resisted that kind of organization, choosing instead to maintain loose networks through an online app. Instead of entering into a vacuum, all of these new entities became part of a larger ecosystem of left-leaning organizations that had long existed to organize the grassroots on behalf of a progressive agenda. The shock of Trump's election also prompted a cascading set of responses by existing organizations that felt their agendas under attack in a new way. Throughout the year following Trump's election, as Lennard writes, all of these organizations, old and new, sought to define what " 'organization' beyond mobilization" means. The uncertainty created by this process of building organization brings to the forefront several key strategic tensions relevant to any movement organization (Lennard 2017).

This chapter examines the ways in which entities in the anti-Trump Resistance responded to two particular strategic dilemmas:

First, how will they address questions of race within their constituencies? More specifically, how will the organizations in the countermobilization address tensions around race in the progressive ecosystem, particularly given distinctions between the constituency base of long-standing groups and the new Resistance organizations? Can older groups that focus on constituencies of color and newer, white-led groups come together into one broader countermovement?

Second, how will they invest in leadership? As these new entities in the countermobilization became more institutionalized, one of the pressures they faced was to invest more in developing the leadership of their base. How much and how will they invest in developing this leadership and in building the democratic capacities of a new group of people?

Neither of these questions has easy answers, and it may be that the countermobilization continues to grapple with these questions without ever fully resolving them or resolving them in different ways at different points in time. Nonetheless, understanding what the questions are, and how organizations are grappling with them, helps us unpack the unfolding dynamics of countermobilization.

In this chapter, we illuminate the questions about constituency and leadership just described by considering two organizations in particular: ISAIAH and Indivisible. ISAIAH is a long-standing, faith-based-community organization in Minnesota, and Indivisible is a new organization that emerged after the election to capture the swell of grassroots anger after Trump won (see Chapter 8). To contextualize these cases, we also describe how they are part of a larger ecosystem of organizations working against Trump and for progressive political change. Both organizations under consideration here grapple with questions around race in their constituency and leadership development. Throughout this chapter, we draw on our own observations of resistance activity throughout 2017, as well as on interviews conducted with movement leaders during this year.

ISAIAH and Indivisible in the Resistance Landscape

Following the unprecedented size of the Women's March, some observers wondered whether people would continue to show up for other resistance activity. In the weeks that followed the Women's March, spontaneous airport protests, a flood of donations to progressive organizations, and the emergence of new vehicles for political activity like the March for Science and Indivisible indicated that we were in a different kind of political moment. As community organizers like to say, "People were in motion." Scholars refer to moments like these as "cycles of contention" in which heightened tensions cause a proliferation of collective action and innovation in forms of contention that are unlike periods of greater stasis.[6] Famed community organizer Tom Hayden captured this idea when he said, "Change is slow, except when it's fast." The emergence of the anti-Trump Resistance represents a moment of contention in which things were "fast."

ISAIAH and Indivisible are distinct organizations in the countermobilization that responded to this moment in different ways. ISAIAH is a faith-based community organizing (FBCO) coalition of over 100 congregations throughout Minnesota, including the Twin Cities, as well as in smaller cities and towns across the state. Founded in 2000, the organization has worked on a wide variety of progressive issues within the state and also nationally as part of the PICO National Network.[7] Its signature campaigns include supporting drivers' licenses for immigrants, racial equity in education, and access to public transit. One of the most prominent campaigns ISAIAH worked on (in coalition with other progressive organizations) was the defeat of racially biased voter identification laws in Minnesota in 2012.

ISAIAH leaders had been planning an event for January 2017 for months prior to Trump's improbable victory in November 2016. Regardless of the election outcome, the January event was designed to kick off ISAIAH's advocacy around the 2017 state legislative session. Many of their existing plans to advance progressive policies through the 2017 state legislative session, however, were rendered moot when Republicans unexpectedly won control of the Minnesota state legislature. In addition, ISAIAH leaders recognized that the Resistance activity sparked by Trump's election changed the meaning of the moment and the structure of political opportunities available to them—and they had to make choices about how to respond to the challenge. We subsequently examine their response, focusing on the campaign they began to call #PropheticResistance to adopt the language of the countermobilization.

Indivisible, in contrast, began haphazardly as a response to the Trump election. Originally not intended to be an organization at all, Indivisible began as a Google document created by Ezra Levin and Leah Greenberg, two former Congressional staffers who wrote a guide for how to pressure members of Congress (see Chapter 8). They published the guide online with an op-ed in the *New York Times*. Much to their surprise, from this guide, an organization developed rapidly. Outraged activists around the country starting forming thousands of Indivisible groups. They used the guide as their basis to draw people in congressional districts together, so that they could direct their anger at elected officials. Levin and Greenberg capitalized on this groundswell to form a national infrastructure to support these groups. Throughout 2017, Indivisible was "flying the plane as it was getting built," trying to figure out what it meant to be an organization in this political moment.

We chose these cases to compare how new and existing organizations responded to the foment of activity following the 2016 election. Looking at Indivisible provides insight into how new organizations within the anti-Trump Resistance evolved, whereas the ISAIAH example shows how leaders in existing organizations responded to the new cycle of contention brought about by the emerging Resistance. We are not claiming that these organizations are representative of Resistance organizations, but rather that their experiences illuminate common challenges that diverse organizations face when they attempt to organize the grassroots as a cycle of contention emerges. To provide a better sense of how Indivisible and ISAIAH fit as cases into the broader resistance movement, in the next section we provide a brief summary of the evolving ecosystem of progressive social movement organizations and their activities. Then, in the sections that follow, we turn to a discussion of how leaders in ISAIAH and Indivisible have grappled with questions about constituency and leadership.

Contextualizing Our Cases

To contextualize these two case studies within the broader landscape of Resistance organizations, we draw on a "map" of the progressive ecosystem that the Democracy Alliance created in the spring of 2017.[8] The Democracy Alliance is a coordinated network of high-net-worth donors to progressive causes led by prominent figures like George Soros.[9] In response to the uncertainty created by the fast-moving resistance activity in 2017, they created a map that sought to make sense of the changing ecosystem. They categorized the Resistance groups into 11 different categories, 7 of which referred to organizations that were not focused on engaging people in grassroots activity; instead, they focused on things like litigation, policy research, and fund raising. The remaining 4 categories included organizations that did engage the grassroots and were labeled by the Democracy Alliance as (1) organizing, (2) pressuring elected officials, (3) planning marches, and (4) electoralizing the grassroots. The last three of these categories focused primarily on new organizations that emerged after the election.

The largest category of grassroots organizations, which the Democracy Alliance called "Organizing," seemed to be an umbrella category used to characterize national, grassroots organizations that existed prior to the 2016 election. Although the map did not list state-based organizations, ISAIAH's national affiliate, the PICO National Network, fit into this category. In addition to PICO, this category included the other largest community organizing networks such as People's Action and the Center for Popular Democracy. Beyond community organizing, this category also included labor organizations like CoWorker.org and the National Domestic Workers Alliance, and digital-first groups like MoveOn and ColorOfChange. Finally, it also included organizations that originated in electoral politics, such as Organizing for Action and Health Care for America Now. All of these organizations develop and mobilize constituencies for issues of interest. They utilize a variety of tactics, including protest, pressuring elected officials, and voter mobilization.

Indivisible fit within the second group—organizations that are focused on "pressuring elected officials" to resist Trump's agenda. Even though Indivisible received more media attention, other groups, like the Town Hall Project, did similar work. The Town Hall Project is an organization run by volunteers dedicated to bringing constituents into face-to-face conversation with their elected officials by organizing opportunities for them to connect through office hours, town halls, and other events. Other groups emerged that looked less like traditional organizations and were more like online apps designed to channel people's activism. One such organization is Wall of Us, which is dedicated to identifying "four concrete acts of resistance curated and personalized [for activists] each week." 5Calls.org and Daily Action are similar online apps that people could download to have suggestions for five phone calls they could make each day or one action they could take each day.

Given the diversity of organizations in the countermovement, finding two organizations that completely captured the breadth and variety of progressive grassroots organizations after Trump's election would be very difficult. ISAIAH and Indivisible, nonetheless, do serve as exemplars of some portion of these groups. Although these two organizations have significant differences arising from disparities in organizational age, purpose, and composition, they share common challenges along with the other organizations in the progressive ecosystem previously described. In the following sections, we use examples from ISAIAH and Indivisible to illustrate how organizations in different parts of the ecosystem confront these challenges.

Organizational Challenges Confronting the Countermobilization

As the countermobilization to Trump evolved from the initial heady days of early 2017, entities in the Resistance, both old and new, began to confront questions about how to build, sustain, and define their work. In an informal interview in March 2017, a long-standing leader in the progressive ecosystem outlined some core questions about the new Resistance organizations:

> Are they going to be doing leadership development and education, are they going to be membership organizations that have lasting capacity in the community, or do you want to help them become that? . . . What are they good for? What can they become? How does that fit into the ecosystem?[10]

Leaders were trying to understand the long-term intentions of the anti-Trump Resistance organizations. Which constituency will they focus on and how? To what extent will they invest in cultivating a devoted base of grassroots leaders, equipping them with skills, and guiding them through diverse experiences of political theater and negotiation? How will they tie these pieces together to have impact?

These questions were not limited to new organizations. In both old and new organizations, we see the struggle of organizations within the countermobilization to define themselves. We highlight two key questions that confront organizations in this cycle of contention as they evolve. First, how do they define their constituency? Who is the base to whom they see themselves accountable, and, in particular, how does this interact with questions of race in the progressive movement? Second, how do they address the question of leadership? How will they invest in people to sustain their activism over the long term? We choose these questions about constituency and leadership development because they are at the heart of understanding what these organizations are and how they intend to evolve.

Defining the Constituency

A core question about constituency confronting organizations like ISAIAH and Indivisible is about race and how central they want to make it. What is the extent to which they want to put the interests of constituents of color at the center of their work? Knowing how a grassroots organization defines its constituency is crucial to understanding that organization's purpose. Given the racially charged nature of political conflicts in the United States, particularly in the wake of Trump's election, interrogating how organizations address race is core to understanding the countermobilization.

The question of race has long bedeviled organizations in the progressive ecosystem. Before looking specifically at the ways that Indivisible and ISAIAH handled the question, it is worth examining the choices around race made by established organizations to understand the backdrop against which ISAIAH and Indivisible were acting. In the decades prior to the 2016 election, the four most prominent multi-issue organizing networks in the progressive ecosystem made a conscious choice to put questions of race and intersectionality at the center of their work. Although all of these networks originated in a race-neutral approach, in recent decades, they moved toward a race-central approach.

For example, in their online statement of values, People's Action writes, "Systems of racism and exclusion that perpetuate violence and deny people even the essentials based on race, gender, and country of origin." The Center for Popular Democracy describes itself as, "strengthen[ing] our collective capacity to envision and win an innovative pro-worker, pro-immigrant, racial and economic justice agenda." The PICO National Network describes its mission as, "Together we are lifting up a new vision for America that unites people across region, race, class, and religion." Finally, the Center for Community Change writes that, "The Center's mission is to build the power and capacity of low-income people, especially low-income people of color, to change their communities and public policies for the better." As Richard Wood and Brad Fulton describe, moving from a race-neutral to a race-central approach was no easy task and was contested within the networks undergoing the transition.[11]

This history contextualizes the critique that Indivisible faced as a new organization in the progressive ecosystem with a primarily white constituency base and, thus far, a race-neutral approach. In any grassroots organizations, there are many ways to define a constituency, such as through ideological or issue concerns (e.g., people who want to stop fracking), demography (e.g., racial groups, gender), or structure (e.g., people who live in a certain neighborhood or who are part of a particular religious congregation). Among newly formed Resistance organizations like Indivisible (see Chapter 8), the default path was to define the constituency based on ideology: People who wanted to resist Trump were the constituency base of these organizations. Race did not play into their understanding of constituency. The challenge was that many of the people who became most active in the new Resistance organizations were white, even as many of the issues the Resistance wanted to address had a strong racial dimension to them, given Trump's own focus on race. Long-standing organizations like ISAIAH, in contrast, had a much stronger focus on constituencies of color, creating distinctions between the old and the new groups in the countermobilization.

After the election, a variety of news sources identified white, middle-class voters, particularly women,[12] as the core of the new organizations in the anti-Trump Resistance.[13] These journalistic data are corroborated by our own observation of a training led by Indivisible for its core leaders. In the fall of 2017, 1 year after the election, Indivisible began hosting trainings for core leaders to prepare them for ongoing Resistance work in their communities and the 2018 elections. At the first training, held in Arizona, evaluation data show that the attendees were 87% white, 75% female, and that 55% had annual household incomes between $50,000 and $150,000.[14] These were the leaders who were most committed to Indivisible, because they were still active with Indivisible even a year after the election.

The white constituency base of organizations like Indivisible presents a particular challenge in the era of Trumpism. The Trump movement racialized its appeal, fueled by online publications like *Breitbart* and events like the white supremacy marches in Charlottesville, but organizations like Indivisible have been somewhat unclear in how they will approach race. This is the case even though many of the issues being worked on by Indivisible leaders were connected to race. Some, like Trump's proposed immigration bans, were explicitly focused on race, whereas others, like health care, had a strong racial dimension. The question that confronted organizations like Indivisible was the extent to which they would take on race as a defining issue of the Resistance. The articulated goal of organizations like Indivisible is to build a multiracial coalition, but the demographics of their base belie that intention. Given long-standing racial divides in both the progressive movement and American politics writ large, the challenge for many organizations in the countermobilization is to see whether it is possible to build a multiracial coalition that counteracts the appeals to whiteness embedded in Trumpism.

ISAIAH's response to similar tensions, however, shows one possible approach. ISAIAH's base is predominantly white, which is unusual among FBCO groups. The National Study of Community Organizing Coalitions in 2011 found that less than half (46%) of organizational members (i.e., congregations) of FBCOs are majority white and that FBCOs as a whole are significantly more diverse than public schools and US counties.[15] Nonetheless, ISAIAH leaders have made a strong commitment to working toward building a multiracial constituency and have been explicitly advocating for racial equality with their predominantly white base since 2009, when the organization coauthored several reports with the Kirwan Institute for the Study of Race and Ethnicity about racial inequality in Minnesota. At their event to launch their #PropheticResistance campaign in January 2017, for instance, the organizers sought to meld practices appealing to the traditional, white-led progressive establishment in Minnesota with a call for a more radical vision of racial justice. The appeal of their event to the political establishment and their ability to bridge these racial divides is exemplified by the fact that elected officials, including former US Senator Al Franken and Minneapolis Mayor Betsy Hodges, were there for the event.

Even though the majority of attendees at the event were white, the message and leadership of the event were both multiracial. The clergy and leaders represented on stage were racially diverse: white, Black, and Latino clergy spoke, including one Latino clergyman who spoke through a translator. The event opened with two, high-energy gospel songs sung by a Black song leader. Although unfamiliar with the cadence of the songs, the primarily older, white attendees clapped along enthusiastically, responding to the energy in the room. Speakers intentionally highlighted the need for racial justice and used the language of "white supremacy" to contextualize the work of resistance. The event itself focused on a call to action for people of faith in Minnesota to resist unjust laws and practices and to defend democracy, but the appeal was strongly grounded in an analysis of the racial injustice in America. Many of the speakers at the event were ISAIAH leaders who shared personal narratives about hardships related to economic and racial inequality. ISAIAH's executive director, Doran Schrantz, contextualized these stories in a broader analysis about the relationship between race and American democracy:

> Let's not get caught up in the question of who in this room is a Democrat and who is a Republican. Because, in this moment, that way of interpreting what is happening will lead you nowhere. It will simply blind you to reality. There is a persistent myth that our politics are paralyzed by two equal and opposing forces in a struggle over tax policy, the role of government, and the size of deficits . . . but would those debates so rouse the passions of the people that we would have

devolved, essentially, two tribes? . . . There is a larger story here. And the center of that story is not President Donald Trump . . . . The center of the story is you—US . . . . The larger story is this—everyone in this room, like it or not, has inherited both the great promise and the titanic struggle that is the United States of America.

Schrantz went on to describe the struggle, in which "democracy cannot be reconciled with White Supremacy," and the contradiction of a country that simultaneously seeks to create a democracy in which ordinary people are "equal co-creators of a nation" but that certain people are deemed less than human. The challenge, she argued, was not to "reconcile the irreconcilable" but to "pick up the mantle and demand that this nation fulfill the promise," to create a country in which people "bathed in the air of freedom and the fullness of our own humanity" are able to "act on behalf of ourselves and our communities." Schrantz connected this broad vision with specific campaigns that ISAIAH was gearing up to work on in the coming spring. These included churches providing sanctuary for immigrants threatened with deportation, fighting against cutbacks on health care, and fighting preemption of local laws.

Schrantz's approach was to make building a multiracial coalition synonymous with reclaiming democracy, and to create a unified sense of community among the people in the room who recognized that people of all racial backgrounds shared pain. Her message, thus, was an effort to push the boundaries of the energy around the Resistance, and to create a vision of American democracy that recognizes the country's racial history but transcends it with something new. Schrantz brought the church to its feet with her vision of a multiracial democracy, as thousands of people thunderously responded to her clarion call. Whether ISAIAH and other organizations like it are able to deliver on building these multiracial constituencies, however, remains to be seen.

The contrasting race-neutral approach of Indivisible and race-central approach of ISAIAH highlight general questions confronting Resistance organizations, their relationship to each other, their understanding of their own constituencies, and their approach to resisting Trumpism. Established, intersectionally focused groups like ISAIAH have to figure out if and how to work with newer, white-led groups like Indivisible under the umbrella of countermobilization. Like ISAIAH, many of the existing groups in the ecosystem focus on questions of race and intersectional constituencies, building up a base among constituencies of color and advocating a race-based approach to understanding political issues. The vast majority of the new leaders and activists in the Resistance, however, are white middle-class folks. Can these groups come together? How are questions of race understood and handled within these organizations, and what kind of constituency work is needed to build a broad base? Finally, can organizations resisting Trump build a multiracial, cross-class constituency that transcends Trumpism? These cleavages around constituency, race, and class highlight the ongoing struggle for organizations in the progressive ecosystem.

Leadership

Questions around leadership are intimately tied to organizational purpose and strategy. Leadership challenges confront both old and new organizations in the Resistance as they grapple with whether they want to invest in building the capacities of their constituencies. The way the questions manifested themselves for Indivisible and ISAIAH, however, were very different. Whereas some organizations, like ISAIAH, originated with a philosophical commitment to building civic skills and political leadership capacities in their constituents, other organizations, like Indivisible, began to confront the question as they faced strategic challenges to their model. Indivisible thus looked to leadership development as one possible solution to emerging strategic dilemmas, whether ISAIAH grappled with questions about whether shifting their leadership development strategies would render them more or less effective in accomplishing their goals.

When Indivisible first began, it focused purely on capturing all the people eager to take action after the election. The sheer numbers of people interested in activism in that moment seemed to obviate the need for Indivisible to develop any of its own strategies for building and maintaining a constituency. People were self-motivated to resist Trump, and Indivisible was scrambling to keep up with the demand. As the heady days of the early Resistance waned, Indivisible and other entities in the countermobilization had to think about strategies for building and sustaining activism. This challenge led them to questions about leadership: Would they invest in developing the leadership and capacities of their base? What tools, tactics, and trainings would make them more effective at harnessing grassroots action for political influence?

Why did leadership development become an important question as Indivisible evolved? When Indivisible first emerged, its entire *raison d'être* focused on teaching citizens how to most effectively pressure members of Congress. Although that strategy generated a robust wave of activity in the early months of 2017, Indivisible leaders began to feel as if they needed to do more. In a conversation with national Indivisible leaders in May 2017, we found that one of the challenges they were facing was maintaining activist commitments. Local groups that initially held events that filled meeting rooms were finding that only a much smaller, core group of people were continuing to show up 6 months after the election. As Guy Potucek, an Indivisible group leader in Northern Virginia said in August 2017, "There are folks who I've talked to both in the leadership team [and outside] who have said it would be great when we can get back to our normal lives, so it's also possible that it just kind of fades away as the immediate threat goes away."[16]

Relatedly, as the local Indivisible groups began to mature, they sought to become less reactive to the Trump agenda and more proactive about moving a progressive agenda forward. In the beginning, the groups were simply reacting out of sheer anger to Trump, protesting and channeling activity to resist his agenda. As the country settled into the early Trump Era, Indivisible leaders started to express a desire to be more proactive about their work. As one article put it, Indivisible "has two ambitious main goals: to stop Trump from achieving anything, and to transform liberal grassroots activism and the way Americans engage with democracy."[17] Thus, although Indivisible continued to run a variety of campaigns to pressure elected officials around issues like Obamacare, Deferred Action for Childhood Arrivals (DACA), and so on, they were simultaneously wondering whether a broader set of strategies was necessary to continue maintaining the organization over time.

These changing strategic imperatives pushed Indivisible leaders to consider leadership development strategies that they witnessed in other organizations in the progressive ecosystem that were facing similar types of challenges. The combination of Indivisible's changing needs—the desire to become more proactive and the need to do more work to keep its constituency engaged—highlighted the lack of experience and training among many Indivisible activists. It raised questions for Indivisible leaders about how much they wanted and needed to invest in training and capacity building to accomplish their organizational goals. They began a "listening tour" of their chapters to hear from leaders what they wanted.[18] They began a conversation with a variety of experienced grassroots organizing groups and other movement leaders, including funders and movement support organizations, to identify ways they could develop a training program for leaders. They wanted to begin teaching their leaders to strategize, build cohesive teams, and develop the kind of civic capacities that have long characterized groups, like ISAIAH, that focus on community organizing or building independent political power.

Undoubtedly, tendencies toward organizational isomorphism are at play here. Organizations in cycles of contention often adopt culturally accepted repertoires for action, and in moments of strategic uncertainty, organizations like Indivisible will intentionally and unintentionally look to other organizations to identity possible solutions.[19] Even as a new organization that relies heavily on online communication, Indivisible could follow the same trajectory identified by Michels in his classic work on political parties through an increasing reliance on expert leaders and ongoing institutionalization of organizational activities.[20] Will the "iron law of oligarchy" hold true for emergent grassroots organizations in the anti-Trump Resistance that use digital platforms to engage people? Given the often-porous boundaries between movement and institutional politics, it is possible that there will be significant overlap in organizational strategies and tactics.[21]

Although ISAIAH's questions around leadership development had a different tilt to them than Indivisible's because the organization had a long-standing leadership development program, the questions were similarly tied up with questions of organizational strategy. The 2,000 attendees at ISAIAH's Prophetic Resistance launch in January 2017 did not emerge overnight. Instead, many of them came because they were already active leaders in a congregation that had a relationship with ISAIAH. Many attendees sat (or stood) with the people they knew from their churches. In a private conversation, one minister ruefully noted that most of his congregants were standing in the back of the church, unable to get seats. "I'm sure I'll hear about that!" he chuckled. Energy from the Resistance amplified the work that ISAIAH was doing, but the organization had already built a complex network of relationships within and among congregations. Many of attendees at the event represented volunteer leaders from across the state who had been organizing in their own congregations for months, years, or in some cases, decades prior to the event. All ISAIAH leaders undergo an intensive leadership development process that includes attending political education events and organizing trainings that ISAIAH offers as well as being mentored one-on-one by organizers.

For ISAIAH, the leadership challenge focused on if and how its long-standing leadership development strategies could and should be adapted to the present moment. The organization's deep leadership development program meant it had an existing base of trained leaders who were prepared to leap into action. When ISAIAH was doing 100 days of #PropheticAction following its kick-off event, ISAIAH leaders were trained and equipped to do everything from organizing protests, to speaking at town hall meetings, to writing op-eds, to creating political education events around white supremacy. The question was whether they could accommodate all the new interest and whether the organization should adapt its program to do so. The January 2017 event, for instance, was filled to overcapacity, and event organizers had to set up satellite feeds at other churches around Minnesota to accommodate the unexpected outpouring of interest in #PropheticResistance.

In a debrief following the event, an ISAIAH staff person noted one particular challenge facing ISAIAH: Given that organizers cannot be everywhere, how can they develop tools to unleash the energy around the Resistance instead of becoming a bottleneck? ISAIAH's primary organizing strategies revolve around time and labor-intensive one-on-one meetings and leadership development. In a moment at which thousands of people are ready to move immediately, could the organization shift its practices to capture that energy? Could they set up similar kinds of programs to provide leadership development at the scale needed to accommodate the countermobilization?

The dilemma confronting ISAIAH thus revolves around the tension between deep leadership development and work at the scale needed for social transformation. This challenge is, historically speaking, somewhat unique. How can organizations in this present moment do their work in a way that maintains deep grassroots roots, but also generates the visibility and scale they need? Although more organizations did this in the past, ISAIAH does not have many models of organizations in the present era that can do both.[22] For example, three of the membership-based organizations with the broadest name recognition in the Democracy Alliance's map were MoveOn, the ACLU, and Planned Parenthood. At the time of the election, they lacked the local infrastructure to be able to provide all people who wanted to find meaningful opportunities for engagement with appropriate channels for doing so. Groups like ISAIAH that did have deep roots, however, did not have the visibility to draw people toward them.

ISAIAH thus will have to make choices about if and how to allocate resources to accommodate the shifting dynamics of countermobilization without having clear repertoires to guide its strategic choices. Its leaders will have to consider a range of questions. Was the outpouring of resistance durable enough that ISAIAH should shift its resources toward developing a different kind of leadership development program to help unleash the new energy? Would developing different leadership development tactics make ISAIAH more effective in leading resistance work, or would it be more effective for the organization to continue investing heavily in one-on-one relationships and smaller-scale leadership development work?

Similarly, questions about leadership development confronting Indivisible are intimately tied to questions about organizational purpose. Indivisible's sense of its own goals shifted as it began to focus on developing more capacity. Founder Leah Greenberg said, "Success is long-term, success means developing a foundational progressive infrastructure at the community level." Indivisible began to develop a plan for the 2018 midterms, to expand the organization's purview to longer-term fights. Levin and Greenberg's articulation of their goals have taken a subtle new tone, though, that focuses not only on winning policy outcomes, but doing so in a way that builds capacity for the kind of infrastructure Greenberg describes. Although Indivisible and ISAIAH face different kinds of challenges, both were grappling with the question of the extent to which investing in leadership development—and how to do it—would be a more or less effective use of their resources. These questions about the purposes and investments of the Resistance organizations are still being negotiated and likely will remain unsettled for some time.

Conclusion

Cycles of contention often begin with an initial shock, but the cycle evolves as that shock triggers a set of cascading responses. A movement develops, a countermovement reacts, and strategic action unfolds as movement players act and react to each other.[23] In this chapter, we have documented some of the ways in which old and new groups that are part of the anti-Trump Resistance acted and reacted to the changing political conditions within them. We used two exemplar organizations—Indivisible and ISAIAH—to examine the relationship of new Resistance organizations to other groups in the progressive ecosystem, and to highlight a variety of strategic dilemmas around constituency and leadership that confront entities in the anti-Trump Resistance. In particular, we highlighted two key challenges for organizations in this moment: (1) How will they define their constituencies, and address questions of race (or not)? (2) How will they invest resources in leadership development, and how will that investment be balanced with strategies to mobilize "at scale" as many people as possible? Our conversations with leaders and observations of organizational activities suggest that Resistance organizations like Indivisible are grappling with how to define their purpose and strategies after the initial burst of resistance activity in 2017. Similarly, older organizations like ISAIAH continue to face unique challenges related to how well their existing strategies match the changing political context. The decisions that leaders make in the face of these challenges will determine whether organizations will build coalitions across race to form a broad-based countermovement.

Questions about constituency and leadership, furthermore, are central to understanding the relationship between these organizations and democracy, and the legacy of social movements in the United States. In calling her constituents to engage in 100 days of #PropheticResistance, Doran Schrantz argued that their choice to engage is about much more than simply resisting Trump. The work she was describing is the work of what she calls "moral citizenship," work that she connects to a long history of social movements and other cycles of contention. We close with her words:

> "We can choose, right now, to be a part of the history of moral citizenship that has always pushed for the promise to be fulfilled, expanding and expanding the circle of who is free, who is seen, who is equal, who is citizen. From the migrant farm workers, The Underground Railroad, the women's suffrage, striking miners and the small farmers movements, the movement for Civil Rights, the poor people's movement, the

movement for Black Lives, to water protectors at Standing Rock and the emerging movement to provide sanctuary, and so many others. This is great, moral citizenship demanding, with faith in the unseen, clear-eyed, that this democracy must be re-imagined, fought for, and defended. Every day."

Conclusion

Trumpism, the Resistance, and the Future
of American Democracy

DAVID S. MEYER

Donald Trump campaigned on an apocalyptic premise: that the United States was in the midst of a critical moment in which its institutions, politics, and culture were failing dangerously, threatening the survival of the Republic. Policies on crime, immigration, and trade had created an "American carnage."[1] He alone, he announced, possessed the judgment and independence to fix it.[2]

Trump's victory in November 2016 created exactly the threat he described for those who would join the Resistance. Figuring out how to resist, however, presented ongoing and fundamental dilemmas. On the one hand, Trump was elected through a process specified in the Constitution, promising action on a range of policies that many Americans opposed. Those opponents have access to ample means of expression for their opinions on matters of policy and can find numerous institutional routes to try to exercise influence. As individuals, they can contact legislators, support interest groups, protest, and engage in elections. This is all part and parcel of the familiar and frustrating practice of democracy (Meyer 2014).

But what if that's not enough? On the other hand, the Trump presidency can represent a threat to the familiar and frustrating practice of democracy. Trump has evinced no knowledge of, much less commitment to, the institutions, rules, and practices of contemporary American politics. Recognizing the extraordinary and particular danger of this president and his own disrespect for norms and conventions can encourage opponents to abandon those same norms.

Critics urged citizens to remember that the Trump presidency was a dangerous departure from the well-established contestation that defines American politics; this presidency, they emphasized, was not normal.[3]

In a moment of risk or crisis, many routines and restrictions no longer seem appropriate, and advocates will try to throw every resource they have into the struggle. In response to the threat, opponents initially grasped at dramatic and desperate strategies, in essence, in denial that someone like Donald Trump could hold the highest office in the land. Activists variously called for preemptive impeachment; the deployment of the 25th Amendment, declaring the president unfit to serve; and the defection of principled members of the Electoral College, who would deny Trump the election he'd won. They hoped for some constitutional *deus ex machina* to rescue the Constitution and democracy from the electoral verdict. The predictable failure of such efforts contributed to the massive turnout at what turned out to be the first Women's March.

That the marchers' prime target, a President Trump, remained in office was, minimally, a disappointment; the need for ongoing and difficult action could be a cause for despair. One year on, however, the Resistance continued to grow and diversify. The Women's March was followed by marches on taxes, the environment, climate, science, the investigation of Russian influence on the election, and taxes—to name just a few. The marches capped a new level of protest and engagement at the local level as well.

The very breadth of the opposition to Trump, however, presents ongoing challenges. Opponents range from conservatives who deplore Trump's rhetoric, bearing, and lifestyle, and fear his destructive impact on their party (and country), to committed activists on the Left, some of whom would have turned out to protest a Democratic president as well. The Resistance includes people and groups at virtually every point in between on the political spectrum. As a result, drawing a sharp line defining the goals, strategies, and tactics of the Resistance is even more difficult than it would be for a narrower and more focused opposition, one limited to a defined set of issues or a partisan identity. Importantly, although the Resistance includes the colorful demonstrations that command attention, it also includes people working less visibly within mainstream politics, a mobilization that isn't normally very obtrusive (Katzenstein 1998).

Activists divide over both ultimate goals and strategies for influence. In a stylized formulation, we can say that one faction remains committed to preservation of our (and their) institutions, essentially offering a stepped-up version of politics as usual. Another sees the preservation of normal politics as a kind of acquiescence to what they define as the unique threat of Trump, not only to existing institutions and norms, but to the welfare and safety of America—and, sometimes, the world. Within the latter group are people and groups whose ambitions far outstrip removal of Trump from office. Going forward, all work in the kind of loose alliance that characterizes social movements in America, but that will always be a volatile relationship.

The Resistance enjoys the advantages of massive and diffuse support but carries all the potential liabilities of the divides within that broad coalition as well. The preceding chapters illustrate these dilemmas, and in this chapter I mean to take account of them while returning to the questions Sidney Tarrow and I raised in our Introduction. We explained that the Trump presidency and the emergent Resistance raise challenges to scholarship on social movements, the political Left, and American norms and institutions. First, we asked about the extent to which social movement theory helps explain the development of the Resistance and what the Resistance can tell us about social movements more generally. Second, we asked just how the Resistance offers a reprise of long-standing divisions within the American Left. And finally, we asked what the Trump presidency and its Resistance tell us about the workings of American political institutions and the future of those institutions. I will address these in turn.

The Resistance and Social Movement Theory

Social protest is one way to make politics in liberal democracies, and some social movements are virtually always staging some kind of protest. Importantly, protest events, including demonstrations and civil disobedience, are generally an addition to, rather than an alternative to, more conventional means of political activity (Meyer and Tarrow 1998). The Trump presidency and the concomitant Resistance press us to examine the ebbs and flows of collective action, what Tarrow (Chapter 9) describes as the "Rhythms of Resistance." We are less interested here in how an individual decides to engage in political action than in the larger patterns of collective challenges to authority and their relationships with mainstream politics.

Mobilization, Opportunities, and Coalitions

Whereas social movement presence is a constant, movements vary in terms of their size, volatility, issues engaged, and constituencies mobilized. A great deal of activism on the Left predated the emergence of Donald Trump as a candidate, but his election provoked a larger number of people to take to the streets to make their claims. As demonstrated in the contributions by Hahrie Han and Michelle Oyakawa (Chapter 11), Dana Fisher (Chapter 5), and Megan Brooker (Chapter 8), the emergence of hostile policies, in conjunction with Republican control of Congress, effectively encouraged educated middle- and upper-income, mostly white, people, who normally enjoyed access to routine means of making political claims, to see protest as a necessary addition to their efforts. This finding contributes to a long-standing debate within the academy about the relation-ship of protest to political opportunities. One stream of literature (e.g., McAdam 1996) has emphasized the importance of encouraging allies in power to the de-velopment of a social movement mobilization, whereas another has emphasized threats and political exclusion (e.g., Meyer 1990). Examination of the Trump Resistance can speak to this question and suggests the utility of looking more closely at *which* constituencies take on protest at different times (Meyer 2004). This examination calls for more serious scrutiny of the mobilization of particular constituencies over time. Activists working on behalf of immigrant rights and Black Lives Matter, for example, certainly continued their efforts (as Zepeda-Millán and Wallace show in Chapter 4); it's not clear that there was less protest. It is clear, however, that their efforts were subsumed in the larger, mostly whiter, political movement, and, to some degree, overshadowed by that movement. We have an opportunity here to understand how differently positioned groups re-spond to changes in the political environment and to each other.

An additional twist to our discussions of political opportunities and mobili-zation is the effect of the Trump campaign and presidency on the mobilization of the racist right. Vigorously, and more or less explicitly, Trump offered racialized positions on immigration and crime. He also periodically picked Twitter fights with targets, like black football players who knelt during the national anthem be-fore their games to protest police violence. Such fights reinforced Trump's iden-tification with white nationalists and legitimated their cause and their efforts. Those white nationalists, normally pressed to the margins of American politics, responded by turning out in response to the support Trump signaled. Trump's first year in office saw organized campaigns in support of Confederate Civil War memorials, and a few dramatic and disruptive demonstrations. Most notably, a Unite the Right assembly in Charlottesville, Virginia, resulted in violent con-frontation between avowed racists and counterdemonstrators, and resulted in the tragic death of one counterdemonstrator.[4] Racists also stepped up their vis-ibility on American college campuses. The Anti-Defamation League (ADL) re-ported a threefold increase in the number of racist incidents on campuses in 2017 over the previous year, identifying more than 300 events (ADL 2018), mostly provocative leafleting emphasizing white identity. The upsurge on the racist right, in response to openings from the Trump administration, is exactly the sort of response McAdam (1996) would predict. Of course, the increased visibility and volatility of white nationalism presents both a provocation and an obstacle for the Resistance.

When we talk about a social movement, we necessarily oversimplify, at least when talking about a very large and diverse campaign like the Resistance. Describing the actions of any movement blurs the diversity of whatever cam-paign is under study: Large and potentially successful social movements comprise a range of groups and assorted individuals cooperating—to some degree—and political figures stepping up, on occasion, to offer support. Participants also disagree on a lot, including goals, ideology, tactics, and just whom they are willing to work with. A particularly salient and provocative threat—and the Trump presidency certainly qualifies as one—makes cooperation more urgent, and therefore a little bit easier to negotiate; common enemies promote cooperation (Meyer and Corrigall-Brown 2005). The dynamics surrounding internal battles about strategy, particularly regarding engagement in mainstream politics, pose pressing questions of practical politics and theory (van Dyke and McCammon 2010).

In addition to the dynamics of cooperation and competition among extant groups, the Resistance also spawned numerous new groups. Hahrie Han and Michelle Oyakawa, in Chapter 11, show how new groups like Indivisible can claim unfilled niches—defined by distinct approaches to political activism—in a larger movement. At the same time, they must be mindful of securing a distinct base of support and line of mobilization. To do so, they must negotiate, more or less explicitly, with the many groups already working in that movement, and figure out how to engage and retain new activists. The evolution of the Resistance, in the context of shifting responses from mainstream political allies and opponents, offers a chance to understand these dynamics and even to assess the wisdom of particular strategic choices and alliances.

Movements, Messaging, and Media

The nature of available means for messaging is fundamentally, and continually, changing the strategies for organizing, both inside and outside the political arena. Social science remains, always, a beat or two behind the next set of organizing innovations. Earlier analyses of movements and media identified two routes for messaging. First, activists could engage in sending a "retail" message that involved more or less direct contact with individuals and face-to-face conversations. Organizers spoke to those they knew, and recruited at meetings of the already organized, in settings like social groups, religious congregations, and classes. This approach allowed personalization and the cultivation of trust but was extremely slow and resource intensive.[5] "Wholesale" recruiting depended on mass media managed largely by businesses interested in selling access to audiences to advertisers. Organizers worked to devise newsworthy events that could convey their political messages to mass audiences (e.g., Ryan 1991). But access to large audiences was mediated, filtered, and framed by third parties with no stake in a movement or its goals. Activists struggled not only to gain coverage for their causes and their efforts, but also to exercise control in defining their messages.

The growth of social media over the past two decades continues to change this media landscape. Savvy activists no longer depend on mainstream media to get their messages out to either adherents or uncommitted audiences. Posting on Twitter or Facebook can reach many more people than the most developed telephone tree in a fraction of the time. At the same time, mainstream media enjoy less influence than in the past. David Karpf's chapter (Chapter 7) shows that organizers within the Resistance have been consistent innovators, devising new ways to get their messages out to potential supporters even before mainstream media are engaged. Increasingly sophisticated use of unmediated communication with potential supporters means that organizers can generate large numbers at events much more easily than in the past, but that the infrastructure supporting those numbers need not be very developed (Tufekci 2017). A participant can self-recruit without signing onto many of the goals of a movement or event, and with minimal connections to anyone else there. This creates the challenge of building movement infrastructure *after* the most dramatic events and finding ways to engage and unite new partisans.

As Berry and Chenoweth show in their chapter (Chapter 3), the Women's March came from an idea floated on Facebook. Established organizations signed onto the effort, but the infrastructure for the event developed in response to a deadline. In contrast, the iconic 1963 March on Washington was first proposed more than two decades earlier and reflected months of active planning by several very well-established groups. The contemporary model is different: The millions who showed up at Women's Marches across the country were the impetus for building a Resistance infrastructure, rather than the outcome of that infrastructure. The appearance of mass events very early in a movement's emergence represents a new development in social movement cycles, one that demands attention. Megan Brooker's story of Indivisible reflects the power of social media in a different way. Activism didn't bubble up from grassroots organizations, but rather, both new and established groups grabbed onto a set of protocols for influence posted in an online memo. In the months following, Indivisible worked to raise money and develop a resilient structure. Again, substantial organization followed events, rather than preceded them.

Hundreds of local and national organizations signed onto the Women's March in the months after Trump's election, and hundreds of local groups soon adopted some part of the *Indivisible Playbook*. They shared agreement on opposition to Donald Trump, but brokered stark differences in emphasis, strategies, and issues, which are playing out over time. At the outset, the Women's March prohibited New Wave Feminists, a group opposed to abortion rights, from officially sponsoring the event,[6] generating some controversy outside the organizing groups. Rival contingents later sought to claim the mantle of the Women's March, offering different rhetoric and distinct approaches to local organizing.[7] Disputes about control, priorities, and strategies are characteristic of social movements in America, including large and successful ones; they are likely to become more evident as mainstream politics responds with the possibilities of partial victories. The demands of managing a coalition developed in the context of a dynamic policy environment pose ongoing questions for our scholarly understanding of the politics of protest.

In summary, examination of the Resistance affords students of social movements the chance to advance long-standing debates about the relationship of mobilization to opportunities, the dynamics of coalitions, and how the ongoing development of mass and social media affects the dynamics of social movements altogether. Even as scholars can look at the Resistance as a particularly interesting example of a contemporary movement, those within the movement note somewhat different challenges. They want to find ways to continue to mobilize effectively, advancing their own ideas and protecting the institutions of American democracy.

A Challenge to the American Left

Cooperation with allies and negotiating with mainstream politics have always been contested issues on the American Left. During the campaign for the Democratic presidential nomination, actress Susan Sarandon, a strong supporter of Bernie Sanders, suggested that "Some people feel that Donald Trump will bring the revolution immediately, if he gets in. Then things will really, you know, explode."[8] Sarandon, appalled by candidate Trump, was eager for the "political revolution" Sanders promised, and apparently as opposed to mainstream Democratic foreign policy as she was to the Trump presidency.

If Sarandon's preferred policies seem quite removed from mainstream politics, advocacy for them is not. The broad Resistance loosely unified vigorous protest on virtually every issue of concern on the Left, but that unity remains tenuous, with strains particularly visible on the radical Left. After Trump was elected, demonstrators appeared in the streets of large American cities and in a few places engaged in confrontations with police and vandalized some property. On the day of Trump's Inauguration—the eve of the Women's March—a range of more aggressive, creative, and destructive protests spread across Washington, DC. The Queer Dance party staged outside incoming Vice President Mike Pence's residence featured a variety of music, costumes, flags, and a lot of glitter.

More aggressively, hundreds of DisruptJ20 protesters launched unpermitted marches through the streets, protesting US foreign policy, inequality, and discrimination, and were less specific about policy demands. As announced on an organizing site, "DisruptJ20 rejects all forms of domination and oppression, particularly those based on racism, poverty, gender, and sexuality, organizes by consensus, and embraces a diversity of tactics." Indeed, public communications from the group emphasized urgency and tactics rather than issues, asserting that, although ideologically and strategically diverse, DisruptJ20 protesters would commit not to help law enforcement maintain public order.[9] A few protesters attacked a limousine with bricks and broke storefront windows, including those at the entrances to targets like Starbuck's and the Bank of America. More than 200 people were arrested for being in the streets when the destruction took place and faced harsh felony charges for conspiracy to riot that could have resulted in decades in prison.[10] The demonstrators certainly had grievances with the incoming Trump administration, but importantly, planning for the demonstration had begun in July 2016, when it appeared that Hillary Clinton was sure to win.

The point is that Donald Trump's policies and persona added little more than a bit of emphasis and perhaps a sense of urgency for some left activists in the United States. It is likely, however, that at least a few others would be convinced that Trump's presidency announced a need for more aggressive politics—as Sarandon predicted. The DisruptJ20 protests followed a well-established routine of disruptive protests at Inaugurations albeit larger, more volatile, and surrounded by less-disruptive events. They presented more mainstream anti-Trump forces with a potential image problem, that of managing an association, often imposed by opponents, with an unruly and unpopular radical flank.

At the other end of the opposition spectrum were more institutionally oriented activists who would normally emphasize far less-disruptive politics. Often members of the Democratic Party, these are exactly the people who are less likely to engage in street protests when Democrats are in power (e.g., Heaney and Rojas 2015). Some political professionals, exemplified by Indivisible (see Megan Brooker's Chapter 8), recognized the loss of institutional access and potential influence, so turned to promoting citizen activism at the grassroots. Indivisible's repertoire included protest actions, as local Indivisible groups organized travel to support national and regional demonstrations. And Indivisible's local groups were filled with people who normally engaged in politics in much more limited ways.

From the outset, the Trump Resistance created a capacious umbrella for groups and individuals who bring very different ideas about strategies for influence and ultimate goals to their efforts. The breadth of the spectrum is perhaps broader and denser than usually the case in American political movements, but it is a difference of degree, rather than kind. The inherent dilemmas are also, therefore, familiar. Organizers need to decide how to orient their efforts both to mainstream politics and to potential allies. For some in the Resistance, protest efforts are a means to an institutional end—stalling unfriendly policy initiatives, mobilizing and educating voters, incubating policy alternatives—and moving back to more routine politics when opportunities appear. For others, protest efforts are a means to end institutional politics as we know it.

The early Trump presidency has made at least tacit cooperation easier than it normally is, but even then there are problems. Should would-be institutional liberals defend protesters who destroy property or call for open borders? Should those with a more radical analysis see voter registration efforts as part of their campaign? Easy answers disappear as institutional efforts advance and public policy comes to the fore.

The Trump administration's policy offerings have put Resistance activists in an unusual and strained position of working to defend institutions and established policies they might normally criticize. American policy toward Russia provides a recurrent example of this stress. During the Cold War, mainstream conservative dogma put an aggressive stance against the Soviet Union at the center of foreign policy. The stance united criticism of Communism with militarized wariness about the Soviet Union's essential nature. This conflation of disparate rationales was apparent at the outset (X 1947). The collapse of the Soviet Union and the end of state Communism ended one set of reasons for massive military expenditures and a harsh stance toward Moscow; candidate Donald Trump had refrained from criticizing Russia on matters of foreign policy or human rights and promised to get along better with its leader. This stance was a departure from mainstream conservativism, and foreign policy hawks, like Republican Senators Lindsey Graham (R-SC) and John McCain (R-AZ), saw it as a threat to their party and to national security. They unsuccessfully challenged the campaign on foreign policy generally but emphasized the threat from Russia. Their challenge continued after Trump took office but found limited support. Resistance activists have to choose whether to support these critics and whether to make the policy of a harsher stance to Russia a focal point in their campaigns.

Cooperation between Russia and the Trump campaign emerged as an issue after the election, quickly resulting in the dismissal of National Security Adviser Michael Flynn after just a few weeks in office. Within months, Trump fired FBI Director James Comey, explaining to both American and Russian media that he hoped it would end the investigation of possible collusion between Trump and Russia (Vitali and Siemaszko 2017). Trump viciously criticized his own attorney general, Jeff Sessions, for recusing himself from the matter and thereby allowing another Justice official to appoint Robert Mueller as a special counsel in the matter. The White House, in conjunction with Republican allies in Congress, has maintained an unending campaign against the integrity of both Mueller and the FBI. Oddly, a damaged and recused AG Jeff Sessions was less dangerous to the future of the Republic than a replacement named as Trump sought loyalty. Still, Sessions was difficult for Democrats to defend. Similarly, standing up for the honor and independence of the FBI was an unusual and awkward position for many in the Resistance. In the meantime, Trump's continued attacks on the FBI and the Justice Department more generally have undermined Republican faith in those institutions (Purdum 2018). On such issues, the organized Left found itself in the unusual position of placing a defense of a new Cold War stance, and its attendant institutions, at the center of its efforts. For activists on the Left, criticism of Russia resurrected a long-dormant version of Cold War liberalism.

Electoral politics makes such issues especially salient. Particularly in the House of Representatives, Democrats often represent constituencies that demand continual and uncompromising resistance to the Trump White House and the Republican agenda more generally. This means that many members of Congress lose nothing by repeatedly announcing their intent to impeach the president, even as the legislators know that it is politically impossible to do so. Many did so, encouraged by activists within the party (Burns 2018). Candidates for office can win allegiance at the Democratic grassroots by affirming their support for very progressive policies, like single-payer health care, even as those same policies remain anathema to the coveted swing voters, who must turn out if Democrats hope to gain ground in Congress or state legislatures.

Fundamentally, activists on the Left need to recognize as allies those who would defend mainstream American politics and institutions from Donald Trump, others who see Trump as a threat demanding vigorous opposition by any means necessary, and a much smaller faction that would use the Trump Resistance to advance a broader revolutionary campaign. This very broad and loose alliance reflects a moment in which the survival of long-standing American political institutions and attendant norms has been called into question. In essence, Trump opponents must decide whether the Trump infestation of the Executive Branch justifies burning down the institutions that house it. Alternatively, activists on the Left can work to defend those institutions against a threat from the occupant of the Oval Office, even if that entails mobilizing and politicizing those institutions.

Politicizing American Institutions

The Resistance has mobilized not only in the streets and in mainstream American political institutions, but also in the institutions of civil society, challenging the norms and legitimacy of those institutions. Look briefly at the tensions within the organization of mental health professionals and within the American academy.

Immediately upon his election, a group of well-established and well-regarded mental health professionals challenged Donald Trump's fitness for office. Mostly psychiatrists, the group leaned on its professional credentials to buttress its claim that a President Trump represented a threat to the well-being of both the United States and the rest of the world (Lee et al. 2017). Citing Trump's statements and behavior, the professionals proclaimed their duty to warn the government and the American public and to call for immediate action, sometimes starting with a professional evaluation of the president's mental health.

Trump himself emphatically proclaimed his own sanity and indeed his genius, but the accuracy of the mental health warning has evoked less debate than the appropriateness of offering professional diagnoses without a serious in-person examination. Citing the American Psychiatric Association's "Goldwater Rule" (no diagnosis without examination), Jeffrey A. Lieberman (2017), a recent president of the Association and chair of the psychiatry department at Columbia University, acknowledged the critical authors' sincerity, but charged them with professional dereliction of duty and moral failures. He announced that their well-intentioned effort "undermines the profession's integrity and credibility."[11]

Unsurprisingly, the critical missive generated extensive debate in the comments section. Although some Trump supporters weighed in to reject the diagnosis, many more comments focused on the moral and professional responsibilities of mental health professionals and citizens than on the sanity of the president. Organizations of mental health professionals include fans of Trump's policies, as well as defenders of their institutions' and professions' credibility. Politicizing and mobilizing means jeopardizing both the comity and the status of the group and the work and undermining the norms of routine politics at the same time. The division among the psychiatrists is an example of divisions among Trump opponents virtually everywhere else. The psychiatrists' dilemma is one that crystallizes a set of problems common to all sorts of professionals and citizens engaging the politics of the Trump presidency, as some advocates worked to enlist their profession in the Resistance.

Those problems reappear in the ongoing political debate about "Dreamers," that is, people who were brought to the United States as children without legal authorization or documentation. Candidate Trump campaigned vigorously against immigrants, but offered periodic expressions of support for the Dreamers, promising to treat them with "heart" (McCaskill 2017). In September of 2017, Trump announced the end of the Deferred Action for Childhood Arrivals (DACA) program, giving Congress 6 months to legislate a solution to the problem of the Dreamers, before deportations could start. Many states grant some kind of official status to these young people; California, for example, allows them to obtain drivers' licenses, and pay in-state tuition to attend state universities. The president of the University of California system, Janet Napolitano, was emphatic in announcing opposition to the end of DACA and support for the Dreamers, announcing

I am deeply troubled by President Trump's decision to effectively end the DACA program and uproot the lives of an estimated 800,000

Dreamers across the nation. This backward-thinking, far-reaching move threatens to separate families and derail the futures of some of this country's brightest young minds, thousands of whom currently attend or have graduated from the University of California.[12]

Ironically, as secretary of Homeland Security, Napolitano had presided over record numbers of deportations. Nonetheless, as president of the University of California she took a strong oppositional position that was largely shared in the American academy (Harris 2017). In addition to formal statements, she joined other academic leaders in lobbying members of Congress and in supporting a lawsuit against the repeal of DACA filed by 15 states.[13] University leaders across the country announced their support for DACA recipients and provided advice and support for students affected by the policy. But universities are subject to federal law and now face pressures to announce their own resistance to cooperation with immigration officials. Leaders of several universities, including the University of Pennsylvania (Trump's alma mater), have declared their commitment not to cooperate with immigration officials, declaring their campuses sanctuaries (Vongkiatkajorn 2017). They are under pressure from students to go further in protecting the Dreamers. The Resistance presents a test of just how far these leaders are willing to go to defend their institutions and their constituencies.

The scope of the Resistance offers opportunities to build alliances that stretch across the political spectrum, but those alliances present dilemmas for all concerned. As long as the threat of the Trump presidency trumps concerns about ultimate ends, organizers can manage those alliances. Concerns about avoiding tainted allies and maintaining the rule of law, however, present recurrent challenges to those organizers. Moreover, the Resistance will succeed only to the extent that it can maintain efforts both in the streets and within mainstream institutions.

A Challenge to Institutions: This Wasn't Supposed to Happen

Donald Trump's presence in the presidency reflects institutional failure. Americans watching the emergence of aspiring authoritarians in other democracies, like Silvio Berlusconi in Italy or, more recently, Recep Tayyip Erdogan in Turkey, have found what turned out to be undue comfort in the institutional design and developed norms of American politics.[14] Trump's express threat to the constitutional design has forced his opponents to consider which elements of that design are actually worth defending.

The Founders focused a great deal of attention on avoiding tyranny—either of a monarch or of a mob. In designing and defending the Constitution, they took pains to design institutional tripwires that would prevent the emergence of a demagogue—or limit the damage that such a leader could do. They offered two sets of remedies: stopping an unqualified person from becoming president; and constraining the autonomy of the presidency.

Protecting the Presidency

Alexander Hamilton focused on the former protection; in Federalist #68, he emphasized the power and importance of the presidency, and touted the newly created Electoral College as a failsafe that would ensure that only qualified men would hold the job. As he wrote,

> The process of election affords a moral certainty, that the office of President will never fall to the lot of any man who is not in an eminent degree endowed with the requisite qualifications. Talents for low intrigue, and the little arts of popularity, may alone suffice to elevate a man to the first honors in a single State; but it will require other talents, and a different kind of merit, to establish him in the esteem and confidence of the whole Union, or of so considerable a portion of it as would be necessary to make him a successful candidate for the distinguished office of President of the United States. It will not be too strong to say, that there will be a constant probability of seeing the station filled by characters pre-eminent for ability and virtue.

The Electoral College never worked exactly the way that Hamilton envisioned, and long before Trump was even born, it had become a vehicle for translating the results of state elections to a national context. Voters chose electors nominated not for their independent judgment, but for their loyalty to one of the major parties.

Although not in the original design, political parties developed as another tripwire to prevent the election of demagogues to the presidency. Party leaders sought electability and compatibility, first through a caucus system, and much later through an extended system of primaries that required sustained engagement and extensive funding. Through the long campaign process, political scientists found, party leaders had developed ways to ensure that their eventual nominee was someone they wanted as a candidate and as a president (Cohen et al. 2008). Donald Trump, who had never served in the military or the bureaucracy, much less elective office, represented exactly the sort of candidate the Republican Party leaders wanted to filter out. Most came to support Trump only when they were convinced that they had no practical alternatives. Even then, the Party housed an unusual number of "Never Trumpers" in its ranks.

As candidate Trump advanced through the electoral process, violating well-established traditions of disclosure and civility, some opponents reached desperately for institutional means to stop him and found only frustration. Republican Never Trumpers called for dramatic action at their convention, but most of the prominent anti-Trump leaders, including two former presidents Bush, skipped the convention altogether, warning that the November election would prove the wisdom of their stance. Much of the Democratic Party's fall campaign focused on the sheer unsuitability of the Republican candidate for public office, emphasizing their widely shared evaluation of Trump's skills, background, and temperament, rather than policy positions, which might be contested and exacerbate conflicts within the party. This strategic choice proved costly, as a substantive debate on contested political issues was overshadowed by endless discussion of Trump's endless liabilities and offenses. Indeed, the chaotic and undisciplined Trump campaign presented recurrent challenges of focus that frustrated the Democrats in 2016 and continue to bedevil and animate the Resistance. Comparing the Trump threat to the one that Silvio Berlusconi posed to Italian democracy, Luigi Zingales (2016) warned against a fixation on what seemed like the simplest opposition strategy:

> Mr. Berlusconi was able to govern Italy for as long as he did mostly thanks to the incompetence of his opposition. It was so rabidly obsessed with his personality that any substantive political debate disappeared; it focused only on personal attacks, the effect of which was to increase Mr. Berlusconi's popularity. His secret was an ability to set off a Pavlovian reaction among his leftist opponents, which engendered instantaneous sympathy in most moderate voters. Mr. Trump is no different.
>
> We saw this dynamic during the presidential campaign. Hillary Clinton was so focused on explaining how bad Mr. Trump was that she too often didn't promote her own ideas, to make the positive case for voting for her. The news media was so intent on ridiculing Mr. Trump's behavior that it ended up providing him with free advertising.[15]
>
> The Democratic Party should learn this lesson . . . an opposition focused on personality would crown Mr. Trump as the people's leader of the fight against the Washington caste. It would also weaken the opposition voice on the issues, where it is important to conduct a battle of principles.

After the balloting, a few activists continued to focus on the visible threat of the Trump persona, downplaying their opposition to the right-wing Republican policies he championed. They tried to convince members of the Electoral College to substitute their own judgment for that of their states' voters, preventing Trump from taking office. Ultimately, just a few "Hamilton Electors" withheld their votes for Trump. Here too, we see the strain in trying to jury-rig an institution to work for a near-term goal. The institutions work effectively as tripwires only when the people operating within them are willing to use their power. Members of the Electoral College chose not to be "faithless," and members of Congress and the Courts have thus far chosen not to hold Trump to previous standards of disclosure or the emoluments clause of the Constitution. The rules work only when people are willing to use them.

Protecting the Republic From a President

If parties and the electoral process both failed to prevent a would-be demagogue from taking office, several institutional checks still gave hope to Trump's opponents. James Madison displayed less faith in the electoral process than did his Federalist Papers coauthor, recognizing that "[E]nlightened statesmen will not always be at the helm" (Federalist #10). Madison claimed, however, that the checks and balances built into the structure of government would prevent both corruption and the violation of citizens' rights. His argument, repeated daily in civics classes across the United States, was that other independent institutions, particularly Congress, would serve as a counterbalance to a renegade president.

Whether the other branches of government can effectively constrain the president's initiatives remains an open question: Trump himself has shown little deference to either the norms or institutional rules of American politics. In his campaign, Trump consistently displayed an ignorance of constitutional strictures, repeatedly promising, for example, to imprison his political opponents. He refused to release his tax returns and pilloried the free press to a degree unusual even in contested American politics. In office, Trump clearly prized loyalty in his appointees above experience or competence, vociferously criticized "unelected" federal judges who supported challenges to his administration's sloppily crafted travel ban (see Dorf and Chu, Chapter 6) and an independent judiciary more generally, and called for Congress to end any rules or practices, particularly the filibuster, that might constrain the majority from supporting him. The independent judiciary and the anti-majoritarian procedures in the Senate are examples of the many rules and routines built into American politics to frustrate majorities—exactly the things that often send Americans out into the streets.

Virtually all national Republican leaders greeted Donald Trump's announcement of his presidential candidacy with skepticism, if not ridicule. Over time, however, elected officials began to sign onto the campaign as alternatives faltered and Trump demonstrated vigorous support among a significant faction of Republican voters. By the time of the Republican National Convention, most party regulars proclaimed support for Trump—as an alternative to Hillary Clinton and the Democrats—but there were significant holdouts, who skipped the convention. Once Trump took office, however, critics, including both Presidents Bush, Ohio Governor John Kasich, and Nebraska Senator Ben Sasse, were silent, or offered only the most measured criticism. Even somewhat harsher critics, like Arizona Senators John McCain and Jeff Flake, continued to vote for the president's agenda. The Republican Congressional leadership defended the president in service to their policy agenda, compromising any commitment to preserving the institutions of American democracy.

The Constitution does not enforce itself. From the moment Trump was elected, ethics experts from both political parties, including the director of the US Office of Government Ethics, have identified visible conflicts of interest resulting from his diverse and complicated business assets—with no visible impact on the White House. The president refused to place his holdings in a blind trust, much less divest them, assigning day-to-day management of his businesses to his sons (Lizza 2017). Trump's casual disregard of previous norms did not generate any response from the Republican-controlled Congress, and a public interest group, Citizens for Responsibility and Ethics in Washington (CREW), filed suit in federal court, charging that he violated the emoluments clause of the Constitution by taking money from foreign interests. In December of 2017, the court dismissed the suit, finding no role for the court in holding the president accountable (Fahrenthold and O'Connell 2017).[16] Judge George B. Daniels made this ruling:

> As the only political branch with the power to consent to violations of the Foreign Emoluments Clause, Congress is the appropriate body to determine whether, and to what extent, Defendant's conduct unlawfully infringes on that power . . . . If Congress determines that an infringement has occurred, it is up to Congress to decide whether to challenge or acquiesce to Defendant's conduct. As such, this case presents a non-justiciable political question.[17]

The judicial system, as Alexander Hamilton wrote centuries ago, depends on the acceptance and enforcement of its decisions by the other branches of government. When Judge Daniels passed the problem to Congress, the Republican-controlled House and Senate did not respond to the verdict at all. CREW announced that it would appeal the decision, and another case on the same issue is pending in another court. Nonetheless, like the lawyers challenging the Travel Ban, the litigants must depend not only on the independence and judgment of the judiciary, but also on the willingness of political actors to respect it. At this writing, we cannot evaluate how resilient that respect is, nor predict whether challengers will continue to bind themselves to the same strictures the White House rejects. The Resistance ultimately depends on people who will never take to the street in a demonstration.

An Independent Media

Independent mass media present another set of institutions that face fundamental challenges in the Trump Era. Since the founding of the United States, elected officials have navigated often-stormy relationships with the media that covered them, which change as the composition of American media has developed from primarily partisan papers, to broadcast media mostly constrained by journalistic norms of objectivity. Politicians and activists now must manage a landscape characterized by narrowcasting, in which neither relies exclusively on mainstream media to get their messages out. David Karpf's chapter (Chapter 7) shows how Resistance figures have taken advantage of the evolving landscape, but they are not alone. Donald Trump has hardly ignored mainstream media, consistently chastising outlets as purveyors of "fake news" and has found Twitter to be an extremely useful tool for reaching his supporters directly and for setting the agenda for mainstream media. The ritual press conference, at which the president responds to questions from a range of mainstream reporters, has been largely superseded by press briefings with foreign leaders, and the press corps have expanded to include formerly marginal Internet outlets. Likely more consequential, Trump and his administration's explicit disregard for veracity has challenged the conventions of reporting. Although all presidents misrepresent the truth from time to time, the pace of Trump's lies has far outstripped anything in the historical record. Moreover, the administration has continued to reiterate lies even when mainstream media have reported them (Leonhardt et al. 2017).

Mainstream media outlets then must make decisions about how to report. Adhering to previously consensual standards that allow political figures to make their own cases, while quoting opponents, no longer seems adequate. But even deciding what words to use ("incorrect," "false," or "lie") to describe fallacious statements from the White House remains controversial among journalists (e.g., Hepworth 2017; Johnson 2017). Trump's ongoing assault on mainstream news has contributed to eroding public respect for the media, and journalists fear that challenging the White House statements more explicitly contributes to that erosion. It's surely not clear what approach is best for preserving an independent and critical press, nor for countering Donald Trump.

American politics advantages the defense, that is, those who oppose change. Donald Trump's election forced his opponents to take on the task of preventing the new president from executing his policies. The future of the American project is dependent on how well the Resistance and the institutional allies it inspires do in using those rules and institutions to frustrate the president's agenda, and how much influence they can deploy on the broader political process.

Coda: How the Resistance Continues

A year after the first Women's March, an anniversary effort produced extraordinary turnouts in hundreds of demonstrations across the country.[18] In mainstream media, the second March was eclipsed by the first shutdown of the federal government during the Trump Era, as Congress encountered a brief standoff on the DACA policy. The large turnouts at the second March, albeit smaller than the first, reflected the diffusion, rather than the dissolution, of the movement.

DACA was a particularly salient issue because President Trump had, months earlier, unilaterally ended President Obama's policy to allow some immigrants who were brought to the country as children to work legally. Trump simultaneously announced his sympathy for the young people and called on Congress to fix the problem he'd exacerbated. The chaos of the DACA uncertainty came embedded in reports of the president's racist rhetoric in Oval Office negotiations to address the problem. The DACA debacle was emblematic of a confused and chaotic presidency, best described as "malevolence tempered by incompetence."[19] The summary story is clear: Those unhappy about a Trump presidency last year had every reason to stay that way—and Trump helped. And organizers had worked over the previous year to build a series of sustainable campaigns.

But the large demonstrations are only dramatic and emphatic punctuation marks in a much larger effort. The first Women's March was about the disappointment of national elections; 2018's events were pointed at the upcoming elections as an opportunity. Activists carrying an extremely broad range of concerns focused on changing the government to address those policies. Trump was not on the ballot, but activists announced their commitment to lash him to every candidate with an R next to his or her name. Resistance organizers encouraged supporters not only to vote, but also to run for office, with some visible success. At least a half-dozen of the new Democratic delegates elected in 2017 to the lower house of Virginia's legislature cited the first Women's March as inspiration. Those women were the leading edge of a much larger trend: Record numbers of Democratic women launched campaigns for office at every level of governance, and many more signed onto campaign work (Traister 2018).

The detailed work of organizing and funding electoral campaigns represents a continuation, not a departure, from protest politics. Such efforts revive and reinforce the primacy of American political institutions—with all of the attendant frustrations and compromises. The future of the Resistance in America depends on its ability to make institutional politics an extension of the protest movement Donald Trump provoked. Success will entail protest in the streets along with restoring the vitality of American political institutions.

Predictions of political apocalypse are *almost* always wrong. At some point, Donald Trump will leave office, and he has evinced little interest or capacity to build an organization that will outlast him. Nonetheless, the consequences of his tenure in office are the critical and thus far undetermined outcomes of the struggle between his administration and the Resistance. There are immediate casualties, including the well-being of immigrants and refugees, the loss of benefits to the truly needy, and the erosion of American commitment to international agreements. The revived racist Right is also unlikely to disappear with the Trump presidency. Trump is undermining the functioning of American institutions, including the bureaucracy, the military, and social welfare programs, both by erratic management and funding and by undermining public support for those institutions. This is a bleak version of an American future.

Alternatively, the Resistance could produce a revitalized civil society and a more engaged and informed citizenry. In the efforts to constrain Trump's influence, activists could build broader communities of engagement and create cooperative and sympathetic connections among different groups. The legacy of an indifferent and incompetent administration could engender a new respect for the importance of American political institutions and a commitment to build and protect them. Ultimately, this could be the legacy of the Resistance.

Acknowledgments: Thanks to Colin Bernatsky, Megan Brooker, Russ Dalton, and Sid Tarrow, for patient readings and helpful comments on earlier versions of this chapter.

Afterword

What the Resistance Means for American Democracy

JACOB S. HACKER

The late economist Paul Samuelson once quipped that stock prices had predicted "nine of the last five recessions."[1] Yet social scientists, in general, are prone to the opposite error: They don't see change coming. The world is complex, and our strongest theories are designed to explain continuity rather than change. During periods of rapid transformation, our data are often dated by the time we analyze them. And when big outcomes hinge on comparatively small causes—a close election, a key strategic choice—forecasting the future can seem a fool's errand.

The election of Donald J. Trump appears a case in point. Few thought the businessman-turned-reality-TV-star could win the Republican nomination, much less defeat his more seasoned Democratic opponent. In the tumultuous two-plus years since Trump launched his improbable bid for the presidency, he has broken virtually every norm of American politics and overseen a campaign and a presidency the likes of which the United States has never seen— one that poses an unprecedented threat to effective governance and, perhaps, to American democracy.

And yet, as the contributions to this timely volume make clear, the rupture of Trump's election emerged out of political, economic, and social trends to which scholars have in fact devoted considerable attention. In particular, Trump's victory and the broad-based response to it are rooted in three fundamental shifts in the American political universe: the intense, ongoing, and asymmetric polarization of the two major parties; the reorientation of American politics around issues of race and immigration in response to shifting demographics and group power dynamics; and the declining responsiveness of political elites to the views of the nonaffluent in an age of skyrocketing inequality. All of these trends have become increasingly prominent, not only within American society, but also within social science.

Even expert forecasts of the 2016 election performed remarkably well. Most correctly predicted a modest Democratic margin of victory in the popular vote.[2] Of course, that margin was irrelevant to the final outcome in the Electoral College. But students of American politics have also been pointing out for years that our distinctive electoral system is becoming more and more favorable to Republicans—in Congressional as well as presidential elections—because of its bias toward less-populous states, successful Republican gerrymandering, and the increasing concentration of Democratic voters (and hence "wasted votes" for Democratic candidates) in America's urban centers.

In short, recent political events constitute an intensification of many of the deepest trends that have reshaped American democracy over the last generation. But that does not make them any less destabilizing—or the political response to them any less fateful. Indeed, it is not too much of an exaggeration to say that the long-term health of American democracy rests on how effectively the organized opposition to President Trump and to the Republican Congressional majority is able to counter the most undemocratic elements of the present governing order.

The chapters in this volume provide a rich picture of this opposition, known by its stalwarts as "the Resistance." In doing so, they draw on a wealth of research about contemporary social movements that predates Trump's election. Ironically, given the Leftward thrust of the Resistance, much of this research has concerned forces on the Right: the surge of white nationalism, the Tea Party movement, the rise of organized Christian conservatism, the coalescence of business groups and conservative donors around billionaire brothers Charles and David Koch. Even before Trump's election, however, students of social movements were also examining new forms of mobilization on the Left, from unconventional strategies and new constituencies, such as Latino chambermaids and janitors, and targets of labor organizing to the protean protests against inequality grouped under the banner of Occupy Wall Street to the wave of mobilization against racially biased criminal justice united by the cry "Black Lives Matter."

The authors in this volume have each tried to grapple with fundamental questions about our current moment raised by these rich new veins of scholarship: How can we understand the Resistance in light of recent social movements and political organizations? How must we change our theories and concepts to reflect what is happening now? And what is the prospect that this current constellation of organized forces will be successful—indeed, what does "success" even mean, given the heightened, some might say existential, stakes of contemporary conflict?

These are the questions that I take up in this brief Afterword, drawing insight and inspiration from the illuminating contributions to this volume. I start with the empirical picture—where we are—and then turn to the analytic challenge—how we understand the forces at work. The Resistance, I shall argue, is propelled by many of the same propulsive forces driving other recent social movements. Yet it is also swimming against powerful tides, tides that ultimately threaten to swamp our basic democratic institutions. The question is not whether the Resistance will change the course of our politics. It already has. The question is whether it will be enough to turn back this fundamental threat and, if so, what it will bring in its place.

A Transformed Political World

"The political parties created democracy," wrote the great American political scientist E. E. Schattschneider in 1942, "and modern democracy is unthinkable save in terms of the parties. As a matter of fact, the condition of the parties is the best possible evidence of the nature of any regime."[3]

Schattschneider was not happy with the regime he saw in the American party system. To him, what was notable was the *weakness* of American parties—the fissures within the Democratic Party between the two-party North and one-party South, the moderate me-tooism of the Republican Party, and the constricted agenda of debate around the Cold War (where the broad center agreed on what to do) and on issues of race (where the broad center agreed on what *not* to do). Schattschneider wanted clearer divisions between the parties, what we would today call "polarization," and a more equal competitive balance between them. In 1950, he headed a special committee of the American Political Science Association that issued a now-famous report calling for a "More Responsible Two-Party System."

Be careful what you wish for! Today, the parties are more polarized than at any point since the 19th century. We are also in the midst of the most intense period of national party competition since the Civil War. Yet the result has not looked anything like "responsible" party government, with two competing parties held electorally accountable for their promises and performance. To the contrary, as the chapters in this volume make clear, a huge disconnect separates voters and their elected representatives. Indeed, American democracy is facing virtually unprecedented threats to its legitimacy and perhaps even its survival—or at least survival in anything like the more robust form that characterized the mid 20th century, notwithstanding all the limits of democratic responsiveness in that era.

If any reminder of the voter–elite disconnect was needed, the first year of the Trump presidency has provided it in abundance. The most popular (and populist) aspects of Trump's campaign—his defense of Medicaid and Medicare, his demand for big infrastructure investments, his call for a fundamentally new US trade policy—were either scaled back or abandoned. Instead, Trump avidly supported the two least popular pieces of legislation in the past quarter-century: "repeal and replacement" of the 2010 Affordable Care Act (which, despite the label, reached well beyond the 2010 law to enact huge permanent cuts to Medicaid) and tax-cut legislation that delivered more than three-quarters of its long-term benefits to the top 1%. Although the health care repeal narrowly failed in the Senate, it came closer to passage than any bill that has polled so badly and would have represented the most significant retrenchment of the American welfare state in history. Bills that garner only 20%–30% support and yet have a good chance of passage indicate a breakdown of responsiveness, not the responsible party government that heightened polarization was supposed to deliver.[4]

Asymmetric Polarization

How can we understand this paradox, which is so central, in turn, to understanding the potential of and threats facing the Resistance? The key is to recognize that polarization has not been symmetric. That is, it has not been driven by the move of Republicans to the Right and Democrats to the Left in more or less equal measure. Instead, it has been fueled by the sharp rightward shift of the GOP on economic issues and by the party's growing incentive and capacity to use wedge issues (race, religion, morality, guns, immigration) to stoke the outrage of its increasingly downscale voting base.[5] As Doug McAdam argues in Chapter 1, the realignment of the parties around race—apparent in the North long before the 1960s, but catalyzed in the South by the national Democratic leadership's belated embrace of civil rights—has caused the GOP and Democrats to switch places. No longer the party of abolition and the Union, Republicans are now the party of the South with strong political incentives to stoke white resentment and anxiety in an increasingly multiracial society.

This shift has buoyed the GOP's electoral fortunes, leading to a near 50–50 battle for the presidency and both houses of Congress. It has also coincided with a sharp hardening of the respective geographic bases of the two parties. Put crudely, Democrats receive their strongest support in urban and coastal areas outside the South; Republicans, the nonurban South, interior West (Montana, Wyoming, the Dakotas), and rural areas. As a result, Republicans and Democrats generally hail from areas where *intra*party competition is fiercer than *inter*party competition—particularly on the Republican side, where conservative primary challengers are often well funded and appealing to disenchanted GOP voters. Thus, close competition for control of national political institutions masks a strikingly uncompetitive electoral system in all but the quadrennial presidential contest.

Fatefully, this Janus-faced system also embodies a significant built-in GOP edge, rooted in in America's peculiar electoral geography as well as the much greater participation of core Republican voting blocs in lower-turnout elections. The United States has the most malapportioned upper house in the rich world: Every state gets two seats in the Senate regardless of population. This bias partly carries over to the Electoral College, because states receive Electoral College votes equal to their total number of Congressional representatives (Senate plus House). It also matters more than in the past, both because population differences across the states have magnified and because less-populous states have become more solidly Republican. And it matters especially in midterm elections (2010, 2014, 2018) because of the higher relative participation rates of core GOP voters in low-turnout elections.

Republicans also enjoy an edge because GOP voters are more geographically dispersed than the urban and coastal regional bases of Democratic Party. Dispersed voters result in more districts with solid but not overwhelming Republican margins. This is especially true because Republicans can use their greater strength in statehouses (courtesy of the very same dispersion, as well as their turnout edge in generally low-turnout state elections) to draw districts in the most favorable way. Democrats, meanwhile, are increasingly crammed into urban areas where most of their lopsided votes for Democratic candidates are "wasted." The result is an estimated five-to-eight-point baseline advantage for Republicans in the battle for Congressional seats.[6] Democrats, in other words, have to win big to win Congress, limiting the extent to which Republicans need to worry that their rightward trajectory threatens their political standing.

Plutocratic Populism

There is a final reason why partisan polarization has not brought responsible party government: skyrocketing inequality. America's unrivaled surge in inequality, which has returned the United States to disparities of wealth and income not seen since before the Great Depression, has reverberated within both parties. Yet it has had very different effects in each. Democrats, in general, have been cross-pressured—torn between their big-money donors and affluent urban professionals, on the one hand, and their traditional supporters, including less-affluent white workers, African Americans, and (more recently) Hispanics, on the other. The ongoing collapse of private-sector labor unions has been a fateful component of this shift, because white workers are much more likely to support Democrats when they are unionized and because unions were so fundamental to Democratic fund-raising and get-out-the-vote efforts as well as to progressive policy drives in Washington.

Republicans, by contrast, have been emboldened. Their conservative economic agenda aligns with the deregulatory and tax-cutting aims of their biggest contributors and organized backers. In particular, Republicans have been strengthened by the conservative donor networks and lobbying organizations that have fed off rising inequality and fed into campaigns and policymaking in the states and Washington, DC. Leading business groups no longer represent a moderate establishment. They are, alternately, fixated on pay and prerogatives of top executives (the Business Roundtable), increasingly partisan, and focused on the narrow demands of individual sectors (the Chamber of Commerce), or dedicated to dismantling the mixed economy altogether (the Koch brothers' network).

To be sure, Republicans now face their own internal tensions, driven by the populist upsurge within their party. Their outraged voting base is a powerful but difficult-to-control force that both helps and creates headaches for national GOP elites. It helps because it undergirds Republicans' significant edge in electoral competition outside urban areas and because it disciplines members of Congress who might otherwise buck the conservative party leadership— members who, thanks to the base, face the constant threat of primary challenges from their right. It creates headaches because the base has a weakness for unelectable extreme candidates (witness defeated Alabama Senate candidate Roy Moore) as well as increasing animosity toward the national party leadership (witness President Trump's simultaneous reliance on and ridicule of Senate Majority Leader Mitch McConnell).

Yet it is crucial to recognize that the antisystem wave that helped to elect Trump was fostered by three decades of GOP attacks on Washington and the liberal, media, and educational elites who putatively control it. Since the mid 1990s, Republicans have run *for* Congress by running *against* Congress. Despite holding the House, Senate, or White House in some combination for virtually this entire period, they have perfected the self-fulfilling critique: Say government doesn't work; then tie the government in knots and starve its key agencies. Say the game is rigged; then pass policies that are highly favorable toward economic elites.

This jujitsu works (more or less) for two main reasons. First, the media environment has shifted, as many of the contributors to this volume point out. Conservative talk radio, Fox News, and ever-more-extreme online sources reinforce Republicans' antisystem messages and insulate core GOP voters from contrary signals. Media isolation and geographic isolation are thus self-reinforcing, creating more and more areas of the country where the incentives for moderation are weak whereas those for intensifying extremism are strong.

Second, the ongoing economic decline of right-leaning regions of the country—virtually all growth is now concentrated in urban centers—has created a widespread sense of resentment and betrayal. In dying industrial towns, in former fossil-fuel capitals, in rural states and regions from coast to coast, a volatile mix of anxiety and anger has proved increasingly pivotal to Republican electoral success. This anxiety and anger found a ripe target in the nation's first African American president, who seemed to many white working-class voters to embody both of the twin trends they saw as threatening their status and well-being: the rise of an educated urban elite and the growing presence and power of nonwhite America.

Of course, the party still depends on the support of white suburban voters, especially in the South. In 2016, Trump benefited enormously from rising "negative partisanship," which led many moderate Republicans to back a man they viewed as unqualified because they couldn't bring themselves to vote for a Democrat.[7] But less-educated white voters constitute the GOP's electoral fire-wall. Despite repeated predictions of a new Democratic majority of younger, more-educated, and nonwhite voters, the Republican Party has held onto its majority by increasing support and turnout among less-affluent white voters (and by pursuing restrictions on voting that they hope will deter the participation of younger and nonwhite voters).

These working-class voters have plenty of reason for grievance, from rising mortality rates to falling wages to stagnant or declining social mobility. But in our age of inequality, GOP policy aims mostly reflect the demands of upscale conservatives. As a result, Republicans have little incentive to embrace economic populism, at least so long as zero-sum wedge issues can keep disaffected voters in the fold. And so, against a broad backdrop of increasing tolerance and diversity in American society, Republican candidates have gone the other way. Coded racial appeals are no longer coded. Attacks on the "mainstream" media have gone mainstream. Even institutions of government once revered by the Right, such as the FBI, are demonized when seen as a threat to GOP governance. To the extent that these attacks work, populism and plutocracy continue their marriage of political convenience. As Marie Antoinette might have said if she lived during the Trump presidency, "Let them eat tweets!"

Enter the Resistance

The Resistance has both responded to and been constrained by the asymmetric polarization of the parties and the plutocratic populism it has wrought. The diversity of the organizations and movements involved make any neat generalizations hazardous. Yet three common features of these groups clearly reflect the contemporary political environment: (1) their movement character, (2) their limited partisan reach, and (3) their ambivalence about whether to adopt outsider strategies of disruption, protest, and consciousness-raising or insider strategies of electoral, legislative, and administrative engagement.

Each of these features marks at least a partial departure from the movement and group dynamics of previous eras. Moreover, each of these features is a double-edged sword, allowing the Resistance to gain rapid and impressive ground but also limiting the scope of its impact—and, in particular, its capacity to protect against the erosion of democracy that current political dynamics are furthering. Understanding these common features is therefore critical to assessing not just the character of the organizations and movements arrayed against President Trump and his allies, but also the prospect that these organizations and movements will foster a significant course correction.

Movementization

The asymmetric polarization of the parties is usually linked to voters, or at least to party activists. And, indeed, polarization has rested heavily on an intensifying cycle of partisan mobilization (particularly on the Right) in which each election becomes more critical to saving the country from the evils of the opposing party than the last. The roots of this transformation, however, are more accurately located within the *institutional* evolution of American politics: in particular, the decline of large mass organizations in favor of smaller (often memberless) issue organizations and lobbying groups, and the rise of the federal government as the central focus and site of political contestation.[8] Put concisely, American politics has simultaneously *nationalized, professionalized,* and *"movementized."*

Nationalization is the easiest trend to explain. On the electoral side, nationalization was furthered by the creation of a competitive party system in the South and by the growing resource needs of parties and candidates in an increasingly media-driven environment. On the governance side, it was furthered by the massive expansion of the federal government as a regulatory and spending power. The greater openness of both campaigns and governance to outside scrutiny and influence—a legacy of transparency and the decentralization reforms of the 1960s and 1970s—added to the shift, undermining closed-door bargains that balanced regional party interests against national priorities and increasing the rewards for campaigns and groups that could attract DC-oriented funders and exploit national media attention.

Professionalization is also relatively easy to understand. Mass-based organizations declined for many reasons, but there is no question that large mass-membership groups were at a disadvantage in the Washington-centered policy struggles to which mature public programs gave rise. What took their place were professional organizations of both the Right and the Left: business and trade groups, which exploded in size and influence in the 1970s and 1980s; and environmental, consumer, and other single-issue groups, which became more central to the Democratic Party's organizational infrastructure as labor unions declined.

Movementization is the puzzling development, given that it initially seems at odds with the shift toward a nationalized, professionalized politics. But it makes more sense once we see it as a response to the first two changes—a strategic adaptation to new realities by groups not naturally organized into this new politics, a strategy that benefited greatly from changes in the media and organizational environment that increased both the ease of grassroots organization and encouraged more traditional groups to adopt hybrid strategies involving both national leadership and ground-level action (even as lobbying groups began relying more on "Astroturf" faux grassroots mobilization). It is crucial to recognize that in almost all these cases, elite organizing strategies were critical in tapping and directing latent publics.

At the same time, grassroots activity was key to these strategies' energy and efficacy—and a major source of their legitimacy. This development has played out on the Right as well as the Left: Evangelical leaders, for example, saw an opening for a mass movement grounded in conservative-values voters who lacked a natural alliance in professionalized groups of either the Left or the Right. Although allied with local labor unions, living-wage campaigns adopted a movement strategy focused on lower-level governance as a response to the national policy stalemate and the weakening pull of traditional unions within the Democratic Party.

Against this backdrop, the Resistance's organizational evolution and strategic repertoire seem natural outgrowths of the movementization seen in other areas. For all the diversity of the groups involved, none looks like a business or public-interest organization. (In fact, some established progressive groups, such as the ACLU, are trying to add a movement element to their traditional legal and lobbying focus.) Nor do any of them—even the most governance focused, Indivisible—have as their prime goal changing laws in Washington. Some may be more policy oriented (though often beneath the national level), but all are now united in a central aim: stopping the Trump presidency and GOP Congress. Given their disadvantages in a Republican-controlled Washington, the strategies of the day are movement strategies, but for most that was true even before Trump's rise.

One-Sided Influence

These very same dynamics, however, limit the Resistance's capacity and reach in ways that many of the authors in this volume note. For starters, social movements in the past often sought to prick the consciousness of the vast middle of the electorate—creating pressure on *both* of the major parties to respond. Trump's unprecedented popularity and the small but real movement of wavering Republican voters into the independent column may reflect in part the Resistance's efforts. Nonetheless, the Resistance has had extremely limited success in pulling Republican voters away from the right pole, and in particular away from President Trump.

The battle over health care is instructive, because it featured the most concerted campaign by the forces of the Resistance to cross-pressure Republicans. Drawing from the Congressionally focused playbook embraced by Indivisible, a variety of groups focused intently on vulnerable members of Congress, prominently protesting in these members' districts and flooding town hall meetings, much as the Tea Party had in the original fight over the Affordable Care Act. The result, however, was relatively meager (though, given that Republicans had only a two-seat majority in the Senate, possibly decisive): Senators Susan Collins of Maine and Lisa Murkowski of Alaska may have been fortified in their opposition by these activities. But ultimately, it was Senator John McCain of Arizona—whose stated concern was the lack of regular Senate order in the debate over the legislation—who killed the bill. In any case, scores of other Congressional Republicans in competitive states were evidently unmoved by these intense activities.

Again, the scope of retrenchment envisioned by the health care legislation was without modern US precedent, and the House and Senate bills polled at bottom-feeding levels. Yet even on this opposition-friendly terrain, the Resistance found GOP support to be near-monolithic. On less-favorable battlefields—the tax-cut legislation that passed not long thereafter, restrictive immigration policies, the call for more aggressive oversight of and greater accountability for the Trump presidency—they have smashed into even greater Republican unity.

Indeed, contrary to the predictions of many pundits, this unity only increased during the first year of the Trump presidency. Apostates, such as Senators Jeff Flake of Arizona and Bob Corker of Tennessee, have one thing in common: They are not running for reelection. (Senator John McCain, an octogenarian battling brain cancer, is also widely presumed to be in his last Senate term.) With occasional defections, often from the GOP's right flank, the rest of the party has largely rallied around the president—a president most of the GOP leadership viewed with either ambivalence or hostility during the 2016 campaign. A big part of this, of course, is that Trump has backed the conservative economic agenda of the GOP leadership. Another part is fear of the Republican voting base, which remains firmly behind the president. And then there is the simple reality that the party's future rests on Trump's future—and thus on suppressing and minimizing the fallout from the ongoing revelations about the president's ties to Russia during the campaign and his efforts to deter, if not illegally obstruct, the investigations of these ties.

Whatever the case, the Resistance has not changed the calculus, or at least changed it enough to offset these powerful centripetal forces. It is as if American politics is playing out in two parallel universes and the Resistance exists only in one. Even relatively recent social movements—from evangelicals to AIDs activists, from gun rights groups to grassroots campaigns for greater corporate responsibility—have had some effect on the "nonaligned" side of the partisan aisle. Not so, it seems, the Resistance. In this regard, its closest counterpart might be the Tea Party, which was clearly an intra-Republican affair. But the Tea Party almost derailed the Affordable Care Act by frightening vulnerable Democrats and emboldening the so-called Blue Dog Caucus in the House and moderate Democrats like Ben Nelson and Joe Lieberman in the Senate. The Resistance, by contrast, does not seem to have had much effect on moderate Republicans, as small in number as they now are, beyond encouraging those remaining to consider retirement.

Beneath the national level and within that party's intellectual coterie, Trump is viewed with much more open disfavor. Although the Resistance did not move many national Republicans, it certainly played some role in strengthening the prominently expressed concerns of GOP governors like John Kasich of Ohio, which did create cross-pressures for the national party. Prominent conservative intellectuals—such as Yuval Levin, editor of *National Affairs*, and Peter Wehner, a senior fellow at the conservative think tank The Ethics and Public Policy Center—have been even more critical of Trump and of the Congressional GOP's alliance with them, and some of this small-r resistance may well reflect the ongoing efforts of the big-r movements. Neoconservative foreign policy writer Max Boot has declared, for example, that the Resistance has helped convince him that the complaints of black and Latino students he dismissed when a college student are in fact rooted in real injustices that government should redress.

Still, these are slender reeds on which to lean. For the present, the Resistance has essentially two live options: (1) shape the agenda of Democrats and the progressive forces around them or (2) work to bring more Democrats into office. And this means that, to an unprecedented degree, the future of the Resistance— and of American democracy—rests on the capacity of the movement against President Trump to contribute to an electoral correction in 2018 and 2020.

The Electoral Imperative

The American electoral system is a creaky relic of 18-century understandings of popular democracy. Not only does it lack the proportional representation and attendant multiparty competition of most affluent democracies; it also leaves near-complete control over the drawing of districts and the administration of elections to state and local authorities. As already discussed, moreover, it translates votes into electoral outcomes and thereby power balances in Washington in a way that can be described only as deeply distorted—and, in recent years, deeply distorted in favor of the Republican Party.

And yet, this very same system is now the central switch-point on the tracks of American democracy. If the 2018 midterm election results in a GOP loss of one or both houses of Congress, the movement against Trump will have advanced dramatically. To be sure, the immediate effect will almost certainly not be GOP moderation. It is a topsy-turvy fact of contemporary politics that even groups seeking moderation tend to pose the biggest electoral threat to marginal, and hence moderate, members of Congress. The Republicans who survive an electoral correction will overrepresent the most conservative precincts of the party, and they will have an ally in the White House wielding his veto pen to preserve the major GOP breakthroughs of 2017, most notably, the tax cuts. Despite all this, the fundamental calculus will change. Without the capacity for Republicans to pass new bills, the plutocratic policy glue that has cemented the party will no longer bind as strongly. And if the correction is very large, it could create a threat to the party's electoral standing from swing voters big enough to compete with the ever-present threat from the party's base.

For this very same reason, however, 2018 will not be a normal midterm election. On the Democratic side, unprecedented numbers of candidates are running. On the Republican side, the big-money backers of the party are promising hitherto-unseen sums to protect vulnerable Republicans. In this environment, the Resistance could be pivotal as a source of grassroots energy and get-out-the-vote mobilization, creating a midterm environment in which Democrats are not at their usual disadvantage in elections not held alongside the presidential contest. Democrats have no shortage of cash, either—though, as usual, both recruitment and fund-raising have proceeded with much less central coordination.

Certainly, the "fundamentals" favor Democrats. The question is whether they do so to an extent that they can overcome Republicans' built-in advantages, as well as the solidification of Trump's base in the face of the Resistance. As this book makes clear, the Resistance has struggled with the president's protean, volatile role in national affairs. In a hyperpolarized world, it is pulled toward strategies that unify both its natural allies *and* its committed opponents. It is drawn toward flashy opposition unmoored from long-term organizational investment and toward litmus tests on policy ("single payer!") and strategy ("impeachment!") that are irrelevant or worse in the absence of a true electoral reversal. Above all, the work of the Resistance almost inevitably hardens the divisions that many of its activists hope to overcome. Whether insisting that black lives matter or that immigrant dreamers deserve a path to citizenship, the Resistance unavoidably reflects and often reinforces the underlying anxieties and animosities that have allowed Republicans to attract less-affluent white voters while pursuing an agenda that offers little of material substance to them.

Yet the history of social movements suggests that the short-term and long-term effects of mass mobilization can be very different. Absent an even-deeper erosion of our democracy—a live possibility, alas, where it once seemed unthinkable—the growing diversity of our nation, the rising influence of younger Americans in the electorate and in positions of power, and the continuing concentration of growth in urban America will create powerful pressures for a more-progressive Democratic Party and, perhaps, a more-moderate Republican Party. As it does, the Resistance will be faced with the hard choices all such movements do: whether to retain an outsider orientation or focus on the difficult work of improving government effectiveness and undoing the GOP assault on the administrative state, and whether to move from opposition to cooperation, including cooperation with disaffected conservatives and defecting Republicans. Resistance groups and their leaders will have to ask, "How programmatic should we be? What levels of government deserve our greatest attention? Do we focus on winning elections or on building organizations? How much of our attention should be aimed at fundamental political and social reforms? How much at perfecting progressive strategies that take for granted the many perversions and inequities of the current political system?"

These are good dilemmas to have. They are signs of success, not failure. But they also pose risks, and if the Resistance is to be more than a spur for electoral correction—as much as that alone could bring—its members and leaders will have to navigate those risks. Already, however, the Resistance has shown both citizens and social scientists something vital. In an era in which inequality seems locked in and grassroots politics locked out, in which movements of the right seem to have monopolized the passion and political efficacy that drove progressive reforms for much of the last century, the individuals and organizations showcased in this book offer a reminder that periods of heightened political stakes bring commitment and democratic vision as well as conflict and democratic vulnerability. By the time this book appears in print, we will know far more about what that commitment and vision have wrought and, more important, whether it has provided the external constraint that the internal checks of American political institutions have not.

Acknowledgments: This chapter draws heavily on my joint work with Paul Pierson, whose ideas are now present in everything I write. I am also grateful to Sid Tarrow and David Meyer, who kindly asked me to reflect on the chapters in this book, generously gave me feedback on an earlier draft of this chapter, and genially tolerated—and I hope at least partly rectified—my evident ignorance of the social movement literature.

NOTES

Introduction

1. https://womensmarch.com.
2. Vogel and Cheney, "Left adopts shock tactics in Obamacare repeal fight."
3. della Porta, *Social Movements in Times of Austerity.*
4. Note that the historic March on Washington in 1963 assembled fewer than half as many protesters in the nation's capital and claimed no sister marches across the country—and around the globe—which the Women's March did.
5. The term "focal point" has been employed by students of contentious politics to designate key moments in a protest cycle that have a galvanizing impact on later protest events. For a stimulating analysis coming from another cycle of protest, see Ketchley and Barrie, "Days of Protest, Fridays of Revolution."
6. Chenoweth and Pressman, "The Women's March Could Change Politics Like the Tea Party Did."
7. For a stimulating debate about the Resistance, see *Mobilizing Ideas: The Anti-Trump Resistance* at Mobilizingideas.wordpress.com, published in September 2017.
8. For example, the index to the first edition of *The Blackwell Companion to Social Movements,* arguably the definitive contemporary resource on the subject, includes exactly two page listings for the term "elections." By contrast "religion" has 21 listings, "emotion" boasts 32, and even "communism" has 15 (Snow, Soule, & Kriesi, *The Blackwell Companion to Social Movements,* 717–754). European scholars are more ecumenical: In the 2015 *Oxford Handbook of Social Movements,* Donatella della Porta and Mario Diani include extensive sections on "Contentious politics," courts and legal systems, democracy, geopolitics, nationalism, party politics, and states.
9. https://www.peoplepower.org/.
10. https://www.indivisibleguide.com/.
11. Lipton, Sanger, and Shane, "The Perfect Weapon."
12. For an astute and detailed journalistic analysis, see Davis, "The Liberal-Left Divide Reshaping American Politics."
13. In addition to McAdam's contribution to this book (Chapter 1), see McAdam and Kloos, *Deeply Divided.*
14. Abramowitz and Webster, "All Politics is National."
15. https://www.congress.gov/bill/109th-congress/house-bill/4437.
16. For an astute analysis, see http://www.ncsl.org/research/immigration/summary-of-the-sensenbrenner-immigration-bill.aspx.
17. The full statement makes clear that Trump was attacking not only the immigrants themselves but the Mexican government, thus combining the anti-immigrant and nationalist themes of his campaign. "*What can be simpler or more accurately stated? The Mexican Government is forcing*

their most unwanted people into the United States. They are, in many cases, criminals, drug dealers, rapists, etc." Lee, "Donald Trump's False Comments Connecting Mexican Immigrants and Crime."

18. There was also another outside stimulus: In the spring, *Adbusters*, an anticonsumerist magazine, published a call for an occupation of Wall Street, for which "20,000 people [would] flood into lower Manhattan, set up tents, kitchens, peaceful barricades and occupy Wall Street for a few months. Once there," it continued, "we shall incessantly repeat one simple demand in a plurality of voices. *Adbusters*, "#Occupywallstreet." For an ethnographic analysis, see Gould-Wartofsky, *The Occupiers*.

19. Office of the Press Secretary, The White House, "Remarks by the President on the Economy in Osawatomie, Kansas."

20. https://www.change.org/p/prosecute-the-killer-of-our-son-17-year-old-trayvon-martin.

21. http://fusion.net/video/55309/having-the-talk-what-black-parents-tell-their-children-about-the-police/.

22. https://drive.google.com/file/d/0B5pPLuvq-gBqZjNDTDI2RmZVVEU/view?pli=1.

23. http://www.thedemands.org/.

24. Blee and Currier, "How Local Social Movement Groups Handle a Presidential Election."

25. *Seattle Times*, "Black Lives Matter Protesters Shut Down Bernie Sanders."

26. For example, Williams, "Clinton Made Her Case to Black Voters." Frey, "Census Shows Pervasive Decline in 2016 Minority Voter Turnout."

27. https://en.wikipedia.org/wiki/Newspaper_endorsements_in_the_United_States_presidential_election,_2016.

28. Fuller, "Anti-Trump Demonstrators Take to the Streets in Several U.S. Cities."

29. Although polls showed some decline in Trump's core support, that decline was most visible in the states most favorable to Republicans anyway, meaning they were unlikely to sway national elections as long as the United States maintained the Electoral College. See Enten, "Trump's Popularity Has Dipped Most in Red States."

30. CODEPINK is a feminist-led direct-action peace group, most visible for theatrical presentations that often disrupt Congressional hearings or party conventions. For its place in the larger peace movement, see Heaney and Rojas, "Partisans, Nonpartisans, and the Antiwar Movement in the United States."

Chapter 1

1. For a more complete story, as well as contemporary analysis, see CNN reports: www.cnn.com/2012/01/23/politics/welfare-queen/.

2. YouTube, Willie Horton 1988 Attack Ad.

3. *Mother Jones* was the first to break the story: www.motherjones.com/politics/2012/09/secret-video-romney-private-fundraiser.

4. Weiser and Kasdan, "Voting Law Changes."

5. Ibid.

6. Cook's Report: http://cookpolitical.com/story/5604.

Chapter 2

1. To fully appreciate the virulence of the grassroots populist backlash in 2016, it is important to bear in mind that the strongest rival to Trump in the Republican primary campaigns was Texas Senator and Tea Party icon Ted Cruz, the *bête noire* of the Washington establishment and an ideological hardliner who routinely accused the party of "betraying" its voters. The Republican establishment eventually rallied behind Cruz in a last-ditch effort to deny Trump the nomination, clearly demonstrating the party leadership's political desperation and its loss of control over the populist currents it had long stirred up, but putatively contained under more "proper" establishment leadership.

2. Following the 2016 elections, the Republican Party controlled the presidency, both houses of Congress, two-thirds of state legislative chambers, and 33 governorships, and it is well positioned to stack the Supreme Court for a generation to come. This institutional dominance

has been achieved despite losing the popular vote in six of the last seven presidential elections and beating the Democrats by a mere 48.3% to 47.3% margin in the national vote for the lower house of Congress in 2016 (http://history.house.gov/Institution/Election-Statistics/Election-Statistics/).

Chapter 3

1. A secret Facebook group is one whose members and posts are not visible to the public.
2. We thank David Meyer for this point.
3. It is important to recall that for many Americans, the legitimacy of the vote outcome was called into question in the weeks after the election for various reasons, including claims of voter suppression, Russian hacking, and a rejection of Electoral College process in the face of a clear majority vote for Clinton.
4. We thank Mary Elizabeth King for this point. On the other hand, Tarrow (Chapter 9 in this volume) argues that Trump provided a focal point that might have been squandered had Women's March organizers tried to hash out concrete policy proposals.
5. See full list here: https://www.womensmarch.com/partners.
6. See the Guiding Vision and Definition of Principles for the Women's March on Washington here: https://static1.squarespace.com/static/584086c7be6594762f5ec56e/t/587ffb31d2b857e5d49dcd4f/1484782386354/WMW+Guiding+Vision+%26+Definition+of+Principles.pdf.

Chapter 4

1. Carrillo, Mario. America's Voice. Personal phone interview. August 28, 2017.
2. Deferred Action for Childhood Arrivals (DACA).
3. Wise, "With Barbs and Bluster."
4. Bialik, "Top Pollsters Expect Clinton To Win."
5. Mercer, Deane, and McGeeney, "Why 2016 Election Polls Missed their Mark."
6. Vogel and Isenstadt, "How Did Everyone Get It So Wrong?"
7. Wagner, Gearan, and DelReal, "Early Voting by Latinos May Help Clinton in Several States."
8. Shepard, "Latino Voting Surge Rattles Trump Campaign."
9. Mascaro, "Latino Support for Clinton Set to Hit Record High for a Presidential Candidate."
10. Benenson, Laurence. National Immigration Forum. Personal phone interview. August 30, 2017.
11. Cuna, Elizabeth. United We Dream. Personal phone interview. October 27, 2017.
12. Carrillo, Mario. America's Voice. Personal phone interview. August 28, 2017.
13. Benenson, Laurence. National Immigration Forum. Personal phone interview. August 30, 2017.
14. Newman, Chris. National Day Laborer Organizing Network. Personal phone interview. October 27, 2017.
15. Benenson, Laurence. National Immigration Forum. Personal phone interview. August 30, 2017.
16. Sacchetti, "Trump Administration Targets 'Sanctuary' Cities In Latest Wave of Immigration Arrests."
17. Banco, "Undocumented Immigrants in Trump's America Now Deported After Running Red Lights."
18. Santiago, "The Big Accomplishment of Trump's First 100 Days?"
19. Carrillo, Mario. America's Voice. Personal phone interview. August 28, 2017.
20. Ibid.
21. Ibid.
22. Cuna, Elizabeth. United We Dream. Personal phone interview. October 27, 2017.
23. Newman, Chris. National Day Laborer Organizing Network. Personal phone interview. October 27, 2017.
24. Benenson, Laurence. National Immigration Forum. Personal phone interview. August 30, 2017.

25. McGreevy and Ulloa, "California Again Steps Up to Trump."
26. Ulloa, "California Lawmakers Approve Landmark 'Sanctuary State' Bill to Expand Protections for Immigrants."
27. Benenson, Laurence. National Immigration Forum. Personal phone interview. August 30, 2017.
28. The survey was conducted after the 2016 election and was in the field from December 2016 through mid-February 2017. The polling firm Latino Decisions fielded the survey in conjunction with Pacific Market Research. Latino respondents were given the choice of taking the survey in Spanish or English. More information about the CMPS survey can be found here: http://www.latinodecisions.com/recent-polls/cmps-2016/.
29. The survey item asked specifically about support for activism on behalf of lesbian, gay, and bisexual rights. The item did not include transgender rights because we did not want to conflate sexuality and gender. Thus we use the term LGB, rather than LGBT, to reflect the survey question wording. For more on the unique nature of transgender rights and struggles, see Curry, "Why Gay Rights and Trans Rights Should Be Separated."
30. https://blacklivesmatter.com/about/what-we believe/.
31. *Washington Times*, "Blacks, Hispanics Nixed Gay Marriage."
32. Cuna, Elizabeth. United We Dream. Personal phone interview. October 27, 2017.
33. Ibid.
34. https://unitedwedream.org/about/projects/quip/.
35. NAACP, "NAACP Files Lawsuit in Defense of DACA Eligible People of Color."
36. https://policy.m4bl.org/platform/.
37. https://now.org/resource/immigration-as-a-feminist-issue/.
38. https://nwlc.org/resources/immigrant-rights-and-reproductive-justice-how-harsh-immigration-policies-harm-immigrant-health/.
39. https://www.womensmarch.com/.
40. https://www.aclu.org/issues/immigrants-rights/immigrants-rights-and-detention/sexual-abuse-immigration-detention-0.
41. Newman, Chris. National Day Laborer Organizing Network. Personal phone interview. October 27, 2017.
42. For evidence on the growing political sophistication of the Dreamers' movement, see the accounts in Jordan, "Futures in Jeopardy"; Alcindor, "Republicans Present Conservative Vision for 'Dreamer' Protection"; and Preston, "How the Dreamers Learned to Play Politics."
43. Linthicum, "Trump's Border Rhetoric Emboldens Officials on Local Level to Target Immigration."
44. Ocampo, "Top 6 Facts on the Latino Vote."
45. For Latino millennials' support for Bernie Sanders over Hilary Clinton, see O'Reilly Herrera, "Grupo Neo-Latino," and Alvarez et al., "Latino Students Speak About the 2016 Elections."

Chapter 5

1. For a full discussion of this point, see Fisher, "Resistance in the Streets."
2. Chapter 1; see also Tarrow, *Power in Movement*; Tilly and Tarrow, *Contentious Politics*.
3. For recent accounts, see Fisher et al., "How Do Organizations Matter?"; Klandermans et al., "Mobilization Without Organization"; Walgrave et al., "Transnational Collective Identification"; Eggert and Giugni, "Homogenizing 'Old' and 'New' Social Movements"; Heaney and Rojas, *Party in the Street*.
4. See especially McAdam, "Recruitment to High-Risk Activism"; Lim, "Social Networks and Political Participation"; Munson, *The Making of Pro-Life Activists*; Saunders et al., "Explaining Differential Protest Participation"; Fisher and McInerney, "The Limits of Networks in Social Movement Retention"; Klandermans et al., "Mobilization Without Organization."
5. Oberschall, *Social Conflict and Social Movements*; Tilly, *From Mobilization to Revolution*; McAdam, "Recruitment to High-Risk Activism"; Marwell, Oliver, and Prahl, "Social Networks and Collective Action"; Gould, "Multiple Networks and Mobilization in the Paris Commune, 1871"; Bearman and Everett, "The Structure of Social Protest, 1961–1983"; Oegema and Klandermans, "Why Social Movement Sympathizers Don't Participate";

Kim and Bearman, "The Structure and Dynamics of Movement Participation"; Loveman, "High-Risk Collective Action"; Kitts, "Mobilizing in Black Boxes"; Polletta and Jasper, "Collective Identity and Social Movements"; Tindall, "Networks as Constraints and Opportunities."

6. Opp and Gern, "Dissident Groups, Personal Networks, and Spontaneous Cooperation."

7. Klandermans and Oegema, "Potentials, Networks, Motivations, and Barriers."

8. Rochford, "Recruitment Strategies, Ideology, and Organization in the Hare Krishna Movement."

9. Anheier, "Movement Development and Organizational Networks"; Passy, "Social Networks Matter."

10. McAdam and Paulsen, "Specifying the Relationship Between Social Ties and Activism"; see also Fernandez and McAdam, "Social Networks and Social Movements."

11. Ohlemacher, "Bridging People and Protest."

12. Klandermans et al., "Mobilization Without Organization"; see also Wahlström and Wennerhag, "Alone in the Crowd"; Fisher and Boekkooi, "Mobilizing Friends and Strangers."

13. Klandermans et al., "Mobilization without Organization."

14. Saunders et al., "Explaining Differential Protest Participation."

15. Verhulst and Walgrave, "The First Time Is the Hardest?"; Saunders et al., "Explaining Differential Protest Participation."

16. Verhulst and Walgrave, "The First Time Is the Hardest?" 455.

17. See particularly Carastathis, "Identity Categories as Potential Coalitions"; Roberts and Jesudason, "Movement Intersectionality"; Wadsworth, "Intersectionality in California's Same-Sex Marriage Battles"; see also Adam, "Intersectional Coalitions."

18. Brown, *States of Injury*; Ehrenreich, "Subordination and Symbiosis."

19. Crenshaw, "Mapping the Margins"; see also Wadsworth, "Intersectionality in California's Same-Sex Marriage Battles."

20. Roberts and Jesudason, "Movement Intersectionality," 313.

21. Terriquez, "Intersectional Mobilization, Social Movement Spillover, and Queer Youth Leadership in the Immigrant Rights Movement," 343.

22. van Dyke, "Crossing Movement Boundaries," 244.

23. Fisher, Dow, and Ray, "Intersectionality Takes It to the Streets."

24. http://2014.peoplesclimate.org.

25. Thorson et al., "Climate and Sustainability|Seeking Visibility in a Big Tent."

26. Worth, "Communities Already Experiencing the Impacts of Global Warming are Often the Least Equipped to Deal With It."

27. Foderaro, "Taking a Call for Climate Change to the Streets."

28. http://2014.peoplesclimate.org; for an alternative estimate, see Munguia, "How Many People Really Showed Up To The People's Climate March?"

29. Dastagir, " 'Largest-Ever' Climate-Change March Rolls through NYC."

30. See map of lineup at http://2014.peoplesclimate.org/lineup/.

31. https://www.womensmarch.com/partners/.

32. https://pcm2017.wpengine.com/.

33. https://ballotpedia.org/Clean_Power_Plan_political_timeline.

34. Fandos, "Climate March Draws Thousands of Protesters Alarmed by Trump's Environmental Agenda."

35. https://pcm2017.wpengine.com/.

36. See maps of WM at https://www.womensmarch.com/map/ and PCM17 and http://pcm2017.wpengine.com/logistics/#map.

37. Bédoyan, Aelst, and Walgrave, "Limitations and Possibilities of Transnational Mobilization"; Fisher et al., "How Do Organizations Matter?"; Fisher, Dow, and Ray, "Intersectionality Takes It to the Streets"; Heaney and Rojas, "Coalition Dissolution, Mobilization, and Network Dynamics in the US Antiwar Movement."

38. Walgrave, Wouters, and Ketelaars, "Response Problems in the Protest Survey Design," 85; Walgrave and Verhulst, "Selection and Response Bias in Protest Surveys"; Lynn and Clarke, "Separating Refusal Bias and Non-Contact Bias."

39. University of Maryland IRB # 332104-1 and IRB # 999342-1, respectively.

40. For a full discussion of this methodology, see Walgrave, Wouters, and Ketelaars, "Response Problems in the Protest Survey Design"; Walgrave and Verhulst, "Selection and Response Bias in Protest Surveys."
41. Fisher, Dow, and Ray, "Intersectionality Takes It to the Streets."
42. For a discussion, see Fisher, Svendsen, and Connolly, *Urban Environmental Stewardship and Civic Engagement.*
43. Fisher, "Resistance in the Streets"; see also Shulevitz, "Year One."
44. See particularly Diani and McAdam, *Social Movements and Networks*; Tindall, "Networks as Constraints and Opportunities."
45. As the question asked respondents to check all that apply, the totals add up to more than 100%.
46. For details see http://newsroom.unfccc.int/unfccc-newsroom/peoples-climate-march-chooses-inspiring-posters/.
47. For a full discussion, see Pew Research Center, "Social Media Update 2016."
48. Fisher, "Resistance in the Streets."
49. Fisher, Dow, and Ray, "Intersectionality Takes It to the Streets."
50. Klandermans et al., "Mobilization Without Organization"; Saunders et al., "Explaining Differential Protest Participation."
51. Fisher, Dow, and Ray, "Intersectionality Takes It to the Streets."
52. For a full discussion of Moral Shocks, see Jasper and Poulsen, "Recruiting Strangers and Friends."

Chapter 6

1. Johnson, "Trump Calls for 'Total and Complete Shutdown of Muslims Entering the United States.'"
2. Johnson, "Donald Trump Now Says Even Legal Immigrants Are a Security Threat."
3. Executive Order No. 13769.
4. Blumenthal, "The Scene at JFK as Taxi Drivers Strike Following Trump Immigration Ban."
5. Bierman, "Trump Administration Further Clarifies Travel Ban."
6. Executive Order No. 13780.
7. *Trump v. Int'l Refugee Assistance Project*, No. 16-1436, 2017; *Hawaii v. Trump*, 859 F.3d 741, 789 (9th Cir.), *cert. granted sub nom. Trump v. Int'l Refugee Assistance Project*, 137 S. Ct. 2080, 198 L. Ed. 2d 643 (2017), *cert. granted, judgment vacated*, No. 16-1540, 2017 WL 4782860 (U.S. Oct. 24, 2017), *vacated*, 874 F.3d 1112 (9th Cir. Nov. 2, 2017).
8. *Trump v. International Refugee Assistance Project*, 137 S. Ct. 2080, 2087 (2017).
9. Proclamation No. 9645 82 Fed. Reg. 186, 45161 (Sept. 24, 2017).
10. *Hawaii v. Trump*, No. 17-17168, 2017 WL 5343014 (9th Cir. Nov. 13, 2017).
11. *Trump v. Hawaii*, No. 17A550, 2017 WL 5987406 (Dec. 4, 2017).
12. *Hawaii v. Trump*, 17-17168, 2017 WL 6554184 (9th Cir. Dec. 22, 2017).
13. Clinton, "Remarks Announcing the Nomination of Ruth Bader Ginsburg to be a Supreme Court Associate Justice."
14. 347 U.S. 483 (1954).
15. Meyer and Boutcher, "Signals and Spillover."
16. Rosenberg, *The Hollow Hope*, 339–419.
17. 135 S. Ct. 2584 (2015).
18. Persily, Citrin, and Egan, *Public Opinion and Constitutional Controversy.* The authors dissect public opinion on various issues and find that Supreme Court decisions may leave public opinion largely unmoved, may legitimate particular viewpoints, may provoke backlash, and may lead to polarization; Frymer, *Black and Blue*, 16–17, 70–97. Frymer does not deny the limits of courts as agents of social change but emphasizes that other government institutions have limits as well, arguing that in some contexts courts can be and have been relatively effective change agents.
19. McCann, *Rights at Work.*
20. Boutcher, "Mobilizing in the Shadow of the Law."
21. McCann, *Rights at Work*, 5–12.

22. Henrike Dessaules, Communications Manager, IRAP, telephone interview by Michael S. Chu, August 7, 2017; Camille Mackler, Director of Immigration Legal Policy, New York Immigration Coalition, telephone interview by Michael S. Chu, August 22, 2017. Unless otherwise noted, all information in the second section comes from interviews and subsequent communications with Henrike Dessaules or Camille Mackler.

23. Bromwich, "Lawyers Mobilize at Nations' Airports after Trump's Order." Telephone interviews with Dessaules and with Mackler also indicate that the refugee advocacy community knew about the Ban before it was effective.

24. Bromwich, "Lawyers Mobilize at Nations' Airports after Trump's Order"; Dessaules, telephone interview, August 7, 2017.

25. Mallon, "The Fight Against Trump's Travel Ban Is Headed to the Supreme Court"; Rubin, Queally, and Tchekmedyian, "Coordinated Chaos."

26. One administrator fielded hundreds of emails from volunteers in just a few days. Given IRAP's presence across the country, volunteers likely came from throughout the United States. Dessaules, telephone interview, August 7, 2017.

27. Bromwich, "Lawyers Mobilize at Nations' Airports after Trump's Order"; Mallon, "The Fight Against Trump's Travel Ban Is Headed to the Supreme Court"; Shear, Kulish, and Feuer, "Judge Blocks Trump Order on Refugees amid Chaos and Outcry Worldwide"; Wiedeman, "24 Hours at JFK"; Dessaules, telephone interview, August 7, 2017.

28. More than 650 lawyers signed up in the first two days alone. Aliyu, "Coalition of Volunteers."

29. Westcott, "Thousands of Lawyers Descend on U.S. Airports to Fight Trump's Immigrant Ban."

30. Rubin, Queally, and Tchekmedyian, "Coordinated Chaos."

31. Frankel, "At JFK's Terminal 4"; Dessaules, telephone interview. August 7, 2017. It is unclear whether these groups were answering IRAP's call to action, were motivated by the news reports, or independently organized events.

32. Whitford, "JFK Lawyers"; Rubin, Queally, and Tchekmedyian, "Coordinated Chaos"; Mackler, telephone interview, August 22, 2017.

33. National Immigration Law Center, "What We Do." The National Immigration Law Center focuses on defending and advocating the rights of low-income immigrants.

34. Mallon, "The Fight Against Trump's Travel Ban Is Headed to the Supreme Court"; Scott, "We Call it the Muslim Ban 3.0."

35. Frankel, "At JFK's Terminal 4"; Mackler, telephone interview, August 22, 2017.

36. Mallon, "The Fight Against Trump's Travel Ban Is Headed to the Supreme Court"; Camille Mackler would later take over as unofficial head lawyer of JFK.

37. It is not clear what specific role IRAP played in the overall organization after these initial hours, though it is clear IRAP had some overall organizational role.

38. Rubin, Queally, and Tchekmedyian, "Coordinated Chaos."

39. Frankel, "At JFK's Terminal 4."

40. Whitford, "JFK Lawyers"; Mackler, telephone interview, August 22, 2017.

41. Blau and Brown, "Lawyers Brave Long Days at JFK Airport Helping Immigrants Panicking Over Trump Travel Ban."

42. Bromwich, "Lawyers Mobilize at Nations' Airports after Trump's Order"; Mackler, telephone interview, August 22, 2017.

43. Whitford, "JFK Lawyers."

44. Bromwich, "Lawyers Mobilize at Nations' Airports after Trump's Order." Slack donated the professional account to the lawyers.

45. Frankel, "At JFK's Terminal 4."

46. Westcott, "Thousands of Lawyers Descend on U.S. Airports to Fight Trump's Immigrant Ban."

47. Becker, "Fighting Back"; Westcott, "Thousands of Lawyers Descend on U.S. Airports to Fight Trump's Immigrant Ban."

48. Rubin, Queally, and Tchekmedyian, "Coordinated Chaos."

49. Bromwich, "Lawyers Mobilize at Nations' Airports after Trump's Order"; Dessaules, telephone interview, August 7, 2017.

50. Westcott, "Thousands of Lawyers Descend on U.S. Airports to Fight Trump's Immigrant Ban."

51. Whitford, "JFK Lawyers"; Mackler, telephone interview, August 22, 2017.

52. *Regents of Univ. of California v. United States Dep't of Homeland Security*, No. C17-05211, 2018 WL 339144 (N.D. Cal., Jan. 9, 2018).
53. Frankel, "At JFK's Terminal 4."
54. Frank, *Law and the Modern Mind*.
55. Smith-Spark and Hanna, "March for Science."
56. Kalhan, "Gray Zone," 1, 5.
57. Ambrogi, "Lawyer Activism Under Trump"; Emerson Collective, "We the Action."
58. Dovere, "Match Site Launches for Progressive Lawyers and Non-Profits."
59. Mackler, telephone interview, August 22, 2017.
60. Ambrogi, "Lawyer Activism Under Trump"; Dovere, "Match Site Launches for Progressive Lawyers and Non-Profits."
61. Posner, "Judges v. Trump."
62. *United States v. Carolene Prods. Co.*, 304 U.S. 144, 153 n.4 (1938).
63. Ely, *Democracy and Distrust*. One of the current authors has referred to Ely's theory that judicial review should aim to correct breakdowns in the democratic process as "the single most perceptive justificatory account of the work of the Warren Court and arguably of modern constitutional law more broadly." Dorf, "The Coherentism of Democracy and Distrust," 114, 1237, 1238.
64. Bump, "President Trump is Now Speculating That the Media Is Covering up Terrorist Attacks."

Chapter 7

1. Sleeping Giants is organized through a Facebook page (https://www.facebook.com/slpnggiants/) and Twitter account (@slpng_giants). Color of Change is a digital activist organization and can be found on the web at www.colorofchange.org.
2. Crooked Media's website is www.crooked.com.
3. Personal correspondence, Anne Thompson, December 21, 2017.
4. https://crooked.com/podcast-series/majority-54/.

Chapter 8

1. Rosenmann, "Rachel Maddow Drops Truth Bomb on the Right."
2. Indivisible's national Policy Director Angel Padilla was interviewed by the author on November 15, 2017, and consented to having his name used in print. Indivisible MDI steering committee members Meredith and Grace were interviewed by the author on November 11, 2017, and November 12, 2017, respectively, and both names are pseudonyms.
3. Levin was an aide to Representative Lloyd Doggett (D-TX) and Greenberg an aide to former Representative Tom Perriello (D-VA), who lost his seat to a Republican challenger in the 2010 midterm election wave influenced by the Tea Party. Padilla served as legislative assistant to Representative Luis Gutiérrez (D-IL).
4. Angel Padilla, personal interview, November 15, 2017.
5. Angel Padilla, personal interview, November 15, 2017.
6. Angel Padilla, personal interview, November 15, 2017.
7. Indivisible's original website was www.indivisibleguide.com, but it later migrated to www.indivisible.org.
8. Angel Padilla, personal interview, November 15, 2017.
9. Angel Padilla, personal interview, November 15, 2017.
10. Angel Padilla, personal interview, November 15, 2017.
11. Angel Padilla, personal interview, November 15, 2017.
12. Meredith and Grace (Indivisible MDI), personal interviews, November 11, 2017, and November 12, 2017, respectively.
13. Angel Padilla, personal interview, November 15, 2017.
14. Meredith (Indivisible MDI), personal interview, November 11, 2017.
15. Grace (Indivisible MDI), personal interview, November 12, 2017.
16. Angel Padilla, personal interview, November 15, 2017.

17. Graphics used by Indivisible MDI are accessible at: https://indivisiblemdi.wordpress.com/graphics/.

18. Meredith (Indivisible MDI), personal interview, November 11, 2017.

19. On July 27, 2017, Ezra Levin (@ezralevin) posted to Twitter declaring, "I just can't stop thinking of the Maine Indivisible groups who drove hours to coordinate protests at every one of Collins' district offices." In replying to his original tweet, he continued: "And the heroes at @AZ_Indivisible, @Indivisible_SAZ and dozens of other local groups who held COUNTLESS local events to apply their power." "And just a week or so ago, talking to Indivisible groups in Alaska on their efforts to blanket Murkowski's district offices repeatedly." (https://twitter.com/ezralevin/status/890811112547000321).

20. Angel Padilla, personal interview, November 15, 2017.

21. Meredith (Indivisible MDI), personal interview, November 11, 2017.

22. Grace (Indivisible MDI), personal interview, November 12, 2017.

23. Angel Padilla, personal interview, November 15, 2017.

24. Angel Padilla, personal interview, November 15, 2017.

25. Angel Padilla, personal interview, November 15, 2017.

26. Angel Padilla, personal correspondence, November 15, 2017.

27. As reported by the *Washington Post*, Democrats flipped at least 15 seats in Virginia, but electoral outcomes were still unresolved in three additional races as of November 8, 2017. Nirappil, "Democrats Make Significant Gains in Virginia Legislature."

28. Angel Padilla, personal interview, November 15, 2017.

29. Angel Padilla, personal interview, November 15, 2017.

30. Angel Padilla, personal interview, November 15, 2017.

Chapter 9

1. In Helena, a Liberian refugee was elected mayor (Bradner, "Democrats Sweep in Virginia, New Jersey").

2. Bullington, "A 'Progressive Ticket' Sweeps Helena."

3. Smith, "Democrats Salute Week That Saw the Emergence of an anti-Trump Coalition."

4. Anapol, "Trump Voter."

5. For a more extended version of this argument, see McAdam and Kloos, *Deeply Divided*, as well as McAdam's contribution to this volume (Chapter 1).

6. See Tarrow, *War, States, and Contention*, chap. 4, which summarizes a wealth of research on Mussolini's rise to power by Italian historians.

7. To be more precise, the future Duce arrived in Rome in a sleeping car while his squads of Fascist thugs marched on city halls around the country.

8. In this respect, I follow David and Ruth Collier who, in their *Shaping the Political Arena*, write that the "mechanisms of production and reproduction" that follow a political shock are more important than the initial shock, turning that shock into a "critical juncture."

9. On the mechanism-based approach to political and social change that informs this chapter, see McAdam, Tarrow, and Tilly, *Dynamics of Contention*.

10. Tarrow, *Power in Movement*, 199.

11. Lieberman, "Trumpism and the Global Liberal Order," 2.

12. McAdam, Chapter 1 of this volume.

13. Schlozman, *When Movements Anchor Parties*.

14. McAdam and Kloos, *Deeply Divided*, chap. 4, on "The Strange Consequential Seventies," tell this story in detail.

15. See Figure 1.1 in McAdam's chapter in this volume (Chapter 1) for the effects of these institutional reforms.

16. Meyer and Staggenborg, "Movements, Countermovements, and the Structure of Political Opportunity," 1648.

17. Grossman and Hopkins, *Asymmetric Politics*.

18. Most scholars have seen populism as a type of political party; I define it as a personal, unmediated relationship between a leader and followers that grows out of certain kinds of

movements, as does Aslanidis, "Populism and Social Movements," and Roberts in Chapter 2 of this volume.

19. http://www.breitbart.com/. Bannon came to the Trump campaign from the Breitbart news web, to which he briefly returned after "being resigned" as Trump's White House adviser, probably at the hands of Trump's daughter, Ivanka, and his son-in-law Jared Kushner.

20. Like the Italian conservatives who thought they could use Mussolini to return to power, the Republican establishment assumed that the presence of the "adults in the room" would moderate Trump's radical appeals. But as Richard Valelly writes; "One of the more dangerous patterns in modern democratic politics is conservative politicians believing that they can manage anti-system radical right forces and harness them for their own purposes." Valelly, "Regeneration or Decay?" 5.

21. With apologies for self-promotion, the major source of my thinking on cycles of contention is my text, *Power in Movement*, chap. 10.

22. See Han and Oyakawa's chapter in this volume (p. 231).

23. *The Guardian*, "ACLU Launching People Power to Resist Trump Immigration Policies in 'Freedom Cities.'"

24. Gabbatt, "Solidarity Sundays."

25. *The Guardian*, "ACLU Launching People Power to Resist Trump Immigration Policies in 'Freedom Cities.'"

26. https://www.indivisibleguide.com/.

27. Criss, "What is Indivisible?"

28. For a general rundown of the major groups that have formed nationally to contest the Trump administration, see *The Guardian*, "Who Are the Key Players In the Resistance Against Donald Trump?"

29. Meyer and Staggenborg, "Movements, Countermovements, and the Structure of Political Opportunity," 1639.

30. Caygle. 2017. "Democrats Demand Hearing after Uptick in Hate Crimes."

31. della Porta and Tarrow, "Unwanted Children."

32. An unexpected event—the exposure in late 2017 of producer Harvey Weinstein's sexual predation—led not only to the diffusion of the "Me Too!" movement around the country but to its amplification into a critique of the routine practices of universities, Congress, and the entertainment industry. Ironically, it was Anita Hill, who was an early victim of sexual harassment in the 1990s, who was put in charge of a commission aimed at cleaning up the Augean Stables in Hollywood after the Weinstein and other revelations.

33. West Savali, "BLM Partners with Other Organizations to Halt Jail Expansion."

34. Randall, "Black Lives Matter Switches Resistance Tactics In Trump Era."

35. For an analysis of movement–countermovement interaction and federalism, see Meyer and Staggenborg, "Countermovement Dynamics in Federal Systems."

36. Wilson, Helmore, and Swaine, "Man Charged With Murder After Driving Into Anti-Far-Right Protesters in Charlottesville."

37. Meyer and Staggenborg, "Movements, Countermovements, and the Structure of Political Opportunity." Also see Mottl, "The Analysis of Countermovements"; Lo, "Countermovements and Conservative Movements in the Contemporary U.S."; and Zald and Useem, "Movement and Countermovement Interaction."

38. Meyer and Staggenborg, "Movements, Countermovements, and the Structure of Political Opportunity," 1631. The definition of a movement they adopt from Tarrow, *Power in Movement*, 3–4. For an examination of a countermovement that "anticipated" the movement against which it was mobilized, see Dorf and Tarrow, "Strange Bedfellows."

39. Meyer and Staggenborg, "Movements, Countermovements, and the Structure of Political Opportunity," 1632. Also see Andrews, "Movement-Countermovement Dynamics and the Emergence of New Institutions."

40. Zald and Useem saw the interaction between movements and countermovements as "a sometimes loosely coupled tango of mobilization and demobilization" (Zald and Useem, "Movement and Countermovement Interaction," 247).

41. Rose-Ackerman, "Administrative Law, the Common Law, and the US Presidential System."

42. A Suffolk University poll toward the end of 2017 found that between June and December, Trump's favorability rating dropped significantly from 90% to 58% among respondents who said they trust Fox over any other news network. See Wilts, "Donald Trump's Popularity Starts to Fall Among Loyal Fox News Fans."

43. Rose-Ackerman, "Administrative Law, the Common Law, and the US Presidential System." *Politico* has kept a rough record of these administrative reforms in a recurring rubric called "Five Things Trump Did This Week While You Weren't Looking." For an example, see Vinik, "5 Things Trump Did This Week While You Weren't Looking."

44. Rose-Ackerman, "Administrative Law, the Common Law, and the US Presidential System." Trump's popularity after his first year in office affected virtually every facet of his base, with the possible exception of Pentecostal Protestants, who were among his first supporters—even as the president's sexual adventures were blaringly publicized in the press. See Sullivan, "Millions of Americans Believe God Made Trump President," for this consistent support.

45. Perhaps nothing was more surprising to liberal opinion than Trump's success in maintaining the support of evangelical groups, like the Family Research Council, that was willing to overlook his personal behavior as long as he continued to deliver on policies—like antiabortion—that catered to their preferences. For a striking example, see Dovere, "Tony Perkins."

46. The best evidence tracking public opinion on the Affordable Care Act during the debate will be found in the Kaiser Family Foundation's "Health Tracking Polls" at https://www.kff.org/interactve/kaiser-health-tracking-poll-the-publics-views-on-the-aca/#?response-=favorable-Unfavorable.

47. Kim Williams has carried out a content analysis of newspaper data on African American attitudes toward immigration through 2013. See her "Black Political Interests on Immigrant Rights."

48. Preston, "How the Dreamers Learned to Play Politics"; Jordan, "Futures in Jeopardy."

49. In December 2017, the Supreme Court held, by a vote of 7 to 2, that the Trump refugee ban from seven countries was legal and could go into effect while further challenges are considered by the courts. See Liptik, "Supreme Court Allows Trump Travel Ban to Take Effect."

50. https://twitter.com/bluelivesmtr?ref_src=twsrc%5Egoogle%7Ctwcamp%5Eserp%7Ctwgr%5Eauthor.

51. For further information on antiprotester bills introduced in state legislatures, see Suh and Tarrow, "The Repression of Protest in the Age of Trump."

52. Bacon, Jr., "Trump and Other Conservatives Embrace Blue Lives Matter Movement."

53. Quoted from Fisher, "American Resistance."

54. Tarrow, *Power in Movement*, 201.

55. For a thorough—and thoroughly frightening—analysis of the dangers of Trumpism to liberal democracy, see Lieberman et al., "Trumpism and American Democracy."

56. Mettler, "This Is Really Unprecedented," 2.

Chapter 10

1. There were certainly episodic large protests during the 1990s and 2000s. See, e.g., Heaney and Rojas, *Party in the Street*.

2. Within each age range, there were substantial splits by gender and by race, with whites and men less opposed to Trump. Combining Millennials and Gen Xers (ages 18–49), only 24% of women approved of Trump's performance, compared with 40% of men.

3. Milkman, "A New Political Generation," analyzes opinion by generation on some of these GSS items but inexplicably compares Boomers with Millennials without discussing GenX, combining them with older generations in an "all others" category. I analyzed the 2016 GSS and am reporting my own conclusions here, with the exception of support for BLM, which comes from Horowitz and Livingston, "How Americans View the Black Lives Matter Movement." Horowitz and Livingston do not break their age ranges down by generation, instead reporting

support for BLM by those under 30 (60%), those 30–49 (46%), those 50–64 (37%), and those 65 and older (26%).

4. Higher proportions of younger than older Millennials agreed it was the government's responsibility to reduce income differences and aid black people, support marijuana legalization, think of themselves as liberal or extremely liberal, and support same-sex marriage; similar proportions of the two Millennial micro-cohorts thought homosexuality was not wrong.

5. The reverse is true for agreement that the government should aid blacks and identifying as liberal.

6. This was also true for respondents with at least some college, who actually had lower support across generations for restrictions on racist speech. The GSS variable is spkrac: "If such a person [who believed Blacks are genetically inferior] wanted to make a speech in your community claiming that Blacks are inferior, should he be allowed to speak, or not?" For respondents with or without some college, there is also no significant difference by generation in whether a racist should be permitted to teach in a college (variable colrac) or whether a book advocating the inferiority of blacks should be removed from a library (variable librac).

7. Data from drfisher.umd.edu.

8. The difference here is not about intersectionality, per se, but the salience of individual issues of racial and gender inequality. Fisher, Dow, and Ray, "Intersectionality Takes It to the Streets."

9. According to Fisher et al.'s data, Generation X participants in the Women's March were similar to Millennials and Baby Boomers in their racial composition, education, and the degree to which they were motivated to attend by Trump's election, as previously discussed.

10. Dreamers are drawn exclusively from Millennials, because only those born in 1981 and later were eligible for legal status under DACA, whereas college sexual assault activists are younger Millennials who were in college during the upsurge of activism from 2011 to the present.

11. Similarly, the majority (60%) of users of the #BLM hashtag on Twitter were 29-years-old or under, but more than half of highly active tweeters about #BLM were older, between 30 and 64 (Olteano Weber, and Gatica-Perez, "Characterizing the Demographics Behind the #BlackLivesMatter Movement"). Unfortunately, Olteano et al. present age breakdowns only graphically, without specific percentages. Ages 30–64 are presented as one group. Virtually no tweets were from ages 65 and up.

12. Recoding into generations is my own.

13. Young activists in the antipipeline movement received training and mentorship from older indigenous activists, with fewer generational divisions (Elbein, "The Youth Group that Launched a Movement at Standing Rock"; Enzinna, "I Didn't Come Here to Lose"; Gauthier, "Youth From Pine Ridge Reservation Vow to Stay at Standing Rock Despite Blizzards").

14. There are differences by education and gender, with Democratic women with postgraduate degrees having the highest rate of protest participation (43%). The report does not break down protest by Republicans by other variables. The report does not break down protest by age combined with gender, race, or degree. Protest rates among Democrats are higher for whites than for Blacks. The vast majority of protest participation across party identification was opposed to Trump (67% vs. 11% in favor); it is thus safe to assume that virtually all the protest participation by Democrats opposed Trump.

15. Generation X leaders were Swing Left (36), Sister District (38), 1 of Indivisible's leaders; Our Revolution (49); Millennials were 5 Indivisible (early 30s); Run for Something (27). No leaders under age 25 are cited in reports. Our Revolution, oriented toward changing the Democratic Party, was founded by Sanders' Millennial-aged former campaign manager and is now headed by Nina Turner, 49, who had been an elected official in Ohio.

16. At the time of the election, it had 2.9-million members (Collins, "Pantsuits Nation on Fire"). By December, 2017, it had 3,840,196 members (Facebook: Pantsuit Nation).

17. Based on my own coding of speakers listed at the Women's March webpage (https://www.womensmarch.com/speakers/). I found speakers' ages online at Wikipedia pages or other biographical sketches, or deduced age from education and employment histories at LinkedIn pages. I established reliable generations for 39 of the 42 speakers; the remaining 3 are omitted from totals for calculating percentages.

18. Data are available at drfisher.umd.edu in Excel form. Recoding into generations is mine. I used the Pew definitions of generations and converted to ages in 2016, but included 18-year-olds with Millennials; micro-cohorts are ages 18–25 and 26–35, Gen Xers ages 36–51, Baby Boomers ages 52–70. The corresponding birth years are Millennials 1981–1997, Gen Xers 1965–80; Boomers 1946–64.

19. Even before the election, Dreamers, Occupy, Standing Rock, and the campus sexual assault movement had older, experienced activist mentors from earlier waves of related movements, but not without tensions (Whittier, "Campus Activism Against Sexual Assault"). For example, Milkman reports that Dreamers "initially accepted the mentorship of older immigrant rights activists" but "grew impatient with the seemingly interminable struggle for comprehensive immigration reform" (Milkman, "A New Political Generation"). In contrast, BLM organizers were more generationally differentiated, intensifying persistent generational divisions within the antiracism movement (Garza, "A Herstory of the #BlackLivesMatter Movement"; Murphy, "The Hope and Burden of the Civil Rights Movement"). Milkman reports that young women involved in the campus sexual assault movement were initially "skeptical" about feminism and had no direct mentoring from feminist veterans, but Reger ("Micro-Cohorts") finds both connections to existing women's movement organizations and conflict and critique coming from older feminists to younger ones. Further, preexisting women's movement organizations had created the political opportunities that the campus sexual assault movement used (through the Violence Against Women Act and the Department of Education's interpretation of Title IX as requiring campus action on sexual assault claims) (Whittier, *Frenemies*). Rape crisis centers, many on college campuses, and earlier frames about rape culture, acquaintance rape, and consent were important resources.

20. The sibling Resistance School at Berkeley lists four speakers, three experienced organizers from in their 40s and 50s and 71-year-old former Labor Secretary Robert Reich. Speakers for sessions listed at http://resistanceschoolberkeley.org/sessions/.

Chapter 11

1. Lennard, "Six Months After the Election."
2. https://www.facebook.com/groups/pantsuitnation/.
3. https://www.womensmarch.com/.
4. Meyer and Tarrow, "A Movement Society"; Tarrow, "Rhythms of Resistance."
5. Skocpol, Ganz, and Munson, "A Nation of Organizers."
6. Tarrow, *Power in Movement.*
7. Wood and Fulton, *A Shared Future.*
8. *New York Times,* "Here's the Democracy Alliance's Resistance Map."
9. Hertel-Fernandez, "How the Right Trounced Liberals in the States."
10. Hahrie Han, personal interview, March 13, 2017.
11. Wood and Fulton, *A Shared Future.*
12. Drum, "Will Women Save Us From Donald Trump?"
13. Tesfaye, "White Women Strike Back."
14. We would like to thank Avi McClelland, graduate student in Communications at University of California Santa Barbara, for this information.
15. Wood and Fulton, *A Shared Future,* 68–72.
16. de Haldevang, "The American Left Has Its Own Tea Party."
17. Ibid.
18. Dickinson, "How a New Generation of Progressive Activists Is Leading the Trump Resistance."
19. DiMaggio and Powell, "The Iron Cage Revisited."
20. Michels, *Political Parties.*
21. Meyer and Tarrow, "A Movement Society."
22. Skocpol, Ganz, and Munson, "A Nation of Organizers." They find that 58 membership-based organizations at the turn of the 20th century could claim more than 1% of the adult US population as members. Nowadays, in the first two decades of the 21st century, an association

would have to have approximately 2.5-million members to cross the 1% threshold. Few organizations other than MoveOn could probably claim that.

23. Tarrow, *Power in Movement*.

Conclusion

1. The phrase is from Trump's inaugural speech. See Blake, "Trump's Full Inaugural Speech Transcript, Annotated."
2. The text of Donald Trump's speech at the Republican National Convention (July 21, 2017) is available at https://www.politico.com/story/2016/07/full-transcript-donald-trump-nomination-acceptance-speech-at-rnc-225974.
3. For example, see Blow, "Donald Trump, This Is Not Normal."
4. Kennedy, "Heather Heyer."
5. Saul Alinsky provided a manual for such efforts in *Rules for Radicals*. A thoughtful academic analysis of the flexibility inherent in face-to-face organizing can be found in Robnett, "African-American Women in the Civil Rights Movement."
6. Graham, "Women's March on Washington Says No to Pro-Life Feminist Group."
7. Stockman, "One Year after Women's March."
8. Kopan, "Susan Sarandon."
9. http://www.disruptj20.org/tag/press/.
10. Most demonstrators refused to negotiate plea agreements. After the first criminal trial of six protesters produced verdicts of not guilty on all charges, the District of Columbia prosecutor dropped all charges against most of the defendants. See Reilly, "Justice Department Drops Felony Charges Against 129 Trump Inauguration Defendants."
11. Although Dr. Lieberman opposes diagnosis at a distance, he has expressed his own worries about President Trump publicly and called for a professional evaluation, as well as legislated standards for mental health adequate to do the job of the presidency. See Lieberman., "Maybe Trump Is Not Mentally Ill."
12. UC Office of the President, "UC President Napolitano denounces decision to end DACA program."
13. For example, McGreevy, "California Sues Trump Administration Over Plan to End DACA."
14. Levitsky and Ziblatt, *How Democracies Die*, offer a systematic analysis of the processes through which democracies erode.
15. In Chapter 7 in this volume, David Karpf notes that the Trump campaign's outlandish rhetoric allowed it to monopolize free media coverage, saving itself money, and far outstripping the attention that rival Republicans received.
16. CREW filed lawsuits in multiple jurisdictions. In Maryland, see O'Connell and Fahrenthold, "Maryland, D.C. Get Subpoena Power in Trump Emoluments Suit."
17. https://www.courthousenews.com/wp-content/uploads/2017/12/EmolumentsDismissal.pdf.
18. Erica Chenoweth and Jeremy Pressman's crowd-sourcing project reported more than 400 demonstrations, totaling between 1.8- and 2.6-million protesters. https://docs.google.com/spreadsheets/d/1vl1MlIZP2i87TFvSVDUY1zkRgmSfe-_-Ae_I3pr-cQA/edit#gid=272855497.
19. The term is from Benjamin Wittes, who was writing only about Trump's first proposed travel ban for Muslims. See "Malevolence Tempered by Incompetence."

Afterword

1. Quoted in Bluedorn, Decressin, and Terrones, "Do Asset Price Drops Foreshadow Recessions?"
2. Campbell, "Forecasting the 2016 Presidential Election."
3. Schattschneider, *Party Government*, 1.

4. Since the tax bill's passage, it has risen in popularity—spurred by prominent announcements by major US companies that they will use some of the windfall to pay higher wages. Nonetheless, the rise is modest—a Pew poll done in late January 2018, found 37% approval—and it does not change the basic fact that the bill polled abysmally at the time Republicans enacted it. Pew Research Center, "Public Has Mixed Expectations for New Tax Law."

5. Hacker and Pierson, *American Amnesia.*

6. Enten, "A Very Early Look At The Battle For The House in 2018."

7. Abramowitz and Webster, "The Rise of Negative Partisanship and the Nationalization of U.S. Elections in the 21st Century."

8. Skocpol, *Diminished Democracy;* Hacker and Pierson, "After the 'Master Theory."

BIBLIOGRAPHY

"About Pantsuit Nation." https://www.pantsuitnation.org/mission.html. Accessed January 4, 2018.

"About Us." 2017. Indivisible. https://www.indivisible.org/about-us/. Accessed January 4, 2018.

Abrajano, Marisa and Zoltan Hajnal. 2015. *White Backlash: Immigration, Race, and American Politics.* Princeton: Princeton University Press.

Abramowitz, Alan. 2017. "Partisanship and the Triumph of Trump." American Political Science Association Annual Conference. San Francisco, CA, August 31–September 3.

Abramowitz, Alan and Steven W. Webster. 2015a. "All Politics is National: The Rise of Negative Partisanship and the Nationalization of U.S. House and Senate Elections in the 21St Century." American Political Science Association Annual Conference. San Francisco, CA, September 3–6. http://stevenwwebster.com/research/all_politics_is_national.pdf.

Abramowitz, Alan I. and Steven Webster. 2015b. "The Only Thing We Have to Fear is the Other Party." In *Sabato's Crystal Ball.* University of Virginia Center for Politics, June 4. http://www.centerforpolitics.org/crystalball/articles/the-only-thing-we-have-to-fear-is-the-other-party/. Accessed January 31, 2018.

Abramowitz, Alan I. and Steven Webster. 2016. "The Rise of Negative Partisanship and the Nationalization of U.S. Elections in the 21st Century." *Electoral Studies* 41: 12–22.

Abrams, Amah-Rose. 2017. "Shepard Fairey Releases 'We the People' Series to Protest Trump." *Artnet News,* January 20. https://news.artnet.com/art-world/shepard-fairey-releases-we-the-people-series-824468. Accessed January 4, 2018.

Adam, Erin M. 2017. "Intersectional Coalitions: The Paradoxes of Rights-Based Movement Building in LGBTQ and Immigrant Communities." *Law & Society Review* 51(1): 132–167.

Adbusters. 2011. "#Occupywallstreet." *Adbusters* blog, July 13. http://www.webcitation.org/63DZ1nIDl. Accessed September 8, 2017.

ADL (Anti-Defamation League). 2018. "White Supremacist Propaganda Surges on Campus." https://www.adl.org/education/resources/reports/white-supremacist-propaganda-surges-on-campus. Accessed February 4, 2018.

Akom, Antwi A. 2006. "The Racial Dimensions of Social Capital." In *Beyond Resistance,* eds. Shawn Ginwright, Pedro Noguera, and Julio Cammarota, 81–92. New York: Routledge.

Agostino, Alexa. 2017. "Millennials Have Every Right to Complain, and Should Do It More." *Boston Globe,* March 28. https://www.bostonglobe.com/magazine/2017/03/28/millennials-have-every-right-complain-and-should-more/IF0BjygWcoepdIGZgTiomI/story.html. Accessed January 5, 2018.

Albertazzi, Daniele and Sean Mueller. 2017. "Populism and Liberal Democracy: Populists in Government in Austria, Italy, Poland and Switzerland." In *The Populist Radical Right: A Reader,* ed. Cas Muddie, 507–525. Abingdon, UK: Routledge.

Alcindor, Yamiche. 2017. "Republicans Present Conservative Vision for 'Dreamer' Protection." *New York Times*, September 25. https://www.nytimes.com/2017/09/25/us/politics/republicans-daca-citizenship.html.

Alinsky, Saul. 1971. *Rules for Radicals*. New York: Random House.

Aliyu, Wale. 2017. "Coalition of Volunteers, Attorneys Camp Out at JFK in Wake of Trump Ban." *NBC New York*, January 30. http://www.nbcnewyork.com/news/local/No-Ban-JFK-Volunteers-Attorneys-Coalition-John-F-Kennedy-Airport-New-York-City-Trump-Immigration-Ban-412204223.html.

Alvarez, Frida, Yariset Rodriguez, Jesus Belmonte, Jarol Torres, Alejandro Salinas. 2016. "Latino Students Speak About the 2016 Elections." Latino/Latin American Studies Lectures. https://digitalcommons.csbsju.edu/llas_lectures/17/. Accessed April 21, 2018.

Ambrogi, Robert. 2017. "Stanford Law Journal Publishes Special Issue on Lawyer Activism Under Trump." *Law Sites Blog*, February 20. https://wp.me/p31n5j-3N9.

Amenta, Edwin, Neal Caren, Elizabeth Chiarello, and Yang Su. 2010. "The Political Consequences of Social Movements." *Annual Review of Sociology* 36: 287–307.

Amenta, Edwin, Neal Caren, and Sheera Joy Olasky. 2005. "Age for Leisure? Political Mediation and the Impact of the Pension Movement on US Old-Age Policy. *American Sociological Review* 70: 516–538.

Amenta, Edwin, Bruce G. Carruthers, and Yvonne Zylan. 1992. "A Hero for the Aged? The Townsend Movement, the Political Mediation Model, and U.S. Old-Age Policy, 1934–1950." *American Journal of Sociology* 98(2): 308–339.

Anapol, Avery. 2017. "Trump Voter: If Jesus Christ told me Trump colluded with Russia, I'd check with Trump," *The Hill*, November 21. http://thehill.com/homenews/administration/361158-trump-voter-if-jesus-christ-told-me-trump-colluded-with-russia-id.

Andrews, Kenneth. 2002. "Movement-Countermovement Dynamics and the Emergence of New Institutions: The Case of 'White Flight' Schools in Mississippi." *Social Forces* 80: 911–936.

Andrews, Kenneth T., Marshall Ganz, Matthew Baggetta, Hahrie Han, and Chaeyoon Lim. 2010. "Leadership, Membership and Voice: Civic Associations That Work." *American Journal of Sociology* 115(4): 1191–1242.

Anheier, Helmut. 2003. "Movement Development and Organizational Networks: The Role of 'Single Members' in the German Nazi Party, 1925–30." In *Social Movements and Networks*, eds. Mario Diani and Doug McAdam, 49–72. New York: Oxford University Press.

Anria, Santiago. Forthcoming. *Movements, Party, and Power: The Bolivian MAS in Comparative Perspective*. New York: Cambridge University Press.

Armstrong, Elizabeth A. and Suzanna M. Crage 2006. "Movements and Memory: The Making of the Stonewall Myth." *American Sociological Review* 71: 724–751.

Art, David. 2011. *Inside the Radical Right: The Development of Anti-Immigrant Parties in Western Europe*. New York: Cambridge University Press.

Aslanidis, Paris. 2016. "Populist Social Movements of the Great Recession." *Mobilization: An International Quarterly* 21(3): 301–321.

Aslanidis, Paris. 2017. "Populism and Social Movements." In *Handbook of Populism*. eds., Cristobal Rovira Kaltwasser, Paul A. Taggart, Paulina Ochoa Espejo, and Pierre Ostiguy, chap. 16. Oxford: Oxford University Press.

Ayoub, Phillip. Forthcoming. "Intersectional and Transnational Coalitions During Times of Crisis: The European LGBTI Movement." *Social Politics*.

Bacon, Jr., Perry. 2016. "Trump and Other Conservatives Embrace Blue Lives Matter Movement." *NBC News*, July 23. https://www.nbcnews.com/storyline/2016-conventions/trump-other-conservatives-embrace-blue-lives-matter-movement-n615156.

Banco, Erin. 2017. "Undocumented Immigrants in Trump's America Now Deported After Running Red Lights." *Newsweek*, July 15. http://www.newsweek.com/2017/08/11/trump-bad-hombres-ice-immigration-636830.html.

Barkan, Steven E. 1986. "Interorganizational Conflict in the Southern Civil Rights Movement." *Sociological Inquiry* 56(2): 190–209.

Barreto, Matt 2007. "Si se Puede! Latino Candidates and the Mobilization of Latino Voters." *American Political Science Review* 101: 425–441.

Barreto, Matt and Gary Segura. 2014. *Latino America: How America's Most Dynamic Population is Poised to Transform the Politics of the Nation.* New York: Public Affairs.

Barreto, Matt, Lorrie Frasure-Yokley, Edward D. Vargas, and Janelle Wong. 2017. *The Collaborative Multiracial Postelection Survey (CMPS), 2016.* Los Angeles, CA.

Bearman, Peter S. and Kevin D. Everett. 1993. "The Structure of Social Protest, 1961–1983." *Social Networks* 15(2): 171–200.

Becker, Olivia. 2017. "Fighting Back: How Volunteer Lawyers Inside JFK Airport Helped Families Affected by Trump's Refugee Ban." *Vice News,* January 29. https://news.vice.com/story/how-volunteer-lawyers-inside-jfk-airport-fought-back-against-trumps-refugee-ban.

Bédoyan, Isabelle, Peter Aelst, and Stefaan Walgrave. 2004. "Limitations and Possibilities of Transnational Mobilization: The Case of EU Summit Protesters in Brussels, 2001." *Mobilization: An International Quarterly* 9(1): 39–54.

Bell, Emily 2016. "The End of the News as We Know It: How Facebook Swallowed Journalism." *Medium.com,* March 7. https://medium.com/tow-center/the-end-of-the-news-as-we-know-it-how-facebook-swallowed-journalism-60344fa50962.

Benford, Robert D. and David A. Snow. 2000. "Framing Processes and Social Movements: An Overview and Assessment." *Annual Review of Sociology* 26(1): 611–639.

Benkler, Yochai, Hal Roberts, Robert M. Faris, Bruce Etling, Ethan Zuckerman, and Nikki Bourassa. 2017. "Partisanship, Propaganda, and Disinformation: Online Media and the 2016 U.S. Presidential Election." Berkman Klein Center for Internet & Society Research Paper. https://dash.harvard.edu/handle/1/33759251.

Berezin, Mabel. 2009. *Illiberal Politics in Neoliberal Times: Culture, Security and Populism in a New Europe.* New York: Cambridge University Press.

Bialik, Carl. 2016. "Top Pollsters Expect Clinton To Win." *FiveThirtyEight,* October 18. http://fivethirtyeight.com/features/top-pollsters-expect-clinton-to-win/.

Bierman, Noah. 2017. "Trump Administration Further Clarifies Travel Ban, Exempting Green Card Holders." *Los Angeles Times,* February 1. https://www.usatoday.com/story/news/2017/01/28/taxi-drivers-strike-jfk-airport-following-trumps-immigration-ban/97198818/.

Black, Duncan. 1958. *A Theory of Committees and Elections.* New York: Cambridge University Press.

Blake, Aaron. 2017. "Trump's Full Inaugural Speech Transcript, Annotated." *Washington Post,* January 20. https://www.washingtonpost.com/news/the-fix/wp/2017/01/20/donald-trumps-full-inauguration-speech-transcript-annotated/?utm_term=.b18e9c7eb4a6. Accessed February 4, 2018.

Blau, Reuven and Stephen Rex Brown. 2017. "Lawyers Brave Long Days at JFK Airport Helping Immigrants Panicking Over Trump Travel Ban," *New York Daily News,* June 16. http://nydn.us/2sBVRZr.

Blee, Kathleen M. and Ashley Currier. 2006. "How Local Social Movement Groups Handle a Presidential Election." *Qualitative Sociology* 29: 261–280.

Blow, Charles M. 2016. "Donald Trump, This Is Not Normal." *New York Times,* December 16. https://www.nytimes.com/2016/12/19/opinion/donald-trump-this-is-not-normal.html.

Bluedorn, John C., Jörg Decressin, and Marco E. Terrones. 2016. "Do Asset Price Drops Foreshadow Recessions?" *International Journal of Forecasting* 32 (April 1).

Blumenthal, Eli. 2017. "The Scene at JFK as Taxi Drivers Strike Following Trump Immigration Ban," *USA Today,* January 28. http://usat.ly/2jJjUOo.

Booher, Jennifer (@JennQuercus). 2017a. "Brand New Indivisible group on Mount Desert Island, Maine." Twitter post, January 30. https://twitter.com/JennQuercus/status/826241949812273154.

Booher, Jennifer (@JennQuercus). 2017b. "55 people here at the first meeting of MDI Indivisible. Not bad for a town of 5,000." Twitter post, January 30. https://twitter.com/JennQuercus/status/826229482432393220.

Boren, Cindy and Des Bieler 2018. "Eagles' Malcolm Jenkins Joins Chris Long and Torrey Smith in Skipping White House Visit." *Chicago Tribune* (reprinted from *Washington Post*), February 5, 2018. http://www.chicagotribune.com/sports/football/ct-eagles-malcolm-jenkins-chris-long-torrey-smith-skipping-white-house-20180205-story.html. Accessed February 9, 2018.

Bornschier, Simon. 2010. *Cleavage Politics and the Populist Right: The New Cultural Conflict in Western Europe.* Philadelphia: Temple University Press.

Boutcher, Steven A. 2011. "Mobilizing in the Shadow of the Law: Lesbian and Gay Rights in the Aftermath of Bowers v. Hardwick." *Research in Social Movements, Conflict and Change* 31: 175–205.

Bradner, Eric. 2017. "Democrats Sweep in Virginia, New Jersey." *CNN*, November 8. https://edition.cnn.com/2017/11/07/politics/2017-us-election-highlights/index.html.

Breiner, Andrew 2017. "Sex Worker Solidarity Sparks More Controversy for Women's March. *Roll Call*, January 18. https://www.rollcall.com/news/politics/sex-worker-solidarity-sparks-controversy-womens-march. Accessed December 8, 2017.

Brazile, Donna. 2017. *Hacks: The Inside Story of the Break-ins and Breakdowns that Put Donald Trump in the White House*. New York: Hachette.

Brooker, Megan E. and David S. Meyer. Forthcoming (2018). "Coalitions and the Organization of Collective Action." In *The Wiley Blackwell Companion to Social Movements*, eds. David A. Snow, Sarah A. Soule, Hanspeter Kriesi, and Holly J. McCammon. Hoboken, NJ: Wiley.

Bromwich, Jonah Engel. 2017. "Lawyers Mobilize at Nations' Airports after Trump's Order." *New York Times*, January 29. https://nyti.ms/2jGwZuh.

Broomfield, Mark 2017. "Women's March against Donald Trump is the Largest Day of Protests in U.S. History, Say Political Scientists." *The Independent*, January 23. https://www.independent.co.uk/news/world/americas/womens-march-anti-donald-trump-womens-rights-largest-protest-demonstration-us-history-political-a7541081.html. Accessed December 8, 2017.

Brown, Wendy. 1995. *States of Injury: Power and Freedom in Late Modernity*. Princeton: Princeton University Press.

Bullington, Joseph. 2017. "A 'Progressive Ticket' Sweeps Helena, Montana's Municipal Elections." *In These Times*, November 10. http://inthesetimes.com/rural-america/entry/20685/progressive-politics-our-revolution-wilmont-j.-collins-helena-montana?link_id=10&.

Bump, Philip. 2017. "President Trump is Now Speculating That the Media Is Covering up Terrorist Attacks." *Washington Post*, February 6. http://wapo.st/2keUB7h?tid=ss_tw&utm_term=.3175f9a64753.

Burciaga, Edelina M. and Lisa M. Martinez. 2017. "How Do Political Contexts Shape Undocumented Youth Movements? Evidence from Three Immigrant Destinations." *Mobilization* 22(4): 451–471.

Burghart, Devin and Leonard Zeskind. 2010. *Tea Party Nationalism: A Critical Examination of the Tea Party Movement and the Size, Scope, and Focus of Its National Factions*. Kansas City, MO: Institute for Research & Education on Human Rights.

Campbell, James. E. 2016. "Forecasting the 2016 Presidential Election: Introduction." *PS: Political Science and Politics* 49(October): 649–654.

Canovan, Margaret. 1999. "Trust the People! Populism and the Two Faces of Democracy." *Political Studies* 47: 2–16.

Captain, Sean. 2011. "The Demographics of Occupy Wall Street." *Fast Company*, October 19. https://www.fastcompany.com/1789018/demographics-occupy-wall-street. Accessed January 4, 2018.

Carastathis, Anna. 2013. "Identity Categories as Potential Coalitions." *Signs* 38(4): 941–965.

Carmines, Edward G. and James Stimson. 1989. *Issue Evolution: Race and the Transformation of American Politics*. Princeton: Princeton University Press.

Caygle, Heather. 2017. "Democrats Demand Hearing after Uptick in Hate Crimes." *Politico*, November 20. https://www.politico.com/story/2017/11/20/democrats-hate-crimes-251006.

Chadwick, Andrew 2013. *The Hybrid Media System: Politics and Power*. New York: Oxford University Press.

Chavez, Leo. 2008. *The Latino Threat*. Stanford, CA: Stanford University Press.

Chenoweth, Erica and Jeremy Pressman. 2017. "This Is What We Learned by Counting the Women's Marches." *Washington Post*, February 7. https://www.washingtonpost.com/news/monkey-cage/wp/2017/02/07/this-is-what-we-learned-by-counting-the-womens-marches/?utm_term=.b84c6e9f4dd4. Accessed December 8, 2017.

Chenoweth, Erica and Jeremy Pressman. 2018. "The Women's March Could Change Politics Like the Tea Party Did." *The Guardian*, January 31. https://www.theguardian.com/commentisfree/2018/jan/31/womens-march-politics-tea-party. Accessed January 31, 2018.

Clinton, William J. 1993. "Remarks Announcing the Nomination of Ruth Bader Ginsburg to be a Supreme Court Associate Justice." *The American Presidency Project*, June 14. http://www.presidency.ucsb.edu/ws/index.php?pid=46684.

Codur, Anne-Marie and Mary Elizabeth King. 2015. "Women in Civil Resistance." In *Women, War, and Violence: Topography, Resistance, and Hope [2 volumes]: Topography, Resistance, and Hope*, eds. Mariam M. Kurtz and Lester R. Kurtz, 401–406. Santa Barbara, CA: Praeger.

Coe, Alexis 2017. "A Brief History Of Women's Marches: From Suffrage Parade To This Week's March On Washington." *Lenny*, January 18. http://www.lennyletter.com/politics/a693/a-brief-history-of-womens-marches/. Accessed December 8, 2017.

Cohen, Marty, David Karol, Hans Noel, and John Zaller. 2008. *The Party Decides: Presidential Nominations Before and After Reform*. Chicago: University of Chicago Press.

Collier, Ruth Berins and David Collier. 1991. *Shaping the Political Arena: Critical Junctures, the Labor Movement, and Regime Dynamics in Latin America*. Princeton: Princeton University Press.

Collins, Eliza. 2016a. "Les Moonves: Trump's Run is 'Damn Good for CBS.'" *Politico.com*, February 29. https://www.politico.com/blogs/on-media/2016/02/les-moonves-trump-cbs-220001. Accessed February 9, 2018.

Collins, Eliza. 2016b. "Pantsuits Nation on Fire." *USA Today*, November 8. https://www.usatoday.com/story/news/politics/onpolitics/2016/11/08/pantsuits-nation-clinton/93500206/. Accessed January 5, 2018.

Confessore, Nicholas and Karen Yourish. 2016. "$2 Billion Worth of Free Media for Donald Trump." *NYTimes.com*, The Upshot, March 15. https://www.nytimes.com/2016/03/16/upshot/measuring-donald-trumps-mammoth-advantage-in-free-media.html?_r=0.

Converse, Philip E., Warren E. Miller, Jerrold G. Rusk, and Arthur C. Wolfe. 1969. "Continuity and Change in American Politics: Parties and Issues in the 1968 Election." *American Political Science Review* 63: 1083–1105.

Cooney, Samantha 2017. "The Women's March Isn't Officially Honoring Hillary Clinton." *Motto*, January 20. http://motto.time.com/4641070/womens-march-excludes-hillary-clinton/. Accessed December 10, 2017.

Crenshaw, Kimberle 1991. "Mapping the Margins: Intersectionality, Identity Politics, and Violence Against Women of Color." *Stanford Law Review* 43(6): 1241–1299.

Criss, Doug. 2017. "What is Indivisible? Political Group Hopes to Be Flip Side of Tea Party." *CNN Politics*, February 12. https://edition.cnn.com/2017/02/11/politics/indivisible-profile-trnd/index.html.

Curry, Tyler. 2014. "Why Gay Rights and Trans Rights Should Be Separated." *Huffington Post*, February 17. https://www.huffingtonpost.com/tyler-curry/gay-rights-and-trans-rights_b_4763380.html.

Cusumano, Katherine 2007. "The Women Of The Women's March: Meet the Activists Who Are Planning One of The Largest Demonstrations in American History." *W Magazine*, January 19. https://www.wmagazine.com/story/womens-march-on-washington-activists-organizers. Accessed December 9, 2017.

Dahl, Robert A. 1971. *Polyarchy: Participation and Opposition*. New Haven, CT: Yale University Press.

Dalton, Russell J. and Martin P. Wattenberg, eds. 2000. *Parties Without Partisans: Political Change in Advanced Industrial Democracies*. Oxford: Oxford University Press.

Dastagir, Alia E. 2014. "'Largest-Ever' Climate-Change March Rolls through NYC." *USA Today*, September 21. https://www.usatoday.com/story/news/nation/2014/09/21/nyc-climate-change-march/16008009/.

Davey, Monica 2017. "At Women's Convention in Detroit, a Test of Momentum and Focus." *New York Times*, October 28. https://www.nytimes.com/2017/10/28/us/women-convention-detroit-march.html?_r=0, Accessed December 8, 2017.

Davis, Pete. 2017. "The Liberal-Left Divide Reshaping American Politics." *The Guardian*, October 26. www.theguardian.com/news/2017/oct/26/the-liberal-left-divide-reshaping-american-politics.

Dean, Claudia, Maeve Duggan, and Rich Morin. 2016. "Americans Name the 10 Most Significant Historic Events of Their Lifetimes." http://www.people-press.org/2016/12/15/americans-name-the-10-most-significant-historic-events-of-their-lifetimes/. Accessed January 4, 2018.

Deerwester, Jayme. 2017. "The Most Memorable Quotes from the Women's March on Washington." *USA Today*, January 21. https://www.usatoday.com/story/life/entertainthis/2017/01/21/most-memorable-quotes-womens-march-washington/96890596/. Accessed January 4, 2018.

De la Torre, Carlos. 2010. *Populist Seduction in Latin America*, 2nd ed. Athens: Ohio University Press.

De la Torre, Carlos, ed. 2015. *The Promise and Perils of Populism: Global Perspectives*. Lexington: University of Kentucky Press.

de Haldevang, Max. 2017a. "A Moderate Republican's Savaging by Voters Shows Why Democrats Think They Can Take Back Congress." *Quartz*, May 12. https://qz.com/981499/congressman-tom-macarthurs-savaging-by-constituents-at-a-town-hall-shows-why-democrats-are-hopeful-about-2018-midterms/.

de Haldevang, Max. 2017b. "The American Left Has Its Own Tea Party, and It's Coming for Donald Trump." *Quartz*, September 16. https://qz.com/1065652/the-american-left-has-its-own-tea-party-and-its-coming-for-donald-trump/.

Delgadillo, Natalie. 2017. "Is Trump's Presidency Actually Inspiring More Millennials to Run for Office?" *Emerge America*, November 15. https://emerge.ngpvanhost.com/news/trumps-presidency-actually-inspiring-more-millennials-run-office/. Accessed January 4, 2018.

della Porta, Donatella. 2015. *Social Movements in Times of Austerity: Bringing Capitalism Back In*. Cambridge: Polity Press.

della Porta, Donatella, Joseba Fernandez, Hara Kouki, and Lorenzo Mosca. 2017. *Movement Parties Against Austerity*. London: Polity Press.

della Porta, Donatella and Sidney Tarrow. 1986. "Unwanted Children: Political Violence and the Cycle of Protest in Italy." *European Journal of Political Research* 14: 607–632.

Dickinson, Tim. 2017. "How a New Generation of Progressive Activists Is Leading the Trump Resistance." *Rolling Stone*, August 24. http://www.rollingstone.com/politics/features/how-progressive-activists-are-leading-the-trump-resistance-w499221.

DiMaggio, Paul and Walter W. Powell. 1991. "The Iron Cage Revisited: Institutional Isomorphism and Collective Rationality in Organizational Fields." In *New Institutionalism in Organizational Analysis*, eds. Walter Powell and Paul DiMaggio, 63–82. Chicago: University of Chicago Press.

Diani, Mario, and Doug McAdam, eds. 2003. *Social Movements and Networks: Relational Approaches to Collective Action*. Oxford and New York: Oxford University Press.

Dorf, Michael C. 2005. "The Coherentism of Democracy and Distrust." *Yale Law Journal* 114(6): 1237–1278.

Dorf, Michael C. and Sidney Tarrow 2013. "Strange Bedfellows: How an Anticipatory Countermovement Brought Same-Sex Marriage Into the Public Arena." *Law and Social Inquiry* 39: 449–473.

Dovere, Edward-Isaac. 2017. "Match Site Launches for Progressive Lawyers and Non-Profits." *Politico*, July 28. http://www.politico.com/story/2017/07/28/match-site-launches-for-anti-trump-lawyers-and-non-profits-241065.

Dovere, Edward-Isaac. 2018. "Tony Perkins: Trump Gets 'a Mulligan' on Life, Stormy Daniels." *Politico*, January 23. https://www.politico.com/magazine/story/2018/01/23/tony-perkins-evangelicals-donald-trump-stormy-daniels-216498.

Downs, Anthony. 1957. *An Economic Theory of Democracy*. New York: Harper and Row.

Dreier, Peter 2017. "The Anti-Trump Resistance and Beyond: Building a Progressive Movement." *Mobilizing Ideas*, July 24. https://mobilizingideas.wordpress.com/2017/07/24/the-anti-trump-resistance-and-beyond-building-a-progressive-movement/. Accessed February 7, 2018.

Drew, Elizabeth. 2012. "Determined to Vote." *New York Review of Books*, December 20, 26–28.

Drum, Kevin. 2017. "Will Women Save Us From Donald Trump?" *Mother Jones*, November 14. http://www.motherjones.com/kevin-drum/2017/11/will-women-save-us-from-donald-trump/#.

Dudziak, Mary L. 2000. *Cold War Civil Rights: Race and the Image of American Democracy*. Princeton: Princeton University Press.

Edsall, Thomas Bryne and Mary D. Edsall. 1991. *Chain Reaction: The Impact of Race, Rights, and Taxes on American Politics*. New York: Norton.

Edwards, Mickey. 2013. "What Is the Common Good? The Case for Transcending Partisanship." *Daedalus* 142: 84–94.

Eggert, Nina, and Marco Giugni. 2012. "Homogenizing 'Old' and 'New' Social Movements: A Comparison of Participants in May Day and Climate Change Demonstrations." *Mobilization: An International Quarterly* 17(3): 335–348.

Ehrenreich, Nancy. 2002. "Subordination and Symbiosis: Mechanisms of Mutual Support Between Subordinating Systems." *UMKC Law Review* 71: 251–324.

Elbein, Saul. 2017. "The Youth Group that Launched a Movement at Standing Rock." *New York Times Magazine*, January 31. https://www.nytimes.com/2017/01/31/magazine/the-youth-group-that-launched-a-movement-at-standing-rock.html?_r=0. Accessed January 4, 2018.

Ellison, Christopher G., Gabriel A. Acevedo, and Aida I. Ramos-Wada. 2011. "Religion and Attitudes Toward Same-Sex Marriage Among US Latinos." *Social Science Quarterly* 92(1): 35–56.

Ely, John Hart. 1980. *Democracy and Distrust: A Theory of Judicial Review*. Cambridge, MA: Harvard University Press.

Emerge America. 2017. Home. https://emerge.ngpvanhost.com/. Accessed January 4, 2018.

Emerson Collective. 2017. "We the Action: Connecting Lawyers with Nonprofits in Need." http://www.emersoncollective.com/articles/2017/7/we-the-action/. Accessed November 30, 2017.

Engler, Paul and Sophie Lasoff. 2017. "Resistance Guide: How to Sustain the Movement to Win." *Momentum*. http://centerfortheworkingpoor.org/resistance guide/ResistanceGuide_Interactive.pdf.

Enten, Harry. 2017. "A Very Early Look at the Battle for the House in 2018." *FiveThirtyEight*, February 15. hattps://fivethirtyeight.com/features/a-very-early-look-at-the-battle-for-the-house-in-2018/.

Enten, Harry. 2017. "Trump's Popularity Has Dipped Most in Red States." *FiveThirtyEight*, September 18. https://fivethirtyeight.com/features/trumps-popularity-has-dipped-most-in-red-states/. Accessed October 25, 2017.

Enzinna, Wes. 2017. "'I Didn't Come Here to Lose': How a Movement Was Born at Standing Rock." *Mother Jones*, January/February. http://www.motherjones.com/politics/2016/12/dakota-access-pipeline-standing-rock-oil-water-protest/. Accessed January 4, 2018.

Fahrenthold, David A. and Jonathan O'Connell. 2017. "Judge Dismisses Lawsuit Alleging Trump Violated Constitution." *Washington Post*, December 21.

Fandos, Nicholas. 2017. "Climate March Draws Thousands of Protesters Alarmed by Trump's Environmental Agenda." *New York Times*, April 29, sec. Politics. https://www.nytimes.com/2017/04/29/us/politics/peoples-climate-march-trump.html.

Farhi, Paul 2017. "The Mysterious Group That's Picking Breitbart Apart, One Tweet at a Time." *Washington Post*, September 22. https://www.washingtonpost.com/lifestyle/style/the-mysterious-group-thats-picking-breitbart-apart-one-tweet-at-a-time/2017/09/22/df1ee0c0-9d5c-11e7-9083-fbfddf6804c2_story.html?utm_term=.72cedebeeb92.

Felsenthal, Julia. 2017. "These Are Women Organizing the Women's March on Washington." *Vogue*, January 10. https://www.vogue.com/article/meet-the-women-of-the-womens-march-on-washington. Accessed December 8, 2017.

Fernandez, Roberto M. and Doug McAdam. 1988. "Social Networks and Social Movements: Multiorganizational Fields and Recruitment to Mississippi Freedom Summer." *Sociological Forum* 3(3): 357–382.

Ferree, Myra Marx, and Aili Mari Tripp, eds. 2006. *Global Feminism: Transnational Women's Activism, Organizing, and Human Rights*. New York: New York University Press.

Fetner, Tina and Brayden G. King. 2014. "Three-Layer Movements, Resources, and the Tea Party." In *Understanding the Tea Party Movement*, eds. Nella Van Dyke and David S. Meyer, 35–54. New York: Ashgate.

Filc, Dani. 2015. "Latin American Inclusive and European Exclusionary Populism: Colonialism as an Explanation." *Journal of Political Ideologies* 20(3): 263–283.

Fisher, Dana R. 2017a. "American Resistance." https://theamericanresistancebook.wordpress.com/2017/09/20/intersectionality-across-the-resistance/.

Fisher, Dana R. 2017b. "Resistance in the Streets." In *American Resistance*. https://americanresistancebook.com/.

Fisher, Dana. 2017c. "Studying Large-Scale Protest: Understanding Mobilization and Participation at the People's Climate March." http://www.drfisher.umd.edu/PCM_PreliminaryResults.pdf. Accessed January 4, 2018.

Fisher, Dana R. and Marije Boekkooi. 2010. "Mobilizing Friends and Strangers: Understanding the Role of the Internet in the Step It Up Day of Action." *Information, Communication & Society* 13(2): 193–208.

Fisher, Dana R., Dawn M. Dow, and Rashawn Ray. 2017. "Intersectionality Takes It to the Streets: Mobilizing Across Diverse Interests for the Women's March." *Science Advances* 3(9): 1–8.

Fisher, Dana, and Paul-Brian McInerney. 2012. "The Limits of Networks in Social Movement Retention: On Canvassers and Their Careers." *Mobilization: An International Quarterly* 17(2): 109–128.

Fisher, Dana R., Kevin Stanley, David Berman, and Gina Neff. 2005. "How Do Organizations Matter? Mobilization and Support for Participants at Five Globalization Protests." *Social Problems* 52(1): 102–121.

Fisher, Dana R., Erika S Svendsen, and James J. T. Connolly. 2015. *Urban Environmental Stewardship and Civic Engagement*. New York: Routledge.

Flanagin, Andrew, Bruce Bimber, and Cynthia Stohl. 2012. *Collective Action in Organizations: Interaction and Engagement in an Era of Technological Change*. New York: Cambridge University Press.

Foderaro, Lisa W. 2014. "Taking a Call for Climate Change to the Streets." *New York Times*, September 21, sec. N.Y./Region. https://www.nytimes.com/2014/09/22/nyregion/new-york-city-climate-change-march.html.

Formisano, Ronald P. 2012. *The Tea Party: A Brief History*. Baltimore, MD: Johns Hopkins University Press.

Fouriezos, Nick. 2017. "The Tea Party of the Left Resisting Trump." *Ozy*, July 7. http://www.ozy.com/pov/the-tea-party-of-the-left-resisting-trump/79451.

Fox-Bevilacqua, Marisa. 2017. "Jewish Women Divided Ahead of March on Washington." *Haaretz*, January 21. https://www.haaretz.com/us-news/.premium-1.766382. Accessed December 8, 2017.

Frank, Jerome. 1963 [1930]. *Law and the Modern Mind*. New York: Anchor.

Frankel, Alison. 2017. "At JFK's Terminal 4, a Good Weekend to Be a Lawyer." *Reuters*, January 30. http://reut.rs/2kkN8GX.

Franklin, Sekou. 2014. *After the Rebellion: Black Youth, Social Movement Activism, and the Post-Civil Rights Generation*. New York: New York University Press.

Frey, William H. 2017. "Census Shows Pervasive Decline in 2016 Minority Voter Turnout." *Brookings Report*. Washington, DC: Brookings Institution.

Fried, Amy. 2017. "How Maine People Moved Sen. Collins and Stopped Trumpcare." *Pollways BDN Blogs*, August 8. http://pollways.bangordailynews.com/2017/08/08/national/collins-deserves-praise-but-lets-not-forget-the-maine-people-who-influenced-her/.

Fry, Richard. 2016. "Millennials Overtake Baby Boomers as America's Largest Generation." Pew Research Center, April 25. http://www.pewresearch.org/fact-tank/2016/04/25/millennials-overtake-baby-boomers/. Accessed January 4, 2018.

Frymer, Paul. 2007. *Black and Blue: African Americans, the Labor Movement, and the Decline of the Democratic Party*. Princeton: Princeton University Press.

Fuller, Thomas. 2016. "Anti-Trump Demonstrators Take to the Streets in Several U.S. Cities." *New York Times*, November 9. https://www.nytimes.com/2016/11/10/us/trump-election-protest-berkeley-oakland.html. Accessed September 21, 2017.

Gabbatt, Adam. 2017. "Solidarity Sundays: Women Resist Trump With Monthly Activism Meet-ups." *The Guardian*, March 31. https: www.the guardian.com/us-news/2017/mar31/trump-resistance.

Gamson, William A. 1990. *The Strategy of Social Protest*, 2nd ed. Belmont, CA: Wadsworth.

Gamson, William A. and Gadi Wolfsfeld. 1993. "Movements and Media as Interacting Systems." *Annals of the American Academy of Political and Social Science* 528: 114–125.

Garcia Martinez, A. 2016. *Chaos Monkeys: Obscene Fortune and Random Failure in Silicon Valley.* New York: Harper Collins.

Ganz, Marshall. 2010. "Leading Change: Leadership, Organization, and Social Movements." In *Handbook of Leadership Theory and Practice: An HBS Centennial Colloquium on Advancing Leadership*, eds. Nitin Nohria and Rakesh Khurana, 527–568. Boston: Harvard Business Press.

Garofoli, Joe. 2017a. "Protesters Target Sen. Feinstein for Not Holding Town Halls." *SFGATE*, February 24. www.sfgate.com/politics/article/Protesters-target-Sen-Feinstein-for-not-holding-10955584.php.

Garofoli, Joe 2017b. "'Pod Save America' about to take its next step." *SFChronicle.com*, December 9. https://www.sfchronicle.com/politics/article/Pod-Save-America-about-to-take-its-next-step-12418780.php.

Garza, Alicia. 2014. "A Herstory of the #BlackLivesMatter Movement." *The Feminist Wire*, October 7. http://www.thefeministwire.com/2014/10/blacklivesmatter-2/. Accessed January 4, 2018.

Gauthier, Liz. 2016. "Youth From Pine Ridge Reservation Vow to Stay at Standing Rock Despite Blizzards." *Indian Country Today*, December 13. https://indiancountrymedianetwork.com/news/native-news/youths-pine-ridge-reservation-vow-stay-standing-rock-despite-blizzards/. Accessed January 4, 2018.

Gillion, Daniel Q. 2013. *The Political Power of Protest: Minority Activism and Shifts in Public Policy.* New York: Cambridge University Press.

Goldstone, Jack A. 2003. "Introduction: Bridging Institutionalized and Noninstitutionalized Politics." In *States, Parties, and Social Movements*, ed. Jack A. Goldstone, 1–24. New York: Cambridge University Press.

Goldstone, Jack and Charles Tilly. 2001. "Threat (and Opportunity): Popular Action and State Response in the Dynamics of Contentious Action." In *Silence and Voice in the Study of Contentious Politics*, eds. Ronald Aminzade, Jack Goldstone, Doug McAdam, Elizabeth Perry, William Sewell, Sidney Tarrow, and Charles Tilly, 179–194. New York: Cambridge University Press.

Gould, Roger V. 1991. "Multiple Networks and Mobilization in the Paris Commune, 1871." *American Sociological Review* 56(6): 716–729.

Gould-Wartofsky, Michael. A. 2015. *The Occupiers: The Making of the 99 Percent Movement.* New York: Oxford University Press.

Gourevitch, Philip. 2012. "Republican vs. Republican." *The New Yorker*, September 3, 17–18.

Graham, Ruth. 2017. "Women's March on Washington Says No to Pro-Life Feminist Group," *Slate*, January 17. http://www.slate.com/blogs/xx_factor/2017/01/17/pro_life_feminist_group_new_wave_feminists_removed_from_women_s_march_partnership.html. Accessed January 25, 2018.

Grossman, Matt and David A. Hopkins. 2016. *Asymmetric Politics: Ideological Republicans and Group Interest Democrats.* New York: Oxford University Press.

Haberman, Maggie, Glenn Thrush, and Peter Baker. 2017. "Inside Trump's Hour-by-Hour Battle for Self-Preservation. *New York Times*, December 9. https://www.nytimes.com/2017/12/09/us/politics/donald-trump-president.html?_r=1.

Hacker, Jacob S. and Paul Pierson. 2014. "After the Master Theory: Downs, Schattschneider, and the Rebirth of Policy-Focused Analysis." *Perspectives on Politics* 12: 643–662.

Hacker, Jacob S. and Paul Pierson. 2016. *American Amnesia: How the War on Government Allowed Us to Forget What Made America Prosper.* New York: Simon and Schuster.

Hadden, Jennifer and Sidney Tarrow. 2007. "Spillover or Spillout: The Global Justice Movement in the United States after 9/11." *Mobilization* 12: 359–376.

Haider-Markel, Donald P. and Mark Josyln. 2008. "Beliefs About the Origins of Homosexuality and Support for Gay Rights." *Public Opinion Quarterly* 72(2): 291–310.

Haines, Herbert H. 2013. "Radical Flank Effects." In *The Wiley-Blackwell Encyclopedia of Social and Political Movements*, eds. David A. Snow, Donatella della Porta, Bert Klandermans, and Doug McAdam. Oxford: Blackwell. http://onlinelibrary.wiley.com/doi/10.1002/9780470674871.wbespm174/full.

Han, Hahrie. 2014. *How Organizations Develop Activists: Civic Associations and Leadership in the 21st Century*. Oxford: Oxford University Press.

Hancock, Ange-Marie. 2007. "Intersectionality as a Normative and Empirical Paradigm." *Politics and Gender* 3(2): 248–254.

Hao, Karen 2017. "Behind the Mystery Group Hitting Breitbart Where It Hurts." *Mother Jones*, March 24. http://www.motherjones.com/media/2017/03/breitbart-sleeping-giants-ads/.

Harris, Adam. 2017. "Colleges Deplore Trump's Threat to DACA. How Far Can They Go to Fight It?" *Chronicle of Higher Education*, September 6. https://www.chronicle.com/article/Colleges-Deplore-Trump-s/241110. Accessed February 4, 2018.

Harris, Fredrick. 2015. "The Next Civil Rights Movement?" *Dissent*, Summer. https://www.dissentmagazine.org/article/black-lives-matter-new-civil-rights-movement-fredrick-harris. Accessed January 4, 2018.

Hawkins, Kirk A. 2010. *Venezuela's Chavismo and Populism in Comparative Perspective*. New York: Cambridge University Press.

Heaney, Michael T. 2017a. "Activism in an Era of Partisan Polarization." *PS: Political Science and Politics* 50: 1000–1003.

Heaney, Michael T. 2017b. "Partisanship and the Resurgence of Women's Protest in the United States." Working Paper, University of Michigan. https://sites.lsa.umich.edu/mheaney/wp-content/uploads/sites/38/2017/02/Partisanship_and_Womens_Protest.pdf. Accessed December 9, 2017.

Heaney, Michael T. and Fabio Rojas. 2007. "Partisans, Nonpartisans, and the Antiwar Movement in the United States." *American Politics Research* 35: 431–464.

Heaney, Michael T. and Fabio Rojas. 2008. "Coalition Dissolution, Mobilization, and Network Dynamics in the US Antiwar Movement." *Research in Social Movements, Conflicts and Change* 28: 39–82.

Heaney, Michael T. and Fabio Rojas. 2015. *Party in the Street: The Antiwar Movement and the Democratic Party After 9/11*. New York: Cambridge University Press.

Henry, Astrid. 2004. *Not My Mother's Sister*. Bloomington: Indiana University Press.

Hepworth, Shelley. 2017. "Tracking Trump-Era Assault on Press Norms." *Columbia Journalism Review*, May 25. https://www.cjr.org/watchdog/tracking-trump-assault-press-freedom-media-attack.php. Accessed February 6, 2018.

Hero, Rodney R. and Robert R. Preuhs. 2009. "Beyond (the Scope of) Conflict: National Black and Latino Advocacy Group Relationships in the Congressional Arena." *Perspectives on Politics* 7(3): 501–517.

Hertel-Fernandez, Alexander. 2016. "How the Right Trounced Liberals in the States." *Democracy: A Journal of Ideas*, 28. https://democracyjournal.org/magazine/39/how-the-right-trounced-liberals-in-the-states/.

Hetherington, Marc J. 2011. "Resurgent Mass Partisanship: The Role of Elite Polarization." In *Controversies in Voting Behavior*, 5th ed., eds. Richard G. Niemi, Herbert F. Weisberg, and David C. Kimball, 242–265. Washington, DC: CQ Press.

Hetherington, Marc J. and Jonathan D. Weiler. 2009. *Authoritarianism and Polarization in American Politics*. New York: Cambridge University Press.

Hochschild, Arlie Rossell 2016. "The Ecstatic Edge of Politics: Sociology and Donald Trump." *Contemporary Sociology* 45: 683–690.

Honan, Matt. 2011. "Generation X is Sick of Your Bullshit." *Gizmodo*, October 18. https://gizmodo.com/5851062/generation-x-is-sick-of-your-bullshit. Accessed January 4, 2018.

Horowitz, Juliana Menasce and Gretchen Livingston. 2016. "How Americans View the Black Lives Matter Movement." http://www.pewresearch.org/fact-tank/2016/07/08/how-americans-view-the-black-lives-matter-movement/. Accessed January 4, 2018.

Hunter, Margaret. 2007. "The Persistent Problem of Colorism: Skin Tone, Status, and Inequality." *Sociology Compass* 1(1): 237–254.

Indivisible. n.d. "About Us." https://www.indivisible.org/about-us/. Accessed January 1, 2018.

Indivisible. n.d. "Statements." https://www.indivisible.org/statements/. Accessed January 1, 2018.

Indivisible. 2016. "Indivisible Guide." *Internet Archive*, December 20. https://web.archive.org/web/20161220114421/, https://www.indivisibleguide.com.

Indivisible. 2017a. "Missing Members of Congress Action Plan." February 14. https://www.indivisible.org/resource/missing-members-action-plan/?wpdmdl=1883.

Indivisible. 2017b. "Prioritizing Key Policy Issues." May 15. https://www.indivisible.org/resource/prioritizing-key-policy-issues/?wpdmdl=11332.

Indivisible435. 2017. "Indivisible Endorsements: A Practical Guide for Endorsing in Primaries and Beyond." November 1. https://indivisible435.org/endorsement.

Indivisible Guide. 2017. "Indivisible: A Practical Guide for Resisting the Trump Agenda." Updated March 9. https://www.indivisible.org/resource/guide-english-pdf/?wpdmdl=1777.

Indivisible MDI (@Indivisible_MDI). 2017. "Thank you Senator, we need you in DC!" Twitter post, October 14. https://twitter.com/Indivisible_MDI/status/919152240354570240.

Inglehart, Ronald. 1984. "The Changing Structure of Political Cleavages in Western Society." In *Electoral Change in Advanced Industrial Democracies: Realignment or Dealignment*, eds. Russell J. Dalton, Scott C. Flanagan, and Paul Alan Beck, 25–69. Princeton: Princeton University Press.

Isserman, Maurice. 1987. *If I Had a Hammer*. New York: Basic Books.

Jasper, James M. and Jane D. Poulsen. 1995. "Recruiting Strangers and Friends: Moral Shocks and Social Networks in Animal Rights and Anti-Nuclear Protests." *Social Problems* 42(4): 493–512.

Johnson, Jenna. 2015. "Trump Calls for 'Total and Complete Shutdown of Muslims Entering the United States.'" *Washington Post*, December 7. http://wapo.st/1YV0ViR?tid=ss_tw&utm_term=.532b8cdb615a.

Johnson, Jenna. 2016. "Donald Trump Now Says Even Legal Immigrants Are a Security Threat." *Washington Post*, August 5. http://wapo.st/2asOfMf?tid=ss_tw&utm_term=.a6a661a12ba3.

Johnson, Jenna. 2017. "A Taxonomy of Dishonesty: Why the Press Should Call out Politicians When They Lie." *The Economist*, February 16. https://www.economist.com/news/books-and-arts/21717019-and-why-lying-isnt-same-talking-nonsense-why-press-should-call-out-politicians. Accessed January 22, 2018.

Jones-Correa, Michael, Sophia J. Wallace, and Chris Zepeda-Millán. 2016. "The Impact of Large Scale Collective Action on Latino Perceptions of Commonality and Competition with African-Americans." *Social Science Quarterly* 97(2): 458–475.

Jordan, Miriam. 2017. "Futures in Jeopardy, 'Dreamers' Get Backing of Big Names and Businesses." *New York Times*, December 7. https://www.nytimes.com/2017/12/07/us/dreamers-shutdown-laurene-jobs.html.

Judis, John B. 2016. *The Populist Explosion: How the Great Recession Transformed American Politics*. New York: Columbia Global Reports.

Kalhan, Anil. 2013. "'Gray Zone' Constitutionalism and the Dilemma of Judicial Independence in Pakistan." *Vanderbilt Journal of Transnational Law* 46(1):1–96.

Kalogeropoulos, A. and Newman, N. (2017). "'I Saw the News on Facebook': Brand Attribution When Accessing News from Distributed Environments." Research Report, Reuters Institute for the Study of Journalism. http://reutersinstitute.politics.ox.ac.uk/sites/default/files/2017–07/Brand%20attributions%20report.pdf.

Karpf, David. 2012. *The MoveOn Effect: The Unexpected Transformation of American Political Advocacy*. New York: Oxford University Press.

Karpf, David 2016a. *Analytic Activism: Digital Listening and the New Political Strategy*. New York: Oxford University Press.

Karpf, David 2016b. "The Clickbait Candidate." *Chronicle of Higher Education*, June 16. https://www.chronicle.com/article/The-Clickbait-Candidate/236815.

Katzenstein, Mary F. 1998. *Faithful and Fearless: Moving Feminist Protest Inside the Church and the Military*. Princeton: Princeton University Press.

Kearney, Laila. 2016. "Hawaii Grandma's Plea Launches Women's March in Washington." *Reuters*, December 5. https://www.reuters.com/article/us-usa-trump-women/hawaii-grandmas-plea-launches-womens-march-in-washington-idUSKBN13U0GW. Accessed December 8, 2017.

Kennedy, Maev. 2017. "Heather Heyer, Victim of Charlottesville Car Attack, Was Civil Rights Activist." *The Guardian*, August 13. https://www.theguardian.com/us-news/2017/aug/

13/woman-killed-at-white-supremacist-rally-in-charlottesville-named. Accessed February 4, 2018.

Ketchley, Neil and Christopher Barrie. 2017. "Days of Protest, Fridays of Revolution: Focal Points and Mass Mobilization in Egypt and Tunisia." Unpublished paper, Kings College, London, June. https://www.academia.edu/36427987/Days_of_Protest_Fridays_of_Revolution_ Focal_Points_and_Mass_Mobilization_in_Egypt_and_Tunisia.

Kim, Hyojoung and Peter S. Bearman. 1997. "The Structure and Dynamics of Movement Participation." *American Sociological Review* 62(1): 70–93.

Kitschelt, Herbert. 1986. "Political Opportunity Structures and Political Protest: Anti-Nuclear Movements in Four Democracies." *British Journal of Political Science* 16(1): 57–85.

Kitschelt, Herbert. 1988. "Left-Libertarian Parties: Explaining Innovation in Competitive Party Systems." *World Politics* 40(2): 194–234.

Kitschelt, Herbert. 1994. *The Transformation of European Social Democracy*. New York: Cambridge University Press.

Kitschelt, Herbert. 1997. *The Radical Right in Western Europe: A Comparative Analysis*. Ann Arbor: University of Michigan Press.

Kitts, James. 2000. "Mobilizing in Black Boxes: Social Networks and Participation in Social Movement Organizations." *Mobilization: An International Quarterly* 5(2): 241–257.

Klandermans, Bert, and Dirk Oegema. 1987. "Potentials, Networks, Motivations, and Barriers: Steps Towards Participation in Social Movements." *American Sociological Review* 52(4): 519–531.

Klandermans, Bert, Jacquelien van Stekelenburg, Marie-Louise Damen, Dunya van Troost, and Anouk van Leeuwen. 2014. "Mobilization Without Organization: The Case of Unaffiliated Demonstrators." *European Sociological Review* 30(6): 702–716.

Klatch, Rebecca. 1999. *A Generation Divided: The New Left, the New Right, and the 1960s*. Berkeley: University of California Press.

Kopan, Tai. 2017. "Susan Sarandon: Trump more likely to bring 'revolution' than Clinton," *CNN Politics*, March 29. https://www.cnn.com/2016/03/29/politics/susan-sarandon-donald-trump-hillary-clinton-bernie-sanders/index.html. Accessed February 4, 2018.

Kotkin, Joel. 2017. "The Screwed Generation Turns Socialist." *The Daily Beast*, February 19. https://www.thedailybeast.com/the-screwed-generation-turns-socialist. Accessed January 4, 2018.

Kriesi, Hanspeter. 2008. "Contexts of Party Mobilization." In *West European Politics in the Age of Globalization*, eds. Hanspeter Kriesi, Edgar Grande, Romain Lachat, Martin Dolezal, Simon Bornschier, and Timotheos Frey, 23–52. New York: Cambridge University Press.

Kriesi, Hanspeter, Edgar Grande, Romain Lachat, Martin Dolezal, Simon Bornschier, and Timotheos Frey. 2008. *West European Politics in the Age of Globalization*. New York: Cambridge University Press.

Kriesi, Hanspeter, Ruud Koopmans, Jan W. Duyvendak, and Marco Giugni. 1992. "New Social Movements and Political Opportunities in Western Europe." *European Journal of Political Research* 22(2): 219–244.

Kriesi, Hanspeter and Takis S. Pappas, eds. 2015. *European Populism in the Shadow of the Great Recession*. Colchester, UK: ECPR Press.

Lach, Eric 2017. "How a Veteran of *Fox News* Boycotts Does It." *NewYorker.com*, April 6. https://www.newyorker.com/news/news-desk/how-a-veteran-of-fox-news-boycotts-does-it.

Laclau, Ernesto. 2007. *On Populist Reason*. London: Verso.

Layton, Azza Salama. 2000. *International Politics and Civil Rights Policies in the United States, 1941–1960*. New York: Cambridge University Press.

Lee, Bandy et al. 2017. *The Dangerous Case of Donald Trump. 27 Psychiatrists and Mental Health Experts Assess a President*. New York: Thomas Dunne Books (St. Martins).

Lee, Frances E. 2016. *Insecure Majorities: Congress and the Perpetual Campaign*. Chicago: University of Chicago Press.

Lee, Michelle Ye Hee. 2015. "Donald Trump's False Comments Connecting Mexican Immigrants and Crime." *Washington Post*, July 8. https://www.washingtonpost.com/news/fact-checker/wp/2015/07/08/donald-trumps-false-comments-connecting-mexican-immigrants-and-crime/?utm_term=.8c750adae3d9.

Lee, Taeku. 2002. *Mobilizing Public Opinion: Black Insurgency and Racial Attitudes in the Civil Rights Era.* Chicago: The University of Chicago Press.

Lemieux, Jamilah 2017. Why I'm skipping the Women's March on Washington. *ColorLines,* January 21. https://www.colorlines.com/articles/why-im-skipping-womens-march-washington-opinion. Accessed 8 December 8, 2017.

Lennard, Natasha. 2017. "Six Months After the Election, What Does 'The Resistance' Mean Now?" *Esquire,* May 13. http://www.esquire.com/news-politics/news/a55038/what-does-the-resistance-mean.

Leonard, Sarah. 2017. "Is Donald Trump Turning Liberals Into Radicals?" *New York Times,* October 20. https://www.nytimes.com/2017/10/20/opinion/sunday/trump-resistance-radicals.html. Accessed January 4, 2018.

Leonhardt, David, Ian Prasad Philbrick, and Stuart A. Thompson. 2017. "Trump's Lies vs. Obama's." *New York Times,* December 14.

Levin, Ezra, Leah Greenberg, and Angel Padilla. 2017a. "To Stop Trump, Democrats Can Learn From the Tea Party." *New York Times Opinion,* January 2. https://www.nytimes.com/2017/01/02/opinion/to-stop-trump-democrats-can-learn-from-the-tea-party.html.

Levin, Ezra, Leah Greenberg, and Angel Padilla. 2017b. "Who Saved Obamacare from the GOP? The American People." *Washington Post,* July 31. https://www.washingtonpost.com/news/posteverything/wp/2017/07/31/who-saved-obamacare-from-the-gop-the-american-people/.

Levitsky, Steven and Lucan A. Way. 2010. *Competitive Authoritarianism: Hybrid Regimes After the Cold War.* New York: Cambridge University Press.

Levitsky, Steven and Daniel Ziblatt. 2018. *How Democracies Die.* New York: Crown.

Lewis, Nicole. 2017. "Think all Millennials Hate Trump? Actually, #It'sComplicated." *Washington Post,* August 5. https://www.washingtonpost.com/news/the-fix/wp/2017/08/05/think-all-millennials-hate-trump-actually-itscomplicated/?utm_term=.ffcc39c444fd. Accessed January 4, 2018.

Lieberman, Jeffrey A. 2017. "Psychiatrists Diagnosing the President—Moral Imperative or Ethical Violation?" letter. *New England Journal of Medicine.* December 27.

Lieberman, Jeffrey A. 2018. "Maybe Trump Is Not Mentally Ill. Maybe He's Just a Jerk." *New York Times,* January 12. https://www.nytimes.com/2018/01/12/opinion/trump-mentally-ill.html. Accessed January 12, 2018.

Lieberman, Robert C. 2017. "Trumpism and the Global Liberal Order." Prepared for the conference on The State of American Democracy in Historical and Comparative Perspective. Cornell University, Ithaca, NY.

Lieberman, Robert C., Suzanne Mettler, Thomas B. Pepinsky, Kenneth R. Roberts, and Richard Valelly. 2017. "Trumpism and American Democracy: History, Comparison, and the Predicament of Liberal Democracy in the United States." Unpublished paper, Cornell University, Ithaca, NY, August 29. https://papers.ssrn.com/sol3/papers.cfm?abstract_id=3028990.

Lim, Chaeyoon. 2008. "Social Networks and Political Participation: How Do Networks Matter?" *Social Forces* 87(2): 961–982.

Lindig, Sarah. 2017. "The Most Inspiring Quotes from the Women's March Speeches." *Elle,* January 21. http://www.elle.com/culture/career-politics/news/a42344/inspiring-quotes-womens-march-speeches/. Accessed January 4, 2018.

Linthicum, Kate. 2016. "Trump's Border Rhetoric Emboldens Officials on Local Level to Target Immigration, Activists Say." *Los Angeles Times,* May 13. http://www.latimes.com/politics/la-na-trump-immigration-20160513-snap-story.html.

Linz, Juan. 1990. "The Perils of Presidentialism." *Journal of Democracy* 1(1): 51–69.

Liptik, Adam. 2017. "Supreme Court Allows Trump Travel Ban to Take Effect." *New York Times,* December 4. https://www.nytimes.com/2017/12/04/us/politics/trump-travel-ban-supreme-court.html.

Lipton, Eric, David E. Sanger, and Scott Shane. 2016. "The Perfect Weapon: How Russian Cyberpower Invaded the U.S." *New York Times,* December 15. https://www.nytimes.com/2016/12/13/us/politics/russia-hack-election-dnc.html?mcubz=0.

Lizza, Ryan. 2017. "How Trump Broke the Office of Government Ethics." *The New Yorker,* July 14. https://www.newyorker.com/news/ryan-lizza/how-trump-broke-the-office-of-government-ethics.

Lo, Clarence 1982. "Countermovements and Conservative Movements in the Contemporary U.S." *Annual Review of Sociology* 8: 107–134.

Lockhart, P. R. 2017. "Trump Rhetoric Pits New Immigrants Against African Americans and Latinos." *Mother Jones*, August 14.

Loveman, Mara. 1998. "High-Risk Collective Action: Defending Human Rights in Chile, Uruguay, and Argentina." *American Journal of Sociology* 104(2): 477–525.

Lucey, Catherine and Tim Reynolds. 2017. "President Donald Trump withdraws White House offer to Golden State Warriors." *NBA.com*, September 23. http://www.nba.com/article/2017/09/23/president-donald-trump-withdraws-white-house-offer-golden-state-warriors#/. Accessed February 9, 2018.

Luthin, Reinhard H. 1954. *American Demagogues*. Boston: Beacon.

Lynn, Peter and Paul Clarke. 2002. "Separating Refusal Bias and Non-Contact Bias: Evidence from UK National Surveys." *Journal of the Royal Statistical Society. Series D (The Statistician)* 51(3): 319–333.

Madrid, Raúl. 2012. *The Rise of Ethnic Politics in Latin America*. New York: Cambridge University Press.

Madrigal, Alexis. 2017. "When the Facebook Traffic Goes Away." *TheAtlantic.com*, October 24. https://www.theatlantic.com/technology/archive/2017/10/when-the-facebook-traffic-goes-away/543828/.

Mahmoud, Ahsha. 2017. "Millennials are the Ones Leading the Resistance against Trump." *Huffington Post*, August 13. https://www.huffingtonpost.com/entry/say-what-you-will-against-millennials-but-theyre_us_598e569ee4b0ed1f464c0acc. Accessed January 4, 2018.

Mair, Peter. 2013. *Ruling the Void: The Hollowing of Western Democracy*. London: Verso.

Mallon, Maggie. 2017. "The Fight Against Trump's Travel Ban Is Headed to the Supreme Court—And Becca Heller Is the Woman Leading the Charge." *Glamour Magazine*, June 15. https://www.glamour.com/story/becca-heller-irap-vs-trump-supreme-court.

Malone, Clare 2016. "Clinton Couldn't Win Over White Women." *FiveThirtyEight*, November 9. https://fivethirtyeight.com/features/clinton-couldnt-win-over-white-women/. Accessed December 8, 2017.

Mann, Thomas E. and Norman J. Ornstein. 2012. *It's Even Worse Than It Looks: How the American Constitutional System Collided with the New Politics of Extremism*. New York: Basic Books.

Mannheim, Karl. 1952 [1928]. "The Problem of Generations." In *Essays on the Sociology of Knowledge*, ed. P. Kecskemeti, 276–332. London: Routledge and Kegan Paul.

Marshall, Josh 2017. "A Serf on Google's Farm." *TalkingPointsMemo.com*, September 1. http://talkingpointsmemo.com/edblog/a-serf-on-googles-farm.

Martin, Andrew W. 2008. "The Institutional Logic of Union Organizing and the Effectiveness of Social Movement Repertoires." *American Journal of Sociology* 113(4): 1067–1103.

Marwell, Gerald, Pamela E. Oliver, and Ralph Prahl. 1988. "Social Networks and Collective Action: A Theory of the Critical Mass. III." *American Journal of Sociology* 94(3): 502–534.

Mascaro, Lisa. 2016. "Latino Support for Clinton Set to Hit Record High for a Presidential Candidate—and for Trump, a New Low." *Los Angeles Times*, November 6. http://www.latimes.com/nation/politics/trailguide/la-na-trailguide-updates-latino-support-for-hillary-clinton-at-1478451714-htmlstory.html.

Masuoka, Natalie and Jane Junn. 2013. *The Politics of Belonging: Race, Public Opinion, and Immigration*. Chicago: University of Chicago Press.

Mayer, Jane 2017. "The Reclusive Hedge-Fund Tycoon Behind the Trump Presidency." *The New Yorker*, March 27.

McAdam, Doug. 1983. "Tactical Innovation and the Pace of Insurgency." *American Sociological Review* 48(6): 735–754.

McAdam, Doug. 1986. "Recruitment to High-Risk Activism: The Case of Freedom Summer." *American Journal of Sociology* 92(1): 64–90.

McAdam, Doug. 1988. *Freedom Summer*. New York: Oxford University Press.

McAdam, Doug. 1996. "Conceptual Origins, Current Problems, Future Directions." In *Comparative Perspectives on Social Movements: Political Opportunities, Mobilizing Structures, and Cultural Framings*, eds. Doug McAdam, John D. McCarthy, and Mayer N. Zald, 23–40. New York: Cambridge University Press.

McAdam, Doug. 1999a. "The Biographical Impact of Social Movements." In *How Social Movements Matter*, eds. Marco Giugni, Doug McAdam, and Charles Tilly, 117–146. Minneapolis: University of Minnesota Press.

McAdam, Doug. 1999b. *Political Process and the Development of Black Insurgency, 1930–70*. Chicago: University of Chicago Press.

McAdam, Doug. 2009. "The Civil Rights Movement: Power from Below and Above, 1945–1970." In *Civil Resistance and Power Politics*, eds. Adam Roberts and Timothy Garton Ash, 58–74. Oxford: Oxford University Press.

McAdam, Doug and Katrina Kloos. 2014. *Deeply Divided: Racial Politics and Social Movements in Post-War America*. New York: Oxford University Press.

McAdam, Doug and Ronnelle Paulsen. 1993. "Specifying the Relationship Between Social Ties and Activism." *American Journal of Sociology* 99(3): 640–667.

McAdam, Doug, Sidney Tarrow, and Charles Tilly. 2001. *Dynamics of Contention*. New York: Cambridge University Press.

McAlevey, Jane. 2016. *No Shortcuts: Organizing for Power in the New Gilded Age*. Oxford: Oxford University Press.

McCammon, Holly, and Karen Campbell. 2002. "Allies on the Road to Victory: Coalition Formation Between the Suffragists and the Woman's Christian Temperance Union." *Mobilization: An International Quarterly* 7(3): 231–251.

McCann, Michael W. 1994. *Rights at Work*. Chicago: University of Chicago Press.

McCarthy, John D. and Mayer N. Zald. 1977. "Resource Mobilization and Social Movements: A Partial Theory." *American Journal of Sociology* 82(6): 1212–1241.

McCaskill, Nolan. 2017. "Trump Says He Will Treat Dreamers 'With Heart.'" *Politico*, February 16. https://www.politico.com/story/2017/02/trump-press-conference-dreamers-heart-235103. Accessed February 4, 2018.

McChesney, Robert W. and Victor Pickard. 2011. *Will the Last Reporter Please Turn out the Lights: The Collapse of Journalism and What Can Be Done to Fix It*. New York: The New Press.

McClain, Paula D., Niambi M. Carter, Victoria M. DeFrancesco Soto, Monique L. Lyle, Jeffrey D. Grynaviski, Shayla C. Nunnally, Thomas J. Scotto, J. Alan Kendrick, Gerald F. Lackey, and Kendra Davenport Cotton. 2006. "Racial Distancing in a Southern City: Latino Immigrants' Views of Black Americans." *Journal of Politics* 68(3): 571–84.

McGreevy, Patrick. 2017. "California Sues Trump Administration Over Plan to End DACA." *Los Angeles Times*, September 11. http://www.latimes.com/politics/essential/la-pol-ca-essential-politics-updates-california-sues-trump-administration-1505150334-htmlstory.html. Accessed February 4, 2018.

McGreevy, Patrick and Jazmine Ulloa. 2017. "California Again Steps Up to Trump, This Time to Stop the Border Wall." *Los Angeles Times*, September 20. http://www.latimes.com/politics/la-pol-ca-xavier-becerra-trump-wall-lawsuit-20170920-story.html.

Mettler, Katie. 2017. "This Is Really Unprecedented: ICE Detains Woman Seeking Domestic Abuse Protection at Texas Courthouse." *Washington Post*, February 16.

Mercer, Andrew, Claudia Deane, and Kyley McGeeney. 2016. "Why 2016 Election Polls Missed their Mark." Pew Research Center, November 9. http://www.pewresearch.org/fact-tank/2016/11/09/why-2016-election-polls-missed-their-mark/.

Mettler, Suzanne. 2017. "Can it Happen Here? Citizenship and the Deterioration of Democracy in America." Prepared for the conference on The State of American Democracy in Historical and Comparative Perspective. Cornell University, Ithaca, NY.

Meyer, David S. 1990. *A Winter of Discontent: The Nuclear Freeze and American Politics*. New York: Praeger.

Meyer, David S. 1993a. "Institutionalizing Dissent: The United States Structure of Political Opportunity and the End of the Nuclear Freeze Movement." *Sociological Forum* 8(2): 157–179.

Meyer, David S. 1993b. "Peace Protest and Policy: Explaining the Rise and Decline of Antinuclear Movements in Postwar America." *Policy Studies Journal* 21(1): 35–51.

Meyer, David S. 2004. "Protest and Political Opportunities." *Annual Review of Sociology* 30: 125–145.

Meyer, David S. 2006. "Claiming Credit: Stories of Movement Influence as Outcomes." *Mobilization* 11(3): 281–298.

Meyer, David S. 2014. *The Politics of Protest: Social Movements in America*. 2nd ed. Oxford: Oxford University Press.

Meyer, David S. and Steven A. Boutcher. 2007. "Signals and Spillover: Brown v. Board of Education and Other Social Movements." *Perspectives on Politics* 5: 81–93.

Meyer, David S. and Catherine Corrigall-Brown. 2005. "Coalitions and Political Context." *Mobilization* 10(3):327–344.

Meyer, David S. and Eulalie Laschever. 2016. "Social Movements and the Institutionalization of Dissent in America." In *The Oxford Handbook of American Political Development*, eds. Richard M. Valelly, Suzanne Mettler, and Robert C. Lieberman, 563–589. Oxford: Oxford University Press.

Meyer, David S. and Debra C. Minkoff. 2004. "Conceptualizing Political Opportunity." *Social Forces* 82(4): 1457–1492.

Meyer, David S. and Suzanne Staggenborg. 1996. "Movements, Countermovements, and the Structure of Political Opportunity." *American Journal of Sociology* 101: 1628–1660.

Meyer, David S. and Suzanne Staggenborg 1998. "Countermovement Dynamics in Federal Systems: A Comparison of Abortion Politics in Canada and the United States." *Research in Political Sociology* 8: 209–240.

Meyer, David S. and Sidney Tarrow. 1998. "A Movement Society: Contentious Politics for a New Century." In *The Social Movement Society: Contentious Politics for a New Century*, eds. David S. Meyer and Sidney Tarrow, 1–28. Lanham, MD: Rowman & Littlefield.

Meyer, David S. and Nancy Whittier 1994. "Social Movement Spillover." *Social Problems* 41: 277–298.

Michels, Robert. 1915. *Political Parties: A Sociological Study of the Oligarchical Tendencies of Modern Democracy*. New York: Hearst's International Library Co.

Mickey, Robert, Steven Levitsky, and Lucan Ahmad Way. 2017. "Is America Still Safe for Democracy? Why the United States is in Danger of Backsliding." *Foreign Affairs* 96 (May/June): 20–29.

Milkman, Ruth. 2017. "A New Political Generation: Millennials and the Post-2008 Wave of Protest." *American Sociological Review* 82(1): 1–31.

Milkman, Ruth, Stephanie Luce, and Penny Lewis. 2013. "Changing the Subject: A Bottom up Account of Occupy Wall Street in New York City." https://media.sps.cuny.edu/filestore/1/5/7/1_a05051d2117901d/1571_92f562221b8041e.pdf. Accessed January 4, 2018.

Millennial Impact Report 2017. "Phase 2: The Power of Voice." http://www.themillennialimpact.com/latest-research. Accessed January 4, 2018.

Miller, Gary and Norman Schofield. 2008. "The Transformation of the Republican and Democratic Party Coalitions," *Perspectives on Politics* 6(3): 433–450.

Minkenberg, Michael. 2017. "The Radical Right in Public Office: Agenda-Setting and Policy Effects." In *The Populist Radical Right: A Reader*, ed. Cas Mudde, 443–457. Abingdon, UK: Routledge.

Moffitt, Benjamin. 2016. *The Global Rise of Populism: Performance, Political Style, and Representation*. Stanford, CA: Stanford University Press.

Molyneux, Maxine 1998. "Analysing Women's Movements." *Development and Change* 29(2): 219–245.

Morris, Aldon. 1986. *The Origins of the Civil Rights Movement*. New York: Free Press.

Mosthof, Mariella 2017. "If You're not Talking about the Criticism Surrounding the Women's March, then You're Part of The Problem." *Bustle*, January 30. https://www.bustle.com/p/if-youre-not-talking-about-the-criticism-surrounding-the-womens-march-then-youre-part-of-the-problem-33491. Accessed December 8, 2017.

Mottl, Tali. 1980. "The Analysis of Countermovements." *Social Problems* 27: 620–635.

Mudde, Cas. 2004. "The Populist Zeitgeist." *Government and Opposition* 39: 542–563.

Mudde, Cas. 2007. *Populist Radical Right Parties in Europe*. Cambridge: Cambridge University Press.

Mudde, Cas. 2013. "Three Decades of Radical Right Parties in Western Europe: So What?" *European Journal of Political Research* 52: 1–19.

Mudde, Cas, ed. 2017. *The Populist Radical Right: A Reader*. London and New York: Routledge.

Mudde, Cas and Cristóbal Rovira Kaltwasser. 2012. "Populism and (Liberal) Democracy: A Framework for Analysis." In *Populism in Europe and the Americas: Threat or Corrective to*

Democracy?, eds. Cas Mudde and Cristóbal Rovira Kaltwasser. Cambridge: Cambridge University Press.

Mudde, Cas and Cristóbal Rovira Kaltwasser. 2013. "Exclusionary vs. Inclusionary Populism: Comparing the Contemporary Europe and Latin America." *Government and Opposition* 48(2): 147–174.

Mudde, Cas and Cristóbal Rovira Kaltwasser. 2017. *Populism: A Very Short Introduction.* Oxford: Oxford University Press.

Mudde, Cas and Cristóbal Rovira Kaltwasser, eds. 2012. *Populism in Europe and the Americas: Threat or Corrective for Democracy?* Cambridge, Cambridge University Press.

Munguia, Hayley. 2014. "How Many People Really Showed Up To The People's Climate March?" *FiveThirtyEight*, September 30. http://fivethirtyeight.com/features/peoples-climate-march-attendance/ (Accessed 8 November 2017).

Munson, Ziad W. 2010. *The Making of Pro-Life Activists: How Social Movement Mobilization Works.* Chicago: University of Chicago Press.

Murphy, Carla. 2015. "The Hope and Burden of the Civil Rights Movement." *Colorlines*, January 16.   https://www.colorlines.com/articles/hope-and-burden-civil-rights-movement Accessed January 4, 2018.

NAACP. 2017. "NAACP Files Lawsuit in Defense of DACA Eligible People of Color," press release, September 18. http://www.naacp.org/latest/naacp-files-lawsuit-defense-daca-eligible-people-color/.

National Immigration Law Center. 2017. "What We Do." https://www.nilc.org/about-us/what_we_do/. Accessed November 30, 2017.

New York Times. 2017. "Here's the Democracy Alliance's Resistance Map." *New York Times*, October 7. https://www.nytimes.com/interactive/2017/10/07/us/politics/document-DA-ResistanceMap-2017.html.

Nepstad, Sharon. 2004. "Persistent Resistance: Commitment and Community in the Plowshares Movement." *Social Problems* 51(1): 43–60.

Nicholls, Walter. 2013. *The DREAMers: How the Undocumented Youth Movement Transformed the Immigrant Rights Debate.* Palo Alto, CA: Stanford University Press.

Nirappil, Fenit. 2017. "Democrats Make Significant Gains in Virginia Legislature; Control of House in Play." *Washington Post*, November 8. https://www.washingtonpost.com/local/virginia-politics/democrats-poised-to-make-significant-gains-in-virginia-legislature/2017/11/07/9c2f4d24-c401-11e7-aae0-cb18a8c29c65_story.html.

Nwanevu, Osita. 2016. "Sleeping Giants' Is Borrowing Gamergate's Tactics to Attack *Breitbart*." *Slate.com*, December 14. http://www.slate.com/articles/news_and_politics/politics/2016/12/sleeping_giants_campaign_against_breitbart.html.

Oberschall, Anthony. 1973. *Social Conflict and Social Movements.* London: Pearson Education, Limited.

Oboler, Suzanne, and Anani Dzidzienyo. 2005. *Neither Enemies nor Friends: Latinos, Blacks, Afro-Latinos.* New York: Springer.

O'Connell, Jonathan and David A. Fahrenthold. 2017. "Maryland, D.C. Get Subpoena Power in Trump Emoluments Suit." *Washington Post*, November 29. https://www.washingtonpost.com/politics/maryland-dc-get-subpoena-power-in-trump-emoluments-suit/2017/11/29/983be4a6-d528-11e7-a986-d0a9770d9a3e_story.html?utm_term=.13a608387545. Accessed February 4, 2018.

O'Reilly Herrera, Andrea. 2016. "Grupo Neo-Latino: Reaching Critical Mass." http://ragazine.cc/2016/08/grupo-neo-latino/. Accessed April 21, 2018.

Ocampo, Lizet. 2015. "Top 6 Facts on the Latino Vote." Center for American Progress, September 17. https://www.americanprogress.org/issues/immigration/news/2015/09/17/121325/top-6-facts-on-the-latino-vote/.

Oegema, Dirk, and Bert Klandermans. 1994. "Why Social Movement Sympathizers Don't Participate: Erosion and Nonconversion of Support." *American Sociological Review* 59(5): 703–722.

Office of the Press Secretary, The White House. 2011. "Remarks by the President on the Economy in Osawatomie, Kansas," press release, December 06. https://obamawhitehouse.archives.gov/the-press-office/2011/12/06/remarks-president-economy-osawatomie-kansas. Accessed September 8, 2017.

Ohlemacher, Thomas. 1996. "Bridging People and Protest: Social Relays of Protest Groups Against Low-Flying Military Jets in West Germany." *Social Problems* 43(2): 197–218.

Olteano, Alexandra, Ingmar Weber, and Daniel Gatica-Perez. 2015. "Characterizing the Demographics Behind the #BlackLivesMatter Movement." Prepared for AAAI Spring Symposia, March 2016. https://arxiv.org/pdf/1512.05671.pdf. Accessed January 4, 2018.

Oluo, Ijeoma. 2017. "When You Brag That the Women's Marches Were Nonviolent." *The Establishment*, January 23. https://theestablishment.co/when-you-brag-that-the-womens-marches-were-nonviolent-b042133ae2bb. Accessed December 8, 2017.

Opp, Karl-Dieter, and Christiane Gern. 1993. "Dissident Groups, Personal Networks, and Spontaneous Cooperation: The East German Revolution of 1989." *American Sociological Review* 58(5): 659–680.

Ostiguy, Pierre. 2017. "Populism: A Socio-Cultural Approach." In *The Oxford Handbook of Populism*, eds. Cristóbal Rovira Kaltwasser, Paul Taggart, Paulina Ochoa Espejo, and Pierre Ostiguy, 73–97. Oxford: Oxford University Press.

"Our Mission." Pantsuit Nation. https://www.pantsuitnation.org/mission.html. Accessed January 4, 2018.

Padilla, Angel. 2018. "2018 Is Here." *IndivisiBlog*, January 3. https://www.indivisible.org/blog/2018-is-here/.

Panizza, Francisco. 2005. "Introduction: Populism and the Mirror of Democracy." In *Populism and the Mirror of Democracy*, ed. Francisco Panizza, 1–31. London: Verso.

Pappano, Laura. 2017. "Liberal Lessons in Taking Back America." *New York Times*, August 4. https://www.nytimes.com/2017/08/04/education/edlife/harvard-resistance-school-liberal-lessons-take-back-america.html. Accessed January 4, 2018.

Pariser, Eli. 2011. *The Filter Bubble: How the New Personalized Web Is Changing What We Read and How We Think*. New York: Penguin Press.

Parker, Ashley and Steve Eder. 2016. "Inside the Six Weeks Donald Trump Was a Nonstop 'Birther.'" *New York Times*, July 2.

Parker, Christopher S. and Matt Barreto. 2013. *Change They Can't Believe In: The Tea Party and Reactionary Politics in Contemporary America*. Princeton: Princeton University Press.

Pasek, Josh, Jon A. Krosnick, and Trevor Thompson. 2012. "The Impact of Anti-Black Racism on Approval of Barack Obama's Job Performance and on Voting in the 2012 Presidential Election." Unpublished paper, Stanford University, Stanford, CA.

Passy, Florence 2003. "Social Networks Matter. But How?" In *Social Movements and Networks*, eds. Mario Diani and Doug McAdam, 21–47. New York: Oxford University Press.

Patler, Caitlin and Roberto Gonzales. 2015. "Framing Citizenship: Media Coverage of Anti-Deportation Cases Led by Undocumented Immigrant Youth Organizations." *Journal of Ethnic and Migration Studies* 41(9): 1453–1474.

Patterson, Thomas E. 2016. "News Coverage of the 2016 Presidential Primaries: Horse Race Reporting Has Consequences." Research Report, Shorenstein Center on Media, Politics, and Public Policy, July 11. https://shorensteincenter.org/wp-content/uploads/2016/07/Election-2016-Primary-Media-Coverage.pdf?x78124. Accessed February 8, 2018.

Perez, Carmen. 2017. "Keynote Address at the Inclusive Global Leadership Institute," Denver, Colorado, August 28. https://www.youtube.com/watch?v=91qaMSq4RcM. Accessed December 8, 2017.

Persily, Nathaniel, Jack Citrin, and Patrick J. Egan. 2008. *Public Opinion and Constitutional Controversy*. New York: Oxford University Press.

Petre, Caitlin. 2015. "The Traffic Factories: Metrics at Chartbeat, Gawker Media, and the *New York Times*." May 7. *Tow Center for Digital Journalism*. http://towcenter.org/research/traffic-factories/. Accessed February 8, 2018.

Pew Research Center. 2014. "Generation X: America's Neglected Middle Child." http://www.pewresearch.org/fact-tank/2014/06/05/generation-x-americas-neglected-middle-child/. Accessed January 4, 2018.

Pew Research Center. 2015. "The Whys and Hows of Generations Research." http://www.people-press.org/2015/09/03/the-whys-and-hows-of-generations-research/. Accessed January 4, 2018.

Pew Research Center. 2016. "Social Media Update 2016." http://www.pewinternet.org/2016/11/11/social-media-update-2016/ (Accessed 10 November 2017).

Pew Research Center. 2017a. "Presidential Approval Detailed Tables," June. http://www.people-press.org/2017/06/20/presidential-approval-detailed-tables-june-2017/. Accessed January 4, 2018.

Pew Research Center 2017b. "Since Trump's Election, Increased Attention to Politics – Especially among Women," p. 2. http://assets.pewresearch.org/wp-content/uploads/sites/5/2017/07/20131437/07–20-17-Political-release.pdf. Accessed January 4, 2018.

Pew Research Center 2018. "Public Has Mixed Expectations for New Tax Law." January 24. http://www.People-press.org/2018/01/24/public-has-mixed-expectations-for-new-tax-law/.

Phillips, Kevin. 1969. *The Emerging Republican Majority*. New Rochelle, NY: Arlington House.

Phillips, Steve. 2016. *Brown Is the New White: How the Demographic Revolution Has Created a New American Majority*. New York: New Press.

Politico. 2017. "50 Ideas Blowing Up American Politics (and the People Behind Them): Leah Greenberg & Ezra Levin." *Politico Magazine*, September 8. https://www.politico.com/interactives/2017/politico50/leah-greenberg-ezra-levin/.

Polletta, Francesca and James M. Jasper 2001. "Collective Identity and Social Movements." *Annual Review of Sociology* 27(1): 283–305.

Posner, Eric. 2017. "Judges v. Trump: Be Careful What You Wish For." *New York Times*, February 15. https://nyti.ms/2lkOJNb.

Preston, Julia. 2017. "How the Dreamers Learned to Play Politics." *Politico*, September 29. https://www.politico.com/magazine/story/2017/09/09/dreamers-daca-learned-to-play-politics-215588.

Principe, Maria. 2017. *Women in Nonviolent Movements*. Washington, DC: United States Institute of Peace Special Report 399.

Prior, Markus. 2007. *Post-Broadcast Democracy: How Media Choice Increases Inequality in Political Involvement and Polarizes Elections*. Princeton: Princeton University Press.

Pugliese, Nicole. 2017. "How These Six Women's Protests Changed History." *The Guardian*, January 21. https://www.theguardian.com/world/2017/jan/21/womens-march-protests-history-suffragettes-iceland-poland. Accessed 8 December 8, 2017.

Purdum, Todd. 2018. "How Conservatives Learned to Hate the FBI: The GOP Has Almost Always Supported the FBI, but Republicans Have Recently Unleashed a Furious Firestorm of Criticism Against The Bureau." *Politico*, February 3. https://www.politico.com/story/2018/02/03/conservatives-fbi-trump-republicans-389076. Accessed February 4, 2018.

Raeburn, Nicole C. 2004. *Changing Corporate America From the Inside Out: Lesbian and Gay Workplace Rights*. Minneapolis: University of Minnesota Press.

Ramshaw, Emily. 2017. "A Black Lives Matter Cofounder on How Immigration Policy in Trump's America is Different and the Same." *Coveteur*. http://coveteur.com/2017/02/22/black-lives-matter-co-founder-opal-tometi-immigration-justice/.

Randall, Amber. 2017. "Black Lives Matter Switches Resistance Tactics In Trump Era." *The Daily Caller*, May 15. http://dailycaller.com/2017/05/05/black-lives-matter-switches-resistance-tactics-in-trump-era/.

Redden, Molly and Sabrina Siddiqui. 2017. "Donald Trump's Accusers Demand Congress Investigate Sexual Misconduct Claims." *The Guardian*, December 12. https://www.theguardian.com/us-news/2017/dec/11/women-accusing-trump-demand-congress-investigate-sexual-misconduct?CMP=Share_iOSApp_Other. Accessed December 21, 2017.

Reger, Jo. 2012. *Everywhere and Nowhere: Contemporary Feminism in the United States*. New York: Oxford University Press.

Reger, Jo. 2014a. "Debating US Contemporary Feminism." *Sociology Compass* 8(1): 43–51.

Reger, Jo. 2014b. "Micro-Cohorts, Feminist discourse, and the Emergence of the Toronto SlutWalk." *Feminist Formations* 26(1): 49–69.

Reilly, Ryan J. 2018. "Justice Department Drops Felony Charges Against 129 Trump Inauguration Defendants but 59 Other #J20 Protesters Will Face Trial." *The Huffington Post*, January 18. https://www.huffingtonpost.com/entry/j20-felony-charges_us_5a6122b4e4b074ce7a06d638. Accessed January 26, 2018.

Resistance School. 2017. https://resistanceschool.com; attendance reports at https://www.resistanceschool.com/semester-two-welcome#featured-speaker session listings at https://www.resistanceschool.com/session-two-3/ listings for spring 2017 and fall 2017. Accessed January 4, 2018.

Rhodes-Purdy, Matthew. 2017. *Regime Support Beyond the Balance Sheet: Participation and Policy Performance in Latin America*. New York: Cambridge University Press.

Riddell, Kelly. 2017. "Pro-life women banned from anti-Trump Women's March on Washington." *Washington Times*, January 17. https://www.washingtontimes.com/news/2017/jan/17/pro-life-women-banned-anti-trump-womens-march-wash/. Accessed December 8, 2017.

Roberts, Dorothy and Sujatha Jesudason. 2013. "Movement Intersectionality: The Case of Race, Gender, Disability, and Genetic Technologies." *Du Bois Review: Social Science Research on Race* 10(2): 313–328.

Roberts, Kenneth M. 1995. "Neoliberalism and the Transformation of Populism in Latin America: The Peruvian Case." *World Politics* 48(1): 82–116.

Roberts, Kenneth M. 2014. *Changing Course in Latin America: Party Systems in the Neoliberal Era*. New York: Cambridge University Press.

Roberts, Kenneth M. 2016. "Populism as Epithet and Identity: The Use and Misuse of a Contested Concept." *Comparative Politics Newsletter* 26(2): 69–72.

Robnett, Belinda. 1996. "African-American Women in the Civil Rights Movement, 1954–1965: Gender, Leadership, and Micromobilization." *American Journal of Sociology* 101(6): 1661–1693.

Rochford, E. Burke. 1982. "Recruitment Strategies, Ideology, and Organization in the Hare Krishna Movement." *Social Problems* 29(4): 399–410.

Rodgers, Daniel T. 2011. *Age of Fracture*. Cambridge, MA: Harvard University Press.

Rohrabacher, Dana. 2017. "Rohrabacher Outraged by Assault on his District Director by 'Indivisible' Mob," press release, February 15. https://rohrabacher.house.gov/media-center/press-releases/rohrabacher-outraged-by-assault-on-his-district-director-by-indivisible.

Romanos, Eduardo. 2017. "Late Neoliberalism and Its Indignados: Contention in Austerity Spain." In *Late Neoliberalism and Its Discontents in the Economic Crisis*, eds. Donatella della Porta, Massimiliano Andretta, Tiago Fernandes, Francis O'Connor, Eduardo Romanos, and Markos Vogiatzoglou, 131–168. London: Palgrave Macmillan.

Rose, Nikolas. 1999. *Powers of Freedom: Reframing Political Thought*. New York: Cambridge University Press.

Rose-Ackerman, Susan 2017. "Administrative Law, the Common Law, and the U.S. Presidential System: The Republican Party Assault on Regulation." https://adminlawblog.org/2017/03/01/1/. Accessed February 8, 2018.

Rosenberg, Gerald. 2008. *The Hollow Hope*. 2nd ed. Chicago: University of Chicago Press.

Rovira Kaltwasser, Cristóbal, Paul Taggart, Paulina Ochoa Espejo, and Pierre Ostiguy, eds. 2017. *The Oxford Handbook of Populism*. Oxford: Oxford University Press.

Rosenmann, Alexandra. 2017. "Rachel Maddow Drops Truth Bomb on the Right: Trump Resistance Far Outpaces Tea Party's Heyday." *Alternet*, February 2. https://www.alternet.org/activism/rachel-maddow-drops-truthbomb-right-trump-resistance-far-outpaces-tea-party-popularity. Accessed April 22, 2018.

Rubin, Joel, James Queally, and Alene Tchekmedyian. 2017. "'Coordinated Chaos': Scores of Volunteer Attorneys Mobilized to Try to Stop Detentions and Deportations at LAX." *Los Angeles Times*, January 31. http://www.latimes.com/local/lanow/la-me-lax-lawyers-20170131-story.html.

Ruiz-Grossman, Sarah 2016. "These Are the Fierce Activists Leading the Women's March on Washington." *Huffington Post*, December 1. https://www.huffingtonpost.com/entry/women-march-on-washington-organizers_us_58407ee8e4b017f37fe388d1. Accessed December 8, 2017.

Rupnik, Jacques. 2016. "Surging Illiberalism in the East." *Journal of Democracy* 27(4): 77–87.

Rupp, Leila and Verta Taylor. 1987. *Survival in the Doldrums*. New York: Oxford University Press.

Ruzza, Carlo and Stefano Fella. 2009. *Re-inventing the Italian Right: Territorial Politics, Populism, and 'Post-fascism.'* London: Routledge.

Ryan, Charlotte. 1991. *Prime Time Activism: Media Strategies for Grassroots Organizing*. Boston, MA: South End Press.

Sacchetti, Maria. 2017. "Trump Administration Targets 'Sanctuary' Cities In Latest Wave of Immigration Arrests." *Washington Post*, September 28. https://www.washingtonpost.com/local/immigration/trump-administration-targets-sanctuary-cities-in-latest-wave-of-immigration-arrests/2017/09/28/9b5e7de2-a477-11e7-ade1-76d061d56efa_story.html?utm_term=.ee1307384570.

Safronova, Valeriya. 2014. "Millennials and the Age of Tumblr Activism." *New York Times*, December 19. https://www.nytimes.com/2014/12/21/style/millennials-and-the-age-of-tumblr-activism.html. Accessed January 5, 2018.

Sampaio, Anna. 2015. *Terrorizing Latina/o Immigrants: Race, Gender, and Immigration Politics in the Age of Security*. Philadelphia: Temple University Press.

Sanchez, Gabriel. 2008. "Latino Group Consciousness and Perceptions of Commonality with African-Americans." *Social Science Quarterly* 89(2): 428–444.

Sanchez, Gabriel R., Edward D. Vargas, Hannah L. Walker, and Vickie D. Ybarra. 2015. "Stuck Between a Rock and a Hard Place: The Relationship Between Latino/A's Personal Connections to Immigrants and Issue Salience and Presidential Approval." *Politics, Groups, and Identities* 3(3): 454–468.

Santiago, Fabiola. 2017. "The Big Accomplishment of Trump's First 100 Days? Terrorizing Undocumented Immigrants." *Miami Herald*, April 26. http://www.miamiherald.com/news/local/news-columns-blogs/fabiola-santiago/article146744789.html.

Saunders, Clare, Maria Grasso, Cristiana Olcese, Emily Rainsford, and Christopher Rootes. 2012. "Explaining Differential Protest Participation: Novices, Returners, Repeaters, and Stalwarts." *Mobilization: An International Quarterly* 17(3): 263–280.

Schain, Martin A. 2017. "The Extreme-Right and Immigration Policy-Making." In *The Populist Radical Right: A Reader*, ed. Cas Mudde, 458–473. Abingdon, UK: Routledge.

Schattschneider, E. E. 1942. *Party Government*. New Brunswick, NJ: Transaction Books.

Schlozman, Daniel. 2015. *When Movements Anchor Parties: Electoral Alignments in American History*. Princeton: Princeton University Press.

Schor, Elana and Rachael Bade. 2017. "Inside the Protest Movement that Has Republicans Reeling." *Politico*, February 10. http://www.politico.com/story/2017/02/protest-movement-republicans-234863.

Scott, Alec. 2017. "'We Call it the Muslim Ban 3.0': The Young Yale Lawyers Fighting Trump's Order." *The Guardian*, October 24. https://www.theguardian.com/us-news/2017/oct/23/dumbledore-army-donald-trump-travel-ban-legal-battle-mike-wishnie?CMP=share_btn_tw.

Seattle Times. 2015. "Black Lives Matter Protesters Shut Down Bernie Sanders; Later Rally Draws 15,000." *Seattle Times*, August 8. http://www.seattletimes.com/seattle-news/politics/black-lives-matter-protesters-shut-down-bernie-sanders-rally/. Accessed September 17, 2017.

Seif, Hinda. 2014. "'Coming out of the Shadows' and 'Undocuqueer': Undocumented Immigrants Transforming Sexuality Discourse and Activism." *Journal of Language and Sexuality* 3(1): 87–120.

Shear, Michael D., Nicholas Kulish, and Alan Feuer. 2017. "Judge Blocks Trump Order on Refugees amid Chaos and Outcry Worldwide." *New York Times*, January 28. https://nyti.ms/2jHS6tQ.

Shepard, Steven. 2016. "Latino Voting Surge Rattles Trump Campaign." *Politico*, November 6. https://www.politico.com/story/2016/11/latino-vote-surge-donald-trump-campaign-230804.

Shulevitz, Judith 2017. "Year One: Resistance Research." *New York Review of Books*, November 9. http://www.nybooks.com/daily/2017/11/09/year-one-resistance-research/?utm_medium=email&utm_campaign=NYR+Milosz+Persian+art+local+news+resistance&utm_content=NYR+Milosz+Persian+art+local+news+resistance+CID_53c5f8974f87366 b31fcc861f996d10e&utm_source=Newsletter&utm_term=Year+One+Resistance+Research. Accessed December 8, 2017.

Shure, Mamie 2017. "*MST3K* for Politics: The Hosts of *Chapo Trap House* Trace Their Podcast's Evolution to the Disastrous Present." Interview, *avclub.com*, August 24. https://www.avclub.com/mst3k-for-politics-the-hosts-of-chapo-trap-house-trace-1797866330.

Silva, Eduardo. 2009. *Challenging Neoliberalism in Latin America*. New York: Cambridge University Press.

Skocpol, Theda. 2003. *Diminished Democracy: From Membership to Management in American Civil Life*. Norman: University of Oklahoma Press.

Skocpol, Theda, Marshall Ganz, and Ziad Munson. 2000. "A Nation of Organizers: The Institutional Origins of Civic Voluntarism in the United States." *American Political Science Review* 94: 527–546.

Skocpol, Theda and Vanessa Williamson. 2013. *The Tea Party and the Remaking of Republican Conservatism*. Oxford: Oxford University Press.

Smith, David. 2017. "Democrats Salute Week That Saw the Emergence of an anti-Trump Coalition." *The Guardian*, November 11. https://www.theguardian.com/us-news/2017/nov/11/democrats-victories-2018-republicans.

Smith-Spark, Laura and Jason Hanna. 2017. "March for Science: Protestors Gather Worldwide to Support 'Evidence.'" *CNN*, April 22. http://cnn.it/2owuScm.

Snow, David A. and Colin Bernatsky. Forthcoming (2018). "The Coterminous Rise of Right-Wing Populism and Superfluous Populations." In *Populism and Citizenship*, eds. Gregor Fitzi, Juergen Mackert, and Bryan S. Turner. London: Routledge.

Snow, David A, Sarah A. Soule, and Hanspeter Kriesi, eds. 2004. *The Blackwell Companion to Social Movements*. London: Blackwell.

Soule, Sarah A., Doug McAdam, John McCarthy, and Yang Su. 1999. "Protest Events: Cause or Consequence of State Action? The U.S. Women's Movement and Federal Congressional Activities, 1956–1979." *Mobilization* 4(2): 239–256.

Staggenborg, Suzanne. 1986. "Coalition Work in the Pro-Choice Movement: Organizational and Environmental Opportunities and Obstacles." *Social Problems* 33(5): 374–390.

Staggenborg, Suzanne. 1988. "The Consequences of Professionalization and Formalization in the Pro-Choice Movement." *American Sociological Review* 53(4): 585–605.

Staggenborg, Suzanne. 1995. "Can Feminist Organizations be Effective?" In *Feminist Organizations*, eds. Myra Marx Ferree and Patricia Yancey Martin, 339–355. Philadelphia: Temple University Press.

Stanley, Ben. 2017. "Populism in Central and Eastern Europe." In *The Oxford Handbook of Populism*, eds. Cristóbal Rovira Kaltwasser, Paul Taggart, Paulina Ochoa Espejo, and Pierre Ostiguy, 140–160. Oxford: Oxford University Press.

Stavrakakis, Yannis and Giorgos Katsambekis. 2014. "Left-Wing Populism in the European Periphery: The Case of SYRIZA." *Journal of Political Ideologies* 19(2): 119–142.

Stein, Perry. 2017. "The Woman Who Started the Women's March With a Facebook Post Reflects: 'It was Mind-Boggling.'" *Washington Post*, January 31. https://www.washingtonpost.com/news/local/wp/2017/01/31/the-woman-who-started-the-womens-march-with-a-facebook-post-reflects-it-was-mind-boggling/?utm_term=.410e79b5330e. Accessed December 8, 2017.

Stockman, Farah. 2017. "Women's March on Washington Opens Contentious Dialogues About Race." *New York Times*, January 9. https://www.nytimes.com/2017/01/09/us/womens-march-on-washington-opens-contentious-dialogues-about-race.html. Accessed December 8, 2017.

Stockman, Farah. 2018. "One Year after Women's March, More Activism but Less Unity." *New York Times*, January 15. https://www.nytimes.com/2018/01/15/us/womens-march-anniversary.html. Accessed January 25, 2018.

Stout, Christopher T., Kristine Coulter, and Bree Edwards. 2017. "Black Representation: Descriptive Representation, Intersectionality, and Politicians' Responses to Black Political Movements on Twitter." *Mobilization* 22(4): 493–509.

Suh, Chan and Sidney Tarrow. 2018. "The Repression of Protest in the Age of Trump: State Legislators, Protest Threat and Political Realignments," American Sociological Association Annual Meeting, Philadelphia, PA, August 11–14.

Sullivan, Amy. 2018. "Millions of Americans Believe God Made Trump President." *Politico*, January 27. https://www.politico.com/magazine/story/2018/01/27/millions-of-americans-believe-god-made-trump-president-216537.

Taggart, Paul. 2000. *Populism*. Buckingham, UK: Open University Press.

Tarrow, Sidney. 1993. "Cycles of Collective Action: Between Moments of Madness and the Repertoire of Contention." *Social Science History* 17(2): 281–307.

Tarrow, Sidney. 2011. *Power in Movement: Social Movements and Contentious Politics*. 3rd ed. New York: Cambridge University Press.

Tarrow, Sidney. 2015. *War, States, and Contention*. Ithaca, NY: Cornell University Press.

Tarrow, Sidney. 2018. "Rhythms of Resistance: The Anti-Trumpian Moment in a Cycle of Contention." In *The Resistance*, eds. David Meyer and Sidney Tarrow. New York: Oxford University Press.

Tarrow, Sidney and Doug McAdam. 2005. "Scale Shift in Transnational Contention." In *Transnational Protest and Global Activism*, eds. Donatella della Porta and Sidney Tarrow, chap.6. Lanham, MD: Rowman and Littlefield.

Taylor, Judith and Kim de Laat. 2013. "Feminist Internships and the Depression of Political Imagination." *Feminist Formations* 25(1): 84–110.

Taylor, Keeanga-Yamahtta. 2016. *From #BlackLivesMatter to Black Liberation*. Chicago: Haymarket Books.

Taylor, Verta. 1989. "Social Movement Continuity: The Women's Movement in Abeyance." *American Sociological Review* 54(5): 761–775.

Taylor, Verta and Alison Dahl Crossley. 2013. "Abeyance." In *The Wiley-Blackwell Encyclopedia of Social & Political Movements*, eds. David Snow, Donatella della Porta, Bert Klandermans, and Doug McAdam. Oxford: Oxford University Press.

Taylor, Verta and Nella Van Dyke. 2004. "'Get up, Stand up': Tactical Repertoires of Social Movements." In *The Blackwell Companion to Social Movements*, eds. David A. Snow, Sarah A. Soule, and Hanspeter Kriesi, 262–293. Malden, MA: Blackwell.

Taylor, Verta, and Nancy Whittier. 1992. "Collective Identity in Social Movement Communities." In *Frontiers in Social Movement Theory*, eds. Aldon D. Morris and Carol McClurg Mueller, 104–129. New Haven, CT: Yale University Press.

Terriquez, Veronica. 2015. "Intersectional Mobilization, Social Movement Spillover, and Queer Youth Leadership in the Immigrant Rights Movement." *Social Problems* 62(3): 343–362.

Tesfaye, Sophia. 2017. "White Women Strike Back: The Demographic that Gave Us Trump Seeks Redemption." *Salon*, November 9. https://www.salon.com/2017/11/09/white-women-strike-back-the-demographic-that-gave-us-trump-seeks-redemption/.

Tesler, Michael and David O. Sears. 2010. "President Obama and the Growing Polarization of Partisan Attachments by Racial Attitudes and Race." Paper presented at the annual meeting of the American Political Science Association, Washington, DC, September.

The Guardian. 2017. "ACLU Launching People Power to Resist Trump Immigration Policies in 'Freedom Cities.'" *The Guardian*, March 9. https://www.theguardian.com/us-news/2017/mar/09/aclu-people-power-freedom-cities-trump-immigration-policies?CMP=Share_iOSApp_Other.

The Guardian. 2017. "Who Are the Key Players In the Resistance Against Donald Trump?" *The Guardian*, March 9. https://www.theguardian.com/us-news/2017/mar/09/the-resistance-now-key-players-donald-trump?CMP=Share_iOSApp_Other.

Thompson, Anne. 2017. "Trump's Disgusting Rally (Even Worse than Fox News)." Mass email, MoveOn.org. August 23.

Thorson, Kjerstin, Stephanie Edgerly, Neta Kligler-Vilenchik, Yu Xu, and Luping Wang. 2016. "Climate and Sustainability|Seeking Visibility in a Big Tent: Digital Communication and the People's Climate March." *International Journal of Communication* 10: 4784–4806.

Tindall, David B. 2015. "Networks as Constraints and Opportunities." In *Oxford Handbook of Social Movements*, eds. Donatella della Porta and Mario Diani, chap. 14. New York: Oxford University Press.

Tilly, Charles. 1978. *From Mobilization to Revolution*. Reading, MA: Addison-Wesley.

Tilly, Charles and Sidney Tarrow. 2015. *Contentious Politics*. 2nd. ed. New York: Oxford University Press.

Tilly, Charles and Lesley J. Wood. 2012. *Social Movements, 1768–2012*. Boulder, CO: Paradigm Books.

Toobin, Jeffrey. 2013. "Casting Votes." *The New Yorker*, January 14, 17–18.

Traister, Rebecca. 2018. "The Other Women's March on Washington." *The Cut*, January 29. https://www.thecut.com/2018/01/women-candidates-2018-elections.html.   Accessed February 5, 2018.

Tronconi, Filippo, ed. 2015. *Beppe Grillo's Five Star Movement: Organisation, Communication, and Ideology*. Surrey, UK: Ashgate.

Trump, Donald and Tony Schwartz. 1987. *The Art of the Deal*. New York: Ballantine.

Truth School. 2017. Class Lists. https://truthschool.org/classes/class-list/11–14-17-old-people-expressing-our-radical-selves/ https://truthschool.org/classes/class-list/10–07-17-teen-empowerment/. Accessed January 4, 2018.

Tsebelis, George. 2002. *Veto Players: How Political Institutions Work*. Princeton: Princeton University Press.

Tufekci, Zeynep 2017. *Twitter and Teargas: The Power and Fragility of Networked Protest*. New Haven, CT: Yale University Press.

Ulloa, Jazmine. 2017. "California Lawmakers Approve Landmark 'Sanctuary State' Bill to Expand Protections for Immigrants." *Los Angeles Times*, September 16. http://www.latimes.com/politics/la-pol-ca-california-sanctuary-state-bill-20170916-story.html.

Urbina, María. 2017. "Indivisible's Electoral Strategy." *IndivisiBlog*, July 31. https://www.indivisible.org/blog/they-voted-for-trumpcare/.

UC Office of the President. 2017. "UC President Napolitano denounces decision to end DACA program, calls on Congress to make protections permanent." September 5. https://www.universityofcalifornia.edu/press-room/uc-president-napolitano-statement-decision-end-daca-program. Accessed February 4, 2018.

Vagianos, Alanna and Damon Dahlen. 2017. "89 Badass Feminist Signs from the Women's March on Washington." *Huffington Post*, January 21. https://www.huffingtonpost.com/entry/89-badass-feminist-signs-from-the-womens-march-on-washington_us_5883ea28e4b070d8cad310cd. Accessed January 4, 2018.

Valelly, Richard 2017. "Regeneration or Decay? That Depends on How, When, and How Much Trump is Repudiated." Prepared for the conference on The State of American Democracy in Historical and Comparative Perspective. Cornell University, Ithaca, NY.

van Dyke, Nella. 2003a. "Crossing Movement Boundaries: Factors That Facilitate Coalition Protest by American College Students, 1930–1990." *Social Problems* 50(2): 226–250.

van Dyke, Nella. 2003b. "Protest Cycles and Party Politics: The Effects of Elite Allies and Antagonists on Student Protest in the United States, 1930–1990." In *States, Parties, and Social Movements*, ed. Jack A. Goldstone, 226–245. New York: Cambridge University Press.

van Dyke, Nella, and Holly J. McCammon, eds. 2010. *Strategic Alliances: Coalition Building and Social Movements*. Minneapolis: University of Minnesota Press.

van Dyke, Nella and David S. Meyer, eds. 2014. *Understanding the Tea Party*. Aldershot, UK: Ashgate.

Verhulst, Joris and Stefaan Walgrave. 2009. "The First Time Is the Hardest? A Cross-National and Cross-Issue Comparison of First-Time Protest Participants." *Political Behavior* 31(3): 455–484.

Vinik, Danny. 2017. "5 Things Trump Did This Week While You Weren't Looking." *Politico*, September 22.   https://www.politico.com/agenda/story/2017/09/22/trump-policy-medicare-regulation-immigration-000533.

Vitali, Ali and Corky Siemaszko. 2017. "Trump Interview with Lester Holt: President Asked Comey if He Was Under Investigation." *NBC News*. May 11. https://www.nbcnews.com/news/us-news/trump-reveals-he-asked-comey-whether-he-was-under-investigation-n757821. Accessed January 28, 2018.

Vogel, Kenneth P. and Alex Isenstadt. 2016. "How Did Everyone Get It So Wrong?" *Politico*, November 9. https://www.politico.com/story/2016/11/how-did-everyone-get-2016-wrong-presidential-election-231036.

Vogel, Kenneth P. and Kyle Cheney. 2017. "Left Adopts Shock Tactics in Obamacare Repeal Fight." *Politico*, May 9. www.politico.com/story/2017/05/09/democrats-funerals-obamacare-repeal-238127.

Vongkiatkajorn, Kanyakrit. 2017. "Colleges Across America Are Fighting Back Against Trump's Deportation Threats." *Mother Jones*, January 5. https://www.motherjones.com/politics/2017/01/sanctuary-campus-college-dreamers-deportation/.

Wadsworth, Nancy D. 2011. "Intersectionality in California's Same-Sex Marriage Battles: A Complex Proposition." *Political Research Quarterly* 64(1): 200–216.

Wagner, John, Anne Gearan, and Jose D. DelReal. 2016. "Early Voting by Latinos May Help Clinton in Several States." *Washington Post*, November 3. https://www.washingtonpost.com/politics/early-voting-by-latinos-may-help-clinton-in-several-states/2016/11/03/41be5a00-a1da-11e6-8d63-3e0a660f1f04_story.html?utm_term=.6e890af44098.

Wahlström, Mattias and Magnus Wennerhag. 2014. "Alone in the Crowd: Lone Protesters in Western European Demonstrations." *International Sociology* 29(6): 565–583.

Walgrave, Stefaan and Joris Verhulst. 2011. "Selection and Response Bias in Protest Surveys." *Mobilization: An International Quarterly* 16(2): 203–222.

Walgrave, Stefaan, Ruud Wouters, and Pauline Ketelaars. 2016. "Response Problems in the Protest Survey Design: Evidence from Fifty-One Protest Events in Seven Countries." *Mobilization: An International Quarterly* 21(1): 83–104.

Walgrave, Stefaan, Ruud Wouters, Jeroen Van Laer, Joris Verhulst, and Pauline Ketelaars. 2012. "Transnational Collective Identification: May Day and Climate Change Protesters' Identification with Similar Protest Events in Other Countries." *Mobilization: An International Quarterly* 17(3): 301–317.

Wallace, Sophia J. 2012. "It's Complicated: Latinos, President Obama and the 2012 Election." *Social Science Quarterly* 93(5): 1360–1383.

Wallace, Sophia J., Chris Zepeda-Millán, and Michael Jones-Correa. 2014. "Spatial and Temporal Proximity: Examining the Effects of Protests on Political Attitudes." *American Journal of Political Science* 58: 449–465.

Warner, Claire. 2016. "6 Petitions to Change the Electoral College That You Can Sign Right Now." *Bustle*, November 10. https://www.bustle.com/articles/194639-6-petitions-to-change-the-electoral-college-that-you-can-sign-right-now. Accessed December 8, 2017.

Washington Times, 2008. "Blacks, Hispanics Nixed Gay Marriage." *Washington Times*, November 8. https://www.washingtontimes.com/news/2008/nov/8/blacks-hispanics-nixed-gay-marriage/.

Waters, Wendall. 2017 "Report From the Women's March on Washington." *Wicked Local Medford*, January 21. http://medford.wickedlocal.com/entertainmentlife/20170121/report-from-womens-march-on-washington. Accessed January 4, 2018.

Weiser, Wendy R. and Diana Kasdan. 2012. "Voting Law Changes: Election Update." Brennan Center for Justice, October 28. http://www.brennancenter.org/publication/voting-law-changes-election-update.

West Savali, Kirsten. 2017. "BLM Partners with Other Organizations to Halt Jail Expansion." *popularresistance.org*, September 29. https://popularresistance.org/black-lives-matter-co-founder-partners-with-orgs-to-halt-los-angeles-jail-expansion/.

Westcott, Lucy. 2017. "Thousands of Lawyers Descend on U.S. Airports to Fight Trump's Immigrant Ban." *Newsweek*, January 29. http://www.newsweek.com/lawyers-volunteer-us-airports-trump-ban-549830.

Westervelt, Eric. 2017. "ACT UP at 30: Reinvigorated for Trump Fight. National Public Radio, April 17. https://www.npr.org/2017/04/17/522726303/act-up-at-30- reinvigorated-for-trump-fight.

Westfall, Julie. 2017. "Hundreds of People Showed up for a Town Hall with California's Rep. Tom McClintock, and Things Got Intense." *Los Angeles Times*, February 4. http://www.latimes.com/politics/essential/la-pol-ca-essential-politics-updates-hundreds-of-people-show-up-for-town-1486246073-htmlstory.html.

Weyland, Kurt. 1996. "Neoliberalism and Neopopulism in Latin America: Unexpected Affinities." *Studies in Comparative International Development* 31(3): 3–31.

"What We Do." 2017. Sister District. https://www.sisterdistrict.com/what-we-do. Accessed January 4, 2018.

Whitford, Emma. 2017. "JFK Lawyers: We Now Have a 'Replicable' System to Keep Fighting Trump." *Gothamist*, February 6. http://gothamist.com/2017/02/06/jfk_lawyers_trump_travel_ban.php.

Whittier, Nancy. 1995. *Feminist Generations*. Philadelphia: Temple University Press.

Whittier, Nancy. 1997. "Political Generations, Micro-Cohorts, and the Transformation of Social Movements." *American Sociological Review* 62(5): 760–778.

Whittier, Nancy. 2016. "Aggregate Level Biographical Outcomes for Gay and Lesbian Movements." In *The Consequences of Social Movements*, eds. Lorenzo Bosi, Marco Giugni, and Katrin Uba, 130–156. Cambridge: Cambridge University Press.

Whittier, Nancy. 2018. *Frenemies: Feminists, Conservatives, and Sexual Violence*. New York: Oxford.

Whittier, Nancy. Forthcoming (2019). "Campus Activism Against Sexual Assault." In *Different Wavelengths II*, ed. Jo Reger. New York: Routledge.

"Who We Are." Run For Something. https://www.runforsomething.net/. Accessed January 4, 2018.

Wiedeman, Reeves. 2017. "24 Hours at JFK: The Hour-By-Hour Account of Two Iraqis' Detainment and Release." *New York Magazine*, January 31. http://nymag.com/daily/intelligencer/2017/01/24-hours-at-jfk-two-iraqi-refugees-detainment-and-release.html.

Wilkinson, Betina Cutaia. 2015. *Partners or Rivals? Power and Latino, Black, and White Relations in the Twenty-First Century*. Charlottesville: University of Virginia Press.

Williams, Joseph P. 2016. "Clinton Made Her Case to Black Voters. Why Didn't They Hear Her?" *US News and World Report*, November 9. https://www.usnews.com/news/politics/articles/2016-11-09/clinton-made-her-case-to-black-voters-why-didnt-they-hear-her. Accessed October 25, 2017.

Williams, Kim M. 2016. "Black Political Interests on Immigrant Rights: Evidence From Black Newspapers, 2000–2013." *Journal of African American Studies* 20: 248–271.

Williamson, Vanessa. 2017. "Could this be the Left's Tea Party Moment?" *CNN Opinion*, February 12. http://www.cnn.com/2017/02/12/opinions/tea-party-of-the-left-williamson-opinion/index.html.

Wilson, James, Edward Helmore, and Jon Swaine. 2017. "Man Charged With Murder After Driving Into Anti-Far-Right Protesters in Charlottesville." *The Guardian*, August 13. https://www.theguardian.com/us-news/2017/aug/12/virginia-unite-the-right-rally-protest-violence.

Wilts, Alexandra. 2017. "Donald Trump's Popularity Starts to Fall Among Loyal Fox News Fans." *Yahoo! News*, December 14. https://uk.news.yahoo.com/donald-trump-popularity-starts-fall-232400037.html?guccounter=1.

Wisckol, Martin. 2017. "Activists' Visit to Dana Rohrabacher's Office Ends with 2-year-old Hit by Door, 71-year-old Hospitalized." *Orange County Register*, February 16. http://www.ocregister.com/2017/02/16/activists-visit-to-dana-rohrabachers-office-ends-with-2-year-old-hit-by-door-71-year-old-hospitalized/.

Wise, Alana. 2015. "With Barbs and Bluster, Trump Barges into 2016 White House Race." *Reuters*, June 16. http://www.reuters.com/article/us-usa-election-trump/with-barbs-and-bluster-trump-barges-into-2016-white-house-race-idUSKBN0OW1ZU20150616.

Wittes, Benjamin. 2017. "Malevolence Tempered by Incompetence: Trump's Horrifying Executive Order on Refugees and Visas." *Lawfare*, January 28. https://lawfareblog.com/malevolence-tempered-incompetence-trumps-horrifying-executive-order-refugees-and-visas. Accessed January 28, 2018.

Wood, Richard L. and Brad R. Fulton. 2015. *A Shared Future: Faith-Based Organizing for Racial Equity and Ethical Democracy*. Chicago: University of Chicago Press.

World Economic Forum. 2017. *Global Shapers Survey*. http://shaperssurvey2017.org/static/data/WEF_GSC_Annual_Survey_2017.pdf. Accessed January 4, 2018.

Worth, Pamela. 2015. "Communities Already Experiencing the Impacts of Global Warming are Often the Least Equipped to Deal With It. UCS is Working to Ensure They Get the Help They Need." http://www.ucsusa.org/publications/catalyst/fa15-where-climate-change-hits-first-and-worst#.WgMkjFtSzX4. Accessed 8 November 2017.

X (George F. Kennan). 1947. "The Sources of Soviet Conduct." *Foreign Affairs* 25(4): 566–582.

Zald, Mayer N. and Bert Useem. 1987. "Movement and Countermovement Interaction: Mobilization, Tactics, and State Involvement." In *Social Movements in an Organizational Society*, eds. Mayer N. Zald and John D. McCarthy, 247–271. New Brunswick, NJ: Transaction Books.

Zengerle, Jason 2017. "The Voices in Blue America's Head." *New York Times Magazine*, November 22. https://www.nytimes.com/2017/11/22/magazine/the-voices-in-blue-americas-head.html.

Zepeda-Millán, Christopher. 2017. *Latino Mass Mobilization: Immigration, Radicalization, and Activism.* New York: Cambridge University Press.

Zingales, Luigi. 2016. "The Right Way to Resist Trump." *New York Times*, November 18.

Executive Orders and Proclamations

Executive Order No. 13769, Protecting the Nation From Foreign Terrorist Entry Into the United States. 82 Fed. Reg. 8977 (January 27, 2017). https://www.federalregister.gov/documents/2017/02/01/2017-02281/protecting-the-nation-from-foreign-terrorist-entry-into-the-united-states.

Executive Order No. 13780, Protecting the Nation From Foreign Terrorist Entry Into the United States, 82 Fed. Reg. 20, 13209 (March 6, 2017). https://www.federalregister.gov/documents/2017/02/01/2017-02281/protecting-the-nation-from-foreign-terrorist-entry-into-the-united-states.

Proclamation No. 9645 82 Fed. Reg. 186, 45161 (Sept. 24, 2017). https://www.gpo.gov/fdsys/pkg/FR-2017-09-27/pdf/2017-20899.pdf.

Cases

Brown v. Bd. of Ed. of Topeka, Shawnee Cty., Kan., 347 U.S. 483, 74 S. Ct. 686, 98 L. Ed. 873 (1954), supplemented sub nom. *Brown v. Bd. of Educ. of Topeka, Kan.*, 349 U.S. 294, 75 S. Ct. 753, 99 L. Ed. 1083 (1955).

Hawaii v. Trump, 859 F.3d 741, 789 (9th Cir.), cert. granted sub nom. *Trump v. Int'l Refugee Assistance Project*, 137 S. Ct. 2080, 198 L. Ed. 2d 643 (2017), cert. granted, judgment vacated, No. 16–1540, 2017 WL 4782860 (U.S. Oct. 24, 2017), vacated, 874 F.3d 1112 (9th Cir. Nov. 2, 2017).

Obergefell v. Hodges, 135 S. Ct. 2584, 192 L. Ed. 2d 609 (2015).

Regents of Univ. of California v. United States Dep't of Homeland Security, No. C17–05211, 2018 WL 339144 (N.D. Cal., January 9, 2018).

Trump v. Int'l Refugee Assistance Project, No. 16–1436, 2017 WL 4518553 (U.S. Oct. 10, 2017).

United States v. Carolene Prods. Co., 304 U.S. 144, 153 n.4 (1938).

INDEX